# Transforming Middle Level Education

## Perspectives and Possibilities

**JUDITH L. IRVIN, Editor**
*Florida State University*

**ALLYN AND BACON**
*Boston London Toronto Sydney Tokyo Singapore*

*Library of Congress Cataloging-in-Publication Data*

Transforming middle level education  :   perspectives and possibilities /
    [edited by] Judith L. Irvin.
        p.     cm.
    Includes bibliographical references and index.
    ISBN 0-205-13472-6
    1. Middle schools—United States.     2. Education—United States—
—Philosophy.     I. Irvin, Judith L., 1947–
LB1623.5.T73     1992
373.2′36—dc20                                                          91-14823
                                                                          CIP

Printed in the United States of America
10  9  8  7  6  5  4                        95  94

# Contents

# Foreword

The extensive discussions, debates, and assessments of public education throughout our country have brought us to the threshold of the twenty-first century with a resounding challenge and obligation to restructure our schools. A window of opportunity now exists to institute significant change in middle level schools throughout our nation. While a continually increasing number of schools have moved to implement interdisciplinary teams, teacher-advisor programs, broad exploratory experiences, skill-development programs, and other recommended characteristics, the basic questions of *what we teach* and *how we teach* remain, for the most part, unanswered and little challenged. Simply doing better what we are currently doing will not meet youths' needs nor adequately prepare them to become productive citizens in the twenty-first century. The noteworthy progress that middle level education has made during the past few decades is itself at risk unless we move forward to address the critical issues of curriculum and instruction as they pertain to the restructuring of our schools.

*Transforming Middle Level Education: Perspectives and Possibilities* will be a valuable resource to all educators involved in this task. Its potential to provide a foundation for informed discussion and informed *action* is apparent. Hopefully, this book will help middle level educators step through the "window of opportunity" and become involved in real programmatic transformation.

We are indebted to all the professionals who have taken the time to develop, write, and edit this informative book. We will profit from the opportunity to read it and to broaden our understanding of the unique needs and issues facing middle level education today.

Sue Swaim, President
*National Middle School Association*
*1991–1992*

# Foreword

Judith Irvin has collected and organized an unusually attractive set of articles that analyze, attempt to resolve, and otherwise deal with some perennial issues, practices, and projections in middle level education. The contributing authors, including several leaders in the field who have already contributed greatly to its literature, and others with fresh viewpoints and statements, all help to produce a timely treatment of these issues as we move into the last decade of the first century in which this all-important level of education has been established. As Lounsbury so well sketches in the opening chapter, the middle level movement has had two major organizations (junior high and middle schools) and corresponding periods, with the current popular middle school now helping the level become universally accepted, although there is continuing need to make the school match all worthy hopes for this level.

Unlike too many collections of this nature, *Transforming Middle Level Education: Perspectives and Possibilities* has a very significant base to hold the various readings together. Most of them give major attention to the concept we now think of as the rationale of today's most popular middle level organization. This is the concept that a special organization between, not of either, the elementary and the secondary school — a middle school usually containing grades 6 through 8 or 5 through 8 — is essential to meeting the unique needs of students in these critical years of transition from childhood to full adolescence. This concept is fully presented in theory and practice in this book, with convincing arguments as to its importance and utility, especially in those chapters that deal directly with the characteristics of adolescents and with their relationships to such important and relevant practices as interdisciplinary teaming, teacher advisory programs, exploratory programs, curriculum, motivation, and instruction.

As in any collection of readings from several different authors, this book will probably be most useful to readers who have specific questions and problems to explore, or particular authors in whom they are interested. The individual issue treatments cover many aspects of middle level education, with some 19 individuals participating in the authorship, so reference to the appropriate chapters should yield much help to individual users. Especially comprehensive and notably promising reservoirs of information and ideas on what may be the most troublesome issues are the expositions on interdisciplinary teaming and social bonding, curriculum, and evaluation and reporting. Extensive lists of references in the chapters provide for further exploration.

Although great progress has been made in less than a century of middle level educational organization, especially in the last 30 years of the middle school's emergence and present popularity, many acute problems remain. Readings are included to remind us of the inextricable ones of growing up, education, and the culture. The continuing need for progress in middle level teacher preparation and certification, and in research, is sounded very effectively in the chapters on these matters. All of the articles mentioned, plus others, focus directly on maintenance, change, and improvement — indeed, the entire book points out clearly how to keep moving forward in middle level education.

All in all, Irvin and her contributors are to be heartily thanked for this ambitious addition to the field. With an ever-growing number of schools in the middle, there is a persistent need for up-to-date materials to inform and guide practitioners and patrons. The various chapters of this book will give substantial help.

William M. Alexander
*Professor Emeritus*
*University of Florida*

# Preface

*Transforming Middle Level Education: Perspectives and Possibilities* is a book for anyone who has an interest in middle level education — teachers, administrators, university faculty, board members, and parents. The past two decades have witnessed tremendous reform in middle level schools and more restructuring is in the offing. Hundreds of schools have implemented team organization, advisory programs, full and rich exploratory programs, flexible schedules, and other innovations that seek to meet better the needs of young adolescents. Middle level educators are driven by one premise: Everything that is done for and with students in a school should be based on what we know about the nature and needs of the age group. This book builds on that premise and seeks to address it from a broader perspective than that of the past or present. I hope that readers will find ways of using the information and viewpoints in this book to improve middle level education.

The book is divided into four parts: (1) developing a sense of identity both with the middle school movement and with young adolescents (Chapters One through Five); (2) developing a sense of responsiveness to the needs of young adolescents through programs implemented in middle level schools (Chapters Six through Twelve); (3) developing a sense of relevance for students through appropriate curriculum, instruction, grouping practices, and evaluation procedures (Chapters Thirteen through Eighteen); and (4) developing a support system for continued improvement through teacher preparation and research efforts (Chapters Nineteen and Twenty).

The contributing authors of this book are seasoned, dedicated middle level educators. Their perspectives sound loud and clear, as do their hopes for the future — the possibilities for middle level education. It is my hope that this book will lay a foundation for those educators, schools, and communities attempting to move from reform to transformation, and motivate some educators to pursue research agendas in areas pertinent to middle level education. Research, courage, and commitment are the necessary ingredients to transform schools for young adolescents that will prepare them to be productive, happy citizens in the twenty-first century.

## Acknowledgments

Middle level educators are wonderful colleagues. The contributors to this book have been patient, cooperative, and enthusiastic about this project. It has been a real joy to correspond with the fine people who have contributed to this book; my gratitude goes out to them. Also, I thank the National Middle School Association, which has been very supportive of this project from its inception, and my friend and colleague, Donna Schumacher, who gave me invaluable help and support. Last, but hardly least, I appreciate the patience of my family, Bruce, Brandon, and Alesha.

Judith L. Irvin

# About the Contributing Authors

**Dr. Joanne M. Arhar** is a faculty member at the University of South Florida. Joanne has been a teacher, a principal, and a professional development specialist for the American Association of School Administrators. Her research explores the social context of teaching and learning in the middle level school, particularly as it relates to collaborative school cultures. She has authored articles on interdisciplinary organization and the role of the middle level teacher. Joanne received two distinguished dissertation awards in 1991, one from the Association for Supervision and Curriculum Development and the other from the National Association of School Principals.

**Dr. Sherrel Bergman** is a member of the faculty of National-Louis University, Evanston, Illinois, where she teaches master's and doctoral students. Sherrel has been involved with middle level education since she began serious study of this age group in her undergraduate work. She went on to become a middle school teacher, counselor, and researcher. Sherrel is the co-founder of the Association of Illinois Middle Schools and an active member of the National Association of Secondary School Principals Council on Middle Level Education. Among her most notable publications are two books: *Discipline and Guidance—The Thin Line in Middle School: What At-Risk Students Say We Should Do* and *Decision-Making Skills for Middle School Students* (with Rudman).

**Dr. Neila A. Connors** is a faculty member in the Department of Middle Grades Education at Valdosta State College in Georgia. Neila has been a teacher working with students in grades K through 9 and was a middle grades specialist for the Florida Department of Education. Her research has been in the areas of teacher-advisory programs and the role of guidance counselors in middle level schools, positive teachers and their characteristics, and homework. She is currently a member of the Executive Council and Board of Directors for the National Middle School Association, the Executive Director of the Georgia Middle School Association, the editor of the Georgia Middle School Association's Newsletter, and a member of the Florida League of Middle School's steering committee. Among her most notable publications are *S.O.S.: Success Oriented Strategies for Teachers of At Risk Early Adolescents* and *Homework: A New Direction*. Neila has presented throughout the country and recently received the Distinguished Service Award Florida League of Middle Schools.

**Dr. James P. Garvin** is the Executive Director of the New England League of Middle Schools and a former president of the National Middle School Association. Jim is a well-respected speaker and consultant. Among his most notable publications are *Learning How to Kiss a Frog, Merging the Exploratory and Basic Subjects in the Middle Level School* and *A Sane Transition,* published by the New England League of Middle Schools. Jim has received the New England League of Middle Schools Distinguished Service Award and the Massachusetts Junior High/Middle School Principals Association's Outstanding Service Award.

**Dr. Judith L. Irvin** is Director of the Center for the Study of Middle Level Education and a member of the faculty at Florida State University. Judith is a former middle school social studies and reading teacher and among her research interests are curriculum, instruction, literacy learning, and leadership in middle level schools. She is currently Chair of the Research Committee of the National Middle School Association and serves as editor of *Research in Middle Level Education.* She also chairs the Reading/Language Issues for Middle Level Learners Committee for International Reading Association and serves on the Steering Committee for the Florida League of Middle Schools. Among her most notable publications are two books: *Reading and the Middle School Student: Strategies to Enhance Literacy* and *Vocabulary Knowledge: Guidelines for Instruction.* She is also a member of the authorship team for the 1993 Harcourt, Brace, Jovanovich basal reading series.

**Dr. J. Howard Johnston** is Professor and Chair of Secondary Education at the University of South Florida. Howard has been a junior high and high school teacher and is now a well-established author, lecturer, and researcher. He has authored over 100 works on middle level education, among the most notable is *How Fares the Ninth Grade, Life in the Three Sixth Grades* (both co-authored with John Lounsbury), *The New American Family,* and *What Research Says to the Middle Level Practitioner.* Howard is the recipient of the National Middle School Association's Presidential Award, the National Association of Secondary School Principals' Distinguished Service Award, and the New England League of Middle Schools' Distinguished Achievement Award.

**Dr. Frances K. Kochan** is presently Director of the University Laboratory School at Florida State University. Fran is principal investigator for the K–12 program focusing on restructuring the governance and operation of schools. She has had extensive experience in developing innovative programs and organizational change. She has worked overseas in the Trust Territory of the Pacific and Guam, where she helped develop multicultural reading and language materials. She is author of a chapter in *Education and the Family* and has published several articles on reforming teacher education and restructuring in schools.

**Dr. Linda R. Kramer** is currently the Director of a collaborative Master's Degree Program and the instructor for middle level education courses at the State University of New York at Brockport. Linda's interest in students' perceptions of school stems from her own experience as a middle level social studies and language arts teacher. She has authored numerous articles and worked with state departments of education, school districts, and individual faculties. She shares the 1989 Quality of Education Award from the California Council on the Education of Teachers with the faculty at La Mesa Middle School and is the recipient of the 1986 Distinguished Dissertation Award from the National Association of Secondary School Principals.

**Dr. John H. Lounsbury** edited the *Middle School Journal* from 1976 to 1990 and continues as Publications Editor for the National Middle School Association. A student of junior high school/middle school education for 40 years, he has written more than 100 articles and co-authored two college textbooks, *Modern Education for the Junior High School Years* (with Vars and Van Til) and *A Curriculum for the Middle School Years* (with Vars). John has conducted five national research projects *(Shadow Studies)* dealing with middle level education and has edited and produced more than 45 monographs for the National Middle School Association. The Dean Emeritus of the School of Education, Georgia College, Milledgeville, he is a frequent speaker and consultant throughout the United States. In addition to other numerous awards, John has been recognized by the National Middle School Association and the National Association of Secondary School Principals for his contributions to middle level education.

**Dr. C. Kenneth McEwin** is Professor of Curriculum and Instruction at Appalachian State University, Boone, North Carolina. Ken is a former sixth-grade teacher and principal of a middle school. As Chair of the National Middle School Association's Committee on Professional Preparation and Certification Committee, Ken provided leadership in the preparation of the first Middle Level Guidelines for the National Certification and Accreditation for Teacher Education/Teacher Preparation Curriculum Guidelines. He is a past president of National Middle School Association and was the recipient of the John H. Lounsbury Award. Ken has authored numerous professional books and articles on middle level education. Among his most notable contributions are *Schools in the Middle: Status and Progress* and *Preparing to Teach at the Middle Level,* both of which were co-authored with William Alexander.

**Dr. Joel Milgram** is a faculty member at the University of Cincinnati. Formerly the Head of the Department of Educational Psychology and the Associate Dean for Graduate Studies in the College of Education, he now teaches both undergraduate and graduate courses in educational psychology and human development. In 1978, he served as a consultant to the Nigerian government, where he and his family lived for one year, and in 1990, he assisted in the evaluation of several educational programs in Ethiopia. His writings have appeared in numerous journals and books, and he is a frequent consultant for school districts, universities, and governmental agencies. Joel taught in the public schools in New York and works closely with members of the Middle School Council of the National Association of Secondary School Principals.

**Dr. Robert Shockley** is Chair of the Department of Teacher Education at Florida Atlantic University at Boca Raton. Bob is a former Chair and Director of the Center of Education for the Young Adolescent at the University of Wisconsin — Platteville, is a former president of the National Middle School Association, and has served as a consultant to numerous school districts and state education agencies throughout the nation regarding middle school program development. Bob is the author of numerous articles on a variety of topics focusing on middle school educational issues. He has been a frequent featured speaker at state and regional educational conferences and his speech was featured by the Carnegie Corporation of New York at the release of their national report on Middle Level Education, *Turning Points.*

**Mr. Robert C. Spear** is Principal of Powder Mill Middle School and Director of Curriculum, Instruction, and Staff Development of the Southwick/Tolland School District. Bob has been a teacher and administrator at the middle level and is a past president of the New England League of Middle Schools. His research interests include middle school curriculum issues, ability grouping, and the process of renewal in middle level schools. Bob is pursuing a doctoral degree at the University of Massachusetts.

**Dr. David B. Strahan** is a faculty member at the University of North Carolina in Greensboro. David has worked with young adolescents in remedial reading settings. He has conducted investigations of young adolescent reasoning development, instructional strategies, classroom discipline, teacher thinking, and remediation processes. David has written over 40 professional articles and has co-authored two monographs: *Positive Discipline* and *Promoting Harmony in the Middle Grades.* For five years, David was editor of *Middle School Research: Selected Studies* for the National Middle School Association.

**Dr. Julia Thomason** is a faculty member at Appalachian State University, Boone, North Carolina, and a past president of the National Middle School Association. She has been Executive Director of the North Carolina League of Middle Level Schools and a member of the Board of Directors of the Association of Supervision and Curriculum Development. Among her most recent publications are *We Who Laugh Last* and *Who They Are: How We Teach.* Julia is also a very successful speaker and consultant.

**Dr. Max Thompson** is a faculty member at Appalachian State University, Boone, North Carolina, and has authored many articles in special education and middle level education. His research and professional work includes at-risk students, critical/creative thinking, and middle grades assessment evaluation.

**Dr. Conrad F. Toepfer, Jr.,** is a faculty member at State University of New York at Buffalo where he teaches courses and advises graduate students in curriculum planning and development. Conrad began his career as a junior high school teacher and administrator. He is a former president of the National Middle School Association and has also chaired the National Association of Secondary School Principals Council on Middle Level Education since 1981. He has worked with middle level schools throughout the United States and Canada and in Europe. His contributions to the general curriculum and middle level education literature over the past 35 years include work in 30 books and monographs and over 100 articles in professional journals. Conrad is the recipient of the National Middle School Association's John H. Lounsbury Award, the National Association of Secondary School Principals' Distinguished Service to Middle Level Education Award, the New York State Middle School Association's recognition of his "Service to Youth Throughout the World," the Wisconsin Association for Middle Level Education's James Stoltenberg Award for Outstanding Leadership and Service to Middle Level Education, and the New

York State Association for Supervision and Curriculum Development's Louis E. Raths Award.

**Dr. Gordon F. Vars** is a faculty member at Kent State University where he coordinates the Junior High/Middle School Staff Development Program. Gordon has been the coordinator of Middle School Division of Kent State University School and been a middle grades teacher. He is best known for his writing and development of the Core Curriculum and has served as Executive Secretary-Treasurer of the National Association for Core Curriculum and editor of the quarterly newsletter, *The Core Teacher*. His most notable books are *Modern Education for the Junior High School Years* (with Lounsbury and Van Til), *A Curriculum for the Middle School Years* (with Lounsbury), and *Interdisciplinary Teaching in the Middle Grades: Why and How*. Gordon is the recipient of the Ohio Middle School Educator of the Year Award and the John H. Lounsbury Award for Excellence in Middle School Education.

**Dr. Karen D. Wood** is a faculty member at the University of North Carolina at Charlotte and is a former middle school teacher and a K–12 instructional coordinator. Karen has authored over 60 articles and chapters on middle level education and reading. She is the author and originator of "Out of Research—Into Practice" column for the *Middle School Journal* and is currently a co-editor for *Reading Research and Instruction*. Among her most notable publications is an edited book, *Exploring Literature in the Classroom: Content and Methods*. Karen is a member of the authorship team for the 1993 Macmillian-McGraw Hill basal reading program.

# Introduction

As a new century looms ahead, it is natural to ponder what middle level students of the 1990s will need to be like and will need to know in order to negotiate successful life in the twenty-first century. I remember reading Orwell's book *1984* as a teenager and thinking how far away that seemed. The movie *2001* also seemed to take place in the far distant future; now I wonder if the theme song will be played at my son's graduation.

When I was a child, a popular dinnertime conversation concerned the possibility of pay television — seeing a movie in your own home. Around the table, the best hypothesis we could muster was that pay television would work by repeatedly inserting quarters into the set. In the current age of VHS and Fax machines, this lack of foresight seems absurd. The new century is on the horizon, and knowledge accelerates at an ever faster pace. Perhaps young adolescents will tell similar stories about their inability to predict the future.

Even more significant than the knowledge explosion, though, are the value questions facing our children. I have read in the paper about a childless couple engaged in an almost incomprehensible dilemma. They both made their significant contribution to a petrie dish and seven fertilized embryos resulted. Since then, the couple divorced. He wanted to destroy the embryos, whereas she wanted to implant some and have children. Who owns them? Suppose she uses two; what happens to the rest? Such decisions could not even have been imagined 10 years ago. What new ethical dilemmas will occur in the next 20 years?

I asked a group of teachers to list what middle level students would *need to know* when they were 25 years old. Their answers included an understanding of technology, sensitivity to the environment, and the ability to communicate, solve problems, and cooperate with others. These teachers concluded that adults of the twenty-first century will need to be able to deal with the changing nature of the family, maintain a sense of values with flexibility, and have confidence in their ability to adapt to new situations.

Notice that this list does not include the ability to identify an adverbial phrase, list the three causes of the American Revolution, name the states and their capitals, know the origin of igneous rocks, be able to syllabicate, know how to alphabetize up to the third letter, or give definitions of words and use them in a complete sentence.

This marked contrast between projected needs and current practice raises significant questions about what we are doing in our classrooms today—and challenges us to ponder what we *should* be doing to prepare students for the century ahead.

Middle level education teeters on the brink of major transformation. Over the last two decades much "readiness" has been built as educators reorganized and reoriented middle level schools in attempts to make them more responsive to the needs of young adolescents. Some critics may liken this activity as little more than rearranging the deck chairs on the *Titanic*. Although there is some validity in claims of minimal real change, it is certain that middle level schools will, indeed, go over the brink and engage in significant and positive change. Many already have.

*Transforming Middle Level Education: Perspectives and Possibilities* attests to this coming transformation. The contributing authors report what is known to date on a variety of topics important to middle level education and then take a peek into the future. Each chapter reflects a knowledge of pertinent literature and research on a topic that has been written by a highly qualified person.

As editor of this book, I did not attempt to alter the "voice" of each contributing author. Rather, I sought to facilitate the "voice" so that it might sound loud and clear. The contributors to this book offer several hundred years of combined experience in middle level education. All of them are active middle school educators and contributing members of the National Middle School Association. These 19 leaders have dedicated their careers to making school life better for young adolescents.

As this book testifies, middle level schools have already engaged in tremendous *reform*. Many schools have corrected weaknesses in climate, program, and organization. Few schools, however, have begun the deeper process of *transformation*—altering the fundamental character or identity of the school. *Transforming Middle Level Education: Perspectives and Possibilities* does not lay out a blueprint for perfect middle level schooling in the United States. It does, however, lay a foundation for some of the thinking that will lead to transforming middle level education across the nation. It is my hope that this text will nudge and challenge educators to move toward a true transformation of schools for young adolescents.

# Developing a Sense of Identity

*Anyone fortunate enough to spend time and share space with one or more young adolescents knows that two needs scream for attention at this age: a need to belong and a need to discover their identity. The self-esteem of young adolescents seems inexorably tied to these two needs. Identity at this age is particularly important because "who one is" is often linked with "who one is with." Communities and families usually provide a person "learning how to be" with that sense of belonging and a sense of identity. Part One of this book views middle level education from the widened horizon of time and community.*

*In reviewing the efforts to structure an organization that is more responsive to the needs of young adolescents, John H. Lounsbury, in Chapter One, provides historical perspectives on the middle school movement and gives us his glimpse of the future based on its roots. John also discusses the middle school movement's own search for identity. In Chapter Two, Joel Milgram reminds us of the foundational characteristics of young adolescents and updates our knowledge of them; a sense of belonging and a search for identity are central themes. Next, in Chapter Three, Linda Kramer helps us to hear the voices of young adolescents by reporting on her naturalistic studies of students' perceptions of middle school and suggests ways to use these perceptions to improve teaching. In Chapter Four, J. Howard Johnston simply tells a story and thereby discusses the socialization of our youth. Howard helps us understand how important a sense of community is for young adolescents. Frances Kochan closes Part One by helping readers to recognize the school as a part of the larger community and the importance of building strong connections between and among the school, home, and community.*

*Developing a sense of belonging—to school, to community, and to family—is important for all of us. As young adolescents search for their*

1

identity, this sense of belonging actually begins to shape the self-concept that will sustain them as they approach their adult years. As all of these authors stress, the school must take a more active role in helping to build a strong sense of belonging and identity.

# CHAPTER ONE

# Perspectives on the Middle School Movement

JOHN H. LOUNSBURY
*Georgia College*

The junior high school has existed long enough, 80 years, for it to be viewed "in perspective." Even the middle school, now a surprising 30 years old, is subject to a reasonably objective analysis. Are the two forms of school organization really part of the same major thrust? Or are they in conflict, as seemed to be the case in the late 60s and early 70s? What factors lie behind the recent burgeoning interest in middle schools? And what might lie ahead? These and related questions need to be addressed if one is to gain an adequate grasp of middle level education.

To many contemporary educators, the junior high school was a failure. It represents the very practices that most middle level schools are seeking to move away from. Its inadequacies have been so well described and detailed that young educators may think the junior high school was a mistake. The recent return of the ninth grade to the high school from which it came seems like a final bit of evidence for concluding that the junior high school never should have been.

But as is always the case, there is much, much more to the situation than meets the initial eye. A brief review of the history of both the junior

---

The information in this chapter is derived primarily from the author's previous writings, most particularly, C. F. Van Til, G. F. Vars, and J. H. Lounsbury, *Modern Education for the Junior High Years* (Indianapolis, IN: Bobbs Merrill, 1961 and 1967); and J. H. Lounsbury and G. F. Vars, *A Curriculum for the Middle School Years* (New York: Harper and Row, 1978).

high school and middle school is needed if one is to gain the perspective required for transforming middle level education and exploiting its possibilities.

## Why and How the Junior High School Came to Be

The movement to reorganize secondary education began in 1888 when President Charles W. Eliot of Harvard University raised the question: Can the school programs be shortened and enriched? The influential Eliot and many of his presidential colleagues subsequently played key roles in a series of national committees that examined the public school program from the perspective of their primary interest — college preparation. In general, the committees supported the idea of adding two years (grades 7 and 8) to secondary education, which, it was charged, were largely given over to repetition and review. This move would achieve earlier and better college preparatory work. *Economy of time* thus became the first byword in this movement to shift from the 8-4 plan, which had been instituted primarily by Horace Mann, to a 6-6 plan. Separating the now six years of secondary education into junior and senior units, although not originally advocated, soon gained favor as a practical and theoretically sound step.

But almost as quickly as consensus was building to turn grades 7 and 8 into college preparatory grades, public school superintendents and college professors began to be involved in the infant reorganization movement. These educators had different perceptions and a different agenda to bring to the discussions. The best here-and-now education of young adolescents was their chief concern. And so, the very first reason for reorganizing began to diminish in importance, even as the first junior high schools were being established. By the 1920s, the economy of time notion, for all practical purposes, went by the board.

A series of major dropout studies that were conducted between 1907 and 1911 then gave administrative and economic support to reorganization proposals. The statistics reported on the "left backs" and the dropouts were appalling. One-third of all children were "retarded" (that's what they called students who had been retained a year or more in the early part of this century). One-sixth of the pupils in any one grade were repeating that grade. Less than half of the students reached the ninth grade in the high school. Since the negative figures reached their peak in the seventh and eighth grades, reorganization was readily supported for what it could do through an enriched and varied curriculum to keep students in school longer.

Vocational training and civics were among programs advocated so that those who left school early might be better prepared for life outside of school. Such courses were also deemed desirable as a means of "Americanizing" the flood of immigrants coming to our country in the 20s and 30s. *Improved holding power* thus became the second byword of the fledgling movement to reorganize education.

Many believed, and rightly so, that one of the major reasons for the high dropout rate between the eighth and ninth grades and during the ninth grade was the great gap in approach and methods between the elementary school and the high school. The jump from a "mother hen" to a flock of single-subject specialists was too great. The notion of a separate transitional unit, a junior high school, between the two seemed to have merit, hence the third byword became *bridge the gap*.

The young and still not fully accepted field of psychology entered the educational picture in the first two decades of this century and had a substantial effect on reorganization proposals. As compulsory education laws began to be enacted in a number of states, the concern for holding power lost much of its impact. Psychological findings supporting reorganization, however, filled the vacuum quickly—and differently.

G. Stanley Hall (1905) authored the first serious published work on the age of adolescence. Two volumes were issued, the first in 1905. According to Hall's recapitulation or "culture-epoch" theory, the future of humankind was, in large measure, determined by the quality of education received at the crucial age of adolescence. He called adolescence a "psychological second birth" and the adolescent "a new kind of being." Those who accepted his views, and there were many, saw the merit in a new school unit for these unique beings going through the "storm and stress" of puberty that Hall wrote about so convincingly.

A second development in psychology that furthered the cause of the junior high school was the individual differences movement. Although everyone knew that individuals differed, early schools operated on the assumption that people were more or less alike mentally. Differences noted in achievement, it was thought, were due to the application of effort more than native ability. The common but usually worthless advice, "try harder," was born in that era because of that assumption.

But such notions about the unanimity of school children could not stand up when psychologists like Thorndike began measuring and testing. The differences, when charted, were surprising, even startling. Differences between individuals were extensive, so were differences within individuals. And nowhere were the individual differences greater than at the seventh-, eighth-, and ninth-grade levels. Organizing a new school that might better deal with these diverse youngsters made sense. The fourth byword of the junior high school movement thus became *meet the needs of young adolescents*. This goal became the movement's basic theme song, and it has prevailed while other goals diminished in importance as conditions have changed.

One major factor that supported the expansion of the junior high school was a supportive culture. The times were ones of growth and of experimentation with new ways taking hold in government, in industry, in patterns of living, in religion, and in economics. Proposals to reorganize schools thus fell on fertile soil.

So the junior high school, which got started as a downward extension of secondary education with a number of clear functions, began to establish an identity of its own, which, theoretically at least, was more child centered than college preparatory centered.

The case for reorganization and for a separate junior high unit was summarized well in the famous 1918 Report of the Commission on the Reorganization of Secondary Education. Though the Seven Cardinal Principles (objectives) set forth in this document are its major claim to fame, it is worth citing the following paragraphs from the report.

> *The eight years heretofore given to elementary education have not, as a rule, been effectively utilized. The last two of these years in particular have not been well adapted to the needs of the adolescent. . . . We believe that much of the difficulty will be removed by a new type of secondary education beginning at about 12 or 13. Furthermore, the period of four years now allotted to the high school is too short a time in which to accomplish the work outlined above.*
>
> *We, therefore, recommend a reorganization of the school system whereby the first six years shall be devoted to elementary education designed to meet the needs of pupils approximately 6 to 12 years of age; and the second six years to secondary education designed to meet the needs of pupils approximately 12 to 18 years of age.*
>
> *The six years to be devoted to secondary education may well be divided into two periods which may be designated as the junior and senior periods. In the junior period emphasis should be placed upon the attempt to help the pupil explore his own aptitudes and to make at least provisional choice of the kinds of work to which he shall devote himself. In the senior period emphasis should be given to training in the fields thus chosen. This distinction lies at the basis of the organization of the junior and senior high schools.*
>
> *In the junior high school there should be a gradual introduction of departmental instruction, some choice of subjects under guidance, promotion by subjects, pre-vocational courses, and a social organization that calls forth initiative and develops the sense of personal responsibility for the welfare of the group (pp. 12–13).*

Notice particularly the recognition given to helping "the pupil to explore his own aptitudes," to the advocacy of a "gradual introduction of departmentalized instruction," and the call for "a social organization that calls forth initiative and develops the sense of personal responsibility for the welfare of the group." These statements seem quite "middle school" and make evident that the problem with the junior high school was not in its intention but in its implementation.

## Early Developments and Status of the Junior High School

The junior high school, first introduced in 1909–1910, took hold fairly quickly. By 1925, there were 880 separate junior high schools; by 1934, there were 1,950; by 1960, the number reached 5,000; and by 1970, the number of junior high schools peaked at close to 8,000. The difficulty of exactly tracing the growth has long been a handicap to reorganization. The U.S. Office/ Department of Education has never recognized intermediate educational institutions and continues to gather statistics using just two categories, elementary and secondary. But as early as the late 1930s, schools deviating from the traditional 9–12 high school had clearly become majority practice. By the late 1940s, the separate junior high school followed by a separate three-year high school became the most predominant single form of school organization in the United States.

Cities and towns, where enough pupils reside to permit varied types of schools, were naturally where the large majority of junior high schools located. Some states and the District of Columbia ultimately reorganized completely, but every state reported some junior high schools by the early 1930s.

The vast majority of junior high schools were composed of grades 7, 8, and 9, which was the most advocated arrangement. However, there have always been a substantial number of other grade arrangements, such as 6–8, 7–8, 7–10, and 8–9. The 7–8 school has continued to be a popular pattern for middle schools, as it was for junior high schools. As early as 1917, there was a 5–8 school reported. And in the late 1940s, the Skokie Junior High (Winnetka, Illinois), composed of grades 6 through 8, included many of the features currently advocated for middle schools—short-term exploratory courses, an interdisciplinary core, flexible scheduling, student-directed activities, and considerable individualized instruction.

Throughout the entire middle level educational movement it has been clear that administrative factors far outweigh educational factors as determinants of how schools are organized. Existing buildings, economy, integration, expanding or declining pupil populations, and related demographic factors are almost always the prime considerations. A supposedly obsolete high school building typically became a city's first junior high school or, more recently, its first middle school.

## Contributions of the Junior High School

Despite all the negative press in the last 20 or 30 years, the junior high school story is a success story, befitting the nation in which the story took place. Its failures—and there are many—should not negate its successes, of which there were also many.

Certainly the numerical dominance of middle level institutions is a credit to the junior high school. School organization in the United States was revolutionized by this precedent-setting institution, which achieved majority status even before the middle school came along. An enriched and expanded curriculum for young adolescents was achieved via the introduction in junior high schools of industrial arts, home economics, laboratory sciences, foreign languages, and many related exploratory areas. Guidance-oriented homerooms were installed in junior high schools and specialized professional counselors were utilized in a way not previously found in seventh and eighth grades in elementary schools. Although viewed as extracurricular or cocurricular, student activities were greatly expanded by junior high schools. Service-oriented or interest-centered clubs and activities were introduced to give young adolescents opportunities to socialize, to develop leadership skills, and to pursue nonacademic interests.

Despite its later reputation as an inflexible, stereotypical school, the junior high school actually served as a center for much experimentation. The core curriculum, block scheduling, resource units, correlation of content, and an overt concern for affective education were all a part of the early junior high school effort. If not for the handicaps noted below, the junior high school might still be seen as the cutting edge institution it started out to be.

## Handicaps to the Development of the Junior High School

The strong traditions of the college preparatory high school and the establishment of junior high schools under the auspices of secondary education quickly took their toll on this newly created intermediate educational institution of grades 7, 8, and 9. First, the school was saddled with a label that was taken too literally, both in terms of the prestige accorded it and in terms of the educational practices employed in it. The very word *junior* in our culture carries something of a demeaning and subservient tone. The lack of prestige was exacerbated by the attitudes people held concerning this new institution. Teachers were hired with the promise that if they took this job they would have the first appropriate vacancy in the senior high. A transfer of an administrator from a junior high school was characterized as a promotion. The resulting almost unconscious attitude of inferiority influenced innumerable decisions and mindsets—and has not yet been completely overcome.

Since the junior high school was originally seen as a downward extension of secondary education, the complete dominance of traditional high school approaches in it was not surprising. And, lacking any other model, such was almost inevitable. Departmentalization was unquestioned as the way to organize these former elementary grades. Junior editions of high school practices, from superlatives to yearbooks, to cheerleaders, to student activities, and even to the courses themselves, were readily instituted. What limited supervisory leadership given the junior high school was naturally high school oriented.

The new junior high school began operation with virtually no appropriate standards, regulations, or policies to guide its proper development. State departments often required one set of reporting procedures for the seventh and eighth grades and another for the ninth grade. The ninth grade carried Carnegie unit credits applicable to high school graduation and thus never really cut the high school apron strings.

The difficulties experienced by the junior high school were further complicated by the facilities in which it operated. Typically, it set up shop in the old high school building when the favored institution moved into the community's new pride—the modern senior high school building. There, the junior high school contended with the very inadequacies that led to the building of a new high school. Less frequently, but no less a handicap, an old elementary school sometimes became the junior high school. Here, the lack of a gymnasium, home economics and industrial arts laboratories, an adequate library, and space itself restricted the program that could be offered.

And finally, the junior high school lacked specially trained teachers. The vast majority of teachers employed in the early junior high schools were prepared as high school teachers who saw themselves as subject-matter specialists. They didn't see their job as guiding social, emotional, and physical development. Although both the junior high pioneers, Thomas Briggs and Leonard Koos, in their separate books published in 1920, pointed out the critical need for specific teacher preparation, none was forthcoming.

In light of these handicaps, it is little wonder that the junior high school, despite some clear theoretical advocacy to the contrary, became the junior version of the high school with all the characteristics attributable thereto. One might say that Charles W. Eliot had his way after all!

## The Middle School Emerges

The inability of the junior high school to stay open, to establish an independent identity, and to fulfill some of its intended functions, while understandable, led to considerable criticism in the 1940s and 1950s. Although a number of efforts were put forth during these decades to resurrect the

earlier intentions and turn the institution around, conditions were not sufficiently conducive for success. History teaches that it is easier to create a new
institution than to change a well-established one, so the proposal for a middle school, a seemingly fresh idea and with a new name, seemed more
acceptable.

The relatively rapid acceptance of the middle school as a valid educational approach was due to at least three major sources: (1) the dissatisfac-
tion with the junior high school as it had evolved; (2) the Sputnik-induced
obsession with academic mastery, particularly in mathematics and sciences;
and (3) the recognition that young people were indeed maturing physically
earlier.

The first factor has been identified previously and need not be
elaborated on again, except to point out that most of the criticism came from
within (i.e., from active junior high educators who readily recognized its
failures to meet the needs of its clientele) rather than from outside.

The second factor is, in many respects, reminiscent of the original im-
petus for the junior high school. As one Harvard President, Charles W. Eliot,
initiated reform for college preparatory purposes, so another Harvard President, James B. Conant (1960) gave the middle school movement a big boost
with his academic reform recommendations in the late 50s. To many who
were concerned about catching up with the Russians, the movement to institute new math and new science in the middle grades and to return the ninth
grade to the high school where a full four-year sequence of technical and
advanced courses could be taken was the way to go.

The third factor resulted from new scientific evidence that documented
the earlier maturation of young people. An English scientist, J. M. Tanner
(1972), was the most widely quoted authority on this matter. If today's sixth-
grader is like yesterday's seventh- or eighth-grader, then that youngster requires the same specialization of program and faculty that has characterized
intermediate education. Whether due to better prenatal development or a
high-protein diet, both boys and girls do display the signs of puberty earlier
than did their grandparents. And even if disapproving of the unfortunately
related earlier sophistication that has characterized our liberal society, many
agree that school organization might as well reflect these changes.

So the new middle school of grades 5 through 8 or 6 through 8 came
on the scene in the 1960s and readily took hold. Like the junior high school
before it, the middle school was able to take advantage of propitious times
and varied arenas of support. These included court-ordered integration, consolidation to reflect changing residential patterns, and related administrative
factors.

Unfortunately, many early middle school advocates used the stereotypical junior high school as a whipping boy. They made comparisons between the *operational* junior high school and the *theoretical* middle school,

which always made the new middle school appear to be the perfect alternative to the "failed" junior high school. Although such comparisons made good copy and aided in the launching of the middle school movement, they were unfair. This was evident in the 1970s, when research studies (Brooks, 1978; Educational Research Services, 1975; Gatewood, 1973) revealed that there were virtually no significant differences between new middle schools and old junior high schools. Grade levels included had been changed, as had the label on the school, but in terms of program and actual practices, differences were virtually nonexistent. Just creating middle schools administratively failed to break the powerful hand of precedent and ingrained institutionalism already set. Many middle schools were simply junior editions of the junior high school with departmentalization moved down one more grade.

The inability of the middle school initially to incorporate real reform did not, however, slow down its acceptance in principle or in practice. The middle school movement established itself strongly in the 1960s and 70s. Alexander's comprehensive survey in 1967–68 revealed 1,101 schools "having at least three but not more than five grades and including grades 6 and 7." Later surveys (Alexander & McEwin, 1989) revealed significant growth throughout the 1970s and 80s, often at the expense of previously established junior high schools but also because many were being established where no intermediate institutions had been before. By the mid-1980s, the 5-3-4 had become the most common single form of school organization in the country, replacing the previously dominant 6-3-3.

Although progress on the program or curriculum front cannot begin to match progress on the administrative organization front, some signs of programmatic reform are evident. The middle school concept has been able to capitalize on some avenues of support that the junior high school was denied. A major professional organization, the National Middle School Association, was founded in 1963 and has grown to be a powerful advocate through its conferences, journal, and publications. NMSA's regions cover all 50 states, the Canadian provinces, and it has 40 state affiliates and even a European affiliate. The National Association of Secondary School Principals, one of the nation's most influential professional associations, declared itself as an advocate and has made tangible its stance in a variety of services during the past decade. Several other university-based centers have been established and have contributed resources and leadership to the burgeoning movement.

Research, both on the nature of the age group and the programmatic characteristics of middle schools, has also expanded considerably in recent years. The results have provided valuable guides to practice. One could conclude rightfully that the middle school movement is much more than a fad or an innovation. It is a genuinely significant and long-term educational reform effort. Though progress is slow and the components of the middle school concept are still more promise than practice, there is real hope for the eventual implementation of its major tenets.

## Handicaps to the Development of the Middle School

With the exception of its name, the middle school has had to face exactly the same set of obstacles that handicapped the advancement of the junior high school. Some progress on each specific stumbling block can be noted, but not nearly enough to move any one of them from being a part of the problem to being a part of the solution.

The lack of understanding about the age of young adolescence remains now, as it has been for 75 years, the major handicap to the implementation of the middle school concept. A narrow view of what comprises an education and what young adolescents are like continues to make it difficult to operationalize many aspects of the middle school concept. For instance, if parents recognized the exploratory nature and needs of young adolescents, they would demand more extensive exploratory experiences rather than fear such might impinge on what they view to be the main aspect of their child's education. Helping to educate parents and the public about these distinctive transitional years between childhood and full adolescence must continue as a direct responsibility of every middle level teacher, counselor, and administrator.

In large part, this lack of understanding underlies the long-standing handicap of having few teachers specifically prepared to work with middle level youngsters. Although some recent progress can be noted in establishing distinctive middle level education certification and related teacher preparation programs, it has been discouragingly slow. This issue is discussed in more detail in Chapter Nineteen of this book.

## *Conclusion*

The junior high school movement began in the 1910s. The middle school movement began in the 1960s. Are they separate, distinct movements? I think not; rather, the middle school movement could well be characterized as the renaissance of the real junior high school. Is the new merged middle level education movement really the rebirth of progressive education? I think so, for, like progressive education, it is based solely on the best understandings about the nature and needs of learners and the accepted principles of learning. Although progressive education as a movement fell into ill repute and presumably died in the 1950s, the questions it raised remain unanswered but still pertinent. These are the questions that have nagged at the hearts and heads of those who stopped to listen to kids, to read the research, to contemplate seriously the broad goals of education. They are questions that will not be washed away by reactions to short-term crises or slogans like "back to the basics." Nor will they be made obsolete by any special programs that treat symptoms rather than causes.

I believe that in middle level education, the United States has its best chance, perhaps its last chance, to carry out educational reforms that will be truly appropriate for youth and effective for the society that needs its youth to be better educated in every respect than any previous generation had to be.

If history is an indication, of course, middle level institutions are not likely to be changed by revolution, however great the contemporary crisis. But change must come and it will come. The question is: Will it come fast enough to keep our society from sliding further down the path to self-destruction that it seems bent on? Perhaps we should take heart from the fact that where one stands is not as important as in what direction one is moving. Middle level education in the 1990s is clearly in motion, and it is on the right track. Nearly every middle level institution sees itself as in process, on the road rather than at rest. We can, therefore, have hope and optimistically exert our individual and collective efforts to make middle level education developmentally appropriate and intellectually sound.

However, consider carefully and thoughtfully the following statements made by two highly respected educators:

*Every new movement in education, if it is to succeed at all, must pass through two critical stages of development before it can find its proper place. The first stage is that in which the new movement struggles for recognition by educators and by the public. The second stage is that in which approval has been won, but actual practice is incomplete, and the character or status of the new movement is still to be established. The success or failure of the movement may be determined at either of these stages.*

*There is abundant evidence that the middle school movement has passed successfully the first stage of its development. Though little more than a decade has passed since its real beginning, it has met with general approval throughout the country. The question now is not so much whether the middle school shall be recognized as a part of our public-school system, but what sort of a middle school shall be established and what sort of an education shall be provided therein. Hundreds of middle schools established in almost all parts of the country testify to the fact that the new institution has met with general approval. They also testify to the fact that the new institution has met with general approval. They also testify, however, to the fact that those responsible for the organization of middle schools differ widely in their conceptions as to what such schools should be.*

*The present is a time when the middle school movement is in a very critical stage of its development. It is a time when the form of reorganization is found in hundreds of school systems, but the real reorganization attempted in but few. It is a time when there is danger of numerous middle schools in name, but few in fact. It is a time when there is great need for clear orientation and for the recognition of educational standards which should obtain in the new type of school. It is of great importance that at this stage of its development a survey be made of the present status of the middle school, defects and merits pointed out, and a constructive program suggested for its development.*

---

*The middle school is accepted in theory, and its possibilities proved so alluring that the movement for reorganization is well under way in both urban and rural districts. The physical redistribution of the grades seems assured; but if, having accomplished that, schoolmen rest content, they will have missed the one great educational opportunity of their generation for real educational reform. There is a demand for purposes so clear and so cogent that they will result in new curricula, new courses of study, new methods of teaching, and new social relationships—in short, in a new spirit which will make the intermediate years not only worthwhile in themselves, but also an intelligent inspiration for every child to continue as long as profitable the education for which he is by inheritance best fitted. In its essence, the middle school is a device of democracy whereby nurture may cooperate with nature to secure the best results possible for each individual adolescent as well as for society at large.*

Those of us caught up in the exciting, vibrant middle school movement ought to ponder the above statements. They were made 70 years ago! The first three paragraphs were from Alexander Inglis's editor's introduction to Thomas Briggs's book, *The Junior High School.* The fourth paragraph is Dr. Briggs's concluding paragraph in this first book on the junior high school, published in 1920. (Note the last sentence—it is a perfect summary of the middle school concept.) The only change made in the wording was to replace *junior high* with *middle.*

We would all do well to consider and to be humbled by the timelessness and continuing validity of these statements from out of the past. Let us not allow history to repeat itself once again. A rare opportunity exists in the 1990s to truly transform middle level schools. We must seize it.

# References

Alexander, W. M. (1968). *A survey of organizational patterns of reorganized middle schools.* Final Report, USDOE Project 7-D-026. Gainesville, FL: University of Florida.

Alexander, W. M., & McEwin, C. K. (1989). *Schools in the middle: Status and progress.* Columbus, OH: National Middle School Association.

Briggs, T. (1920). *The junior high school.* New York: Houghton Mifflin.

Brooks, K. (1978). The middle school—A national survey. *Middle School Journal, IX*(2), 6–7.

Commission on the Reorganization of Secondary Education. (1918). *Cardinal principles of secondary education.* Bulletin No. 35. Washington, DC: United States Department of the Interior, Bureau of Education.

Conant, J. B. (1960). *Education in the junior high school years.* Princeton, NJ: Educational Testing Service.

Educational Research Services. (1975). *Summary of research on middle schools.* Arlington, VA: Author.

Gatewood, T. E. (1973). What research says about the middle school. *Educational Leadership, 31*(3), 221–224.

Hall, G. S. (1905). *Adolescence, Vol. 1.* New York: D. Appleton Century.

Koos, L. V. (1920). *The junior high school.* New York: Harcourt, Brace and Howe.

Tanner, J. M. (1972). Sequence, tempo, and individual variation in growth and development of boys and girls aged twelve to sixteen. In J. Kagan & R. C. Coles (Eds.), *Twelve to sixteen: Early adolescence* (pp. 1–24). New York: Norton.

# CHAPTER TWO

# A Portrait of Diversity: The Middle Level Student

JOEL MILGRAM
*University of Cincinnati*

A well-known middle school educator was asked at a workshop to describe the general characteristics of the American young adolescent. "How would I know?" he replied, "I only have three of them." This is another way of saying that attempting to try to describe the characteristics of such a diverse group is a risky venture.

No single characteristic describes an 11-year-old or a typical 14-year-old; there are vast differences among them, too vast for anyone to hold a single model of the All-American Young Adolescent. Despite the diversity, however, certain characteristics appear to apply to many, if not most, of the boys and girls between the ages of 10 and 15.

This chapter describes selected characteristics of middle grade students and will provide a context for succeeding chapters in this book. Physical, social, emotional, and cognitive characteristics will be described within the context of two generalizations: (1) young adolescents experience significant change and (2) emotions reach the extremes of high and low during this time of development.

Change and growth for young adolescents can be grouped into four areas: physical, social, emotional, and intellectual. Students change dramatically during a relatively short period of time, which means that the changes themselves and the speed in which they occur have an impact on students. Introspection is difficult for most people during the best of times, but when change occurs so dramatically, it becomes particularly difficult. As an adult, you can look at a photograph of yourself taken three years earlier and have a strong identification with the image you see. A 13-year-old who sees a photograph of herself or himself at 10 years old might view the person as a perfect stranger. Teachers sometimes describe middle level students as "the strange ones": they are indeed strange, particularly to themselves.

The 10- to 15-year-old seems to be on an emotional roller coaster, going through different moods, often within a single day. Mood changes add a degree of unpredictability in behavior and no doubt some excitement to a teacher's life; it serves as a destabilizing influence, often causing an emotional imbalance (Coleman, 1980). Some educators argue that this emotional variability places all young adolescents at high risk of making decisions that may have a negative impact on their future health and/or success. Sensitivity is a necessary quality for adults who work with young adolescents.

Given the previously stated two generalizations—the amount of change and the emotional state of young adolescents—it may be helpful to examine characteristics in the areas social, emotional, cognitive, and physical development in more depth. It is important to remember that the development of these four areas do not take place in isolation from each other. The breakdown of categories is but a writer's convenience. In reality, they are very much interconnected, and often these changes do not take place at the same pace but seem to overlap with each other. One can think of the young adolescent as a school orchestra during rehearsal. The woodwinds, the brass, and the strings all play separately but they are all interconnected and they play, most often, at the same time. And, like the school orchestra, young adolescents are often out of tune as they attempt to cope with significant change.

## Physical Characteristics

Physical appearance is foremost in the mind of most young adolescents. They think about how they look to others and they wonder if the others know about their secret imperfections. Most young adolescents yearn to be physically normal and many perceive themselves not to be. They tend to worry about their breast size, penis size, thigh size, nose size, shoe size, pimple size, and all else that is physically measurable.

The development of the primary and secondary sexual characteristics and the growth spurt represent the most significant physical events of this age group. Both girls and boys are going to grow at a greater rate than they have ever experienced, with the exception of when they were infants. Girls will start their growth spurt around two years earlier than boys, and for a while many girls will tower over some of their male counterparts. During the approximate two years of the growth spurt, 9 to 10 inches of growth for boys and 7 inches for girls is not uncommon. For a time, girls will not only be taller but heavier than boys (Marshall & Tanner, 1974).

Some parts of the body grow faster than others and until all parts catch up with each other the middle level child appears to resemble someone with mismatched parts. The length of the legs most often reach their peak first, followed by the trunk. This may result in ungainly movements; uncomplimentary nicknames often appear at this time (Tanner, 1978).

Girls generally tend to be overly concerned with the development of their body contours. The two most noticeable changes during their growth spurt is breast development and the rounding of the hips. Girls who perceive themselves as shapeless are generally self-conscious, though it is also true that a girl who has developed a particularly large bust will be equally self-conscious. Another major bench mark of physical development for girls is their first menstrual flow, or menarche. The menarche may be a traumatic event associated with shame, or it may be a time of celebration, depending on the degree of preparation and general attitudes of the family (Ruble & Brooks-Gunn, 1982). Regardless, most young women will experience some degree of mood changes sometime during their cycle. Though the first menstrual period might occur somewhat late in puberty, early menstrual periods are not uncommon. Ovulation, however, usually starts 12 months after menarche.

For boys, the growth of facial and pubic hair is perceived as the initial entrance to manhood. Although most facial hair waits for the later stages of adolescence, pubic hair can appear even before the growth spurt. The amount of pubic hair as well as the size of the penis is often associated with a boy's degree of manliness. About a year after the growth spurt begins, most boys experience their first ejaculation during sleep, known as nocturnal emissions. For some boys, this event is a chief topic of conversation, for others it is something they prefer not to share. Like girls, individual reactions depend on family preparation and attitudes (Atwater, 1988).

For both boys and girls, comparisons within the same sex is a major preoccupation and it begins with a preoccupation of one's own body. Most young adolescents examine themselves closely in front of a mirror, undressed, in the privacy of their own homes. Imperfections, or perceived imperfections, are duly noted and, if possible, compensated for by padding a bra, standing taller, starting to lift weights, or covering pimples. Comparisons are usually done quietly and covertly until one is convinced the particular attribute in question fares well against others of the same age and sex. Then, the attribute is flaunted.

Girls, in general, seem more concerned about their physical appearance than boys (Rice, 1990). One could reason that girls become aware at an early age of the emphasis society places on how a person looks. Females in our culture are often judged in terms of attractiveness, whereas their male counterparts can get away with athletic ability and perhaps "rugged good looks." Boys, on the other hand, are more conscious of height than girls, height being another indicator of manliness. Regardless, it is clear that both boys and girls are extremely aware of their appearance and this awareness becomes a major priority in their lives (Rice, 1990).

Most young adolescents make comparisons with their own sex, but cross-sex comparisons increase during those times when what is supposed to be isn't. That is, it is generally expected by both sexes that boys will be stronger, heavier, and taller than most girls. But, because girls' growth spurt begins at around age 12 and the boys not until two years later, girls between the ages of 12 and 14, on the average, will be taller than boys, and between the ages of 10 and 14 will be heavier than boys (Tanner, 1978).

If young adolescents seem bigger than in previous generations it is because they are bigger. The accelerated growth trends over the years (known as the secular trend) has resulted in the average girl being ½ to 1 inch taller than her mother and reaching menarche nearly a year sooner. In the late 1800s, boys did not reach their full adult height until they were at least 23 years of age; currently their adult height is reached by age 18 (Bullough, 1981; Tanner, 1978).

The pace of the physical changes taking place is different for each child and for each sex. In the egocentric, comparative world of the young adolescent, these differences are generally translated into feelings of inadequacy and deficiency, clearly for some more than others. The overweight, short female and the skinny, acned boy without pubic hair may have more negative feelings to overcome than their peers. It is important to remember that all adolescents at one time or another feel badly about some part of parts of their bodies, and that derogatory remarks or jesting comments about physical features by a peer or an adult is extremely hurtful and potentially harmful to the fragile self-esteem. It is within this social context that young adolescents must adjust to new bodies.

## Social Characteristics

A developmental need for socialization is strong for all people, but this need is particularly strong for middle level students. Children do not select their parents and, for the most part, they do not select their teachers. Therefore, friends represent an important act of choice for young adolescents. Choosing and rejecting individuals for interaction provides students the opportunity to engage in this activity, preparing them, in part, for a role in the adult world (Atwater, 1988).

Friends serve a number of purposes for us — one of which is that they help expand our world. Friends allow us to compare families, contrast values, and take risks. Their reactions to our dress, our jokes, our athletic ability, and our appearance allow us to measure our ability in these areas. The question becomes how much deviance from the accepted norms can a friend-ship group tolerate?

Most research on friendship patterns for young adolescents shows that friends are selected on the basis of similarity to one's self. Although a group or a clique may develop a personality of its own, the individual members tend to be like each other and, quite often, will attempt to look like each other. This need to conform manifests itself in similar hair styles, color of socks, or even the gait of walk.

Participation in various school and nonschool clubs and social activities is one vehicle to social acceptance. For girls, being part of a prestigious social group is perceived as an important asset leading to general social acceptance. Boys, on the other hand, still rate athletics as one of the keys to popularity. For both boys and girls, personal qualities are ranked very high as factors determining popularity.

For many young adolescents, shyness is a problem in relating to peers. Often the shy adolescent is unaware that others may also feel the same way, even if they do not *appear* to be shy. Outward manifestations of shyness might include blushing, nervous stomach, sweating, and increased pulse rate. But none of these symptoms may show on some students who, in fact, con-sider themselves extremely shy. The basis of shyness is often the fear that others will view an individual in a negative way (Connolly, White, Stevens, & Burstein, 1987). Though it often has its roots in childhood, young adolescents show an increase in shyness due to sudden growth, developing interests in the opposite sex, and increased fear of making mistakes in front of others (Ishiyama, 1984).

Peer influence and peer pressure to conform is at its strongest between the ages of 11 and 17, although a number of studies report a decline after the age of 15. Many parents and teachers view such strong influences with alarm, but peer pressure *not* to indulge in self-destructive behavior (such as drug abuse) often occurs. Whether or not the influence is to conform with peer rules, the susceptibility to group action demonstrates how dependent middle students are on peer approval (Larson, 1980). Young adolescents who are truly fond of their parents seem to have less need to conform to the demands of peers. Adolescents who come from dysfunctional families seem to be more subject to, and have a greater need for, peer approval (Sebald, 1986).

Peer association, part of the normal development of the young adoles-cent, is an important aspect of learning at this age. The undersocialized middle level student often misses out on many learning opportunities and, in some ways, is not achieving one of the developmental tasks for this age group. The social isolate, common in every school, may reflect family problems, lack of interpersonal skills, or some emotional disorder. Social isolates need careful watching and concern, and will benefit from a well-functioning middle school that regards socialization as part of its purpose.

Gender plays an important role in friendship and socialization patterns. In fact, gender is the single most influential factor in friendship patterns for young adolescents (Atwater, 1988; Schofield, 1981). Despite significant changes in sex-role socialization in our society, middle level students follow same-sex friendship patterns and continue to do so until later adolescence. Boys and girls see themselves as very different from each other in interests, sports, and other activities. Also, cross-sex relationships are often interpreted as romantic in nature and subject to a lot of teasing by friends (Schofield, 1981). Although cross-sex friendship patterns generally do not begin until middle adolescence, exceptions exist. Television advertising and the behavior of some parents have resulted in a small percentage of middle level students having enduring cross-sex friendships (Felson & Gottfredson, 1984).

Educators who fail to recognize the developmental social needs of young adolescents and enforce restrictive rules in situations where socialization would be appropriate are depriving youngsters of growth opportunities. Middle level students, with or without permission from adults, will pass notes, meet in the wash rooms while on "authorized errands," and whisper to each other when the teacher's back is turned. Their needs are better met when conversation is regarded as an important aspect of education, where groups work on reports together, and where kid-talk is respected by the adults who are there to help them socialize into our society. Social validation is important for young adolescents to build and to maintain a positive self-concept (Milgram, 1985).

## Emotional Characteristics

With the monumental changes that occur during this period of growth, it seems natural to wonder how any emotional equilibrium can be maintained. Some educators claim that it is not maintained at all and that there is more emotional turmoil in the life of the young adolescent than existed in earlier periods of childhood.

This age group is in a major transitionary period that naturally creates a multitude of needs, some of which seem contradictory and all of which cannot be met. This contradiction appears in the home as well as the classroom.

A middle level student might still love his teddy bear but want his own room. She may sit on her dad's lap but just die if he held her hand in public. He might delight in a little note from his mother stuck in his lunch bag but would rather swallow it than have it discovered. She might demand a ride to school because it is raining but asked to be dropped off a block away from the main entrance before she is seen with a parent. He may cry in his bedroom then mock his sister for crying. She might join a crusade in cleaning up the neighborhood of litter but allow her room to become an environmental health hazard (Rice, 1990).

In school, he might crave to play basketball but decline when his team must remove their shirts. She might absolutely relish science but opt for the future homemakers club instead. He might know the right answer but give the wrong one. She might pledge friendship forever and break a trust an hour later (Yarcheski & Mahon, 1984). Young adolescents often say yes when they mean no and they laugh when they really want to cry.

Crossing over the line from childhood to adolescence is difficult because the line is not clear and there are inherent risks involved. It is an emotional leap as well as a physical one, and maintaining a balanced sense of self becomes increasingly difficult. Strang (1957) suggested four variations of the self-concept that young adolescents must reconcile if a degree of emotional stability is to be achieved:

1. *General self-concept:* The adolescent's evaluation of himself or herself; the perception of his or her abilities and roles
2. *Temporary self-concept:* A temporary evaluation, perhaps influenced by a recent event or remark
3. *Social self:* The way the adolescent believes others view him or her
4. *Ideal self:* How the adolescent would like to be

By the time a person reaches adolescence, self-concept usually stabilizes. The ages of 10 to 14 is a period of growing, changing, and general instability. Perceptions of self at this time often guide decisions about social situations, cognitive activities, and a general feeling of self-worth (Rice, 1990).

Teachers' and parents' well-meaning responses to adolescent emotions are sometimes thwarted by a failure to understand the seriousness of the situation as viewed by the child. Often the difficulty lies in the fact that the adult naturally perceives action through adult eyes. Young adolescents generally do not perceive their world in the same way as adults. For example, one could easily imagine a teacher comforting a crying young lady of age 13 who just found out that her steady boyfriend of three weeks broke off the relationship. The teacher, as an adult, knows that this is not the end of this student's romantic life and can easily imagine this youngster finding another boyfriend in a few weeks. To comfort her, the teacher might assure the young girl by saying, "Don't worry, Jane, there will be others." Instead of being comforted, Jane might burst into more tears and cry even louder than before. Was not the assurance of future boyfriend a comforting statement? Not necessarily. If a close and significant person in your life suddenly departed without warning, would the assurance of "Don't worry, there will be others" comfort you (Milgram, 1986)?

Many young adolescents do a good job of hiding their fragility as they make the transition from childhood to adolescence. Looking tough, or looking mature, or turning away from offers of help or affection are just some of the ways middle level students let their teachers and parents know that they are developing an emotional autonomy. Also, they may seek to prove their independence and may even get involved in delinquent acts. Though the more serious acts of delinquency emerge in middle and late adolescence, the minor offenses increase from late childhood into early adolescence. Young adolescents under the age of 15 partake in what is called *nuisance behavior,* and yet 1 out of 7 burglaries are committed by this age group (U.S. Bureau of the Census, 1988).

Autonomous behaviors, the ability to handle tasks appropriate to their age with little or no supervision, during the middle grades are increasingly displayed but there are different kinds of autonomous behaviors. Middle level students start to develop and move toward behavioral autonomy. Students generally behave more independently than when they were younger. A part-time job delivering the local newspaper, completing an independent study project, and setting one's own alarm are all examples of *behavioral autonomy.* Often this kind of autonomy is confused with *emotional autonomy,* often defined as the ability to take criticism and rejection and rely on one's own self for encouragement and support (Steinberg, 1985).

Most middle level students have not developed a strong sense of emotional autonomy and are easily discouraged and lose self-confidence. A school's emphasis on content and academic excellence at the expense of strong emotional support at this age does not contribute to the general well-being of its students. Although middle level students do not need to have happy-face stickers put on their papers and foreheads, they do need to be surrounded by adults who manifest caring and interest in their problems. Emotional autonomy will develop in varying degrees as children approach adulthood. But the fact that some of the boys shave and some of the girls appear to be adult women should not lead us to believe that middle level students are adults with little need for strong emotional support. The growth of emotional maturity is facilitated not only by good role models but by young adolescents' advances in intellectual development (Fasick, 1984).

## Cognitive Development

The transitional features of early adolescence also apply to cognitive development. Transition affects the way students are capable of thinking. This is the time for formal thought; that is, having the ability to deal with abstract concepts, ideas, and symbols. The brain now becomes a more powerful thinking machine than it was previously. Although it is generally believed that the formal operational stage of thinking begins at about age 11 or 12, considerable research exists that a percentage of adolescents never reached this stage (Keating, 1980; Linn, 1983). There appears to be little or no relationship between intelligence and the attainment of formal thought, or social class and the attainment of formal thought, but there is evidence that suggests there may be cultural differences (Dasen, 1977; Johoda, 1980; Rogoff & Lave, 1984). For example, U.S. children between the ages of 13 and 15 are more advanced in formal thought than the same aged group in Hong Kong (Rice, 1990).

The transition to formal thought is not unrelated to social competence. The ability to see another's point of view, to empathize, and to put one's self in the other person's shoes is characteristic of abstract thinking. In turn, it also produces a heightened level of awareness, self-consciousness, and even a pronounced awkwardness of thought (Steinberg, 1985). Decision making may be more painful because of the power to examine more of the possibilities and options. Awkwardness also occurs because the young adolescent is in the beginning stages of learning to use this new mental power. Using this new powerful tool requires some practice and the initial use may result in its inappropriate use. For example, adolescents with newly acquired formal thought tend to give overly complex solutions to relatively simple problems. Sometimes referred to as *pseudostupidity,* bright individuals may seem to regress intellectually as they accommodate to their new mental powers (Elkind, 1978).

A logical outcome of the ability to deal with concepts in an abstract fashion would appear to be a heightened increase in creativity. The creative process often calls for a new interpretation or novel arrangement of existing notions. The more powerful thinking machine of the adolescent appears ready-made for great leaps into imaginative thought. Surprisingly, adolescents are often less creative than younger children (Wolf & Larsen, 1981). It may be that the social inhibitions and fears of not conforming contribute to this phenomenon (Earl, 1987).

One must also question whether the schools for young adolescents are allowing for and rewarding the creative process. Very often, young adolescents are questioned by their teachers and often discover that there was only "one right answer." A teacher-initiated question that begins with "What is the significance of . . ." followed by a single-student response and then another teacher-initiated unrelated question sends messages to the students that *the* right answer has been given and whatever other answers they had in mind were incorrect. Of course, a term such as *significance of* may yield discussion and debate and be open to creative interpretations. Young adolescents are not cognitive risk takers, and with the teacher's help, will willingly conform.

Although it is still not clear whether it is biologically or socially based (or both), there do appear to be gender differences in intellectual abilities during early adolescence. Prior to puberty, both boys and girls show little or no difference on measures of verbal and spatial abilities. After puberty, girls score higher on the verbal and boys higher on the spatial ability measures (Maccoby & Jacklin, 1974). If environmental influences do play a part in these outcomes, then middle schools must be sure they are not contributing by advising boys into certain areas of study and girls into others.

Often, parents and teachers will describe the personality of a young adolescent as more difficult than a younger child. Fifth-grade teachers are often heard to describe their colleagues in the seventh grade as "nuts" for wanting to teach at that age level. When pressed for specifics, one of the characteristics about young adolescents that teachers and parents do not like is the appearance of being argumentative. An explanation for this behavior is that they are not more argumentative, but better arguers. Students tend to be more facile in engaging in debate, in use of language, and in finding inconsistencies in the other person's reasoning. All of this gives the impression that they argue more. In reality, though, the young adolescent has a way to go before he or she can match adult experiences or social maturity; cognitively, they are coming closer to full adult intellectual capacity.

Because of the wide variability between and within young adolescents in their ability to reason abstractly, it becomes clear that schools with a diverse and flexible curriculum seem to be in the best position to meet the needs of all students. Failing is internalized and failure effects all aspects of young adolescents' development. It is not the act of learning that is frustrating, it is the act of not understanding. The introspective abilities of the middle level student leads them to dwell on failure and builds upon itself to effect social and academic areas.

## Conclusion

As discussed earlier, the breakdown of the characteristics of middle level students into the physical, social, cognitive, and emotional areas seems artificial. No boundaries separate these areas; they are intertwined and interact with each other in a complex and not easily understood manner.

Human beings are complex and young adolescents are particularly so, especially to themselves. They are sometimes confused and surprised by their own behaviors and usually develop various ways to protect themselves from the contradictions and fears they experience. Forgetting seems to be an effective defense against painful outcomes. The student who forgot to bring in his book report on Monday, and again on Tuesday, and then again on Wednesday may not have written it. But then again he may have completed the report and he doesn't think much of it or the book. Rationalizing, projecting, denying, forgetting, and suppressing are all mechanisms of defense against painful situations and thoughts. To the extent that a young adolescent regards school as a painful experience has much to do with such things as social and emotional maturity, values, and family relationships. The middle school has a responsibility to recognize the distinct needs of young adolescents and be responsive to those needs.

But to recognize effectively the needs of young adolescents requires a complete understanding of the human condition. Continued research efforts should focus on the relationship between developmental characteristics and the interaction with social class, gender, and race. We must find out if the program components that are associated with the middle school movement are appropriate for all middle level schools, regardless of ethnic composition. We need to understand the impact of world crises (such as the Gulf War) on the middle grade students' sense of safety and security. We must learn how to bring out the inner voice of children so that they can teach us what they are really about. What we know now about middle level students has helped to shape some of our schools. What we continue to learn must modify what we now practice. If our schools of the next century are not different, then we have failed to discover and incorporate new knowledge.

# References

Atwater, E. (1988). *Adolescence*. Englewood Cliffs, NJ: Prentice Hall.

Bullough, V. (1981). Age of menarche: A misunderstanding. *Science, 213*(4505), 365–366.

Coleman, J. C. (1980). *The nature of adolescence*. London: Meuthuen.

Connolly, J., White, D., Stevens, R., & Burstein, S. (1987). Adolescents' self-reports of social activity: Assessment of stability and relations to social adjustment. *Journal of Adolescence, 10*(1), 83–95.

Dasen, P. R. (1977). *Piagetian psychology: Cross cultural contributions*. New York: Gardner.

Earl, W. L. (1987). Creativity and self-thrust: A field of study. *Adolescence, 22*(86), 419–432.

Elkind, D. (1978). *The child's reality: Three developmental themes*. Hillsdale, NJ: Erlbaum.

Fasick, F. A. (1984). Parents, peers, youth culture and autonomy in adolescence. *Adolescence, 19*(73), 143–157.

Felson, M., & Gottfredson, M. (1984). Social indicators of adolescent activities near peers and parents. *Journal of Marriage and the Family, 46*(3), 709–714.

Ishiyama, F. I. (1984). Shyness: Anxious social sensitivity and self-isolating tendency. *Adolescence, 19*(76), 903–911.

Johoda, G. (1980). Sex and ethnic differences on a spatial perceptual task: Some hypotheses tested. *British Journal of Psychology, 71*(3), 425–431.

Keating, D. (1980). Thinking processes in the adolescent. In J. Adelson (Ed.), *Handbook of adolescent psychology* (pp. 211–246). New York: Wiley.

Larson, L. E. (1980). The influence of parents and peers during adolescence. In R. E.

Muuss (Ed.), *Adolescent behavior and society* (3rd ed.) (pp. 142–152). New York: Random House.

Linn, M. C. (1983). Content, context and process in reasoning. *Joural of Early Adolescence, 3*(1), 63–82.

Maccoby, E., & Jacklin, C. (1974). *The psychology of sex differences.* Stanford: Stanford University Press.

Marshall, W. A., & Tanner, J. M. (1974). Puberty. In J. A. Davis & J. Dobbong (Eds.), *Scientific foundations of pediatrics.* Philadelphia: Saunders.

Milgram, J. (1985). The ninth grader: A profile. In J. H. Johnston (Ed.), *How fares the ninth grade?* (pp. 5–9). Reston, VA: National Association of Secondary School Principals.

Milgram, J. (1986). The inner world of the sixth grader. *Principals, 65*(4), 17–20.

Rice, F. P. (1990). *The adolescence* (6th ed.). Boston: Allyn and Bacon.

Rogoff, B., & Lave, J. (1984). *Everyday cognition.* Cambridge, MA: Harvard University Press.

Ruble, D. N., & Brooks-Gunn, J. (1982). The experience of menarche. *Child Development, 53*(6), 1557–1566.

Schofield, J. (1981). Complimentary and conflicting identities. In S. Asher & J. Gottman (Eds.), *The development of children's friendships* (pp. 53–90). Cambridge: Cambridge University Press.

Sebald, H. (1986). Adolescents' shifting orientation toward parents and peers: A curvilinear trend over recent decades. *Journal of Marriage and the Family, 48*(1), 5–13.

Steinberg, J. (1985). *Adolescence.* New York: Knopf.

Strang, R. (1957). *The adolescent views himself.* New York: McGraw-Hill.

Tanner, J. M. (1978). *Fetus into man: Physical growth from conception to maturity.* Cambridge, MA: Harvard University Press.

U.S. Bureau of the Census, Department of Commerce. (1988). *Statistical abstract of the United States.* Washington, DC: U.S. Government Printing Office.

Wolf, F. M., & Larsen, G. L. (1981). On why adolescent formal operators may not be critical thinkers. *Adolescence, 16*(62), 345–348.

Yarcheski, A., & Mahon, A. E. (1984). Chumships, relationships, altruistic behavior, and loneliness in early adolescents. *Adolescence, 19*(76), 913–924.

# CHAPTER THREE

# Young Adolescents' Perceptions of School

LINDA R. KRAMER
*State University of New York,*
*Brockport*

*It's not like elementary school where everyone is always watching you or you're in just one classroom. It's a lot of hard work and you have to be really organized, because if you're not organized you're not going to be able to find your way through. Some people think, "Why do we have English?" or "Why do we have to do this in math?" They don't know [why] now because they don't really use it in their everyday life, but I'm sure it's going to pay off in the future. I think it's going to be useful, because why would they be teaching it? They wouldn't teach us for nothing! I admit, sometimes I say, "Why do we have to do it?", but I think about it, and it must mean something.* —EIGHTH-GRADE GIRL

    Young adolescents are not passive recipients of teaching, no matter how uninvolved they may appear to be. Students think about school; their interpretations of school life and the meanings they confer on teachers' actions, classroom processes, and school events have real consequences for how much they learn. Researchers and practitioners increasingly agree that students' perceptions of school influence instruction and achievement as much as the behaviors of teachers. It has even been suggested that differences in how students perceive school may be the missing link between instructional strategies and achievement outcomes, explaining why some students are more successful in specific contexts than others (Weinstein, 1989).

    Despite a growing awareness of the importance of students' perceptions, educators have tended to ignore how school appears to students from their point of view. Indeed, much of what we know about the subjective experiences of students has not come from observing them in school and asking questions. Instead, researchers have inferred student perspectives from objective studies of programs, curriculum, and teachers. This is to say that systematic investigations of schooling from the student perspective, particularly the point of view of young adolescents, have not been undertaken.

The need to understand more about how students perceive school is closely tied to what we know about motivation. It appears that making the most of the middle grades is not simply a question of individual aptitude, nor is it solely related to the structure or the quality of the experiences students encounter in school. Rather, motivation is related to a combination of personal and school factors that are mediated by students' interpretations. In a review of research on motivation, Berliner (1989) concluded that a "profound truth that emerges from this cumulative set of studies is that environments do not influence motivation in any direct fashion, rather it is the perception of those environments that influences motivation" (pp. 317–318). In other words, it is not the experience, but the *interpretation* of the experience that has consequences.

The process through which student perceptions act on motivation is a complex one. On a broad scale, how students view their overall experiences in school is a critical factor. Do they believe they have opportunities to be successful? Do they perceive learning as interesting and worthwhile? Do they feel accepted and valued? On a smaller scale, research indicates that perceptions act as filters through which students selectively and differentially respond to classroom events. In fact, studies show that there may be great individual differences in how students within one classroom perceive and interpret events. For example, studies of high and low achievers illustrate students' sensitivity to teacher behaviors and teacher-student interactional patterns. Rich descriptions from these studies indicate that students monitor teacher behavior for clues about their smartness relative to peers, and consequently behave in ways that "fit" the expectations they perceive their teachers hold for them.

Other examples of the ways perceptions differentially shape students' behaviors are studies that investigate how carefully students attend to the structure of lessons. Students who do poorly on specific lessons are less likely to have noticed or attended to the strategies used during instruction. In contrast, students who did well could name specific techniques used by the teacher to point out important information and summarize key material. These studies show that what students perceive during lessons may not match the experiences teachers planned and intended (Weinstein, 1989).

How can a better understanding of students' perceptions help educators concerned about the middle grades improve teaching and increase student motivation? First, as Elkind (1984) noted, young adolescents are particularly sensitive to the psychosocial environment. Their concern with the impressions others have of them leads to the construction of an imaginary audience by which they feel constantly scrutinized and criticized. Adults who are unaware of the power of the imaginary audience may fail to respond in ways that help students feel valued and accepted, thus creating situations that can hinder communication between students and teachers. In fact, researchers have found that students' views of what happens in their classrooms are not always rational, nor are they synonymous with teachers' or observers' views. To build positive student attitudes, educators must set aside their own assumptions and actively seek a better understanding of student perceptions of school life.

Second, when student perceptions are taken into consideration, educators can more effectively plan school and classroom improvements. Attention to the ways students view the processes inherent in schooling can help us design strategies and programs that lead students from egocentric to more sociocentric perspectives, and that help students understand their own attitudes and the impact of their attitudes on learning. "Teaching can be better understood, and improved, by knowing its effect upon the learner's thoughts that mediate achievement" (Wittrock, 1986, p. 297).

In this chapter, student views about middle level schools will be explored through selected research studies and interviews conducted by the author with young adolescents across five states. This chapter will address the following: (1) the kinds of teachers young adolescents prefer, (2) how perceptions of teacher attitudes influence student behavior, (3) students' interpretations of instructional processes, and (4) students' definitions of the ideal learning environment. The goal of this chapter is to portray how school appears through the eyes of young adolescents, using, as often as possible, their own words to tell the story.

## Person-Centered Teachers

In conversations about school, the ideas and opinions about teachers held by young adolescents surface frequently. As the following interview excerpts illustrate, teachers are central to almost every school experience they discuss.

### Interview #1

*Observer:* (to Jan, who is repeating eighth grade) What's the difference between this year and last year?

*Jan:* Well, this year, I'm reading. It's like last year I didn't read, but this year I'm reading a lot harder. You know, Spanish and English give me a little trouble.

*Observer:* You're a native Spanish speaker and last year you didn't read English as well?

*Jan:* I read English. Yeah, I read English well, but some of the words I mumbled. I used to . . . I used to stop at the sentence, not even finish. I used to look and stop, not reading. So this time, I'm reading it, not just following the words. So I'm doing much better this year.

*Observer:* That's great. Who helped you figure out what you were doing wrong last year?

*Jan:* It was one of our teachers. One of mine that stayed after school and I said O.K. [I would stay]. So I started reading.

### *Interview #2*

*Observer:* (to a seventh-grader who has told the observer there is no one at school he can talk to about his problems) Do you have any idea what makes a teacher the kind you can talk to?

*David:* Umm . . . Some teachers don't give a care about their students. They won't try to find out what's making them fail or anything. All they want is the money.

*Observer:* How do you know that?

*David:* 'Cause I've had a teacher like that. My teachers here are terrible. There's one who tries but the kids get him down. He's tired. Just when he gets the kids settled down, some new kid comes along and disturbs things.

How students describe or categorize teachers and their actions, and the collection of traits they attribute to teachers is referred to in the literature as *person perception*. Most of the studies concerned with young adolescents' perceptions of teachers have focused on teacher personalities and attitudes toward students.

### The Preferred Teacher

During early adolescence the key task is one of self-definition. This job of finding out about ourselves "is facilitated by being with people who know us well and who give us useful information about ourselves. The more people who know us well, the more likely we are to get a balanced picture of ourselves . . ." (Elkind, 1984, p. 144). Perhaps this is why students in the middle grades overwhelmingly prefer teachers who possess personal as well as academic knowledge of the students they teach, and who demonstrate caring and concern in the classroom. During interviews, students describe good teachers as: "Teachers who are understanding. They give me good grades and they suport me. They don't let me down," or "Teachers who really listen to you and care about what's going on. Every time I have a problem they want to talk about it, and they tell me to get it off my chest."

Veaco and Brandon (1986) asked students in seven middle schools to nominate a Teacher of the Year using an open-ended questionnaire in which students were asked to name and describe in detail an outstanding middle school teacher. Students' statements written about the most frequently named outstanding teachers were selected and analyzed by searching for patterns or categories. From the 1,305 statements that were selected, the following characteristics of preferred teachers emerged: (1) nice; good-humored and nonthreatening; (2) easy to talk to; (3) willing to listen; (4) fair; not prejudiced or disposed to favoritism; and (5) explains things well and makes learning fun.

One of the most important findings of this study was that "the teacher's mode of interacting or relating to his or her students can be seen by young adolescents as more important than the subject matter being presented" (p. 221). Veaco and Brandon noted that students' descriptions of the preferred teacher closely matched the person-centered teacher described by Carl Rogers. That is, teacher traits that were most important to young adolescents in the study were genuineness, acceptance, empathy, and understanding.

The degree of concern students believe their teachers possess plays a major role in positive or negative perceptions of teachers, and ultimately in students' satisfaction with school. Unfortunately, Goodlad (1984) found that as students advanced through the grades, teacher support, both personally and academically, declined, and that the decline was especially noticeable during the middle level years. Other studies cited by Eccles and Midgley (1989) also indicate a decline in student ratings of teacher support and concern, particularly true when students move into more traditional junior high schools without team organizations. Eccles and Midgley conclude that, as young adolescents enter junior high, they experience a decline in the quality of personal relationships with teachers and an increase in teacher control.

It seems that at a time when students are defining their own identities and when person-centered teachers are most preferred, young adolescents' relationships with teachers are least likely to meet their needs. Although the academic side of teachers is important to students in terms of teachers' abilities to communicate subject matter clearly and to make learning fun, young adolescents view teachers who provide them first with a personal support base as the most desirable teachers (McEwin & Cross, 1982; Thornburg & Glider, 1984). As one eighth-grader explained:

*I learn most with Mrs. B. She's really nice. She's been listening to me and a lot of other kids. Like one day in class we got to talking about suicide and she asked if anyone ever thought about doing it and some kids raised their hands. She asked them to come back later and talk to her and I think they did.*

Teachers in the middle grades need to be aware that developing a nurturing relationship with their students need not detract from rigorous, content-based teaching and an emphasis on achievement. Rather, as young adolescents see it, warm student-teacher relationships foster the motivation and the desire to learn that are prerequisites to achievement. In fact, successful students identify "nice teachers" as one of the major reasons for their success in school (Beane & Lipka, 1986).

## Perceptions of Teacher Attitudes

Given young adolescents' perceptions of the ideal teacher as student centered, it is not surprising that they are constantly alert to clues about teachers' attitudes toward them. Consider the thoughts of Nicole, a seventh-grader, who had been identified as at-risk by her school counselors and who was failing two classes at the time of this interview.

*Nicole:* People here don't have many people to talk to. I don't. The teachers . . . some of them don't care about their students. They say, "They [administrators] want me to teach and I'm going to do it no matter what." I don't like that. I like them to say, "I'm here to teach and help you because I care." That's what I like. But a lot of them are just saying, "I'm here to teach so I'm gonna teach." I don't think that's right.

*Observer:* Do they actually say that?

*Nicole:* It's more an attitude, and they do say it. Like Ms. G. She's like . . . she never says it, but you know, she's just there and she just wants to teach, but she doesn't want to explain the whole deal.

*Observer:* How do you know that?

*Nicole:* I could feel it. The way she acts and the way she does things. She's been here seven years and all the kids I've talked to that have had her before say, "OOOh! You have Ms. G.!" Just like that.

*Observer:* But a teacher who really cares, how do they act?

*Nicole:* Like Mr. P. He really cares about his students. He's helping me a lot and he tells me, "I'm not angry with you, I just care about you." He's real caring and he does teach me when he cares.

Many middle level schools utilize interdisciplinary team organizations to promote closer and more positive student-teacher relationships. Though few studies have focused on teaming from the student point of view, evidence does show that breaking large schools into smaller units contributes to students' feelings of being well known, liked, and supported (Hawkins & Berndt, 1985). Team organizations foster the development of positive relationships by their very nature. Students and teachers who share the same schedule and the same area of the school, and who work together on common goals, develop a closeness that is difficult to achieve in other arrangements.

In fact, when students are asked to describe teams, they most often describe them first in terms of student-teacher relationships, and second in terms of activities students and teachers do together, such as having a team newspaper or team contests (Kramer, 1985). As one sixth-grade member of a team explained, "It's funner on this team because you're closer to your teachers. You're like a big family, but if you're in the whole school you don't feel that way. This makes you feel like doing your work more."

We know that being liked by teachers is important to young adolescents who believe that being liked by teachers and getting along with them lead to more opportunities in the classroom. More opportunities increase the likelihood of doing well (Kramer, 1987, 1989). Whether it is teachers' feelings of acceptance communicated to students and perceived as positive appraisals that lead to better achievement, or whether achieving and behaving appropriately lead to teacher acceptance and approval, it seems clear that positive perceptions of teachers' attitudes are important to young adolescents.

A study conducted by Davidson and Lang (1960) illustrates this idea. Researchers asked fourth- through sixth-graders to rate a series of adjectives using the stem "My teacher thinks I am . . ." to provide a measure of perceived teacher feelings. Students later responded to the same items using the stem "I think I am . . ." to provide a measure of self-perception. Teachers in the study rated pupils on academic achievement and behavioral characteristics. The results of the study clearly indicated that positive perceptions of teachers' attitudes were related to positive self-perceptions, higher achievement, and better behavior as rated by teachers. Two additional findings are important: (1) girls and students from higher social classes perceived more favorable teacher attitudes and (2) differences were found among classrooms in students' perceptions of positive teacher attitudes.

Davidson and Lang's study leads to other important questions. How are teachers communicating genuineness, acceptance, empathy, and understanding in those classrooms where students hold significantly more positive perceptions of teachers' attitudes? Are students' perceptions of teachers' attitudes flexible? It appears that for some students, once a decision is made that a teacher's attitude toward them is negative, little can be done to change it.

*Observer:* What class gives you the most problems?

*Student:* Miss K., my English teacher.

*Observer:* Why is that?

*Student:* Because we don't get along. I don't know why.

*Observer:* Well, if you could make a suggestion to her about what she could do so that the two of you would get along better, what would you suggest?

*Student:* She should leave school.

*Observer:* Let's say that she has to stay here. What else could she do to make things better between you?

*Student:* I could get out of her class.

When young adolescents perceive that teachers have negative feelings toward them, they often exhibit a decrease in motivation and an increase in deviant classroom behavior (Kramer, 1985, 1989). Nancy's experiences illustrate this point. Nancy was a seventh-grade gifted student who had recently moved to the community and was new at her middle school. It was difficult for her to sit still, she broke rules, failed to complete her homework, and, when she worked in class, it was frequently on assignments related to other subjects.

Observations during the year revealed an increase in incidents of misbehavior. Nancy reported having feelings of guilt and confusion about her ability and her motivation to do school work. She believed that her teachers did not really listen to her and that at team meetings they were "making things up about her." During interviews, Nancy indicated that she gave a great deal of thought to her relationships with teachers, but that she was at a loss as to how she could improve them. She described what she believed to be happening as "getting a reputation" within her team. Interestingly, Nancy's peer group, other gifted and high-achieving girls, was observed to interact with her less and less frequently over the course of the year, and when interviewed, explained: "She (Nancy) is getting a bad reputation with teachers."

Whether Nancy's behaviors led to teachers' attitudes, or teachers' attitudes contributed to Nancy's behavior, this case illustrates the importance of breaking the cycle. As with Nicole's description of Mr. P., teachers can take issue with poor behavior while still communicating positive feelings toward students. A teacher's ability to do this is perceived by students as a caring attitude, and this perception motivates students to want to change poor behavior.

Research on academically at-risk adolescents also suggests that attitudes of teachers toward marginal students are critical factors in students' decisions to stay in school. Using journal writing and interviews to compare students retained in seventh grade with students who had similar academic histories, but who were more successful in seventh grade, Strahan (1988) noted that teacher attitudes, student attitudes, and achievement outcomes seem to be interconnected. How teachers formed attitudes and how these attitudes were communicated to students, however, were not investigated in this study.

Students' perceptions of teachers and their perceptions of teachers' feelings toward them affect motivation to learn and openness to instruction in complex ways. The following interview with one eighth-grade boy summarizes what can happen when negative student perceptions close down relationships with teachers, leaving students alienated and alone.

*Observer:* What advice would you give a new student here?

*Student:* Don't hang around with the wrong people.

*Observer:* Who are the wrong people?

*Student:* You can tell because they're always together, hanging around, saying bad words and doing drugs. This year there's some I hang around with, but most of them quit school. They hang around after school.

*Observer:* Do you ever think of quitting school?

*Student:* Yeah.

*Observer:* I guess you decided not to?

*Student:* I didn't decide it, but they say I have to be 16 to quit.

*Observer:* So in the next years you could quit if you wanted? How are you going to make that decision?

*Student:* With myself, I guess. Just by myself.

The ramifications of believing there is no one to confide in, as compared to believing that teachers support you, can have long-term effects. For some young adolescents, positive perceptions of teachers' attitudes may mean the difference between seeking objective assistance and deciding to "go it alone."

## Perceptions of Instruction and Classroom Environments

Teachers who work with young adolescents are not surprised by studies suggesting that how students perceive instruction is not always synonymous with what the teacher believes students are learning, or what other adults observing in the classroom might predict. We know, for example, that observers' rates of on-task, attending behavior do not always match students' descriptions of their behavior when they watch replays of lessons on videotape. What students think during instruction, or whether students are learning from a particular instructional strategy, is not easily observed. However, several studies suggest that unless we find ways to assess students' thought processes during instruction, as well as their perceptions of classroom environment, we cannot fully understand variations in achievement within the classroom.

### Student Perceptions during Instruction

Winne and Marx (1982) conducted a series of interviews with older students in elementary schools to find out what students thought about instructional behaviors that had been previously identified by their teachers as important. Students were asked to recall how they responded to instructional strategies, that is, what they thought or felt during instruction.

The researchers found that what students reported did not always match what teachers intended students to think about during instruction. This mismatch between student perceptions of intent and teacher intent was particularly apparent during teachers' use of strategies to engage students emotionally. For example, teacher attempts to make the lessons enjoyable were not perceived by students who tended to focus, instead, on the content of the task involved. Interestingly, the researchers found that students' perceptions of teacher intent improved when activities were well practiced and students were more familiar with the material, as opposed to when a great deal of information was presented at once.

Young adolescents often comment about teachers who "just talk and talk and we listen, but I don't know what they're talking about," or teachers who "give us assignments and we just do them. It's quiet and nobody's talking." These perceptions may relate to the findings reported by Winne and Marx. When too much information is presented to students with inadequate time for interaction and practice, students may not perceive the intent of instruction. Although they may comply with the teacher's directions, they are unable to distinguish why or what they are learning.

In a related study, sixth-graders' perceptions of teachers' instructional behaviors were measured and compared to their academic achievement (Stayrook, Corno, & Winne, 1978). The goal of the study was to find out if student perceptions of teacher structuring, soliciting, and reacting behaviors during instruction predicted achievement. *Structuring behaviors* included outlining content, stating objectives, and summarizing ideas; *soliciting* included asking high- and low-order questions; and *reacting* included praising, prompting, and providing reasons for correct responses.

Trained teachers were given specially prepared scripts for a two-week unit, including lesson content and methods of instruction. All class sessions were observed by trained observers who counted the occurrences of structuring, soliciting, and reacting behaviors. Finally, an instrument used to measure student perceptions of these instructional behaviors was administered at the end of the two weeks, along with a multiple-choice test to measure student achievement. The results of the study indicated that, beyond the effects of student ability and actual frequency of behaviors, student perceptions of structuring and reacting behaviors predicted student achievement.

A similar study of fifth- and sixth-graders was conducted to find out what students actually think about during classroom instruction. Students were shown videotapes of lessons in which they had participated, and interviewed about their thoughts (Peterson & Swing, 1982). Student comments were then analyzed and compared with student achievement scores.

The researchers found that students' reports of their thinking during instruction predicted their subsequent achievement scores more accurately than did either measures of their initial ability and attitudes or observers' reports of their behavior during lessons. One of the most interesting findings from this study was that students who reported using specific thinking strategies during instruction such as "repeating and reviewing information to oneself, relating information to prior knowledge, anticipating an answer to a teacher's question, . . . and motivating oneself with self-thoughts" tended to have higher scores on the achievement measure than those who did not (p. 487).

Strubbe (1990) conducted a study to determine students' attitudes toward integrating curriculum across subject areas. In her study, she asked students in the sixth through eighth grades who were completing interdisciplinary units to evaluate them using a Likert-type questionnaire. Strubbe found that interdisciplinary units appealed to students because they provided an integration of subject matter that was more meaningful. Student self-reports indicated that integrating skill development and content across subject areas was motivating, challenging, and fun.

Interestingly, students' perceptions of learning were related to the degree of organization they perceived within the unit; that is, they felt they learned more when the goals and objectives for the unit were clearly communicated. Students also believed that incorporating a variety of activities, offering students choices, and providing opportunities for students to share their knowledge through projects promoted learning. Strubbe concluded that assessing students' perceptions of curriculum not only provided data to support interdisciplinary instruction but provided valuable clues for the improvement of future units. Student perceptions can help "clarify the effective and ineffective components of instruction" (p. 38).

Taken together, these studies indicate that the effect of instruction on achievement is indirect; that is, teaching affects student achievement through student thought processes. Students who do not perceive the intent of instruction or teachers' behaviors aimed at helping them to organize and to retain content are less likely to achieve as much as those who do. Similarly, students who are not actively engaged in perceiving, interpreting, and questioning during instruction are less likely to do well on subsequent achievement tests.

These studies lead us to believe that teachers should make every effort to question students about their thought processes during instruction. Additionally, teachers should attempt to instruct students in thinking strategies that can be used during both instruction and independent work. Young adolescents can be taught to listen for objectives, as well as teachers' structuring and reacting behaviors, and can be given practice in identifying these behaviors during instruction. Teachers can also help students develop their perceptual awareness during instruction by thinking aloud about the content of the lesson, or the problem being solved, to demonstrate productive cognitive strategies. As a result, young adolescents who recognize these strategies will be less likely to say of their teachers, they "just talk and talk and we listen, but I don't know what they're talking about."

### Students' Perceptions of Ideal Classrooms

Shadow studies in which observers follow and record the interactions of selected young adolescents have produced rich descriptions of students' daily routines (Lounsbury & Johnston, 1985, 1988; Lounsbury & Clark, 1990). These studies are helpful because they allow researchers and practitioners, who are typically familiar with only small slices of the students' day, to gain a holistic view of what middle level students experience as they move from classroom to classroom.

The resulting portraits of students illustrate the diversity that exists in classroom environments within the same school, as well as the differences in perspectives of subgroups of students within the same classroom. For example, Mergendoller, Swarthout, and Packer (1982), in their shadow study of Beth, Ernie, Tammy, and Wayne, found that student perceptions of classrooms relate to both social and academic contexts, and that perceptions of environments are bound up in relationships with teachers.

A comparison of elementary classroom environments with those in junior highs is a good place to begin a discussion of young adolescents' perceptions of ideal classrooms. Research has shown that as students move from the elementary grades into traditional junior high schools, they experience many changes. Chief among these changes are a greater emphasis on teacher control, fewer personal and positive student-teacher relationships, and fewer opportunities to engage in decision making (Eccles & Midgley, 1988, 1989).

These differences are not as evident in nontraditional junior highs and middle schools using team organizations and other student-centered strategies; nonetheless, it appears that many young adolescents today are striving for independence in classrooms with fewer opportunities to exercise needed skills than were afforded in the elementary grades.

Do we find evidence of these general findings in interviews with students? The answer is a definitive yes. Student-teacher relationships and opportunities for input and decision making figure prominently in the thinking of young adolescents when they discuss their favorite classes. In the following conversation, Brian, a seventh-grade honors student, describes the class in which he felt he was learning the most. Brian's comments illustrate the importance of perceived levels of input and decision making.

*Brian:* There's this one class I'm in. The teacher selected me and I get to see other students. I think I learn a lot there.

*Observer:* The teacher selected you and you see other students? What does that mean?

*Brian:* We're all in a big group. It's during a separate part of the day every week and we have discussions.

*Observer:* Do you know what the class is called?

*Brian:* Not really. They didn't tell us. But we talk about conflicts, resolutions, and stuff like that. I get to help people work things out.

Overwhelmingly, interviews indicate that students do not believe they are engaged in decision making or given enough opportunities for input in their daily class work. These perceptions may stem from students' beliefs that they are maturing and ready to assume more responsibility than their teachers believe is appropriate.

Do teachers' perceptions of ideal classroom environments compare with the perceptions of young adolescents? Studies have been conducted that look at differences between middle level students' and teachers' perceptions of actual and preferred learning environments. The results of one such study of seventh- through ninth-graders in science and social studies classes indicated that, in comparison to the classroom environments they perceived as actually existing, both teachers and students preferred classrooms with the following: (1) more emphasis on teacher-student interaction; (2) greater concern for personal growth; (3) more opportunities for active learning, problem-solving, and inquiry; and (4) a greater emphasis on individual learning styles and preferences. Students, however, believed that there was a greater discrepancy between actual and preferred environments in the above areas than did the teachers.

A second important finding of the study was that teachers were satisfied with the levels of decision making they allowed students in their classrooms; they perceived no discrepancy between actual and preferred levels. This was not the case for students who perceived a need for more opportunities to have control over their own learning (Fraser, 1982).

Other studies support the idea that both young adolescents and their teachers prefer a more favorable psychosocial classroom environment than they perceive as being actually present, but that teachers perceive the classroom environment more favorably than the students they teach perceive it (Fisher & Fraser, 1983). Does this difference really matter? Researchers have found substantial evidence of a relationship between young adolescents' perceptions of the classroom environment and their achievement and attitudes (Evertson, Anderson, Anderson, & Brophy, 1980; Fraser & Fisher, 1982.) These studies emphasize the importance of nurturing teachers along with high degrees of student involvement, participation, and decision making. In classrooms with these characteristics, students exhibit greater achievement and more positive attitudes toward school.

Providing young adolescents with the kinds of classroom environments they prefer and in which they perform best is referred to as *person-environment fit* (Eccles & Midgley, 1988). Evidence exists, however, particularly in the area of decision making, that there is a "developmental mismatch" between young adolescents and the classroom environments they experience before and after entering middle level schools (Midgley & Feldlaufer, 1987).

Because student and teacher perceptions of the ideal classroom environment differ substantially during the middle grades, teachers would benefit from using any of the short versions of classroom environment scales that presently exist to assess their own classrooms. Teachers' assessments of their classrooms have proven to be highly successful ways to view the environment through students' eyes, and to plan for change and improvement (Fraser, 1981; Fisher & Fraser, 1981). Though again, student perceptions may not be rational or synonymous with teachers' perceptions. Understanding how students think about the environment and comparing their thoughts to the developmental stage characteristics of young adolescents will enable teachers to provide more meaningful learning environments.

## Using Student Perceptions of School to Improve Teaching

In his book, *Control Theory: A New Explanation of How We Control Our Lives,* William Glasser (1984) names four psychological needs that he believes are encoded in the human genes: (1) the need to belong—to love, share, and cooperate; (2) the need for power—to have a lasting effect on our environment; (3) the need for freedom—to make choices; and (4) the need for fun—to play and enjoy the work we do.

These four needs are startlingly apparent in the voices of young adolescents as they speak about their daily lives in school. From their point of view, the things that define a good school are nurturing relationships, decision-making opportunities, activities in which they can provide input, and curriculum that is meaningful. Although individual students are likely to perceive Glasser's four needs and their school's ability to satisfy them in different ways, their collective voices provide convincing evidence that middle level schools must do more to meet these needs.

One way to respond to Glasser's needs is to begin using student perceptions to plan for educational improvement. Teachers can design classroom activities that help students become aware of their own perceptions and how their perceptions influence their behavior. Such activities might include the following: asking students' overall opinions about units of study, why they liked or did not like the content, how the unit will be important to students in the future, how learning activities might be improved, and how they would assess their own performance or ability to use the content.

These kinds of activities indicate to students that teachers care about how they feel. They also provide valuable data about student perceptions that can be used to make curriculum more meaningful, and to make students more aware of how positive attitudes lead to productive behavior. For example, the behaviors of the eighth-grader, whose comments introduced this chapter, would have been very different had she perceived her courses as useless rather than deciding that they would "pay off in the future." Understanding and utilizing student perceptions to improve classrooms can actually help students become more responsible for their own learning. Through discussions of the ways perceptions effect attitudes, and attitudes behaviors, teachers can open the door to conversations that lead to more positive attitudes toward school.

## Conclusion

Studies reviewed in this chapter point to the importance of determining whether students actually perceive and understand the intent of instruction by soliciting frequent feedback from students. Questioning strategies and other assessment techniques can be used to direct students' thought processes during instruction, and to alert them to important phases of a lesson, such as when a teacher engages in outlining content, summarizes main ideas, or provides reasons for correct answers. As teachers are engaged in instruction, they need to devise ways to get inside the thoughts of their students in order to know if students actually understand the content. To simply assume that young adolescents recognize the main points of a lesson because a teacher perceives that they have been adequately covered is a dangerous assumption. Students' perceptions of instruction do not always match the teacher's perceptions, even when they are paying close attention to the lesson at hand.

Few educators may be aware of the pivotal role of student perceptions in learning and achievement. It may seem too time consuming to encourage young adolescents to discuss their perspectives, or to monitor student thought processes in the ways that have been described in this chapter. It may also seem uncomfortable. Developmentally, young adolescents are argumentative; searching for their own voices, they often contradict themselves as well as adults. However, the students, whose perspectives permeate this chapter, have suggested that educators who try to understand schooling through their eyes are ones who inevitably are more responsive to their needs. By actively listening to young adolescents, we promote not only their growth as individuals but the development of positive relationships with adults and educational improvements that can greatly enhance the potential of students.

## References

Beane, J. A., & Lipka, R. P. (1986). *Self-concept, self-esteem, and the curriculum.* New York: Teachers College Press.

Berliner, D. C. (1989). Furthering our understanding of motivation and environments. In C. Ames & R. Ames (Eds.), *Research on motivation in education: Vol. 3. Goals and cognitions* (pp. 317–342). San Diego: Academic Press.

Davidson, H. H., & Lang, G. (1960). Children's perceptions of their teachers' feelings toward them related to self-perception, school achievement, and behavior. *Journal of Experimental Education, 29*(2), 107–118.

Eccles, J. S., & Midgley, C. (1988, October). *Understanding motivation: A developmental approach to person-environment fit.* Paper presented at the Annual Meeting of the National Middle Association, Denver, CO.

Eccles, J. S., & Midgley, C. (1989). Stage-environment fit: Developmentally appropriate classrooms for young adolescents. In C. Ames & R. Ames (Eds.), *Research on motivation in education: Vol. 3. Goals and cognitions* (pp. 139–185). San Diego: Academic Press.

Elkind, D. (1984). *All grown up and no place to go.* Reading, MA: Addison-Wesley.

Evertson, C., Anderson, C., Anderson, L., & Brophy, J. (1980). *American Educational Research Journal, 17*(1), 43–60.

Fisher, D. L., & Fraser, B. J. (1981). Validity and the use of the My Class Inventory. *Science Education, 65*(2), 145–156.

Fisher, D. L., & Fraser, B. J. (1983). A comparison of actual and preferred classroom environments as perceived by science teachers and students. *Journal of Research in Science Teaching, 20*(1), 55–61.

Fraser, B. J. (1981). Using environmental assessments to make better classrooms. *Journal of Curriculum Studies, 13*(2), 133–144.

Fraser, B. J. (1982). Differences between student and teacher perceptions of actual and preferred classroom learning environment. *Educational Evaluation and Policy Analysis, 4*(4), 511–519.

Fraser, B. J., & Fisher, D. L. (1982). Predicting students' outcomes from the perceptions of classroom psychosocial environment. *American Educational Research Journal, 19*(4), 498–518.

Glasser, W. (1984). *Control theory: A new explanation of how we control our lives.* New York: Harper & Row.

Goodlad, J. I. (1984). *A place called school.* New York: McGraw-Hill.

Hawkins, J. A., & Berndt, T. J. (1985, April). *Adjustment following the transition to junior high school.* Paper presented at the Meeting of the Society for Research in Child Development, Toronto.

Kramer, L. (1985). Gifted adolescent girls: Self-perceptions of ability in one middle school setting. *Dissertation Abstracts International, 47*(1), 71A.

Kramer, L. (1987). The ability/achievement dilemma of gifted middle school girls. In *Schools in the middle: A report on trends and practices.* Reston, VA: National Association of Secondary School Principals.

Kramer, L. (1989). *A comparison of at-risk and successful students' school experiences in a multicultural junior high.* Paper presented at the American Educational Research Association Annual Conference, Boston, MA.

Lounsbury, J. H., & Clark, D. C. (1990). *Inside grade eight: From apathy to excitement.* Reston, VA: National Association of Secondary School Principals.

Lounsbury, J. H., & Johnston, H. J. (1985). *How fares the ninth grade? A day in the life of a ninth grader.* Reston, VA: National Association of Secondary School Principals.

Lounsbury, J. H., & Johnston, H. J. (1988). *Life in the three sixth grades.* Reston, VA: National Association of Secondary School Principals.

McEwin, C. K., & Cross, A. H. (1982). A comparative study of perceived victimization, perceived anonymity, self-esteem, and preferred teacher characteristics of gifted and talented and non-labeled early adolescents. *Journal of Early Adolescence, 2*(3), 247–254.

Mergendoller, J. R., Swarthout, D. W., & Packer, M. J. (1982). Lipsticks and backpacks: Life as a seventh grader. *Journal of Early Adolescence, 2*(4), 389–415.

Midgley, C., & Feldlaufer, H. (1987). Students' and teachers' decision-making fit before and after the transition to junior high school. *Journal of Early Adolescence, 7*(2), 225–241.

Peterson, P. L., & Swing, S. R. (1982). Beyond time on task: Students' reports of their thought processes during classroom instruction. *Elementary School Journal, 82*(5), 481–491.

Stayrook, N. G., Corno, L., & Winne, P. H. (1978). Path analyses relating student perceptions of teacher behavior to student achievement. *Journal of Teacher Education, 29*(2), 51–56.

Strahan, D. (1988). Life on the margins: How academically at-risk early adolescents view themselves and school. *Journal of Early Adolescence, 8*(4), 373–390.

Strubbe, M. A. (1990). Are interdisciplinary units worthwhile? Ask students! *Middle School Journal, 21*(3), 36–38.

Thornburg, H. D., & Glider, P. (1984). Dimensions of early adolescent social perceptions and preferences. *Journal of Early Adolescence, 4*(4), 387–406.

Veaco, L., & Brandon, C. (1986). The preferred teacher: A content analysis of young adolescents' writings. *Journal of Early Adolescence, 6*(3), 221–229.

Weinstein, R. S. (1989). Perceptions of classroom processes and student motivation: Children's views of self-fulfilling prophecies. In C. Ames & R. Ames (Eds.), *Research on motivation in education: Vol. 3. Goals and cognitions* (pp. 187–221). San Diego: Academic Press.

Winne, P. H., & Marx, R. W. (1982). Students' and teachers' views of thinking processes involved in classroom learning. *Elementary School Journal, 82*(5), 493–518.

Wittrock, M. C. (1986). Students' thought processes. In M. C. Wittrock (Ed.), *Handbook of research on teaching* (3rd ed.) (pp. 297–314). New York: Macmillan.

# CHAPTER FOUR

# Youth as Cultural and Economic Capital: Learning How to Be

J. HOWARD JOHNSTON
*University of South Florida*

Not long ago, I was having a conversation with a seven-year-old girl and her grandmother about how important grandparents were in the lives of children. This young African-American girl, who was to inherit the legacy of many generations of strong, independent, resourceful women, told me that grandmothers were most important of all. "They're the ones," she said, "who show you how to be."

That statement reminded me of a book encountered in an undergraduate course many years ago, *How Does a Poem Mean?*, by Ciardi (1959). Ciardi said that "the usual question one hears of poetry is 'What does a poem mean?' I'm interested in rather in 'How' the poem means, how it goes about being a performance of itself" (p. 663).

That's what grandmothers do: They show you *how* to be—how to perform the role of "you" in the setting that has been provided for you. Indeed, anthropologists have made a science out of studying this intergenerational transmittal of cultural norms, roles, and behavior, known to seven-year-old girls (and boys) as "how to be."

Most study of culture can probably be reduced to two fundamental areas of inquiry. The first is how we learn to be. The second is best expressed by Bower's succinct definition of *culture* as "the way we do things around here." In essence, then, our interest in culture, as educators, can best be represented by a single, two-part question: *How do we learn to do things the way we do things around here?*

To be sure, a large portion of the burden of teaching children how to be and how we do things around here falls on the adult generations of the family or the community, often in formalized systems such as schools. In fact, that system of intergenerational transmittal of virtually everything anyone needs to know works quite well, producing some of our most tenacious qualities and characteristics as human beings, as members of certain ethnic groups, or as members of a community.

Unfortunately, that system is also most effective when the adult generations are in firm control of the way we do things around here, and are able to predict, with a measure of certainty, the kinds of life events that their children and grandchildren will face. For several thousand generations, those assumptions were fairly reasonable ones to make. Adults basically ran things; things did not change too quickly; and by living as we were shown how to live by our parents and grandparents, we could be assured of reasonable success in handling life events, with the possible exception of a volcanic eruption or an ice age, which did not occur in every generation.

After World War II, however, the rate of change began to accelerate dramatically. Adults seemed to remain in control of things, but the consensus on how we were to do things around here began to break down as communication between heretofore isolated communities and diverse groups began to introduce novel ideas about other ways things could be done around here. Severe economic and social hardships introduced by the war and its aftermath also rearranged traditional roles and norms. Suddenly, the way we do things around here is a matter of negotiation, depending largely on a set of instrumental economic values dealing with the need to provide for economic survival and in a vastly different context than which existed even a short time ago.

As a result of this vastly accelerated change, the ability of parents, grandparents, aunts, and uncles to predict the kind of life events that would confront their children and grandchildren diminished. In short, their ability to educate children adequately for the future declined. And with the diminished ability came a diminished status as useful and reliable sources of help for the future, both in the eyes of the children and in the social and economic system of the times. In fact, evidence can be found to contradict even some of the (al)most external verities that have long been the stock and trade of adult transmitters of cultural values, such as "Hard work and effort will be rewarded," or "Education is the key to a successful future." Just ask one of the working poor in the United States if hard work and effort are justly rewarded, or if a college education was the key to a successful future for a San Francisco cab driver. Today, by the time they reach early adolescence and can astutely observe their surroundings, youth can see a mountain of evidence that their sources of childhood wisdom, parents and grandparents for the most part, really may *not* know how things are done around here anymore.

The net effect of this rapid change is to render, in the eyes of young adolescents, the wisdom of previous generations rather antique, even quaint, but certainly not very useful. Given this view, the collected wisdom of the culture, transmitted as it is both through informal mechanisms in families and formal mechanisms of schooling, is not likely to be very highly prized by a group who believes that they have to figure everything out for themselves. The answers and solutions to life's problems that are remembered by parents as serving them so well (whether they did or not) often are not helpful to youngsters facing a much more complex and ambiguous world. Indeed, parents are often seen as pitifully naive about modern life. When parental solutions are *imposed* on adolescents, because "it's what we did when we were your age," the result is likely to be rejection, rebellion, and the ultimate adolescent admonishment, "You just don't understand!"

Instead of transmitting answers, learning "how to be" and "the way we do things around here" becomes an exercise in observation, analysis, and trial and error. In other words, it is like negotiating an alien terrain with no map, filled with false starts, abrupt stops, and unplanned perils. The wisdom of adults, in this view, is like being given a map of another territory from another planet. Interesting, maybe, but not very useful. What is needed, say these youthful explorers, is help in figuring out how to cope with unknowns, to some extent with unknowables. So the way one learns from one's culture in the late twentieth century is not by studying what others have done but by learning how to read one's environment quickly and adjust behavior to an adaptive stance rather than a rigid one. In other words, you no longer learn the culture, you learn *from* the culture how to figure out the way we do things around here.

Along with this rapidly accelerating rate of change also comes a fundamental change in the way children are viewed by the social and economic system in the western world. Coleman and Husen (1985) postulate that changes in the family and the status of children can be defined in three broad economic phases: bare subsistence or poverty, economic respectability, and affluence. Furthermore, they argue that "these phases correspond roughly to phases of a society's social and economic development, ranging from a subsistence economy, through an industrial economy, to a post-industrial affluent economy" (p. 43).

It is these two phenomena, the relative inability for adults to predict what will happen in their children's lifetimes and the changing status of both children and the elderly in the economy, that become the major issues in culture and how it is learned by youth and, ultimately, how it affects their learning. That, then, is the focus of this chapter.

## Socialization of Youth

Three domains of socialization can be extrapolated from the literature on adolescent development and provide a framework for assessing the school as a socializing agency of particular significance for young adolescents. Two European studies sponsored by German Shell (Deutsche Shell, 1975, 1977), unique for both the enormity of their scope and their focus on socialization over a broad range of ages (12 to 22 years), articulate these social domains most clearly:

1. *Primary socialization,* which occurs in the family, among playmates, and in the early years of schooling, is directed toward achieving emotional stability, cooperative abilities, respect for authority (both parental and nonparental), and forming affective relations.
2. *Secondary socialization* is the result of formal schooling, leisure activity, and other forms of experience, and results in cognitive competence, preparation for more specialized learning, and socialization into both political structures and work.
3. *Tertiary socialization* occurs in legal, religious, social, and voluntary organizations, through media and contact with the political-legal-economic systems. Its goals are the integration of the individual with the social order, recognition as a unique entity in the system, and the development of vocational competence and independent responsibility.

The evidence is growing, however, that the socialization functions may be changing and becoming less clearly differentiated as we approach the end of the twentieth century, with a greater role played by institutions in the primary socialization of youth. As personal care responsibilities fall increasingly to institutions chartered specifically for the purpose of caring for the very young and the very old, the influence of the family and its members is being shared with institutions that operate on the basis of more widely negotiated and somewhat more fluid norms than have previously existed in the relatively isolated context of the home.

Thus, it is critical for all institutions, especially schools, to examine carefully the new roles that may be demanded of them in the acculturation of youth to common social beliefs and norms. For young adolescents in particular, suspicious of utility of parental assistance in coping with a changing society, the shared norms of our culture must first of all be clearly articulated, then reinforced in ways that neither denegrate the child's home life nor deprive anyone of the chance to be successful in adult life. To do so requires the examination of the cultural, economic, and social context in which modern socialization forces operate.

### Children as Resources/Liabilities

Youth, according to Coleman and Husen (1985), has become a stage of redundancy. The importance of the period between the ages of approximately 11 and 15 (referred to as *early adolescence* by middle level educators) as the time when youth are socialized into adult roles through various types of structured and unstructured affiliations with adult institutions (work, in particular) has declined dramatically in the past few decades. Indeed, recent history has shown the inability of the economy to absorb new entrants into adulthood into meaningful work roles, and we have witnessed the alarming growth of an "underclass" of minority students who drop out of school and who have even less chance of being employed than their high school graduate agemates (Wilson, 1986).

At least part of this condition can be attributed to the evolution of western economies from subsistence level to relative affluence. In a model of economic growth, which Coleman and Husen argue parallels in a general way the evolution of economic status of families in the society, the declining importance of children as a family resource becomes evident. As the social and economic conditions of a group passes through the three phases of the model, the status of children in the group changes dramatically (Coleman & Husen, 1985).

In *Phase I,* children are absolutely essential for family survival and, indeed, are often exploited. In this case, households are at or slightly above subsistence level and are historically in agricultural communities, although certain village cultures also exhibit these qualities. Generally, households produce virtually everything they consume, and the exchange of either labor for wages or any form of money for goods and services is minimal.

In such societies, the labor of children is useful and the labor of adolescents is absolutely essential. Because of the labor intensity of the household, there are numerous tasks for children to perform that have a direct bearing on the welfare of the household. Thus, families tend to have numerous children and exploit their labor with little regard for the effect of this exploitation on the child's future or opportunities. In fact, such groups tend to be focused inward, fixated on the present, and have little regard for extending the opportunities of their members.

Indeed, parental approval is given for the early assumption of adult roles, and the U.S. idiom is filled with standard phrases that praise hard work. "He does a man's work," or "She'll be a good wife for someone" are two that raise the hackles of modern child advocates and feminists, but most of the readers of this book can recall those accolades from their own childhood and youth. In short, adolescence, as a prolongation of maturation and a transition between childhood and adulthood, simply does not exist in this phase.

In such societies, the purpose of the school is to protect children from exploitation by the family and to raise children's expectations and opportunities beyond that of their families. Schools and families, then, are frequently antagonistic toward one another, and a primary objective of school and government officials in such settings is to simply get families to allow children to *attend.* Both the early history of U.S. education and some of its most compelling lore documents this relationship between the public and the school.

Among these groups, schools tend to serve best those whose families are able to envision a better future for their child. Even though they may lack the necessary tools and skills to encourage their child to broader aspirations, they sense the importance of the school as a vehicle for improvement of their child's lot in life, so they nurture and encourage the school's efforts. The families who have this vision, however dim it may be, are the precursors of the majority of families in phase 2.

*Phase 2* societies tend to be urban, industrialized, and postagricultural. For the most part, they are engaged in manufacturing and commerce, with a small portion of the population engaged in the now specialized agricultural activity that is sufficient to feed the entire populace. Because of this specialization, this is an exchange economy, in which most workers labor at full-time, specialized jobs for which they are paid with currency. In turn, they use their wages to purchase goods and services from other specialized workers. Children's labor is no longer a major contributor to the subsistence of the family, although it may contribute to comfort or convenience. Adolescents are generally viewed as necessary contributors to family welfare, but usually through indirect mechanisms such as providing childcare so parents can work, or earning their own money so they do not drain family resources away from the common welare.

In this phase, children are viewed as a long-term capital investment, rather than as a short-term source of labor. Now, they are seen as an opportunity for the family, by the next generation, to improve its status, economic circumstances, and influence. In phase 1, a large number of children assured a secure future; in phase 2, it is the accomplishments of each individual child, among the relatively fewer now born to each family, that assures security.

In this phase, transition to adulthood is critical, for it is this transition that will determine the status of the child as an adult and, thereby, affect the entire family's fortune. Families, then, become very concerned about both the economic and status quality of marriages, beyond their ability to produce laboring offspring, and the specific preparations that can be made for careers that represent an advancement in family fortunes.

Among the many implications of this change that are noted by Coleman and Husen (1985) is the fact that demands increase for prolonged, readily available universal education. The family is now the school's ally, not its antagonist. Schooling is seen as the key to a successful future, and motivation for schooling is instilled in children from their earliest years. "Schooling is the principal avenue by which the family can achieve, through its children, status mobility in the next generation" (p. 45).

Because both the family and the society at large value academic achievement, it tends to be very high, both in individuals and in society at large.

School achievement is directly linked, in belief and in practice, to a successful economic future for both the child and his or her family. This is the phase in which most contemporary adults were raised, and certainly the value set that is most clearly articulated by present school arrangements.

*Phase 3* is a postindustrial society. In large measure, it is a welfare state with a high degree of affluence. The family as a producing economic unit has all but vanished. It has become only a consuming unit, not a producing one, whose functional role is devoted primarily to childrearing and the provision of an emotional and physical home base in an otherwise highly institutionalized world.

Many of the family's functions have been taken over by large governmental, industrial, and commercial institutions. As welfare functions are taken over by these organizations, the family has less and less reason to cohere in order to maintain one another's economic status, physical survival, or general welfare. Fewer households are multigenerational, so the tendency is toward individualistic rather than family-deliberated solutions to problems, and toward opportunistic, environmentally determined behavior rather than that which is dictated by historical norms and long-standing family traditions.

In general, the goal orientation shifts toward individual rather than family goals, since the fundamental survival and welfare of individual family members (children, the elderly, the handicapped) is assured by institutions outside of the family. Thus, individual members of the family, particularly young people, are freed from some of the demands of providing for the family's welfare and are permitted to become considerably more self-indulgent. At the same time, the obvious importance of their membership and contribution to the family declines in their own eyes and those of the family itself.

Because the concept of family welfare no longer spans several generations, the family's interest in the future of its elderly or its children is somewhat diminished. Indeed, because everyone's future is assured, however minimally by one social institution or another, the obligation to insulate children against the storms of the future is reduced, so less attention really needs to be given to preparing them for it.

Most western countries are in phase 2, with some becoming affluent enough to approach phase 3. In those societies, many families are already at phase 3, and, because these families are often the most affluent and the most powerful, a number of social institutions are changed, through their influence, to suit their needs for childcare and other support services (ranging from planned recreation to provisions for securing quick meals). This produces a climate that not only supports additional phase 3 development but also creates a psychological condition among other families who take advantage of these restructured institutions, creating a "psychological condition of Phase 3 [beyond what] their own affluence would dictate" (Coleman & Husen, 1985, p. 45).

Tangible resources for children are in abundance in phase 3 societies: televisions, computers, per-pupil school expenditures, leisure resources, and so on. Intangible resources for children, however, decline markedly (Hanushek, 1981): the amount of time that parents and children spend together is greatly reduced; the overt transmission of values about the importance of schooling declines, with its resulting motivational benefit for children; the modeling of productive labor by parents and other adults disappears as more work is either too abstract for children to understand or conduct, too specialized to allow children to see its finished product, or devoted almost solely to the preservation of a given institutional setting or order.

Along with the decline in intangible resources comes awareness on the part of youth that they are irrelevant to the social or economic welfare of either the family or the society as a whole. They produce nothing; their care only consumes resources. In short, they become aware that they are irrelevant and develop a phase 3 mentality, characterized by dependence and lack of strong achievement motivation.

For young adolescents, the issue starts to crystalize around the value of schooling as preparation for the future. If their school work makes no immediate contribution to the welfare of their family or community, and if existing institutions and training seem poorly positioned to prepare them for a future that no one can predict very well, the purpose of going to school seems, even to the youngsters, to be to provide institutionalized care for them until they are able to leave the home. Thus, with young adolescents' growing conviction that school has no present or future relevence to their lives, the drive to excel, or even to comply with school demands, diminishes greatly.

At the same time, achievement in school is highly related to the norms, values, and expectations transmitted to children by the family. It is viewed as children's "work" and they are expected to do it well. Both implicit and explicit achievement training, identified by Clark (1985), convey messages about the importance of schooling for future success. However, to a large extent, these messages are most commonly found in phase 2 families and those who operate very close to subsistence existence, such as the urban poor identified by Wilson (1986). Family affluence may contribute to the *material* aspects of school success, such as freedom from the distractions of poverty and the enrichment of the environment at home, but may have little to do with the actual values associated with school achievement. Indeed, among very affluent children, even teachers often note a belief that the children's school performance is irrelevant to their futures; parental resources will secure a fine college credential, or family contacts will help the child connect with a lucrative work life.

If the amount and quality of education one receives has little to do with economic success for affluent children, and holds little promise of reversing the cycle of poverty and unemployment for disadvantaged youth, it is not

likely to be highly prized by young adolescents. In fact, for many of these children, arguments can be successfully mounted that schooling is, indeed, irrelevant to their futures. Under these circumstances, it is little wonder that so many students view the primarily cognitive functions of schooling as unconnected to either their immediate or their future world.

Successful schools for a transitional society, or one already at phase 3, then, are those that can replicate the parental interest, attention, and other intangible resources that encourage students to take full advantage of the wealth of tangible resources available to them. In the absence of strong compulsions to excel at school from either the family, the social group, or the economic system, the school must work to become a viable competitor for the attention of youth in a time when they recognize that there are other influences on their transition to adulthood: youth-oriented commercial interests, the peer group, and the media.

Coleman and Husen (1985) conclude, "As the family's continuity through generations breaks down, the society and the school as its agent takes an increasing share of responsibility for the transition from childhood and youth to adulthood. This includes not merely a transition from school to work, but a transition from to adulthood in other ways as well" (p. 47). Thus, in the transition between a phase 2 and phase 3 society, and in a phase 3 society itself, the school moves from a strictly secondary socialization role to a more central role in assuring that the child is given membership in a productive group that is engaged in important work that is clearly connected to the future welfare of both the individual and the species. That, ultimately, should guide the school reform efforts of the second millennium.

### The School's Role in Socialization: Circa 2000

School reform efforts of the last decade have produced arguments over the *content* of the curriculum. Shaped by the roles assigned to schools in their historical positions as the developers of intellectual competence, the teachers of respect for institutional authority, and the trainers of vocational competence, that debate has centered largely on the intellectual content of school learning. Acrimonious debate has occurred over the relative value of different types of learning, with some writers even characterizing it as a struggle between useful and ornamental knowledge (Vallance, 1985). Almost absent from most reform discussions, though, has been any consideration of the role of the school as a principal socialization agent in a transitional society.

Increasingly, the school is in the unique position of having both the resources and the compelling self-interest to assure that children are socialized, appropriately, into both vocational competence and a productive adulthood. The resources are those tangible elements that an affluent society can provide for specialized purposes: money, personnel, technology. The self-interest is bred from a growing conviction on the part of many individuals that they can manage *their* child's education better than the school can, by either contracting privately for schooling in a setting over which the individual parent has more control, or by acquiring resources (in the form of materials, tutors), technology (computers, television), and experiences (travel, organized leisure pursuits) that can replace or greatly enhance formalized schooling. As long as the school promotes its function as only the development of intellectual competence and vocational competence, the parents are correct: It can probably be done better in other ways.

To a large degree, then, it is the school's ability to make itself indispensable in a transitional society where the obligations of adequate socialization are falling more heavily on institutions that will determine its continued existence in a form that most of us will recognize.

In rethinking educational reform, it will be necessary to examine the content of schools' *socialization* curricula as well as their intellectual and vocational ones. As a minimum, it appears that this curricula might focus on several major domains.

## Membership

In phase 1 and phase 2 societies, membership in the social group is assured by the importance of children in the economic system and as contributors to the welfare of the family. As societies change the role of children from that of producer to that of consumer, both the child's sense of obligation to the group and the group's influence on individual behavior diminishes. Thus, it falls to the schools to assure that all children are members of a productive, functional, contributing social organization that is officially sanctioned by the larger social order that supports it. It is this membership that will socialize children into productive adult roles.

Membership, according to Hirschi (1969), depends on social bonding, the extent to which an individual forms meaningful and satisfying links with a social group and the extent to which the group encourages the formation of those bonds. Social bonding has four elements: attachment, commitment, involvement, and belief.

*Attachment* refers to the social and emotional bonds to others, characterized by whether an individual cares what others think of him and his behavior. It is reciprocal; an individual will not care about others if she believes others do not care about her.

*Commitment* is the logical part of bonding. It is the belief that remaining connected to a group is the rational thing to do to preserve one's own self-interest. Commitment can be based on immediate needs (as it is in phase

1 societies where we band together for safety) or on long-term, internalized goals, where remaining with the group will help one achieve some desired end for one's self. In the absence of obvious short- or long-term benefit, continued membership in a group is irrational.

*Involvement* describes the extent of an individual's participation in the activities of the group or institution. For students, this means participation in school activities: academic, social, and leisure time. Failing to become engaged, or withdrawing from engagement, often heralds early school leaving.

*Belief* is faith in the institution or group's legitimacy, efficacy, potency, and continued benefit to the individual. It is a feeling that the group is good for me and that I am good for the group. In short, it determines if a student believes that the school will lead to his or her desired goals.

In an excellent study of schools with lower than expected dropout rates, Wehlage, Rutter, Smith, Lesko, and Fernandez (1989) indicated that successful schools are those that give explicit attention to creating a sense of membership for at-risk youth. Wehlage and colleagues argued convincingly that school success can be greatly enhanced by explicitly reducing the effects of impediments to membership: difficulty of coping with school norms; incongruence between home, community, and school; isolation of students from the mainstream of school activity; and maladjustment to the large, impersonal social setting of many schools for adolescents.

## Learning to Work

The second major domain of socialization is that of learning to work. In *Becoming a Worker,* Borman (1986) explored the various dimensions associated with socialization into the role of productive worker. In subsistence societies, work is relatively informal. It is determined by natural cycles of agriculture or by normal events associated with existence. Families are intimately connected with the work that needs to be done, so they are the primary resource to connect children with work. In industrialized societies, work is specialized. Children are occasionally linked to their future work through family ties, such as in a small business or a trade to which children might be apprenticed through the efforts of a family member. But, for the most part, work is not performed in front of children, but in specialized places (factories, offices, laboratories). Thus, the role of the family in linking children to future work begins to weaken. Rather than learning to work by watching people work, and being introduced to the workplace by a family member, children must learn to work by doing children's work, which in industrialized societies means going to school.

In the late twentieth century, then, learning to be a worker has less to do with the learning of specific knowledge or an ordained set of skills (as

in learning to be a blacksmith or a pilot) than with the development of attitudes, knowledge, and skills that enable a individual to

1. Accept the value of work as a necessary condition of success and
   independence
2. Figure out the conditions under which work is performed, and the
   behaviors which facilitate the accomplishment of that work
3. Find meaningful work
4. Adapt one's occupational competencies to the changing demands of
   the economy and the workplace, or even develop new competencies
5. Manage one's own resources, including time, work effort, and money

   Thus, the principal objective for a school in the cultivation of a productive work orientation is to provide opportunities for meaningful work
that is linked both to the improvement of conditions of life and to meaningful rewards for students. In times past, students learned to work by working at home or in some home-related activity. Now, the opportunities are
often no longer present for making meaningful contributions to the welfare
of the family, so work, particularly the kind done in school, is often seen
as arbitrary—something to "occupy" the child. A major goal of schooling
must be to shape a value among children that encourages meaningful work,
eschews meaningless work, and clearly links student work to valued rewards,
including status, discretionary time, and public gratitude.

## Social Heterogeneity and Urbanization

Unfortunately, the little girl who thought that grandmas are the ones who
teach us how to be must soon learn that grandma's world was much more
circumscribed than any in which she will ultimately live as an adult. Grandma
could probably learn "how to be" and expect that to remain fairly stable
throughout her life. Today's children will have no such luxury.
   Children must learn gender roles that accommodate familial, occupational, and civil conditions they will face in adulthood (Boulding, 1966). Incredibly, though, they must learn them from adults who have never had to
face the demands that they will face in their adult lives. Thus, the most appropriate social learning that can probably take place is for children to learn
how to form mutual support networks to ease the transitions that many of
them will make across traditional gender-specific role boundaries in their
families, their careers, and their political system.
   Beyond the formation of these networks, children will also have to cope
with an increasingly heterogenous society. By 2010, one in three people in
the United States will be nonwhite, and well over one-half of the school

population will represent culturally diverse people (Hodgkinson, 1985). Religious groups will be increasingly active in public and civic affairs, and other special interest groups will have increasing public influence. Global affairs will have a direct effect on the most minute aspects of life, from job security to the availability of products. And, in a vitally important development for most Westerners, the utilization of the earth's resources will become more a matter of global concern and less the province only of those who can afford to extract and use them.

All of this will also take place in the context of greater institutionaliza-tion. People will spend more of each day in institutions (from childcare to centers for elderly care), beginning at an earlier age and ending at a later age. More jobs will be in large organizations with fewer opportunities to see the "whole picture." Mass media will consume more attention during the day and take on an increasing share of the responsibility for the instantaneous transmission of culture.

Urbanization will be the norm for demographic change, and children will grow into adulthood in agglomerations of housing in complex physical units with new forms of "taboos" mandated by the physical proximity of people. In short, there will be more of us, in greater variety than ever before, sharing space more densely, and spending more and more time together in institutionalized settings.

Because of the relatively homogenous nature of any given family unit, it is almost perfectly designed to be *unable* to socialize students into this heterogenous setting. Schools, on the other hand, which can structure both the nature of the tasks to be performed and the composition of the group to perform it, are perhaps the most promising agent for this type of socialization.

## Collaboration and Collective Action

As the United States has become more inextricably connected with a global economy, and as our basic industries have had to reshape their age-old prac-tices to become more competitive in global markets, it is clear that the key to successful large-scale competition is the amount of cooperation and col-laboration that exists within the competing unit. Some U.S. business leaders have gone so far as to say that the American system will not survive another generation that knows only how to compete with one another. What is needed are individuals who can and will collaborate with others in order to solve problems, improve their own efforts, and support one another.

Such collaborative behavior has historically been taught in the family. However, because families are having fewer children, there is less opportunity

or need for children to learn the skills associated with negotiation, cooperation, and compromise among peers. Further, as families become less interdependent on one another for the satisfaction of basic needs, individual
goals are more easily satisfied, even in the most trivial areas. For example,
food packaging now permits everyone to have a different type of meal; the
availability of multiple televisions and other entertainment devices frees
children from having to negotiate with anyone over "what to watch"; and
the way in which an individual spends his or her free time has little to do
with the ultimate welfare of the family. In this kind of environment, there
is little opportunity to see the benefits of collective goal setting, negotiation
of priorities, or the exercise of sound interpersonal skills.

Because the opportunities for learning to collaborate are becoming
scarcer in homes, schools are one of the few remaining childhood institutions that might be expected to begin laying the foundation for the development of collaborative attitudes and skills among their students and, ultimately,
their graduates. Historically, though, schools tend to be among the least collaborative institutions in U.S. society. Thus, to achieve the new goals mandated by changing economic and social demands in the 1990s and beyond,
fundamental changes are necessary in the way schools conceive of their functions and execute their responsibilities. Further, those who work in schools
will have to learn new roles and new ways of working with colleagues in order
to be successful models of collaboration for students.

As currently organized, schools are models of isolation and individual
competition rather than collaboration (Rosenholtz, 1989). Teachers are
organized into departments or into relatively isolated and autonomous units
that share an interest in a subject or an intellectual discipline rather than
a common group of clients. Thus, when English teachers share professional
information, it tends to be about teaching English, not about teaching English
to a given student. The reason for this is evident: Two English teachers share
only an interest in the subject. Because they do not serve the same students,
they do not share a common interest in the well-being of any student in particular. Furthermore, because their responsibility is only for the teaching of
English, they tend to focus on cognitive objectives rather than on broader
issues of socialization. As a result, they can talk only about teaching English
in general, not about the kind of English teaching that Bill or Latesa or Jose
needs. And while English serves as the example in this case, the same conditions are true in virtually all subject areas.

At the same time as the organization of schools mitigates against collaboration, so too does the very strong norm of noninterference and tolerance
that exists in most schools. Reinforced by the belief that the individual teacher
is alone responsible for the conduct of his or her class, and never having
been encouraged to see teaching as an interdependent task, getting help is
actually something to be avoided. Traditionally, teachers have held the

noton that it makes little difference if they collaborate with colleagues, because "Once I close my door, I'm responsible, so I do as I please." In fact, few values are as deeply ingrained in any profession as this one is in teaching: A teacher is solely responsible for his or her classroom.

As a result of this value, professional educators not only *expect* to be left alone and not have their individual instructional decisions challenged or questioned by a colleague, but they, in turn, grant that exemption from professional criticism to their colleagues as well. Thus, an almost palpable silence exists in schools about the way in which anyone chooses to exercise his or her responsibility to run a classroom or to deliver instruction. Although individual teachers may have opinions about the practices of another teacher, and may even share those with a close friend, it is unlikely that they will ever engage another teacher in a discussion of their teaching.

In those rare instances when a teacher invites a comment on his or her teaching, others tend to be cautious in offering criticism. To do so would open up their own practices to scrutiny and would violate the long-standing norm of nonconfrontation that exists in the profession. So teachers remain isolated from one of the best sources of professional assistance available to them—the collaboration of colleagues on problems that are shared across a group of students.

This system also discourages the recognition of any single teacher as an expert in anything other than his or her subject area. Because it is not appropriate to criticize another teacher, and because we are reluctant to offer advice to other teachers for fear it will lead to questions about our own practices, and because of norms that tolerate incredibly diverse (and sometimes destructive) teaching practices, no one ever advances himself or herself as "expert" in the craft of teaching—only as expert in a subject area. In fact, debates on teaching strategies are often cut off by statements such as, "Well, that may work in math, but in English we have to do it quite differently." By and large, we buy that argument because it is a social norm, not because of its intrinsic intellectual worth.

Similar conditions exist for students. We begin early to sort and select students into groups that are isolated from one another. The best athletes make the team, the best musicians are in the band, good jumpers and dancers are cheerleaders, and the "brains" are on the Honor Roll. We even group students on the basis of perceived ability, so that we substantiate and validate the differences that exist among people, not in order to use their individual talents to help the group but to shelter their talents from possible contamination by those who have different gifts.

In short, we segment people into factions and ask them to compete for limited rewards. The result is that students learn that it is every person for himself or herself, and the seeds of destructive, instinctive hyper-competitiveness are sown early in our youth.

In such an environment, it is difficult to learn the complex skills, values, and attitudes that are required for the development of a social conscience, the acceptance of the social contract in a democratic society, and practice of skills essential for taking collective action for the common good. Instead, highly competitive systems produce intense, self-centered competition among individuals of the type that is antithetical to recent views of the needs of U.S. society and its economy (Cawelti, 1989).

## Conclusion

The role of society as an educator of children has not changed much in the past two millennia; only the agents of that education have changed. Now, the responsibility for basic socialization is shifting increasingly to youth-serving institutions. Among those, the school is of particular importance. In its most desirable manifestations, schools will represent in each of their settings the increasing diversity of the U.S. population and the increasing interdependence of the global community. It is in school that students will learn, or not learn, how to cope with human diversity; in school, habits of productive work will be learned; and finally, schools will be where our children learn to work together for broad, mutually beneficial goals. It will be in school that youth are organized for collective, publically beneficial action, and in school that the engagement in youth in meaningful service and mutual support will take place.

If they are successful, schools will become even more central to American life, for they will shape the values of the new millennium. If, however, schools are permitted to define their goals only in intellectual terms and are held accountable only for student performance on highly individualized measures of information processing and verbal recall, the increasingly critical mission of productive socialization will be ignored, and schools will have failed to deliver the most important outcome—children who are bonded to their community, to each other, and to habits of productive effort. If that happens, schools, as we know them, will ultimately become superfluous to the human condition.

## References

Borman, K. (1986). *Becoming a worker.* Norwood, NJ: Ablex Press.

Boulding, K. E. (1966). Expecting the unexpected: The uncertain future of knowledge and technology. In E. Morphet and C. Ryan (Eds.), *Prospective changes in society by 1980* (pp. 117–131). Denver: Designing Education for the Future: An 8 Year Project.

Bower, M. (1966). *The will to manage.* New York: McGraw Hill.

Cawelti, G. (December, 1989). *What America needs in its school graduates.* Speech to the Association for Supervision and Curriculum Development's Middle Level Education Institute, Williamsburg, VA.

Ciardi, J. (1959). *How does a poem mean?* Boston: Houghton Mifflin.

Clark, R. (1985). *Family life and school achievement.* Chicago: University of Chicago Press.

Coleman, J. S., & Husen, T. (1985). *Becoming adult in a changing society.* Paris: Organization for Economic Cooperation and Development.

Deutsch Shell. (1975). *Jugend swischen 13 und 24 — Vergleich uber 20 Jahre — Schste Untersuchung zur Situation der deutschen Jugend im Bundesgebiet.* Jugendwerk der Deutschen Shell.

Deutsch Shell. (1977). *Jugend in Europa. Ihre Eingliederdung in die Welt der Erwachsenen.* Analyse swischen der Bendesrepublik Deutschland, Frankreich, und Grossbritannien. Siebente Untersuchung zur Situation der Jugend, anlasslich "75 Jahre Shell in Deutschland."

Hanushek, E. (1981). Throwing money at schools. *Journal of Policy Analysis and Management, 10*(1), 113–121.

Hirschi, T. (1969). *Causes of delinquency.* Los Angeles: University of California Press.

Hodgkinson, H. (1985). *All one system: The demographics of education.* Washington, DC: Educational Leadership Institute.

Rosenholz, S. (1989). *Teachers' workplace: A study of social organizations.* New York: Longman.

Vallance, E. (1985). Ways of knowing and curricular conceptions: Implications for program planning. In E. Eisner (Ed.), *Learning and teaching the ways of knowing. Eighty-Fourth Yearbook of the National Society for the Study of Education* (pp. 199–217). Chicago: University of Chicago Press.

Wehlage, G. G., Rutter, R. A., Smith, G. A., Lesko, N., & Fernandez, R. R. (1989). *Reducing the risk: Schools as communities of support.* Philadelphia: Falmer Press.

Wilson, W. J. (1986). *The truly disadvantaged.* Chicago: University of Chicago Press.

# CHAPTER FIVE

# A New Paradigm of Schooling: Connecting School, Home, and Community

FRANCES K. KOCHAN
*Florida State University*

The middle school movement in the United States has been at the forefront of educational reform for the past two decades. In fact, current recommendations for school restructuring such as teacher decision making, integrated curriculum, cooperative learning, and preparing students to think and work together have long been associated with suggested middle level school organization. Team building, team teaching, interdisciplinary curriculum, and advisor/advisee programs contain elements of what others are now labeling "a restructured school."

Middle level educators can be proud of the progress they have made in meeting the needs of young adolescents. In exemplary middle schools, the curriculum, the operations, and the goals of the school have been developed around the notion that the needs of students must be met. Strategies to meet these needs are ingrained in middle level education literature, as is the belief that middle level education, structured and operated around these characteristics, will meet the physical, social, emotional, and intellectual needs of students and prepare them for the world of tomorrow.

The last decade, however, has been a period of rapid and comprehensive change in our society, which necessitates that we reexamine, reevaluate, and revise our ideas about the needs of the middle school child and the place of the school in meeting those needs. In my opinion, we are presently operating from a vision that is too narrow. Instead of thinking in terms of the needs of the young adolescent by focusing primarily on the individual, we must begin to take a more holistic view. Our focus should also encompass the needs of the young adolescent *within the context of the culture in which he or she exists and in which he or she must function in the future.* Likewise, it is time to consider moving away from the concepts of reform and restructuring of the school, and creating new visions of substantive change and transformation.

In this chapter, I will address the needs of the young adolescent as related to the cultural milieu in which he or she exists and present what I believe the response of the school should be when attempting to meet those needs. I will begin by examining the changes in our society that have made an impact on our students and our schools. Next, I will present a new paradigm of schooling that I believe is an appropriate one for our rapidly changing society and suggest strategies for implementing this paradigm. Developing strong connections and building a sense of community between and among the school, home, and community is imperative. This chapter will not only provide specific strategies for implementing this new paradigm but will also create a new frame of reference about the role of the school in the society of today and tomorrow.

## Examining the Social Context

We are living in a time of immense cultural and societal upheaval. In Toffler's (1981) terms, we are living in the dawn of a new civilization. Our lives are marked not by traditions and stability as in the past, but by temporariness, which results in feelings of impermanence and insecurity. Our social and cultural structures have changed and often our concepts of what is, in many cases, is far from reality.

### A Child's View

During the last year, I have asked numerous groups of adults to reflect on the word *childhood* and to share the words that they associate with it. Among the most frequent responses were words such as *play, fun, happy, carefree,* and *love.* These words seem to typify our concept of childhood. Our concept comes from our own backgrounds and the myths of our society. Yet, when we speak to children, we get a very different picture. A recent survey of students ages 9 through 16 asking them about their major concerns found their greatest concerns were divorce, violence in their home, violence in their community, and pressure to use drugs (Davis & Foster,

1989). In another survey (Foster, 1989) that asked students to identify areas in which they needed help, the responses were equally revealing:

- 66 percent needed guidance in understanding how to get along with others.
- 42 percent wanted to know how to communicate with and relate to parents and teachers.
- 33 percent needed help in dealing with loneliness and grief.
- 25 percent wanted assistance in dealing with alcoholic or drug-addicted parents.

The childhood of today and the concerns of the young adolescent seem to include problems and concerns well beyond those typically connected to physical changes and the social and emotional trials of growing up. This seems to be the cultural context within which our young adolescents must learn to cope, to survive, to adjust, and to succeed.

### A New View of Family

A closely related institution around which we have built mythical concepts is the family. A colleague recently asked his undergraduate education majors to work in groups and create murals of the family. Invariably, they drew mom, dad, two children, and a dog, all with white skin and all with appropriate smiles on their faces. Yet, today only a small percent of U.S. families fit the pattern known as the "typical traditional family"—mother staying at home, father in the workplace, two bright and happy children, the family intact and secure (Johnston, 1990).

Nearly half of all marriages in the United States now result in divorce. Almost 20 percent of this nation's households are headed by a single parent, most of them female. Families are becoming increasingly culturally diverse, and in the next decade minority populations as a group will outnumber those now considered the majority. Structurally, the family is also extremely diverse, including numerous configurations of single, blended, foster, and stepparents (Johnston, 1990).

In the cultural sense, family has changed dramatically. It was through the family that values, morals, traditions, historical roots, and parenting skills were made visible and transmitted to younger generations, with several generations often living in close proximity to one another. The true essence of family in past generations extended beyond blood relations. Family also included neighbors and ethnic or religious groups who helped inculcate cultural and family norms into children. The culture itself, through the national psyche, a consistently verbalized moral code, the spoken ideals of democracy, equality, freedom, and the promise of a better life, helped create a sense of history, of belonging, and of connectedness.

But as we view our world today, at the very time when families are struggling for survival, the support systems that helped make them and our children strong are no longer there. Generations are separated by space and differing value systems. Neighborhoods have become conclaves of isolation. The influence of religion in the community and home has decreased. Values are often transmitted by media heroes. Many parents, under pressure to survive economically, have neither the financial nor time resources to meet the growing demands placed on them. Family interaction has decreased, resulting in a drop in academic achievement in school as well as an increase in the suicide rate among young people (Coleman, 1989).

The economic and lifestyle realities of family life today often result in stress and create problems as parents try to find a balance between the demands of work and family. When families are under stress, children are under stress. When children are under stress, schools cannot ignore the implications, the problems, or the changes that must take place. This demand is particularly true in the middle level years when young adolescents are particularly vulnerable as they struggle with the changes within them and as they face a turbulent present and uncertain future.

## Creating a New Paradigm

Given the social structures that surround our students, for schools to focus on being responsive to student needs by dealing only with the internal school setting is to operate like a horse being led through a fire; in the midst of crisis, we seem to be wearing blinders. Just as we must think of the child, in his or her culture, we must think of the school within the society. The changes in our society have had a great impact on the school. Rather than dealing with this impact as if it could be solved at the school through such things as curriculum changes, restructuring management, or adding student service resources, we must address the issue in a more holistic way.

I believe that what is required is a fundamental change in the paradigm of the school. It will be extremely difficult for the school to be successful unless changes occur within and outside of it. It is time to view the school not as an independent entity but as part of a multidimensional, interdependent, coordinated system that includes the home and the community as partners in the educational and community development process. It is time for schools to become catalysts for change within and beyond their own institutions.

Creating such a paradigm may enable schools to become a strong force in stimulating what Alinsky (1971) labels the "re-creation of community" in our society. To do so will require building and encouraging the development of support systems in the school, the home, and the community to replace those that no longer exist in our society. It means "reconnecting" people and resources, and involves changing roles, relationships, and responsibilities between and among teachers, students, parents, and community personnel.

### Developing Community in the School

A first step in this process is to build a sense of community in the school. The lack of community in our society and the changing nature of the family structure make it vital that our schools provide numerous opportunities for students to think and to operate as family and community units. This necessitates developing or strengthening support systems for students, teachers, and staff within that environment.

*Turning Points* (Carnegie, 1989) suggested that middle school students should be grouped into "communities of learning." These communities provide students with a support system within the school. They also assist students in gaining the skills, knowledge, and attitudes necessary for them to create strong families and strong communities in the future. These communities could likewise be mechanisms through which children acquire not only cognitive skills but the ability to live and work together in harmony.

Middle schools are in a unique position to create such environments because the patterns and concepts are already present in the "schools within a school," the organizational structure, and the advisor/advisee programs. In forming such units of support, it is important to stress the idea of community or family units, rather than teams or schools. The use of concept and value-laden terms as *family* and *community* carries a power of its own, which helps unite and strengthen the bond between students in these units (Weick, 1985).

The concepts of family and community could also be incorporated into the curriculum. Family living and family development courses provide students with meaningful opportunities to think and talk about the importance of strong families in their lives, in school, in home, and in the families they will create in the future. Advisor/advisee programs, social studies classes, and school governance activities could likewise focus on such issues.

In addition to these strategies, we should structure the culture of the school so that the people who work there are supported and nurtured. Ouchi (1981) has suggested that organizations of the future must operate as if they were a family. He stressed that, because of the impersonal nature of our society, organizations must meet individual as well as institutional needs.

Policies of the school should be developed to support the employees so that their own families are strengthened. Job sharing, flexible hours, allowing children of family and staff to attend the school, and providing release time for staff to attend school activities in which their own children are engaged are options that schools can provide. Once again, middle schools already have a structure in place, through teacher teams, that can be used and augmented to develop strong bonds and unity among members. Middle school teacher teams could be reconceptualized into family or community groups. Systems of support could include all members of the staff, as well as teachers, creating a wholeness to the school that recognizes the talents, contributions, and needs of every member.

Like students, teachers and staff should be part of "communities of learning." This is an excellent mechanism for providing them with opportunities to think and reflect on their teaching and work, as well as on the needs of one another. It is imperative for schools to address the issue of limited time and accommodate this constraint in building these communities (Chapman, 1990). Common planning times among teachers is one solution; adding half days for planning to the schedule and providing release days are additional avenues for meeting the necessary time requirements for planning, reflecting, and socializing.

### Uniting with Parents

A second step in creating a changing paradigm of the school is to expand relationships with parents. We know that parents must be welcomed into schools and that parental involvement is a vital factor in school success (Johnston, 1990). Educators also know that this involvement seems to decrease in middle school. The authors of *Turning Points* (Carnegie, 1989) suggested that we must "reengage families in the education of their children." This reengagement includes not only welcoming parents into the school but helping to empower them in the parenting process.

Middle schools should consider providing training in parenting and building strong family relationships. School personnel might conduct such sessions or connect with community agencies to assure that they are available. Another activity could be developing a lending library of videotapes and books or creating partnerships with the local library to inform parents of available resources. An additional strategy could be creating and disseminating newsletters with meaningful information about successful parenting techniques.

In addition to inviting parents into schools, providing parent training, and assisting them in locating needed resources, middle schools could work with parent groups to develop outreach programs. Consideration should be given to such activities as conducting home visits, sending "homework packets" and parenting materials to the home, conducting grade level and school social activities to unite people, or developing "welcome wagons" run by parents to orient new families to the school.

Whatever the specific activities a school decides to implement, it is necessary to develop a mindset in the school that includes the expansion of connections between and among parents and community members as a top priority. Just as the middle school child is vulnerable, the middle school parent is also vulnerable. This is a time of turbulence for families and students. Not only is the society in upheaval, the child is in upheaval. Having a "buddy parent," a "parent ombudsman," a teacher who can talk as a friend, or a social agency one could turn to in time of need can make this a period of survival rather than despair. Uniting these resources for families can be of benefit not only for the individual family in need but for the student, the school, and the community.

We need to consider expanding our concept of parental involvement to include not only inviting parents into the school and reaching out to them but involving them in the operation of the school. Involvement would not be thought of in a paternalistic manner that says, "Come on in. Here is what we can do for you." Nor would it be handled in a demanding manner that says, "Come on in. Here is what you can do for us." Rather, it would be framed in a cooperative manner that says, "Come on in. Let's combine our resources to support and strengthen one another." Thus, the relationship is conceived of as a partnership of equals in which the knowledge of each group is shared to expand the knowledge of both.

In addition, school-parent advisory groups can focus not only on the needs of the school but on the needs of the families and communities served by them. Schools can become involved in meeting family and community needs through school-based and community development activities. One such effort resulted in the formation of a school-based "Caring Connection" where parents helped one another in time of crisis. Allowing parents to identify needs of families and to assist in formulating solutions to those needs helps to improve environments within and outside of the school.

## Networking with the Community

The third step in this process of change is for the school to become an active participant in "connecting schools with the community" (Carnegie, 1989). This connecting begins by placing students in "youth service." Allowing each class, grade level, or the school as a whole to select a worthy project and to develop the concept of service to the community is an essential component of this effort. These experiences serve to bind students together, give them a sense of accomplishment, and strengthen the bonds between the school and the community.

A second component in creating this connection is networking with community resources to meet the needs of students and families. Uniting with other groups, such as recreation departments, youth organizations, and private dance and/or music schools, to provide before- and after-school care would be one technique to assist families and students and to strengthen the relationship between the school and community. Joining with community educators to serve the educational needs of adults is another avenue for creating a school that meets community as well as personal educational needs. Creating mechanisms for networking with social service agencies to meet family needs is an important aspect of creating community connections. Some schools have expanded this idea to include locating human services at the schools so they can become an integral part of the social services system.

Reaching out to families and connecting them to resources can transform not only the community but the school. One school principal joined forces with members of the sheriff's department, the recreation department, the Girl Scouts, and the families in an impoverished, crime-ridden neighborhood to make it a more safe and secure place. Their efforts not only transformed the neighborhood but the lives of students and families and thus improved the school.

## Developing a New Vision

As we approach the twenty-first century, middle level educators should take a leadership role in redefining not only the structure of schools but their role and function. This expanded role includes educating children to create strong families and communities in the future and developing and expanding support services to sustain them and their families in the present.

It will become increasingly difficult for schools to be successful if the society in which our children live is unable to support them and their families. The problem is particularly difficult at the middle school level where parental support subsides and the needs of children become more acute. Therefore, we must consider forming a new paradigm of the middle school that binds all of our forces together to re-create community in our schools and our lives.

This vision involves creating connections between and among the school, home, and community, which would provide systems of support for all of them. Creating such a paradigm requires boldness, commitment, and the creation of a new vision transforming what we do, how we operate, and who we are. With this newly formed vision, and a community of common thought, middle schools help generate stronger family and community ties. This unity creates stronger schools today and more successful students in the years ahead.

# References

Alinsky, S. D. (1971). *Rules for radicals.* New York: Random House.

Carnegie Council on Adolescent Development's Task Force on Education of Young Adolescents. (1989). *Turning points: Preparing youth for the 21st century.* Washington, DC: Carnegie Council on Adolescent Development, a program of Carnegie Corporation of New York.

Chapman, J. (1990). School based decision-making and management implications for school personnel. In J. Chapman (Ed.), *School-based decision-making and management* (pp. 221–244). Briston, PA: Falmer Press.

Coleman, J. S. (1989). *Do students learn more in private rather than in public schools?* Paper presented at the Fifth Annual Critical Issues Symposium, Center for Policy Studies in Education, Tallahassee, FL.

Davis, T., & Foster, G. (1989). *Student survey data analysis report: F/S/C/Partnership Program.* Unpublished Report, Florida State University School, College of Education, Tallahassee, FL.

Foster, G. (1989) *Report of student needs: F/S/C/Partnership Program.* Unpublished Report, Florida State University School, College of Education, Tallahassee, FL.

Johnston, H. J. (1990). *The new American family and the school.* Columbus, OH: National Middle School Association.

Ouchi, W. S. (1981). *Theory Z.* Reading, MA: Addison Wesley.

Toffler, A. (1981). *The third wave.* New York: Bantam Books.

Weick, K. (1985). Sources of order in unorganized systems. In Y. S. Lincoln (Ed.), *Organizational theory and inquiry* (pp. 106–139). Newbury, CA: Sage.

# PART TWO

# Developing a Sense of Responsiveness

In the summer of 1989, when the Carnegie Council on Adolescent Development released Turning Points: Preparing Youth for the 21st Century, the report startled educators and the public alike because of its thorough presentation and analysis of the plight of our country's youth. The Task Force claimed that "early adolescence (aged 10 to 15) is a time when many youth choose a path toward a productive and fulfilling life. For many others, it represents their last best chance to avoid a diminished future" (p. 8). Additionally, they concluded that middle grade schools must be more assertive in the role they play in the lives of young adolescents.

After an examination of U.S. youth and how well middle grade schools, health institutions, and community organization serve them, the Task Force formulated eight recommendations:

1. Create small communities for learning.
2. Teach a core academic program.
3. Ensure success for all students.
4. Empower teachers and administrators to make decisions about the experiences of middle grade students.
5. Staff middle grade school with teachers who are expert at teaching young adolescents.
6. Improve academic performance through fostering the health and fitness of young adolescents.
7. Reengage families in the education of young adolescents.
8. Connect schools with communities (pp. 9–10).

These recommendations coincided with the existing advocacy of middle level educators and associations such as the National Middle School Association. A flurry of new activity relative to middle schools has resulted in state departments of education and local school districts. Work toward evaluating current practices and implementing changes in line with the Carnegie recommendations is ongoing in nearly every state and school district.

Within the last few years, several other significant studies have helped middle level educators understand the conditions of our nation's middle level schools. The most widely known and used are listed at the end of this introduction to Part Two. These studies point out that although many schools have changed their organizational structures and programs to be more responsive to young adolescents, much remains to be done.

The middle school, as an institution, appears to be in the best position to lead the educational transformation in the United States. Programs commonly associated with the middle school movement, such as interdisciplinary teaming, block scheduling, and teacher advisory, are examples of significant restructuring efforts already underway and increasingly advocated, even for high schools. These efforts go far beyond typical school improvement efforts at other levels. They focus attention on the way the school is structured, the climate in which teachers work, the way content is organized, and the best environments for learning to take place.

In Part Two, new organizational structures and programs are reviewed at length. J. Howard Johnston discusses climate and culture as mediators of school values and collaborative behavior in Chapter Six. He presents disadvantaged youth as a special case and suggests ways to create a learning community for all students. In Chapter Seven, Robert Shockley elaborates on the need for developing a sense of mission in middle level schools and discusses the role of leadership in developing and maintaining that mission. Robert Spear, in Chapter Eight, presents a case study for change to the middle school concept that is based on theoretical change literature.

In Chapter Nine, Joanne Arhar presents research on interdisciplinary team organization and discusses the value of teaming in terms of interracial relationships, student behavior, and the social bonding of students to peers and teachers. In Chapter Ten, Neila Connors summarizes literature on advisory programs and discusses ways to make such programs successful. Sherrel Bergman, in Chapter Eleven, discusses exploratory programs in an historical context and presents program models and related issues. James Garvin has been known to say that "beginning a middle school is the easy part, maintaining one is more difficult." Jim shares his many years of experience working in middle schools by discussing ways of maintaining middle schools in Chapter Twelve.

Epstein and Mac Iver (1990) point out that many middle level schools have not begun to restructure. Evidence from their survey and others indicates, however, that many schools have changed their orientation and organization to be more responsive to the needs of young adolescents. A few of these schools have worked through reform and are now struggling to transform. Other schools are so immersed in restructuring that they have little time to think about "the big picture" and any meaningful sense of mission. A few schools, under the leadership of charismatic principals, may be transforming and restructuring at the same time. However the sequence evolves, transformation must occur if educators are to develop a sense of responsiveness to young adolescents.

## References

Alexander, W. M., & McEwin, C. K. (1989). Schools in the middle: Status and progress. Columbus, OH: National Middle School Association.

Carnegie Council on Adolescent Development's Task Force on Education of Young Adolescents. (1989). Turning points: Preparing American youth for the 21st century. Washington, DC: Carnegie Council on Adolescent Development, a program of Carnegie Corporation of New York.

Cawelti, G. (1988, November). Middle schools a better match with early adolescent needs, ASCD survey finds. ASCD Curriculum Update. (Available from the Association for Curriculum and Supervision Development, Alexandria, VA, 22314-2798.)

Epstein, J. L., & Mac Iver, D. J. (1990). Education in the middle grades: National practices and trends. Columbus, OH: National Middle School Association.

Keefe, J. W., Clark, D. C., Nickerson, N. C., & Valentine, J. (1983). The middle level principalship. Reston, VA: National Association of Secondary School Principals.

Lounsbury, J. H., & Clark, D. C. (1990). Inside grade eight: From apathy to excitement. Reston, VA: National Association of Secondary School Principals.

Lounsbury, J. H., & Johnston, J. H. (1988). Life in the three sixth grades. Reston, VA: National Association of Secondary School Principals.

Lounsbury, J. H., & Marani, J. (1962). The junior high school we saw: One day in the eighth grade. Alexandria, VA: Association for Supervision and Curriculum Development.

Lounsbury, J. H., Marani, J., & Compton, M. (1980). The middle school in profile: A day in the seventh grade. Reston, VA: National Association of Secondary School Principals.

National Education Longitudinal Study of 1988. (1988). National Center for Education Statistics, Office of Educational Research and Improvement. Washington, DC: U.S. Department of Education.

# CHAPTER SIX

# Climate and Culture as Mediators of School Values and Collaborative Behavior

J. HOWARD JOHNSTON
*University of South Florida*

For all of the dissimilarities that exist among effective schools, one variable has emerged as being central to their success: the presence of clear, public values that support achievement and excellence while discouraging mediocrity and failure (Boyer, 1983; Brookover, Beady, Flood, Schweitzer, & Wisenbaker, 1979; Coleman, Hoffer, & Kilgore, 1982; Good & Brophy, 1987; Hampel, 1986; Lightfoot, 1983; Metz, 1978; Phi Delta Kappa, 1980; Rutter, Maughan, Mortimore, Ouston, & Smith, 1979; United States Department of Education, 1986). In fact, core values that define and direct an institution's mission are recognized not only in the scholarly literature on organizational effectiveness but in the popular literature and mythology about high-achieving organizations (Deal & Kennedy, 1984; Peters & Waterman, 1982).

Although much research attention has been given to the manner in which effective schools operate, little systematic attention, beyond simple descriptions of the values held by high-achieving schools, has been given to the ways in which these core values are transmitted, how they interact with the value set brought to the institution by its workers and clients, and how they ultimately affect student performance and learning.

School climate is of special importance in middle schools, where students are making a variety of decisions about themselves as students and as members of the school community. It is during this time that the value framework that guides the remainder of their lives is reorganized and re-formed (Toepfer,1988), and it is in the middle school years that students begin to make concrete decisions about their school future. Thus, these critical years are ones when a student decides whether school is a good place for "people like me" (Lipsitz, 1981).

Equally important, the decision to remain connected to the school and become a full participant in its programs and rituals may be largely a func-tion of the school's climate. Wehlage, Rutter, Smith, Lesko, and Fernandez (1989) suggest that the intangible feelings that a school conveys, just as much as its program, leads students to bond with or abandon the institution. For middle grades youth, decisions about the importance of schooling and the decision to drop out or remain in seem to be largely a matter of how the students *feel* about the school. When asked why they dropped out of school, 35 percent of the males and 31 percent of the females studied by Hammack (1986) reported, "School was not for me; I didn't like it." Another 27 per-cent said, "I couldn't get along with teachers."

In virtually all of Hammack's cases, students who left school did so, in part, to restructure their social relationships. Some girls left to get mar-ried (23 percent) or because they were pregnant (11 percent); 27 percent of the males left to go to work. In contrast, while *in* school, these individuals cut classes (54 percent), had discipline problems (41 percent), or were sus-pended (31 percent). Because they did not connect with the school, they formed friendship groups that did not prize education. They and their friends saw themselves as less likely to attend class, less popular, less likely to get good grades, less interested in school, and much less likely to go to college or get a job requiring college education than other students in their grade. Clearly, the decision to leave school reflects, in part, a desire to abandon an unhealthy climate in favor of a more congenial one, either in the workplace or in creating one's own family.

## Effects of Values and Culture

When the study of school effects on achievement began on a broad scale in the 1960s and 70s (Coleman, Campbell, Hobson, McPartland, Mood, Weinfeld, & York, 1986; Jencks, 1972), the focus was on traditional, resource unit variables such as per-pupil expenditure, libraries, recency of textbooks, educational attainments of faculties, breadth of course offerings, and availability of specialized instructional space. These variables showed little consistent relationship with student achievement.

More recent studies (Rutter et al., 1979; Brookover et al., 1979) have looked at process variables in relation to school achievement with encouraging results. Schools do, these studies assert with some certainty, make a difference in student achievement. Such investigation has also led to a large number of studies that examine specific classroom practices (as exemplified by Brophy & Rohrkemper, 1988) designed to identify those specific teacher behaviors and operations that produced the most demonstrable effects on student learning as measured by standard achievement tests.

Currently, the more complex nature of schooling as a social and intellectual enterprise is being recognized. More attention is given to the school as a social system or a culture with discreet norms, expectations, beliefs, and circumscribed patterns of behavior that lead to success or failure (Johnston, 1987; Johnston & Ramos de Perez, 1985; Sarason, 1982).

In all of this complexity, the centrality of values and the transmission of these achievement values through the mechanisms of the school's culture is evident in successful schools. The extent to which these values are widely shared within the school and between the school and its community have an especially profound influence on the success of the school (Coleman, Hoffer, & Kilgore, 1982; Lightfoot, 1983).

Lightfoot (1983) describes these values as a clear ideological stance that gives the institution both coherence and control. In the absence of a clear ideology, institutional efforts can become fragmented, and competitive subcultures can arise within it. Even successful schools can suffer from this alienation syndrome when the drive for success (college admission, high SAT scores, high grades), unguided by a central purpose or ideology, provokes harsh and destructive competition among students and between teachers. Speaking of the institution's workers and clients, Lightfoot argues for inclusivity of this ideology: "Without a common bond, without a clear purpose, the school fails to encompass them and does not take psychological hold on their energies" (1983, p. 321).

The articulation of a clear ideological stance is insufficient, however, to assure commitment and devotion to the school's purpose. Successful schools are also characterized by very clear boundaries, albeit permeable ones, that delineate the time and place where these values are operational (Lightfoot, 1983). Inside of school, the values guide the lives of students, regardless of the values that may exist in the world outside of the school. In private schools, parents support the "values and ideological stance of the teachers and the clear separation between school life and community norms" by opting to send their children to the school (Lightfoot, 1983, p. 322). In Quaker schools, the children often begin the day with several minutes of silence to mark the transition to school life from community influences. These moments separate them from the bustle of life and prepare them to be engulfed in the school's culture.

Among potential dropouts, alienation from the school's culture is usually quite nearly complete. In electing alternative schools, students most often indicated that they were looking for "attachment . . . belonging . . . safety . . . a real home." (Boyer, 1983, p. 246). Central to the success of these schools in retaining students was a close relationship between the potential dropout and a counselor or teacher—an adult who helped mentor the student into the value position of the school by teaching behaviors that were supportive of institutional norms and school success. This need for community, coupled with specific help in learning its standards of membership, proved to be an effective combination in preventing dropouts.

People tend to act on the basis of their psychological identification with a group rather than any formal, legal membership status or compulsory attendance at an institution. Thus, the effectiveness of group norms for shaping student behavior in school is dependent on the extent to which students feel a part of the group that enforces the norms and standards (Rutter et al., 1979). In this regard, values associated with student behavior and achievement must not only be explicit, they must also be "owned" by the groups that are expected to be governed by them: teachers and students. The ways in which this ownership is invited and confirmed are found most explicitly in the climate of the school.

## School Climate and Culture

The term *school climate* has been used to describe so many different phenomena, from school client demographics to classroom practices to school rules and discipline codes, that it is important to categorize these conceptualizations for discussion. Current studies tend to focus on one dimension of climate—the social-system dimension (Anderson, 1982). Other dimensions that have been practically ignored are proposed by Tagiuri (1968) and Miskel and Ogawa (1988): ecology, milieu, and culture. These are also consistent with the dimensions of climate identified by Johnston and Ramos de Perez (1985) in a study of particularly effective middle level schools.

In virtually all cases, the effects of climate on school achievement have been significant, although precise descriptions of generalizable school climate variables have been elusive (Anderson, 1982). Various conceptualizations of climate, not surprisingly, seem to produce different effects on student achievement.

*Ecological* aspects of climate deal with the material aspects of schooling on the performance of students. Physical facilities, including the age of buildings, appearance of school facilities, maintenance of facilities, and allocation of physical resources, have been studied in some detail (Phi Delta Kappa, 1980; Rutter et al., 1979; Tagiuri, 1968; Weber, 1971). As might be expected, the facilities themselves had a relatively small effect on student learning, except when they failed to achieve some minimum aspect of inhabitability (warmth, light, shelter from the elements).

However, Johnston and Ramos de Perez (1985) indicated that both students and teachers in the schools took the nature of the school facility and the condition in which it was maintained as a rather explicit indicator of how highly education was valued by the community. More specifically, those who worked in school saw in the facilities a physical manifestation of the level of commitment that the community offered its school programs.

*Milieu* dimensions of climate are associated with the presence or absence of groups or individuals in an organization. Numerous studies have focused on the presence or absence of teacher characteristics and the effect on student achievement (Miskel & Ogawa, 1988); other studies have examined student characteristics as predictors of student achievement, including family background, racial composition, intellectual talent, and a variety of others (Brookover, Beady, Flood, Schweitzer, & Wisenbaker, 1979; McDill & Rigsby, 1973; Schneider, Glasheen, & Hadley, 1979).

More recently, the nature, purpose, and functioning of groups created by schools has been the target of study, and promising evidence has emerged from studies of collaborative arrangements, alternative forms of student grouping, and cooperative learning arrangements (Arhar, 1990; Johnson & Johnson, 1975; Rosenholtz, 1979; Slavin, 1986).

The *social system* dimension of climate, including the administrative and instructional organization of schools, has also been linked to student achievement. Among the variables indicated in this collection of research studies is the extent to which teachers are involved in decision making about schools, the norms of collaboration and cooperation that exist among faculty, the nature of relationships among teachers, the ways in which classroom instruction is conducted, the nature of student-teacher relationships, and the standards of decorum present in the building (Anglin, 1979; Brookover & Lezotte, 1979; Edmonds, 1979; McDill & Rigsby, 1973; Phi Delta Kappa, 1980; Rutter et al., 1979; Weber, 1971; Wynne, 1980).

Finally, elements of the *cultural dimension* of school climate have been shown to influence school achievement. The schoolwide expectations, the emphasis placed on academics (in comparison or contrast with other potential activities), the commitment of teachers to improving student performance, and the nature of norms/values shared among students and by teachers and students have been linked with explicit achievement outcomes in a variety of academic areas and skills (Brookover & Lezotte, 1979; Brookover et al., 1978; Edmonds, 1979; Johnston & Ramos de Perez, 1985; McDill & Rigsby, 1973; Phi Delta Kappa, 1980; Rutter et al., 1979; Weber, 1971).

Virtually all of the existing research, however, suffers from the treatment of climate or cultural data as static phenomena that, once measured, remain relatively unchanged. Further, the study of school climate or culture has also centered on the artifacts produced by the climate and culture (such as order, clear expectations, opinions about school achievement) rather than the processes by which the culture is transmitted or the climate is altered and manipulated to enhance student achievement and academic excellence. This has led to the gross temptation simply to lift the artifacts from a successful school site and install them in another, thinking that such a move will actually re-create the culture that produced the artifacts of achievement in the effective school site (Johnston, 1987).

Intriguing areas remain unexplored. In the ecology dimension, Pfeffer (1982) posits that six qualities of physical facilities are related to organizational functioning: size, quality, flexibility, arrangement, privacy, and location. These factors, he claims, affect the amount of interaction, affective reaction to job and organization, and affective reaction and orientation toward others. Later research by Rosenholtz (1979) has shown that proximity of workspace and opportunity for interaction are major variables in the amount of collaboration among teachers in schools. Arhar's research (1990) points to organizational arrangements as mediators of social bonding among students and teachers.

Further study in the milieu dimension is indicated by studies on the effects of the demographic composition of groups on student achievement (Beckerman & Good, 1981). The creation of learning groups through ability grouping or tracking arrangements also show a strong relationship with student achievement (Slavin, 1986) and the ways in which teachers treat groups of students (Good & Brophy, 1987). Teacher demographics also affect performance, specifically, innovativeness, type of control system, intraorganizational conflict, career processes, and administrator succession.

Social system data constitute a legion, yet are not entirely conclusive. Differential treatment of marginal and disadvantaged students is well documented in the literature on classroom instruction (Corno & Snow, 1986; Good & Brophy, 1987; Harris, Rosenthal, & Snodgrass, 1986; Jackson, 1968; Johnston & Markle, 1983; Kulik & Kulik, 1982; Metz, 1978; Rutter et al., 1979; Slavin, 1986; Wallace, 1988). More important, however, disadvantaged students generally receive treatment that is counterproductive to educational achievement, thereby perpetuating their educational disadvantage. This process of acculturation, labeled by Robinson (1980) as "school debilitation," creates and sustains an educational underclass that receives an education "suited to their needs" *as perceived, and typically underestimated, by the educational institution.*

Less clear is the extent to which peer-group norms and other, individual, student-coping mechanisms influence school achievement or success. Little insight exists about the manner in which teachers decide who merits their best efforts or about what kind of treatment by the teacher is, in fact, rewarding and productive for disadvantaged students.

The cultural dimension of school climate is concerned with the system of beliefs, values, meanings, and cognitions of organizations (Tagiuri, 1968). Smircich (1983) identified several views of culture represented in organizations, which provide a useful framework for the study of school cultures. Three of these views focus on three concepts of culture: culture as cognition, culture as symbol, and culture as unconscious processes and organization. Although studies of school *organizational* cultures proliferate, relatively little attention has been given to the other conceptualizations of institutional culture.

Shared cognitions, or a system of knowledge and beliefs, help shape how individuals make sense of organizations and their practices. Although studies have indicated that shared cognitions are common among cohesive group members (Bougon, Weick, & Binkhorst, 1977), little information from schools is available, and no systematic study has been undertaken to identify how young adolescents come to interpret and make sense of the school's environment and operations.

The symbolic perspective views culture as a form of symbolic discourse (Smircich, 1983). Promising research has been conducted in this area (Cusick, 1973, 1983; Gronn, 1983; Wolcott, 1973), but again, no attention has been given to the ways in which middle level youth process and understand the symbolic discourse systems that operate in schools. Further, there is no information about the ways in which individuals come to prize certain symbols in the discourse system, especially symbols that are related to school performance and scholastic success.

From the unconscious processes point of view, culture is viewed as projections of deeply imbedded psychological structures. For example, Mitroff (1983) argues that managerial behavior reflects the information processing tendencies of individuals, a contention supported by O'Brien's (1984) work on the intuitive criteria used by supervisors to judge instructional effectiveness and quality.

Consistent with any cultural view is the possibility for subcultures to exist in the larger cultural context (Gregory, 1983). When schools concentrate large numbers of students who hold values that are not supportive of institutional goals, as is the case when large numbers of disadvantaged students are concentrated in a school, school outcomes are generally less productive (Rutter et al., 1979). However, the effects of these subcultures on their members' acceptance of mainstream values and goals has never been adequately addressed with respect to the formation of school achievement norms by disadvantaged youth, a readily identifiable subset of virtually any urban school. Further, no evidence exists about the ways in which subculture groups come to accept and promote mainstream goals or objectives, or what effect the existence of a subculture group has on the formation of institutional norms and policies.

## Culture, Climate, and Disadvantaged Youth: A Special Case

Within schools, identifiable faculty and student cultures exist (Metz, 1978). To the extent that these cultures share similar core values, schools succeed. When the groups' values are in opposition to one another, or when the values are unclear or misunderstood, school performance suffers, student achievement declines, and teacher satisfaction evaporates.

In the absence of clear values, widely shared and securely held, choices about teaching style, student decorum, classroom rules, and individual behavior become matters of personal choice, with no nondisruptive alternative having any more value than any other (Metz, 1978). When decisions about teacher or student behavior are left to individuals, with no fundamental values to serve as guides, both the behavior and individual reactions to it are highly idiosyncratic. When one teacher responds to student behavior from one value set and another teacher responds from a quite different value orientation, students tend to view both reactions as capricious. For disadvantaged and minority students in particular, this is just more evidence that they cannot understand this alien institution called school.

Lacking a coherent vision of mission, purpose, and value, or having one that is not inclusive but exclusionary, schools create disorder (Payne, 1984). The shallowness of relationships between students and teachers in many urban schools creates a sense of anonymity that encourages asocial (if not overtly antisocial) behavior by students. The situation is further exacerbated by the existence of school norms that prohibit the expression of any surprise by teachers or administrators over bad news or outrageous circumstances. Thus, the norms are constantly expanded to include ever more counterproductive behavior by students and colleagues.

The cycle of diminished expectations, poor student performance, classroom practices that value control over learning, and further diminishment of expectations creates student "nobodies." Stinchcombe (1964) explains the effects on students by arguing that misbehavior among disadvantaged youth results from their ritual poverty. By giving them little to symbolize their worth, schools force students to create symbols of their own, a process experienced by the school as misbehavior. Sennett and Cobb (1972) say, "Breaking the rules is an act 'nobodies' can share with each other. This counterculture does not have to come to grips with the labels their teachers have imposed on these kids; it is rather an attempt to create among themselves badges of dignity that those in authority can't destroy" (p. 84).

The extent to which the culture of schools can be transmitted to disadvantaged youth, in a form that is acceptable and credible, has not been fully investigated, nor has the way in which students interpret the school climate and take signals from it about their worth as students and as potential achievers. How the collective and common wisdom about schooling shapes school performance by disadvantaged youth still eludes us, although two studies have touched on the way in which cultural heroes can focus student attention on collective goals.

Schools with strong cultures not only have clear values, they have different kinds of heroes who personify those values for students and for teachers. Lightfoot (1983) described those heroes as "stars." Johnston and Ramos de Perez (1985) stated that they represent a panoply of opportunities for students to model their behavior after a variety of culturally acceptable archetypes, all of whom are human and *show* students how to act. Most important, the heroes are diverse enough so that virtually every student in the school can find at least one with whom to identify.

## Creating a Learning Community for All Students

All of the discussion about culture and how it influences the school experiences of middle level youth remains very abstract until the cultural framework is applied to a specific case. Such an examination points out the ways in which cultural dimensions affect the quality of school life for students, teachers, and parents. It also illustrates specific practices that transmit cultural messages associated with a particular core value. For the purposes of this chapter, it is useful to examine the ways in which schools transmit (or fail to transmit) the values associated with creating and sustaining the fundamental middle level school elements of membership — belonging and collaboration. This analysis is based on studies of particularly effective middle level schools that has been underway since 1983 (see Johnston & Ramos de Perez, 1985).

The call for creating collaborative environments in schools has become so common that it scarcely bears repeating. *An Agenda for Excellence* (1984) from the National Association of Secondary School Principals, The Carnegie Council on Adolescent Development's *Turning Points* (1989), and a host of other educational reports have joined California's *Caught in the Middle* (1987) in stating, unequivocally, that collaboration is essential for successful middle level education.

As is often the case, schools are expected to begin laying the foundation for this kind of collaborative attitude among their students and, ultimately, their graduates. Ironically, though, schools tend to be among the least collaborative institutions in our society. Thus, to achieve the new goals outlined for schooling in the 1990s and beyond, fundamental changes are necessary in the way schools conceive of their functions and execute their responsibilities. Further, those of us who work in schools will have to learn new roles and new ways of working with our colleagues in order to be successful models of collaboration for our students.

## Organizational Responses

A number of innovations have been offered as ways to break down the isolation that characterizes schools and teaching. Most of these are organizational and procedural in nature.

Perhaps the most widespread and commonly practiced organizational innovation in middle level schools is the use of interdisciplinary teaming. In general, this concept, which has a group of teachers sharing a group of students and a common planning time, solves some of the problems of conventional school organization. Most importantly, this organizational plan places teachers together who share a common group of students. Since the subject expertise of each team member is already established, the discussion can focus on instructional approaches as they are employed with groups of children or on an individual child in whom all of the teachers have a common interest.

In addition, teaming builds a sense of community among the teachers and the students. Social bonds tend to be stronger, students feel less anonymous, and teachers feel supported by their colleagues and more effective in the classroom.

Advisory programs are also often used to build strong group membership. Competitions are sometimes organized among team homerooms or advisory groups, operating on the theory that people will bond to a group if they perceive challenges arising from outside that group.

Specific programs can be used to build group cohesiveness. Cooperative learning in academic areas, the production of plays or musical performances, and team activities in intramural or physical education programs can all contribute to the sense of collaboration that exists among students. Even specialized programs, such as "ropes courses" in the physical education class, team retreats, or field trips, exist for the purpose of building group membership and cohesiveness.

All of these interventions can be quite successful in enhancing the spirit of collaboration in schools. Unfortunately, they are often "add-ons" to the basic academic program, and are seen as "frills" or "touchy-feely" stuff by some parents, students, and teachers. For true collaboration to exist, something more is needed.

## A New Value Set

At the center of every institution is a set of core values that drive its decisions, practices, and policies. In schools, those core values generally deal with such concepts as achievement, individual growth, and the development of social membership and responsibility. Historically, schools have focused on the first two of these, and left the development of a social conscience to other agencies: the church, the home, the peer group, and others. Increasingly, though, it is essential that schools work, systematically, to shape not only individual achievements but the attitudes that support group membership and collective action—the very foundations of collaboration.

The components of this new value set are simple, but in many they represent a fundamental shift in how schools view their functions and their modes of operation. The new values are pervasive caring for all members of the group, a willingness to challenge regularities, and the celebration of diversity and unique contributions.

## Pervasive Caring

Collaborative groups care about their members and their welfare. They recognize that the success of the entire group depends on the success of any individual in it, so they support that person without making him or her dependent. They are alert to each other's needs and take care of them without fanfare.

In one school, teachers routinely call colleagues who are sick with offers of help. Most of the time, of course, the illness is minor and no help is needed, but the simple gesture of caring helps build bonds among the faculty that withstand disagreements over institutional procedures, new policies, or annoying practices.

In another school, teachers call the homes of children who are absent. This action is not designed to check up on the kids, but to inquire about their absence and to help them, if necessary, make up school work or take care of other school business that the child may be missing. In a variation on that theme, one school uses a group of student volunteers to make those calls to absent peers.

Another school maintains a clothing bank for students whose families cannot afford appropriate school clothes. The clothes are donated by local manufacturers and stores or purchased by the school from local outlets. They are distributed, in private, before school or during school hours by parent volunteers. There is not a lot of hoopla about it; the school just takes care of that particular need.

Other examples abound. Schools provide childcare during evening school events or on election day. Tutoring materials are made available to parents to help their children at home. Calls are made to parents with *good* news about their child's performance or behavior. A principal stands in the school doorway and greets each of the nearly 800 students by name each morning! In short, the message goes out: We care about you here—we're all in this together.

## Challenging the Rituals

Schools do so many things because "that's the way we do things around here."
Unfortunately, many school practices go unexamined because they are so
common and so long-standing. Challenging the rituals means that schools
take a courageous and unblinking look at their practices to determine what
the effects of the practices are on students.

A number of school policies can have devastating effects on student
"membership" in the school. Grading policies that fail to take into account
individual abilities, effort, or other mitigating circumstances tell a student
that the system is more important than the child. We may know that students
have special needs, but if we do not respond to them, the message is pretty
clear that we can't be bothered to go out of our way for certain students—
even a little bit.

In one case, a seventh-grade boy was late for school every morning.
Because the tardiness was unexcused, he served detention every afternoon.
A research associate asked the boy what the problem was and found that
he was responsible for getting his younger brother and sister to school because
his mother had to be at work at 7:00 A.M. Because the elementary school
opened after the middle school, and because he was unwilling to allow his
younger siblings to wait outside the school in their often dangerous urban
neighborhood, the price he paid for his vigilance was habitual tardiness. He
also gave his lunch money to a friend to collect his brother and sister at their
school at the end of the day and walk them to the middle school so that he
could take them home after serving his detention. When asked why he didn't
tell someone about his problem, he replied, "What for? No one can do
anything about the rules." What a cynical view for a 12-year-old—the rules
punish you for acting responsibly. It would be very hard to affiliate with
an institution that is perceived to be so insensitive.

Schools must examine their practices and the effects of those practices
on students. Does missing three assignments get Debbie an F, even if she
can't go home some nights because her Mom and Dad are fighting? Does
everyone have to climb the rope because the curriculum says so, even if Tom
is overweight and embarrassed about his size? Does everyone have to read
aloud because "that's the way we do things around here"?

## Celebration of Diversity

This value has two components: the recognition of unique contributions and
the rewarding of all achievements. As it stands, most schools reward a very
limited range of accomplishments, and few of them have to do with collaboration. We reward the "best" athletes, not necessarily the whole team. We

reward superior musicians, not those who back them up, and we celebrate the successes of our highest achieving students, not those whose achievements are remarkable because of the odds they must overcome.

In one of my favorite schools, a boy in a wheelchair proudly showed visitors his varsity letters. They were real, and they were given for computer programs he had written to make the librarian's life easier, for the quality of the stage design he had done for the school's holiday music program, and, most important, for the volunteer work he did at a local nursing home. This boy, who will never take an unassisted step in his life, goes to the local nursing home and reads to people who, in his words, "are really sick and can't read for themselves." And the school rewards that unselfish service with a varsity letter—the same kind you get for running the high hurdles or playing baseball for three years.

In that school, you can earn a letter for being a musician, or being an athlete, or building houses for poor people, or working in the school's childcare center on open house nights, or working with the elderly, or cleaning up local streams and rivers. In other words, they reward the things they value, and the things they value are the things that will make the world not only an entertaining place but a more humane and compassionate place as well.

## Conclusion

America's middle level schools participate in the formation of value frameworks in young adolescents that will serve them for their entire lives. The values they form in these years will guide decisions they make, both as teenagers and as adults. It is an awesome responsibility, a demanding task, and much too important to be left to chance. By celebrating our diversity, showing young adolescents how to care for one another, and changing our systems to fit human needs, we will create the kind of world in which we can be pleased to raise our children, live out our careers, and grow old.

Our students learn something in school every day. On bad days, they probably only learn stuff—like California exports wine, or Ohio grows soybeans. On the best days, they will learn a value about how to care for themselves or for one another. The clearest responsibility middle level educators have is to model those values. All of our futures depend on it.

## References

Anderson, C. S. (1982). The search for school climate: A review of the literature. *Review of Educational Research, 52*(3), 368–420.

Anglin, L. W. (1979). Teacher roles and alternative school organization. *Educational Forum, 43*(4), 439–452.

Arhar, J. M. (1990). *The effects of interdisciplinary teaming on the social bonding of middle level teachers and students.* Unpublished doctoral dissertation, University of Cincinnati.

Beckerman, T. M., & Good, T. L. (1981). The classroom ratio of high and low aptitude students and its effect on achievement. *American Educational Research Journal, 18*(3), 317–327.

Bougon, M., Weick, K., & Binkhorst, D. (1977). Cognition in organizations. *Administrtive Science Quarterly, 22*(4), 606–631.

Boyer, E. (1983). *High school.* New York: Harper and Row.

Brookover, W. B. (1979). *School systems and student achievement: Schools make a difference.* New York: Praeger.

Brookover, W. B., Beady, C., Flood, P., Schweitzer, J., & Wisenbaker, J. (1979). *School systems and student achievement: Schools make a difference.* New York: Praeger Press.

Brookover, W. B., & Lezotte, L. W. (1979). *Changes in school environment coincident with changes in school achievement* (Occasional Paper 17). East Lansing, MI: Michigan State University, Institute for Research on Teaching.

Brookover, W. B., Schweitzer, J., Schmeider, R., Flood, P., & Wisenbaker, J. (1978). Elementary school social and school achievement. *American Educational Research Journal, 15*(2), 301–318.

Brophy, J., & Rohrkemper, M. (1988). *The classroom strategy study: Summary report of general findings.* Lansing, MI: Institute for Research on Teaching, Michigan State University.

Carnegie Council on Adolescent Development's Task Force on Education of Young Adolescents. (1989). *Turning points: Preparing youth for the 21st century.* Washington, DC: Carnegie Council on Adolescent Development, a program of Carnegie Corporation of New York.

*Caught in the middle: Educational reform for young adolescents in California public schools.* (1987). Sacramento, CA: Bureau of Publications, California State Department of Education.

Coleman, J. S., Campbell, E. Q., Hobson, C. J., McPartland, J., Mood, A. M., Weinfeld, F. D., & York, R. L. (1986). *Equality of educational opportunity.* Washington, DC: United States Office of Education.

Coleman, J., Hoffer, T., & Kilgore, S. (1982). *High school achievement: Public, catholic and private schools compared.* New York: Basic Books.

Corno, L., & Snow, R. E. (1986). Adapting teaching to individual differences among learners. In M. C. Wittrock (Ed.), *Handbook of research on teaching* (3rd ed.) (pp. 605–629). New York: Macmillian.

Cusik, P. A. (1973). *Inside high school.* New York: Holt, Rinehart and Winston.

Cusik, P. A. (1983). *The egalitarian ideal and the American high school.* White Plains, NY: Longman.

Deal, T., & Kennedy, A. (1984). *Corporate cultures.* Reading, MA: Addison-Wesley.

Edmonds, R. (1979). Effective schools for the urban poor. *Educational Leadership, 37*(1), 5–24.

Good, T., & Brophy, J. (1987). School effects. In M. Wittrock (Ed.), *Third handbook of research on teaching.* New York: Macmillan.

Gregory, K. L. (1983). Native-view paradigms: Multiple cultures and culture conflicts in organizations. *Administrative Science Quarterly, 28*(3), 359–376.

Gronn, P. C. (1983). Talk as work: The accomplishment of school administration. *Administrative Science Quarterly, 28*(1), 1–21.

Hammack, F. M. (1986). Large school systems' dropout reports: An analysis of definitions, procedures, and findings. In G. Natriello (Ed.), *School dropouts: Patterns and policies* (pp. 20–37). New York: Columbia University Press.

Hampel, R. (1986). *The last little citadel.* Boston: Houghton Mifflin.

Harris, M. J., Rosenthal, R., & Snodgrass, S. (1986). The effects of teacher expectations, gender, and behavior on pupil academic performance and self-concept. *Journal of Educational Research, 79*(3), 173–179.

Jackson, P. W. (1968). *Life in classrooms.* New York: Holt, Rinehart and Winston.

Jencks, C. (1972). *Inequality.* New York: Basic Books.

Johnson, D., & Johnson, R. (1975). *Learning together and alone.* Englewood Cliffs, NJ: Prentice-Hall.

Johnston, J. H. (1987). Values, cultures and the effective school. *NASSP Bulletin, 71*(497), 79–88.

Johnston, J. H., & Markle, G. C. (1983). What research says about ability grouping. *Middle School Journal, 14*(4), 28–30.

Johnston, J. H., & Ramos de Perez, M. (1985). Four climates of effective schools. In G. Melton (Ed.), *Schools in the middle.* Reston, VA: National Association of Secondary School Principals.

Kulik, C. C., & Kulik, J. A. (1982). Effects of ability grouping on secondary school students. *American Educational Research Journal, 19*(3), 415–428.

Lightfoot, S. L. (1983). *The good high school.* New York: Basic Books.

Lipsitz, J. (1981, March). *Early adolescence: Psychological and social issues.* Address at the annual meeting of the Association of Supervision and Curriculum Development, St. Louis, MO.

McDill, E. L., & Rigsby, L. C. (1973). *Structure and process in secondary schools: The academic impact of educational climates.* Baltimore: John Hopkins University Press.

Metz, M. H. (1978). *Classrooms and corridors.* Berkeley: University of California Press.

Miskel, C., & Ogawa, R. (1988). Work motivation, job satisfaction and climate. In N. J. Boyan (Ed.), *Handbook of research on educational administration* (pp. 279–304). New York: Longman.

Mitroff, I. (1983). *Stakeholders of the organizational mind.* San Francisco: Jossey-Bass.

NASSP Council on Middle Level Education. (1984). *An agenda for excellence.* Reston, VA: National Association for Secondary School Principals.

O'Brien, M. J. (1984). *Instructional competencies as perceived and applied by training managers.* Unpublished doctoral dissertation, University of Cincinnati.

Payne, C. M. (1984). *Getting what we ask for.* Westport, CT: Greenwood Press.

Peters, T., & Waterman, R. (1982). *In search of excellence.* New York: Warner Books.

Pfeffer, J. (1982). *Organizations and organizational theory.* Marshfield, MA: Pitman.

Phi Delta Kappa. (1980). *Why do some urban schools succeed?* Bloomington, IN: Author.

Robinson, A. (1980). The effect of negative school environment on urban youth. In S. Ruffin (Ed.), *Urban education in the 80s* (pp. 11–17). Reston, VA: National Association of Secondary School Principals.

Rosenholtz, S. (1979, April). *Modifying the effects of academic status.* Paper presented at the meeting of the American Educational Research Association, San Francisco.

Rutter, M., Maughan, B., Mortimore, P., Ouston, J., & Smith, A. (1979). *Fifteen thousand hours.* Cambridge, MA: Harvard University Press.

Sarason, S. B. (1982). *The culture of the school and the problem of change.* Boston: Allyn and Bacon.

Schneider, J. M., Glasheen, J. D., & Hadley, D. W. (1979). Secondary school participation, institutional socialization, and student achievement. *Urban Education, 14*(3), 285–302.

Sennett, R., & Cobb, J. (1972). *The hidden injuries of class.* New York: Vintage.

Slavin, R. (1986). *Ability grouping and student achievement: A best-evidence synthesis* (Occasional Paper). Baltimore: Center for Research on Elementary and Middle School Education, The Johns Hopkins University.

Smircich, L. (1983). Concepts of culture and organizational analysis. *Administrative Science Quarterly, 28*(3), 339–358.

Stinchcombe, A. (1964). *Rebellion in high school.* Chicago: Quadrangle.

Tagiuri, R. (1968). The concept of organizational climate. In R. Tagiuri & G. H. Litwin (Eds.), *Organizational climate: Explorations of a concept.* Boston: Division of Research, Graduate School of Business, Harvard University.

Toepfer, C. (1988, February). *Critical issues in adolescent development.* Address at the annual convention of the National Association of Secondary School Principals, Anaheim, CA.

United States Department of Education. (1986). *What works: Research about teaching and learning.* Washington, DC: Author.

Wallace, J. E. (1988). *Differential teacher behavior toward students of varying ability within heterogenously grouped secondary classrooms.* Unpublished paper, Cincinnati: University of Cincinnati, College of Education.

Weber, G. (1971). *Inner city children can be taught to read* (Occasional Paper 18). Washington, DC: Council on Basic Education.

Wehlage, G. G., Rutter, R., Smith, G., Lesko, N., & Fernandez, R. (1989). *Reducing the risk: Schools as communities of support.* New York: Falmer Press.

Wolcott, H. F. (1973). *The man in the principal's office.* New York: Holt, Rinehart and Winston.

Wynne, E. A. (1980). *Looking at schools: Good, bad and indifferent.* Lexington, MA: D. C. Heath.

# CHAPTER SEVEN

# Developing a Sense of Mission in Middle Schools

ROBERT SHOCKLEY
*Florida Atlantic University*

Much of the rhetoric surrounding calls for educational reform has focused on the issue of school restructuring. Efforts to restructure schools at the middle level appear to be intricately linked to the redefinition of the school's mission and purpose. Consequently, the middle school, as an institution, appears to be in a unique position to lead the reform movement to restructure schools. Programs commonly associated with the middle school movement, such as interdisciplinary teaming, block scheduling, and teacher advisory programs, are examples of significant restructuring efforts already underway. These efforts go far beyond current school improvement efforts existing at other levels by focusing attention on the way the school is organized, the climate in which teachers work, the way content is organized, and the way that young adolescents learn.

In addressing the issue of restructuring schools, Michaels (1988) identified the following components:

1. Decision making rests at the individual school.
2. A collegial, participatory environment exists among both students and staff members.
3. There is flexible use of time.
4. There is an increased personalization of the school environment with a concurrent atmosphere of trust, high expectancies, and sense of fairness.

5. The curriculum focuses on students' understanding what they learn — knowing "why" as well as "how."
6. Emphasis is on higher-order thinking skills for all students.

Interestingly, these components are directly related to arguments cited for school reform in the middle school literature (Alexander & George, 1981; Johnston & Markle, 1986; Lounsbury & Vars, 1978).

Many educators believe that changing the organizational structure of the middle level school is the driving force behind the middle school movement and, consequently, at the heart of the redefined middle school mission (Alexander & George, 1981; Eichhorn, 1966; George, 1977; Johnston & Markle, 1986; Lounsbury, 1984; Lounsbury & Vars, 1978; Wiles & Bondi, 1986). These authors consistently advocate the interdisciplinary team organization as opposed to the more traditional departmentalized structure. Interestingly, there is now a growing number of research studies that support the effectiveness of the use of the interdisciplinary team organization in the middle school as a way to structure the instructional day (Eccles & Midgeley, 1989; Mac Iver & Reuman, 1988; McPartland, 1987; McPartland, Coldiron, & Braddock, 1987). The ultimate rationale behind these efforts is the need to:

1. Establish a structure that empowers middle school teachers to address better the educational and developmental needs of the young adolescent.
2. Redefine the mission and purpose of the middle level school.

## School Mission

Research on effective middle level schools indicates that teachers and administrators in these schools have a strong belief system that sets them apart from elementary or high school teachers (Lipsitz, 1981). These beliefs are supported by a common understanding about the role, function, and mission of the middle school (Manasse, 1984). Kerewsky (1986) concluded that middle school philosophy was a frequent point of reference in discussions in effective middle schools.

Defining the mission of the middle school is complicated by the historical identification of this level of schooling with elementary and/or secondary education. In fact, currently the United States Department of Education does not recognize the existence of middle level schools; their data gathering and classification systems are based only on elementary school and secondary school data. Additionally, teacher and administrator certification in many states continues to be based on the elementary/secondary model.

Unfortunately, this lack of identity is reflected in educational programming, curriculum development, school organization, and in-service education at the school and district level. Consequently, redefining the middle school mission (separate from elementary school and high school) is at the heart of reform efforts at the middle level.

Therefore, it becomes essential for the faculty of a middle school to define the school's uniqueness and sense of purpose. Parents and the public at large have a fair understanding of the purposes of both the elementary and high school. However, considerable confusion exists regarding public perceptions of the purpose of the middle school.

This lack of public understanding of the middle school has been perpetuated by a historical and societal neglect in regard to the middle grades of schooling. This neglect is evidenced in teacher education, federal and state funding practices, educational research, school intervention programs, teacher certification, school facilities, and the lack of appropriately developed curriculum materials. A growing awareness of the formative nature of this period of human development, combined with a growing concern about problems and changes in our society, has caused educators to examine how effectively our schools are preparing youth, resulting in calls for educational reform (Carnegie, 1989).

Clearly defined mission statements for middle schools usually include a number of common denominators. These are:

- A recognition of the uniqueness, importance, and formative nature of the young adolescent years of human development.
- A common commitment to build curricular and instructional programs and practices that are sensitive to the unique developmental needs of young adolescents.
- A recognition of the transitional nature of the middle school. The school is commonly described as a bridge connecting the elementary school to the high school. Consequently, common commitments exist to make these student transitions as smooth as possible (e.g., smallness to largeness, student centered to subject centered).

These points are usually reflected in the school's values, symbols, and beliefs, and consequently establish what is important in the school.

## Culture Building and School Mission

A school's values, symbols, and beliefs are the cultural ingredients that establish what is important in a school. Parents, students, teachers, superintendents, school boards, and community members' understanding and acceptance of these values enable the educational program in the school to move toward accomplishing its educational objectives. An accepted school mission promotes people working toward common goals.

Evolving from this newly defined sense of purpose is the evolution of school norms, which define what people should accomplish and how. Through these norms, teachers and administrators in the school can gain a sense of meaning and significance from their jobs (Sergiovanni, 1984). For middle level educators to derive a sense of purpose and significance to their roles, it is important that they recognize those factors that separate their roles from that of elementary and/or high school educators (Shockley, Holt, & Meichtry, 1985).

Middle schools that are able to develop a tightly structured value system enhance the motivation, commitment, enthusiasm, and loyalty of staff. Teachers have ample opportunities to find meaning and purpose in their work, have a reasonable amount of control over work activities, and experience success. A restructured middle school should encourage practices that empower teachers within a value system that recognizes the unique developmental needs of young adolescents.

Effective middle schools promote culture building. Culture building in schools empowers teachers to articulate answers to these questions:

1. What is the school about?
2. What is really important in this school?
3. How is a middle school unique?
4. How do I fit into the scheme of things?

Cultural building enables a school to define and to strengthen those values and beliefs that give the school its unique identity (Sergiovanni, 1984).

The net effect of culture building is a bonding of teachers, students, and others committed to the mission and beliefs of the school. Their work and their lives take on a new importance with a richer meaning, including an expanded sense of identity because of a new feeling of belonging to something special (De Bevoise, 1984; Sergiovanni, 1984).

The concept of culture building is not new. In 1957, Selznik stated:

> *To institutionalize is to infuse with value beyond the technical requirements of the task at hand. The prizing of social machinery beyond its technical role is largely a reflection of the unique way it fulfills personal or group needs. Whenever individuals become attached to an organization or a way of doing things as persons rather than as technicians, the result is a prizing of the device for its own sake. From the standpoint of the committed person, the organization is changed from an expandable tool into a valued source of personal satisfaction (p. 17).*

Effective middle level schools are value driven. In these schools the values that make the middle school mission separate from that of the elementary and/or high school is a driving force that both school staff and community recognize.

## Role of School Leadership

Clark and Clark (1989) have identified the following leadership criteria necessary to bring about middle school restructuring:

1. A passion for middle level education
2. Willingness to share decision making
3. Concern for the well-being of all persons in the school
4. Opportunity orientation
5. A good self-concept
6. Model of school norms

In his research in instructionally effective middle schools, Garvin (1986) concluded, "These schools were primarily effective because they had committed, informed, courageous and dynamic leadership." He further identified three dominant characteristics of these leaders:

1. Strong human relations skills
2. Strong management skills (able to manage the delegation of authority)
3. Strong technical skills (informed, competent, and involved educators).

These demands for educational reform at the middle school level will require effective leadership. However, restructuring efforts may also force us to take a new look at the way we commonly view leadership. For necessary changes to take place in middle schools, leaders must:

1. Have a clear sense of what the middle school mission should be.
2. Be able to articulate this vision of the school through daily routine activities in the administration of the school.
3. Build and reinforce a strong school culture that communicates the values and beliefs of the school.
4. Encourage and allow leadership to emerge from others in the school.
5. Be proactive in school advocacy efforts.

Leaders reinforce the value and belief systems of a school through a continuous stream of symbolic actions. This type of modeling behavior is sometimes called *purposing*. By a school's formal leadership, purposing clarifies and encourages consensus and commitment to the school's basic mission. Consequently, teachers and other school staff gain a clearer picture of "what is important" in the school.

Findings from a five-year study by the Far West Laboratory for Educational Research and Development suggested that effective principals exercise leadership in subtle ways (Dwyer, 1984). This study compiled approximately 10,000 pages of notes from over 1,000 hours of observations and interviews with teachers, students, and principals. This information was collected in schools that were identified as effective by their district supervisors. The study concluded that administrators assist in clarifying the school's mission and purpose through routine daily actions.

A common form of purposing behavior is story telling. The leader identifies situations and everyday events or accomplishments in the school, where the actions of staff reinforce the mission of the school. These events are then shared with others, both formally and informally. The retold stories of these actions positively reinforce the behaviors involved, as well as send appropriate messages as to what values are important in the school.

Another reflection of purposing behavior by leaders is through the rewards/recognition programs for both staff and students. An effective leader makes sure that the reward systems in the school reinforce the values and mission of the school. The leader who demonstrates modeling and purposing skills sends a strong message to others in terms of what is important in the school (Sergiovanni, 1984).

Effective leaders have a clear sense of vision for their school and they fully understand their leadership role in making that vision a reality. Effective leaders establish plans and processes to implement programs in the school that reflect the school's mission. Leadership styles vary from one individual and situation to another, but a knowledge of one's personal leadership style, strengths, and weaknesses is absolutely essential (Manasse, 1984). Leaders must recognize individuals whose abilities complement their own and rely on these individuals as "leadership substitutes" (Shockley, Holt, & Meichtry, 1985).

Schlechty (1988) stated, "It's time to recognize that instructional leadership inherently resides in the role of the teacher. Inherent in the role of the principal must be the expectation that one will lead leaders" (p. 2).

These leadership substitutes can be either formally or informally designated. Assistant principals may serve this purpose or teachers within the school frequently take on strong leadership roles. School principals must be adept at recognizing and relying on these individuals to complement their own leadership. Murphy (1988) states that effective leaders "draw on their strengths, but also accept their weaknesses and develop a capacity to cope" (p. 655).

Above all else, the middle school principal serves as a symbol to teachers, other staff, community, and parents. The personality, appearance, and behaviors of the school's leader symbolizes the very essence and values of the school. Consequently, the belief systems and management practices of the principal must be philosophically compatible with the mission of the middle level school (as articulated in *Turning Points* [Carnegie, 1989] and other national recommendations and reports).

## School Mission and Faculty Involvement

In his research on award-winning middle schools, Garvin (1986) observed that these schools had a mission statement that was part of a master plan that gave meaning, direction, and context to existing programs. He further concluded that these plans were developed by representatives of many groups, including extensive faculty participation. Furthermore, faculty and parents clearly understood the stated school mission and could articulate it well.

The redefined structure of the middle school, including interdisciplinary teams of teachers, creates an environment in the school that promotes faculty participation and involvement. By breaking large impersonal schools down into smaller more manageable units, the interdisciplinary team school organization enables teachers to maintain more control of major instructional decisions, including:

- Grouping and regrouping of students
- Flexible use of instructional time
- Interdisciplinary teaching and reinforcing concepts/practices across the curriculum
- Student discipline policies and practices
- Parent communication
- Coordination of homework, tests, and projects

More importantly, this model of school organization enables and empowers teachers to be active participants in the articulation of the school's mission. No longer is the school mission an abstract statement, developed for a school accreditation visit. It now becomes a concrete, living statement that guides everyday decisions in the school—decisions that are collectively made by teachers and administrators.

## *Conclusion*

Recent national reports are calling for educational reform that includes school restructuring. The middle school is in a unique position to lead this reform movement. A clearly articulated mission for the middle level school is critically needed if true reform is to occur. Without this sense of mission, schools in the middle will continue to be susceptible to the traditional forces in our society and profession that would make these schools miniature high schools or extended elementary schools, that are ill-defined and inappropriate to the development needs of this age group, as well as ill-equipped to deal with the multifaceted societal problems that are currently reflected in our schools.

## References

Alexander, W. M., & George, P. S. (1981). *The exemplary middle school.* New York: Holt, Rinehart and Winston.

Carnegie Council on Adolescent Development's Task Force on Education of Young Adolescents. (1989). *Turning points: Preparing youth for the 21st century.* Washington, DC: Carnegie Council on Adolescent Development, a program of Carnegie Corporation of New York.

Clark, S., & Clark, D. (1989). School restructuring: A leadership challenge for middle level administrators. *Schools in the middle: A report on trends and practices.* Reston, VA: National Association of Secondary School Principals.

De Bevoise, W. (1984). Synthesis of research on the principal as instructional leader. *Educational Leadership, 41*(5), 14–20.

Dwyer, D. (1984). The search for instructional leadership: Routines and subtleties in the principals role. *Educational Leadership, 41*(5), 32–38.

Eccles, J. S., & Midgeley, C. (1989). Stage environment fit: Developmentally appropriate classrooms for early adolescents. In R. Ames & C. Ames (Eds.), *Research on motivation in education: Vol. 3. Goals and cognitions.* San Diego: Academic Press.

Eichhorn, D. H. (1966). *The middle school.* New York: Center for Research in Education.

Garvin, J. (1986). Common denominators in effective middle schools. *Schools in the middle: A report on trends and practices.* Reston, VA: National Association of Secondary School Principals.

George, P. S. (1977). *The middle school: A look ahead.* Columbus, OH: National Middle School Association.

Johnston, J. H., & Markle, G. C. (1986). *What research says to the middle level practitioner.* Columbus, OH: National Middle School Association.

Kerewsky, W. (1986). Site visitor's report on effective middle schools. *Schools in the middle: A report on trends and practices.* Reston, VA: National Association of Secondary School Principals.

Lipsitz, J. (1981). Educating the early adolescent. *American Education, 17*(8), 13–17.

Lounsbury, J. H. (1984). *Perspectives: Middle school education, 1964–1984.* Columbus, OH: National Middle School Association.

Lounsbury, J. H., & Vars, G. (1978). *A curriculum for the middle school years.* New York: Harper and Row.

Mac Iver, D. J., & Reuman, D. A. (1988). *Decision making in the classroom and early adolescents' valuing of mathematics.* Paper presented at the annual meeting of the American Educational Research Association, New Orleans.

Manasse, A. I. (1984). Principals as leaders of high performing systems. *Educational Leadership, 41*(5), 42–46.

McPartland, J. M. (1987). *Balancing high-quality subject-matter instruction with positive teacher-student relations in the middle grades* (CREMS Report 15). Baltimore, MD: Center for Research on Elementary and Middle Schools, The Johns Hopkins University.

McPartland, J. M., Coldiron, J. R., & Braddock, J. H. (1987). *A description of school structures and classroom practices in elementary, middle, and secondary schools* (CREMS Report 14). Baltimore, MD: Center for Research on Elementary and Middle Schools, The Johns Hopkins University.

Michaels, K. (1988). Caution: Second-wave reform taking place. *Educational Leadership, 45*(5), 3.

Murphy, J. (1988). The unheroic side of leadership: Notes from the swamp. *Phi Delta Kappan, 69*(9), 654–659.

Schlechty, P. (1988). Issue. *ASCD Curriculum Update.* (Available from the Association for Supervision and Curriculum Development, Alexandria, VA, 22314-2798.)

Selznick, P. (1957). *Leadership in administration: A sociological perspective.* New York: Harper & Row.

Sergiovanni, T. (1984). Leadership and excellence in schooling. *Educational Leadership, 41*(5), 4–13.

Shockley, R., Holt, L., & Meichtry, Y. (1985). Leadership in the middle level school: An imperative for excellence. *Schools in the middle: A report on trends and practices.* Reston, VA: National Association of Secondary School Principals.

Wiles, J., & Bondi, J. (1986). *The essential middle school.* Tampa, FL: Wiles, Bondi and Associates.

# CHAPTER EIGHT

# The Process of Change: Developing Effective Middle School Programs

ROBERT C. SPEAR
*Southwick/Tolland Regional*
*School District*
*Southwick, Massachusetts*

The improvement of middle level schools is a necessary and significant change effort in U.S. education. Over the last three decades, many middle level schools have reorganized their grade structure and their educational programs. The Carnegie Council on Adolescent Development reports in *Turning Points* (1989) that "a volatile mismatch exists between the organization of middle grade schools and the intellectual and emotional needs of young adolescents" (p. 8). Recent data suggest that many schools and school districts are moving to middle school organization (Alexander & McEwin, 1989; Epstein & Mac Iver, 1990; Florida Department of Education, 1990; Cawelti, 1988).

Although many middle level educators have attempted this transition and succeeded, others have had less than desirable results. The purpose of this chapter is to explore the process of change. Individual and organizational change will be examined and common principles linking these change efforts to each other will be investigated. A case study, illustrating the components of change, will be presented.

The involvement in, and support and intensity of advance planning for the opening of new middle schools increased significantly over the last 20 years (Alexander & McEwin, 1989). However, all too frequently, change is not managed in productive ways, which results in somewhat frustrating outcomes. Knowledge of individual and educational change can help educators prepare themselves, other individuals, communities, and schools for initiation, implementation, and sustained change. "All sectors of the society must be mobilized to build a national consensus to make transformation of middle grade schools a reality" (Carnegie, 1989, p. 9). The principles described in this chapter can be adapted to complement the many change efforts required to develop and to sustain effective middle schools.

The change to middle school philosophy involves more than the transition from junior high school (or other grade configuration) to a middle school grade configuration. The transition to a middle school concept involves a change in the values, beliefs, and culture of the school. It involves developing, implementing, and sustaining interdisciplinary team organization, an advisor/advisee program, transition/articulation programs with elementary and high schools, exploratory programs, and the improvement of learning environments for young adolescents (Alexander & George, 1981).

Organizational restructuring cannot be effective without changing the orientation of individuals within the organization. Groups of individuals comprise an organization. If individual needs are not considered, and time for learning, reflection, and experimentation is not available, then individuals may be resistant to change. If an individual's beliefs and behaviors do not change, then changes within the organization will not be significant or long lasting.

## Issues of Individual Change

> *When I accept myself as I am . . . I change.*
> *When I accept others as they are . . . they change.*
> (AUTHOR UNKNOWN)

If the heart of the middle school is the interdisciplinary team, the muscle and nerves that make interdisciplinary teaming work are teachers. Becoming a team member often necessitates changing individual behavior. Frequently, in schools, teaching is an individual activity. Teachers spend most of their day in their classrooms, rarely having an opportunity to interact with colleagues. This perception may have its roots in the one-room schoolhouse but it is still pervasive today.

Goodlad (1984) observed that "classroom cells in which teachers spend much of their time appear to be symbolic and predictive of their relative isolation from one another and from sources of ideas beyond their own background of experience" (p. 186). As school enrollments increased, classrooms were added and schools became larger; however, teachers remained in their classrooms. Interdisciplinary teaming, a component of middle schools, breaks down the barriers of teacher isolation, bringing together professionals to enhance learning for young adolescents through discussion, planning, and problem solving.

To work effectively on an interdisciplinary team, teachers must acquire new behaviors and new attitudes about their role as a teacher. The research on adult development has been prolific (Belenky, Clinchy, Goldberger, & Tarule, 1986; Harvey, Hunt, & Schroeder, 1961; Levinson, 1977; Loevinger, 1976; Neugarten, 1977; Whitbourne, 1986) and the research on teacher development is advancing (Burden, 1982; Burke, Christensen, Fessler, McDonnell, & Price, 1987; Levine, 1989; McNergney & Carrier, 1981; Oja, 1979; Sprinthall & Thies-Sprinthall, 1982). The use of such readily available and potentially rich knowledge about human growth can be extremely valuable to those who work with adults (Glickman, 1990, p. 45).

Schools, as humane institutions, recognize that people are different. Adults learn at different rates and in different ways. Improvement is personal, which can rise from individual desire. The utilization of this information by those interested in individual change can be highly effective in promoting individual change.

### Concerns Based Adoption Model (CBAM)

The Concerns Based Adoption Model was developed at the Research and Development Center for Teacher Education at the University of Texas at Austin. The model addresses the stages of concern that most individuals pass through as a change effort develops. "Research on the CBAM has identified seven stages of concern. These stages have been initially verified, measurement procedures have been developed, and they have been used extensively in research and practice" (Hall & Loucks, 1979). This model has been useful to leaders in transition to middle school philosophy. The seven stages are listed in Table 8–1, with a statement that typifies each stage.

**TABLE 8–1** • *Concerns Based Adoption Model (CBAM)*

| Level of Use | Stage of Concern | Statements about Concerns and Typical Behaviors |
| --- | --- | --- |
| Renewal | Refocusing | User seeks effective alternatives to established use of innovation. |
| | | "We could use team planning better if we kept a daily log and set up regular appointments." |

**TABLE 8–1** • *Continued*

| Level of Use | Stage of Concern | Statements about Concerns and Typical Behaviors |
| --- | --- | --- |
| Integration | Collaboration | User makes a deliberate effort to coordinate with others. |
| | | User makes changes to increase outcomes. |
| Refinement | | "Let's teach about mapping skills in a combined unit." |
| Routine | | User makes a few changes and has an established pattern of use. |
| | | "The team meets daily for 40 minutes." |
| Mechanical | Consequence | User attempts innovation in a poorly organized manner and makes changes. |
| | | User asks: How is my use affecting my kids? |
| | | "If I make a more specific calendar for my advisory activities, the kids will know what to expect and will feel more comfortable." |
| Preparation | Management | User prepares to use innovation. |
| | | User seems to spend all of time getting ready. |
| | | "The interdisciplinary unit could be fun and exciting. How will we find the time to organize it?" |
| | Personal | User asks the question: How will this affect me? |
| | | "Will I have to change the way I teach?" "Teaching on a team sounds like more work, Is it?" |
| Orientation | Informational | User seeks information about the innovation. |
| | | User would like to know more about innovation prior to commitment. |
| Nonuse | Awareness | User takes no action with respect to innovation and is not concerned about it. |
| | | "That middle school isn't of interest to me. I don't know much about it, but it doesn't sound much different." |

*Source:* Adapted from Kasak, 1988, p. 14.

It is important to note that at each of the stages, change can be negatively effected. For example, in the awareness stage, if change does not "touch" an individual, the likelihood of that person moving to the next stage is remote. If pertinent information is not investigated and employed, the change effort will be negatively effected.

For each of the stages of concern, questions can be asked and potential solutions explored, so that individuals may move more easily from one stage to another:

- Will the effect of this change be too great for me to sustain?
- Will management issues be all consuming and unmanageable?
- Will the change be too stressful for me?
- If the change will not positively affect my student's learning, why should I do it?

Individual concerns can be assessed and strategies can be developed to enhance individual change. Thinking about individuals in light the Concerns Based Adoption Model can provide information that is useful in facilitating the transition to new behaviors.

*Any improvement effort must begin with an acknowledgement of the complexity, richness, and diversity of the adult population of the school. In any school building, teachers and administrators are exploring diverse life tasks and stages. These multiple perspectives and realities must be considered and planned for. Left unacknowledged, they can challenge, disrupt, and undermine the most carefully constructed change effort. (Capelluti & Eberson, 1990, p. 3)*

## Issues of Organizational Change

Organizational change can be viewed from different perspectives. The larger organization is made up of many smaller groups; for example, an interdisciplinary team or a close group of personal friends within the school. Viewing change as a three-dimensional chess board helps illustrate its complexity. Consideration must be given to the individuals involved, their subgroups, and the entire organization. To develop a complete picture requires careful consideration. Movement at one level will affect outcomes within a subgroup and at another level.

Individual interactions with pairs or triads are complex and difficult. Two people can have one interaction; three people have up to nine interactions. Interactions geometrically progress at a rapid rate as groups become larger. In organizations, interactions are complex and therefore should be carefully considered. All too frequently, those interested in change see it as simplistic; however, change is complex and therefore unpredictable. Information gathered and utilized will improve the possibility of sustaining desired change.

As schools wish to move to a middle school organization there are factors that, when considered carefully, may enhance this change effort. The second part of this chapter will deal with the conditions that promote effective educational change.

## Stages of Organizational Change

Ralph Tyler (1989) stated that "it takes approximately three to five years to accomplish significant educational change." Developing an effective middle school takes time and is an enduring effort. Berman and McLaughlin (1978) contended that "any significant innovation or new project in school districts takes about two years to 'get off the ground,' another two years to be fully implemented, and one or two years more to produce a stable effect on student outcomes" (p. 35). If change is too fast, there may be a sense of being overwhelmed; if the pace is too slow, frustration over not making progress may develop.

According to Berman and McLaughlin (1978), mobilization, implementation, and institutionalization are the three stages of the organizational change. The *mobilization* stage is the foundation on which the change process is built. This stage answers the key question: Why is this change effort important? In this stage, people explore options concerning the implementation of change.

During the *implementation* stage, those involved take initial steps toward building a vision. In this stage, changes in individual behaviors and changes in the operations of the school occur.

It is during the *institutionalization* stage that stabilization of the change takes place. "Institutionalized change occurred when project-related change became part of the standard educational repertoire at both the district and classroom levels. . . . Institutionalized projects planned for the eventual continuation [of the project] from the onset" (Berman & McLaughlin, 1978, p. 20).

While implementing the three stages of the change process, it is important to envision them as overlapping. That is, the mobilization phase will overlap the implementation phase, which will in turn overlap the institutionalization phase. No clear boundaries exist; one phase will flow into another.

### Mobilization: Stage I

Four components comprise the mobilization stage: identifying change, planning for change, generating internal support, and generating external support for the change effort. All too frequently, there is not a clear definition of what the change effort will be. Although this step seems simplistic, it is important to allow individuals the opportunity to gain a complete understanding of the task at hand. Spending time in the initial stages will enable participants to comprehend better the advantages of the change.

Changing a school organization to a middle school concept is a complex process. It is important for each teacher to have a clear understanding of what is expected of him or her, and why this change effort is being introduced. It is helpful to clarify terminology and develop consensus as to the meaning of new terms. It is also helpful to include the purpose of the change. For example, interdisciplinary team organization will necessitate scheduling changes. The change to an advisor/advisee program will necessitate a change in teacher-student interactions. The change to active classroom learning environment necessitates a change of teacher behaviors in the classroom. A change in school climate and culture necessitates a change in attitudes, feelings, thoughts, and behaviors. Being clear about the necessary changes involved in the transition to a middle school concept is an important first step, and will enhance communications as the process of change moves forward.

#### Identifying the Change

The staff at Powder Mill Middle School in Southwick, Massachusetts, worked together to identify areas of perceived strength and areas that were perceived to need change or renewal. Teachers first wrote down their strengths and wishes individually, then they worked in pairs, then in groups of four, and finally as a large group. Strengths were identified so that they could be preserved and built upon.

Group consensus was reached on areas that were in need of renewal. Perceived areas of concern ranged from lack of materials in classrooms, to lack of respect by the community in recognizing the mission of the school.

#### Needs Improvement List

1. Disciplinary code needs to be defined
2. Curriculum organization
3. Lack of flexibility in schedule
4. Lack of student pride and achievement for some
5. Physical appearance of building
6. Need for student handbook

7. Teacher morale low
8. Lack of materials and supplies
9. School image low
10. Formal program for gifted and talented
11. Duty schedule unequal
12. Use of library
13. After-school athletic programs
14. Copy machine needed
15. High guidance/student ratio
16. Student arrival procedure
17. Standard of what defines excellence
18. Large class size
19. Student disrespect for people and equipment

These ideas were generated from individuals, with priority and consensus determined by small groups and then the large group. The list of needs was then regrouped. A priority list was developed that provided a focus for the immediate change effort and a guide for future efforts.

### *Regrouped Needs List*

#### *Immediate Attention*

1. Disciplinary code needs to be defined
6. Need for student handbook
11. Duty schedule unequal
12. Use of library
16. Student arrival procedure
17. Standard of what defines excellence

#### *Resources Needed*

5. Physical appearance of building
8. Lack of materials and supplies
10. Formal program for gifted and talented
13. After-school athletic programs
14. Copy machine needed
15. High guidance/student ratio

#### *Middle School Issues*

2. Curriculum organization
3. Lack of flexibility in schedule
4. Lack of student pride and achievement for some
5. Physical appearance of building
7. Teacher morale low
9. School image low

13. After-school athletic programs
15. High guidance/student ratio

The Powder Mill Middle School community then began to develop and implement changes on those items needing immediate attention. By the end of the school year, five of their first six items had been addressed. Plans were developed to obtain the resources necessary to implement changes in the second section. Within two years, all of the issues had been addressed. The planning for change to a middle school was completed within a year and implementation was to begin the next school year.

### Planning for the Change

The second step in the mobilization stage is to plan the change. The principal and other educators in leadership positions play an important role in change effort. Leadership characteristics of effective principals usually include having a clear, succinct, well-articulated *vision* of the school. Principals share their vision with those with whom they work and constantly focus on it. "Clarity of organizational vision, ability to communicate that vision, commitment to empowering others, and ability to cultivate trust in the organization's functioning are distinguishing characteristics of effective leaders" (Bennis & Nanus, 1985; Hickman & Silva, 1984). "The central characteristics is vision; the presence of a clear image of the future state of the organization" (Rogus, 1990, p. 6). Through discussion, reading, and planning with faculty, parents, and community, a clear consensus vision may energe—one that most, if not all can support.

*Establishing a Timeline*    To implement this vision, the important next step is to develop a timeline. The timeline should be developed with a rigid beginning and end. The points along the timeline should be viewed as flexible, which will enable the modifications to the plan to be made as needs arise. At times, such as the pressures of increasing enrollment or the completion of a new facility, schools do not have the luxury of a flexible timeline. Developing a timeline under these restraints can also be beneficial. It can enable leaders to focus on critical issues and help facilitate important decisions based on time available.

The following timeline was developed for the Powder Mill Middle School. Although this was a rapid timeline, considering other factors such as a climate for change and a new principal, it met the needs of this school.

Sept.    Issues identified
Oct.    Establish committees, process, procedure

| Nov. | Visitation to other schools |
| | Committee work |
| | Gather data |
| Dec. | Synthesize information |
| Jan. | Outside consultant |
| | Individual and small group assessment |
| Feb. | Decision to change to a middle school |
| Mar. | Prepare for change |
| | Consultant |
| Apr. | Development of schedule |
| | Teams identified |
| May/ | Teams develop schedule, procedures, rules, and student |
| June | orientation process |

Garvin (1990) suggests a two-year plan:

| Year 1 | Gather data, form working committees, report results, develop recommendations, gain board approval |
| Year 2 | Development plan for faculty and parents |
| |    Understanding young adolescent needs |
| |    Understanding the middle school concept |
| Fall | Organizational possibilities |
| |    Teaming overview |
| |    Scheduling possibilities |
| | Organizational decisions |
| | Select teams |
| | Adopt schedule |
| Winter | Select school staff |
| | Intensive training of team |
| Spring | Assign students |
| | Develop orientation process |

These general categories can serve as an outline. They will be explained more fully as the issues of changing to a middle school are discussed further.

*Planning Evaluation*   Another function of the planning step is to identify how the change effort will be evaluated. Evaluation is a tool to help gauge effects. The two kinds of evaluation, formative evaluation and summative evaluation, are useful for different purposes. Formative evaluation is most useful to guide work of the change effort; summative evaluation is used at the end of a particular time period.

Tyler (1989) correlated the formative evaluation process to the methodology of the medical profession. A physician will gather data by looking at a patient's medical history, asking questions of the patient, making judgments about appearance, and identifying the location of pain and frequency of occurrence. At the conclusion of an evaluation, the doctor will prescribe a treatment. After a period of time, the doctor will reassess the condition: Has it improved? What symptoms remain? Are there any side effects or new developments? What is the rate of recovery? If improvement is not acceptable, perhaps another treatment will be tried. The process repeats itself until an effective treatment plan is formed and the ailment is controlled and healing.

Likewise, formative evaluation should guide the process of educational change. As the process of change begins, questions will naturally arise, such as: When will an evaluation take place? How will the process be guided? In what ways will data be gathered? The formative evaluation methodology and the points at which assessment will take place should be identified in the timeline.

Formative evaluation procedures illuminate specific issues so that they can be addressed. If incidents of student altercations are reduced, a formative evaluation process might begin to look at the reasons for the reduction. This information is important so that efforts can continue, building on successes.

Summative evaluation takes place at the conclusion of the change effort or at a specific time if change is ongoing. One may argue that the transition to a middle school may never be fully realized, but at some point a summative evaluation may be of assistance. Certain questions will help validate the change effort and provide direction for further renewal: Have we reached our goals or objectives? What is the impact on student learning? Has the climate of the school changed?

Some of the simplest data that can be used for summative evaluation are school attendance records, discipline records, test scores, and climate surveys. If there are fewer discipline referrals to the office after a change such as interdisciplinary team organization has been implemented, it is logical to make some assumptions, such as teachers are working with students in more appropriate ways, teachers are taking more ownership for discipline in the classroom, or a cooperative environment has been created that supports students working with each other. Conversely, if the discipline rates get worse, questions need to be asked and action taken. The data collection merely indicates that results of a problem have changed. Care must be taken to explore other possible reasons for change. Other data sources might include student questionnaires and interviews, school climate surveys, academic grades, and test scores.

Results of student, staff, and parent questionnaires and interviews can provide valuable summative evaluation data in the implementation process.

Phone or mail surveys to parents can help assess the impact of change to a middle school program.

Formal summative evaluation instruments are available to help assess the impact of change efforts in a middle school. The New England League of Middle Schools (1988) has developed an instrument to assist schools in identifying areas of strength and improvement based on the characteristics of middle schools. The instrument correlates the programs and activities in a school with identified middle school components described in *This We Believe* (Alexander, Arth, Cherry, Eichhorn, Toepfer, Vars, & Lounsbury, 1982). Another instrument that some middle level educators have found helpful is produced by the Center for Early Adolescence, titled *Middle Grades Assessment Program* (Dorman, 1981). Each of these instruments, as well as others, may be helpful as school personnel consider summative evaluation.

### Generating Internal Support

School leaders who initiate a change effort should employ strategies for generating internal support. One strategy is informally talking with staff members. In any organization there are key people who need attention. They may or may not be supportive to change efforts. Consideration of the role of the "priests and priestesses" in a school is necessary. Their role is to "bless" the change effort. Without this blessing, many others may not be supportive. It is important to talk informally with staff to show support, gain insights, identify problems or issues, and validate the person's worth to the organization. It is also important to identify leaders and involve them in the change effort.

Leaders must visibly support the innovation. This support may be demonstrated by providing release time, supplying instructional materials, visiting other outstanding programs, or providing resources for staff development. The dissemination of the timeline in and of itself may increase internal support by enabling staff members to see the progress of the change effort.

It is important to identify an individual's role and responsibilities in the change effort during the annual evaluation process. For example, when interdisciplinary teaming is an expectation, often the evaluation process does not identify competencies of teachers who are expected to work within a teaming environment.

Providing positive reinforcement for people who are strengthening the change efforts is also essential. Their efforts should be recognized by leaders, colleagues, and the larger organization. Announcements at school board, faculty, or parent meetings and in newspapers, newsletters, or professional journals are some ways of providing recognition. Perhaps the most effective recognition is the personal thank you or praise for a job well done from leaders, parents, or students.

One of the key ingredients of changing to a middle school philosophy is to provide time for teachers to share ideas. My experience suggests that in a teacher's busy day there is little time for collegial support, problem solving, or reflection. When given opportunity, teachers can identify and work through issues of concern. Often, expressing concerns and talking about possible directions is a very productive staff development effort. Given time and appropriate facilitation, teachers can solve problems, set direction, and develop realistic alternatives to problematic issues. Little (1982) concluded that development activities are most effective when they provide time for teachers to talk together about their work, to develop opportunities for teachers to watch each other teach, and to encourage teachers to develop accepted norms of collegiality, experimentation, and risk taking.

Another key for generating internal support is to focus the change effort on the needs of students. This strategy is powerful because students are the ultimate concern of parents, teachers, and administrators. Students provide a focus for discussion: What will this enable our students to accomplish? In what ways will this change effort enhance student learning?

Identifying staff who might resist change and specifically addressing their concerns in appropriate ways also generates internal support. Resistance is often viewed as negative, but when leadership takes a proactive approach it can enhance change efforts. Educators seem to resist change; it requires giving up tried practices that may have proven successful for them. People generally do not resist change itself; they resist loss or the possibility of losing something familiar (Burke, 1982).

Staff members most resistant to change are often the most supportive after the change effort is institutionalized, particularly if they feel that their views have been valued as the process developed. Thus, it is necessary to include those perceived to be resistant in the planning process. Karp (1984) contended:

> *Two basic assumptions central to dealing with resistance creatively must be reinforced. The first is that people will always resist, knowingly or not, those things that are not in their best interest. Secondly, resistance needs to be honored and dealt with respectively. If handled from this perspective, resistance becomes an organizational asset and can develop, rather than injure the relationship between the demander and the resistor. . . . There are four steps: surfacing, honoring, exploring, and rechecking. . . . There is one pre-condition that is absolutely essential if the work is to be successful; you must be clear about what you want from the resistor. (p. 69)*
>
> *The need to resist is a powerful part of the human makeup. It is neither good nor bad, but an attribute that can be used to strengthen individuals, families, and organizations. (p. 73)*

### Generating External Support

For the change effort to be sustained, external support must be generated. Usually a change effort will have strong external support when its impact is understood and when it is viewed as worthwhile and important by those outside the school organization (Berman & McLaughlin, 1978). The move to a middle school organization will usually be unsuccessful if parents and community do not understand what the impact of this innovation will be and therefore are not supportive of the change.

*Community Support*   The community needs to be consulted, involved, and, in some cases, convinced that this change effort is important and worthwhile. Some researchers hypothesize that one reason the middle school concept is becoming more widely implemented is that it really does address the needs of young adolescents. Alexander and McEwin (1989) found that a comparison of the reasons that were given (from 1968 to 1988) for the establishment of the new middle schools revealed that there was an increased use, over the years, of the argument that this organization served better "the preadolescent/young adolescent age group, rather than primarily for administrative expediency" (p. 46). It is relatively easy to talk with communities about the benefits of a middle school educational program because the reasons are grounded in the needs of the students they serve.

Data collected from parent surveys and information sessions are examples of external support strategies. Data generated from parents and communities can be powerful when talking with school boards, superintendents, and teachers while building support for movement to a middle school organization. Data can also be used to help assess progress. "Projects designed to have a great deal of community involvement appeared to have a direct effect on promoting teacher change . . . projects aimed at direct parent involvement produced more teacher change and were more likely to be continued by teachers" (Berman & McLaughlin, 1978, p. 23).

Other community resources should be utilized. Nearby colleges, universities, or businesses can be supportive of change efforts. Chambers of Commerce and service groups might be particularly interested and can be emotionally, politically, and financially supportive. Private and government grant opportunities can also provide necessary resources for change efforts. Whatever the community resources are, an effort should be made to connect with them. The mission of these groups is to serve the community; using such resources for purposeful change can enhance the effort in numerous ways.

*Central Office Support*   Another factor that indicates external support is district office "blessing." In large systems, a lack of support from the district level administrative team can be problematic. If support is not generated, building level administrators may feel that the movement and development of a middle school is not supported. To help reduce barriers and provide for discussion and common understandings, common in-service activities are helpful for district personnel.

Community representatives, such as the school board, should be involved at approprite intervals. Minimally, they should be informed of the goals, potential benefits, and perceived outcomes at the onset of a project. As the plan is in the formative stages, frequent briefings keep the board informed. Briefings should include (1) a timeline to chart tasks to be completed and activities in process and (2) discussions to keep citizens advised of the progress of the work.

*Using Outside Consultants*   Inviting outside experts to speak with staff is an external support strategy. This activity can be energizing, motivating, and informative. Consultants can also provide a staff with a validating experience. When experts from outside visit a school and draw on their experience to support teachers in their efforts to change, it can have a very positive effect. Consultants must be relevant, timely, and connected to the change effort.

### Factors that Support Mobilization

Research results of the Berman and McLaughlin study (1978) indicated the following factors enhance change efforts:

1. A clear school goal that has a shared sense of vision is evident.
2. The quality of innovation or change is important; that is, it is not a minor change effort but a substantial change effort.
3. The change is tied to the local agenda by addressing specific issues needing attention locally.
4. The change to a middle school has a reasonable fit to the local setting, not only to the district but also the needs of the community.
5. There is evidence of a clear, well-structured process.
6. There is evidence of an active advocate or champion who understands the model and supports it.
7. Principals and teachers are involved in the change.
8. Data collection is evident and formative evaluation is used as the change takes shape.
9. There is evidence of high-quality training for key people.

### Implementation of Change: Stage II

In the mobilization stage, the direction has been set. Staff-development activities have been identified and some have been completed. The time for the actual implementation is at hand. For those moving to middle school philosophy, one indicator of the implementation stage of change is the organizational and personal change required to modify the schedule to accommodate interdisciplinary team teaching.

One caveat: Implementing change does not happen at a distinct point in time. There is not a time when all mobilization activities end and all implementation begins. If an advisor/advisee program is to be developed for a middle school, there will be a time when small groups will meet with teachers for the first time, but this is only one piece of the implementation stage and other efforts will follow.

New behaviors associated with interdisciplinary teaming must be demonstrated, such as the different roles and responsibilities of team members, developing a team schedule, and assessing team relationships. As each behavior evolves, it becomes part of the implementation of change.

As the implementation stage begins, it is helpful to reflect on the stages of concern (CBAM) discussed earlier. The management level and the personal level are related to the implementation stage of change. The consequence and collaboration levels may also be involved. To illustrate, as interdisciplinary teaming begins (after a successful mobilization stage), a high degree of enthusiasm and commitment is usually evident (high morale, low productivity). As the tasks of teaming become evident (which might be different from what was first envisioned), concerns often develop: How can we continue to do all that is expected, or that we choose to do, as a team (low morale, low productivity)? Questions such as this are a natural and important part of the change process. When solutions are discussed and found, management issues begin to be resolved and direction beomes clearer (low morale, moderate productivity). If team members attend to the role and function of the team, eventually the team will become a high-performing team with high morale and high productivity (Hersey & Blanchard, 1988).

Teachers will need time to reflect on and discuss issues associated with a new structure. Teaming provides a forum for this discussion. Grade level or school needs may need to be addressed. In my experience, some of the most informative and worthwhile staff-development programs have taken place when teachers have the time to share in productive ways. Frequently teachers do not have time to reflect on their experience. "Learning does not take place by the experience alone, learning takes place upon the reflection of the experience" (Tyler, 1989).

Consequences of actions is a level of concern for individuals and teams. As a team, how is our work affecting students? Is there spirit on the team? Is there improved parent-school communications? Is student self-esteem improving? Is curriculum enhanced by the use of interdisciplinary units? These questions grow from the change to a middle school and correlate to a level of concern.

As answers to these questions are being formulated, teachers move to the next level of concern—collaboration. Collaboration indicates that the group is moving to the next stage of the change process, the sustaining of change. Questions at this stage sound like: Can we coordinate this activity with another team in the seventh grade? Are we doing what other teams are doing? What are the differences or similarities? Can we work together on this next unit to integrate study skills? How can we be a more effective team? This collaborative effort bonds a school, a grade level, and a team, and is an important piece in the implementation puzzle. Experience indicates that movement up and down the levels of concern is common. Awareness of where individuals, groups, grade levels, and schools might be helpful in monitoring change.

Evaluation is not right or wrong, good or bad, but a process to help shape, renew, and/or improve a program process or procedure. Formative evaluations can begin to identify problems and guide solutions. The medical model discussed previously can be applied to the educational setting and may be helpful. To illustrate, as teams develop, concerns will be raised. Data can be gathered and treatments prescribed. Constant assessment of the teams' development will not only help cure ailments but will be preventive medicine as well, keeping problems small and manageable. It is important that teams develop skills in assessment in order to encourage open discussion and to identify problems and issues that naturally arise.

Formative evaluation procedures are dependent on the nature of the problem, the people involved, and the context of the situation. Considering the implementation of a middle school concept, there are a number of data collection sources that can be helpful. Assessing the variety of instructional approaches used in the classrooms and the nature and content of the curriculum before, during, and after the change effort may provide useful information.

A possible outcome of the movement to a middle school philosophy is that teachers might be more aware of and act on the characteristics of young adolescents. For example, knowing that young adolescents have a short attention span and that their bodies are growing suggests that student movement will occur at frequent intervals in the classroom. Assessments in classrooms will provide informative data to see if teachers are meeting the needs of young adolescents.

Berman and McLaughlin (1978) have identified enhancing factors for successful implementation of a significant change effort. They are:

- A serious commitment for "doing it right"; to make the best possible effort
- Stable leadership at the principal and central office levels
- Administrative commitment and support

- High-quality and appropriate evaluation procedures
- A line of clear responsibility, coordination, and orchestration of the team
- Shared control over implementation
- Establishment of a steering committee
- Flexible implementation
- Adequate financial resources for training, technical assistance, and release time
- Rewards for teachers early in the process
- Empowerment, collegiality, meeting individual needs
- Peer support
- Frequent and sincere encouragement

During implementation, staff-development issues should become more individualized. Small groups, teams, and individuals will identify needs and issues. The staff-development program should become very flexible to address a variety of needs identified; however, they should be contained within the vision developed.

### Institutionalization: Stage III

Institutionalization or sustaining a change effort is the stage at which change is accepted and becomes part of the culture of the organization. Institutionalization, the last phase of innovation, marks the final transition of a change effort to an accepted part of the regular district operations or to its ultimate disappearance (Berman & McLaughlin, 1978). "A cardinal fact of change is that people will always misinterpret and misunderstand some aspect of the purpose or practice of something that is new to them" (Fullan, 1982, p. 167). Continued communication is important; it is through communication that the change effort is shaped to address ever-changing, flexible needs as they develop.

Teaming, as an organizational structure, provides a forum for teachers to communicate and work with each other. As change occurs, discussions, communications, and problem-solving strategies can be utilized to continue institutionalization of the rites and rituals, procedures, and culture of the middle school concept. As new team members become part of the team, the orientation can be positively effected, thus ensuring a smooth transition.

Formative evaluation processes have shaped the change effort to a point where outcomes are predictable, where processes are manageable, and where a general feeling of success about the change effort is evident. Summative evaluation process can then take place. If the effort is the transition to a middle school, a return to the original plan and an assessment of effects of this change effort is appropriate. Reporting of data to all involved is necessary. If the evaluation indicates a need for improvement, then the process of educational change continues.

### Conditions that Enhance Institutionalization

Some enhancing factors identified by Berman and McLaughlin (1978) are:

- Stable program leadership exists.
- Roles, procedures, rites, and rituals become institutionalized.
- Resource allocation continues so that the functions of the change effort can continue.
- Change effort is linked to other change, such as curriculum renewal or improved classroom instruction.
- Competing practices are removed.
- Adequate supply of trainers exists to carry on these change efforts. Local people will assist others with the skills necessary to continue on with the change effort. Again, peer support and the team networking within the school and across the schools is critical for continuation of the change effort.

The institutionalization of change must have sustained attention. As new personnel enter the system, as resources change, as demands on the system from the community change the school, the organization needs to adjust. Change is constant, but a clear vision, formative assessment, and goals will sustain the organization. Figure 8–1 shows that certain processes of mobilization lead to certain processes of implementation and then to certain processes of institutionalization.

## Staff Development

Glatthorn and Spencer (1986) defined *staff development* as "a systematic and continuing effort in which principals and teachers work together to improve schools and solve emerging school problems. Staff development efforts help administrators and teachers bond effectively to address the special needs of early adolescents" (p. 213). The most effective staff-development efforts are linked to the needs of the individuals *and* organizations. Staff development is not something done *to* teachers, but something done *by* and *for* teachers. During the transition to a middle school organization or in the sustaining of the middle school, staff development "is the glue of successful schools. It

**FIGURE 8–1** • *Paths of Innovation*

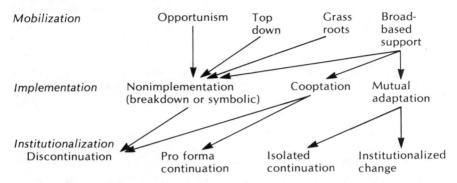

Source: P. Berman and M. M. McLaughlin, *Federal Programs Supporting Educational Change, Vol. VIII: Implementing and Sustaining Innovations.* Santa Monica, CA: Rand Corporation, 1978.

bonds together the discrete elements of instructional effectiveness into a whole school action" (Glickman, 1990, p. 4).

Enhancing characteristics of effective staff-development programs include sustained efforts that provide adequate opportunity for the development of necessary skills or programs. Timing is critical; staff development must be offered when teachers need the acquisition of new skills or the development a new programs. If, in the process of developing a more responsive middle school, an advisor/advisee program is desired as an important component, the needs of teachers must be met in relationship to the planned implementation of the advisor/advisee program. For example, teachers may feel uncomfortable with group process activities; they may need training in techniques for this type of activity. Also, it would make little sense to provide in-service for the advisor/advisee in the beginning stages of moving to a middle school organization, if implementation of this part of the middle school is two years away.

The principal and other administrators should be active members of the staff-development effort, but they should not dominate. Teacher involvement is critical to identify issues, design how the effort will develop, and identify expected outcomes.

Staff development should center on the needs of teachers as they perceive them. The program should be developed carefully so that real needs are established that will address the issues raised. For example, often the issue of ability grouping is met with resistance by teachers. My experience suggests teachers may be unsure of how to work effectively with a diverse classroom of students. Teachers identifying the need to gain skills necessary to work with a heterogeneous classroom is different from teachers insisting that effective instruction is not possible unless groups are homogeneous because the underlying reason is that they are unsure of the skills necessary to be successful.

Another important consideration in the transition to a middle school organization is the consideration of the unique needs of young adolescents. The merging of these issues with school programs provides a powerful partnership to improve student learning and create many topics for staff development.

Teachers should play an active role in planning and facilitating staff-development efforts. Staff development should consider the needs of the adult learner. These needs are not unlike those of the student learner. That is, adults will be motivated to learn if a need is established.

When planning and conducting effective learning experiences for adults, there are some important principles to keep in mind (Wood & Thompson, 1980):

1. *Adults will commit to learning when the goals and objectives are considered realistic and important to the learner.*
2. *Adults will learn, retain, and use what they perceive is relevant to their personal and professional needs.*
3. *Adult learners need to see results of their efforts and have accurate feedback about progress toward their goal.*
4. *Adult learning is ego-involved. Learning a new skill, technique, or concept may promote a positive or negative view of self.*
5. *Adults come to any learning situation with a wide range of previous experiences, knowledge, skills, self direction, interests, and competence. Individualization, therefore, is appropriate for adults.*
6. *Adults want to be origins of their own learning; that is, involved in selection of objectives, content, activities, and assessment.*
7. *Adults will resist learning situations which they believe are an attack on their competence.*
8. *Adults reject prescriptions by others for their learning, especially when what is perceived is viewed as an attack on what they are presently doing (pp. 375–77).*

Staff development is effective when participants are actively involved. Active learning includes demonstrations, developing materials, roleplaying or case studies, hands-on experience, simulation, peer interaction, and cooperative games. If a new skill is required, an opportunity to practice this skill is needed. Transfer of training will be enhanced if an opportunity is provided to apply new skills, ideas, and strategies in the classroom and then receive feedback and support from colleagues (Joyce & Showers, 1988).

This support or "coaching" has been viewed as an effective method to enhance transfer of training.

> *Coaching has several purposes. The first is to build communities of teachers who continually engage in the study of their craft. Second, coaching develops the shared language and set of common understandings necessary for collegial study of new knowledge and skills. Third, coaching provides a structure for the follow up to training that is essential for acquiring new teaching skills and strategies. (Showers, 1985, pp. 43–44)*

Professional development is a holistic experience. In fact, Capelluti and Eberson (1990) maintained that

> *Professional development is not a matter of simple training. It is a richer, more complex, and ultimately more satisfying human accomplishment. Authentic staff development places the teacher at the center of the activities as an active participant, reflective learner, competent decision-maker, and empowered professional. (p. 7)*

Staff development involves many activities based on need and combined to achieve a goal, through collaboration among supervisors, peers, and other educational leaders. Teachers, as professionals, are capable of identifying areas of improvement, renewal, or investigation. Activities might include reading professional journals, attending conferences, trying a new methodology, or participating in study groups or discussion groups. When two or more individuals share the same need or desire to improve skills or programs, collaborative work is possible. "Cooperative professional development is a process by which small teams of teachers work together using a variety of methods and structures for their own professional growth" (Glatthorn, 1987, p. 31).

School-based activities might involve early release programs, day-long in-service opportunities, or three- to five-day institutes. When staff needs are served in large group meetings and not based on teacher concerns, collegial interactions, or teacher-developed goals, staff development may not be meaningful to a majority of teachers. While working with students in a classroom, if a teacher addresses the group needs with little attention to the individual needs, there will be students whose needs will not be met. Thus, staff development based on individual teacher needs will be meaningful for the greatest number of participants.

"Data indicate that teachers rise to challenges. Ambitious and demanding innovations seem more likely to elicit the commitment of teachers than routine projects" (Berman & McLaughlin, 1978, p. 25). The transition to a middle school is an ambitious and demanding innovation, and requires staff-development needs. Assessing those needs and developing options for teachers often is the responsibility of a steering committee.

A steering committee, comprised primarily of teacher representatives, would ensure that teacher viewpoints are considered. Subcommittees can be utilized to research specific topics, which will involve more staff in the process of change effort. Garvin (1990) suggests that four committees be established, each addressing these areas:

1. Organizational issues, which involve grade structure, scheduling, grouping and staffing issues
2. Curriculum, which involves subjects, guidance cocurricular activities, evaluation, and individual pursuits
3. Community impact subcommittee, which addresses enrollment, articulation, parent involvement, and community resource issues
4. Facilities planning, which addresses issues of a new building or usage of the existing plant

A variety of staff-development options are available that address identified needs. The following is a list of options developed at a leadership academy about staff development conducted by the Massachusetts Department of Education in the summer of 1989:

### Possible Staff-Development Activities

Early release or half days

Full-day workshops where substitutes are provided

Visitations to other schools

Common planning times during the school day

After-school workshops

Summer workshops

Summer institutes

Weekly consultant visits

Regular staff meetings

State-funded meetings and experiences

College coursework

Demonstrations and coteaching

Teachers' support groups/study teams

Peer coaching

Mentoring

Teacher-sharing sessions

Journal keeping

Professional reading

Development of a speakers' bureau

Modeling of the principal

Development of a newsletter

Conference attendance

Teacher supervision

Celebrations and rewards for jobs well done

Faculty meetings can also be professional-development opportunities. Unfortunately, faculty meetings often become vehicles to pass along information and may be viewed negatively. Talking, sharing concerns, and identifying problems can become common activities and expectations for faculty meetings.

Staff incentives are important in encouraging change. Rewarding teachers for their work is essential — purchasing additional classroom materials and supplies or other resources for use by teachers who participate in staff development can be an incentive. In-service credit awarded to those who participate in a course and the reimbursement of costs for college coursework is common. Attendance at conferences, of the teachers' choice, can also be an incentive. This could be based on the number of staff-development hours a teacher attends. Another option for teacher incentive is the use of flexible in-service days. For example, for every six hours of staff-development work outside of the regular school day, teachers might earn six hours of release time. (Often this is restricted to previously scheduled early release days or day-long professional days, but systems may choose not to limit this option.) Numerous incentives will support, nurture, and encourage staff members to try a new idea.

The best teacher incentives will be those based on needs of the individual. A variety of options should be explored. For some individuals, release time will be a motivator; for others, materials; for many others, intrinsic motivation is all that is needed. Incentive programs should be flexible to meet the diverse needs of the staff population.

Research by Berman and McLaughlin (1978) indicated that change is easier if:

- It is significant and moderately difficult to achieve.
- People can control their fate or at least have significant influence to steer or guide the effort.
- It will have an impact on an outcome or there is a valued reason for the change.

- It will foster understanding.
- It will help clarify a role.
- It provides an opportunity to pursue deeply held beliefs and values.
- It brings status.
- It brings a chance for more collegial relationship.
- It relieves boredom and routine.

These guidelines are intended to increse the transfer of knowledge, which will enhance the staff-development effort. "Research indicates that staff development can be most important in facilitating lasting change, . . . [and] could significantly improve the effectiveness of teachers and the implementation of local reform efforts" (Berman & McLaughlin, 1978, pp. 42–43).

Reflecting on the conditions that support and enhance staff development as identified by Berman and McLaughlin (1978), it is clear that there are a number of factors that should be considered before any change takes place.

1. Strong administrative support is necessary, both at the building level and at the district level.
2. A culture of experimentation and receptivity to change within the school within the district enhances the change effort.
3. Consistency for the duration of the change effort is important. Consistency manifests itself not only in staff and leadership but also in commitment to budget.
4. There should be a caring, sensitive, and interpersonal interaction associated with the change effort. This respects the notion that change is difficult and is a very individual activity. Not all people will change at the same rate and in the same way.
5. There should be a sustained staff-development effort. One program or even a series of programs will not necessarily have all staff members functioning at the desired levels.
6. There should be flexibility in achieving the vision. If the vision is the transition to a middle school, the vision is a clear articulation of what this school will look like when the goal is achieved. The flexibility comes in how we arrive at that vision. Which road will be chosen? Which direction should we go in? How we get there will be decided along the way. The road map should always be consulted and options considered, but the destination is always clear, enabling the design of the change effort and effective staff-development efforts to guide the journey for safe arrival.

## A Case Study in Progress

The following case study* describes the change process at East Lyme Junior High School in East Lyme, Connecticut, as the school moves to a middle school organization. The principal, Jerome Belair, has described this transition. While this process has worked for this school and this staff, a caveat should be noted: It is important to develop an appropriate process for each school. I would like to thank Jerry for his time, effort, and energy in developing this description of the process of change.

### Year One: The Mobilization State Begins

East Lyme Junior High School was organized as a grade 6 through 8 departmentalized junior high school in 1970. The professional staff is characterized as mature, experienced, and highly educated, with 79 percent having taught for 20 or more years. The town is a residential shoreline community of some 14,000 located in the greater Groton/New London area and has high expectations for its school system. Many residents are prominent in the marine, nuclear, defense, and pharmaceutical industries that dominate the economy of the area.

In July 1987, a new principal was hired for the school and began his tenure by gathering a community snapshot of the junior high program. Prior to Thanksgiving, he interviewed staff, students, and many members of the parent community, asking each group to assess the strengths of the school, identify areas of concern, and share dreams for their school. At the December faculty meeting, Jerry shared his snapshot with his colleagues and asked for a group of volunteers to explore more fully how the school community could improve its school program.

Seven members of the professional staff and both administrators met and formed a study group in January 1988. Previously, the faculty had organized intervention and school effectiveness committees to address specific schoolwide issues. However, both initiatives were never brought to closure. The purpose of the newly formed study group was to examine the various organizational designs for middle schools and to share their findings with the professional staff.

At the February faculty meeting, study group members presented survey questions and reviewed the meaning of each question with the staff. The faculty survey was to be completed by the end of February. The results would

*Special thanks to Thomas F. Reale, Director of Curriculum and Instruction, for his support throughout the change process.

be shared at a future meeting and the staff was assured that this initiative would, indeed, be brought to closure and any change would be agreed to by the faculty.

In mid-March, the study group met and tallied survey results. The results revealed the need (1) for common planning time for teachers who teach the same students in order to communicate and share information about students and subject matter; (2) to create a more supportive environment for both students and staff; (3) for opportunities to communicate across disciplines with other school personnel and with parents; (4) for consistent academic and behavioral expectations in the same grade level; (5) to coordinate homework, testing schedules, and academic skills within all subjects; (6) to provide enrichment opportunities for all students; and (7) to provide a variety of activities to meet the physical, intellectual, social, and emotional needs of the student population. The results reflected a willingness on the part of staff to explore other organizational and scheduling designs to address the needs of the student community and the professional staff.

Five members of the study group attended the seventh annual New England League of Middle School Conference in late March to expand their own knowledge of middle school programming. At the April faculty meeting, these members reported on the many workshop sessions attended at the conference. They highlighted their new learning and possibilities for East Lyme Junior High School. Results of the survey were presented and validated by the staff. Three members of the study group led a brainstorming session, gathering ideas to address the problems identified in the survey. A fourth member facilitated a staff discussion as to what the next step should be in the school improvement study. At the next study group meeting, suggestions and concerns expressed at the April faculty meeting were examined. Ideas were categorized into short- and long-term objectives.

The superintendent of schools was invited to meet with the entire study group in early May. An overview of the initiative was presented and his questions were answered. It was clear by the end of the meeting that the superintendent supported the study group's efforts. Confident of the superintendent's support, the study group informed the Board of Education of its plans and outlined the middle school initiative in the next Parent Teacher Association newsletter. The group was expanded to include PTA parents and Board of Education members. A professional library, including readings and tapes, was established to broaden faculty awareness of middle level programming and the middle school concept.

A timeline for the remainder of the school year and the next school year was drafted with a series of planned events for schoolwide improvement. The development of a common vision was a top priority. The superintendent would be kept informed of progress on a monthly basis. Frequent reports to the Board of Education would be made by the study group.

Opportunities to attend middle level conferences would be made available to all staff. School visitations to exemplary middle schools would be arranged. Professional development days for the 1989–90 school year would be reserved so the entire staff could focus on middle level education, and faculty meetings would address a practitioner's approach to middle level programming.

In May, study group members presented the timeline of activities to the staff for review and acceptance. A collaborative process would be used to address the various timeline components, and all faculty were encouraged to be involved in the exploration and determination of what would be best for East Lyme Junior High School. The study group stressed that a successful change process involved everyone. The timeline reflected staff input and a commitment to design the very best organizational structure that would meet the needs of students, parents, and staff. Most of 1988–89 school year would be used to collect information. During the spring, the faculty would make a decision regarding its future organizational structure.

The study group wanted the decision to be an informed one, drawing from an excellent data base, learning from research and middle level practitioners. East Lyme Junior High would be involved in a firsthand investigation of available options. This plan would bring efforts of past initiatives to fruition. The study group received the superintendent's support to use districtwide professional development days for its initiative.

Following the May faculty meeting and the staff's endorsement of the 1988–89 timeline of activities, the study group was expanded to include four additional faculty members, a parent representative from each of the three elementary schools, and two members of the Board of Education. A meeting with a consultant was scheduled for July to review the plan.

After meeting, the study group drafted a more specific plan to expand the knowledge base of all staff regarding middle level programming and organization. Faculty meetings would be used for guest practitioners as well as faculty discussion. Weekly professional articles would be distributed to all staff and round-table discussions would be organized to discuss them. All faculty would be strongly encouraged to visit other middle level schools. A variety of professional conferences would be available to all interested staff and the middle level professional library would be expanded. A plan for the three full days of professional development was designed.

Eleven exemplary schools throughout the state of Connecticut were identified, and a questionnaire was designed to gather information on effective ways to organize a successful middle level school. Two formal parent programs were scheduled with guest consultants. These programs would highlight the physical, intellectual, social, and emotional characteristics of young adolescents and how the school could best address these needs. In addition, a series of meetings were scheduled to inform parents of the initiative, up-date progress, and address parent concerns. Direct mailings were planned to keep the community informed of progress as the faculty explored the question: What is the best organizational design to meet the needs of young adolescents at East Lyme Junior High School? Minutes of all study group meetings would be recorded and distributed to keep the faculty informed of happenings and progress.

In early August, the principal attended the National Association of Secondary Schools Middle Level Colloquium II. Later in the month, the study group met to review and modify plans for the 1988–89 school year. A recap of the middle level colloquium was shared as well as the highlights of the visit with the consultant. The timeline of activities was reviewed, modified, and accepted, along with a staff-development plan for the new school year. A parent component of staff development was reviewed and an agreement was reached. School visitations and the questionnaire were reviewed. A listing of all professional development library materials was presented to study group members. The creation of a middle level library for parents was discussed and approved. A faculty notebook for professional readings and study group minutes was approved for distribution to each faculty member.

### Year Two: The Process Continues

At the first faculty gathering in September, the study group brought the faculty up to date with a revised timeline of activities for the new school year. All staff were encouraged to become involved in the study process. A listing of school visitations, conferences, professional library materials, professional-development activities, and a middle level initiative notebook was distributed. Each future monthly faculty meeting would include a study group update.

The first round-table discussion began in mid-September. All staff received a copy of a professional article relating to young adolescence and middle level education. Two round-table discussions were planned each month throughout the new school year. The September discussions focused on the physical and intellectual development of young adolescents. Notes were taken during the discussion and shared with the entire staff. All round-table and study group meetings were open to the entire faculty and each study group member was encouraged to invite a colleague.

A mailbox was established in the faculty workroom through which any faculty member could leave questions or concerns for study group response and consideration. This source of communication allowed the study group to keep a finger on the pulse of progress. A consultant was a guest at the September faculty meeting and spoke to the following question: If middle school is the answer, then what is the question? Later that evening, he met with parents and presented a program titled: How to Kiss a Frog. The first professional development in-service day took place in late September. Another middle level educator was the guest and reviewed characteristics of the young adolescent learner and the implications for curriculum and programming. The afternoon session was devoted to developing a mission statement for the school community. The faculty worked in 10 interdisciplinary groups. Following the group work, each group selected a representative to be part of a schoolwide committee to develop further a mission statement for the school community. This committee met on six occasions to draft many mission statements with guiding principles. Each draft was shared with the faculty and was modified according to input and consensus.

In October, the staff began its visitations to exemplary schools throughout Connecticut. Prior to each visitation, a profile was posted on the staff-development board describing each visiting school, and a voluntary sign-up list accompanied each profile. Faculty from different disciplines and grade levels comprised each visitation team. This team completed a formal report that was distributed to all staff. Presentations highlighting each visit were made at faculty meetings.

The study group began to sense apprehension on the part of some faculty members and determined it was necessary to reexplain the group's purpose and reassure staff that all of their input was valued and encouraged. At the October faculty meeting, representatives of the study group presented an overview of early progress and reminded everyone that the first half of the school year would be spent collecting information and the second half processing that information. The staff was reminded that the study group was formed due to faculty displeasure with the present structure and, again, invited all interested members to join the study group. It was stressed that in order to make an informed decision regarding the East Lyme Junior High School organizational structure, everyone needed to research the various options available.

During November, various visiting teams reported back to the faculty on their visitations. Highlights from each visit were shared and possible ideas for consideration were noted. The Principal's Column in the November PTA newsletter provided an update to the parent community regarding initiative activities. In late November, the principal provided a formal presentation to the Board of Education, informing them of the junior high activities and plans for the remainder of the school year.

During one of the November study group meetings, it was suggested that students join the study group. Rather than include students at this time, a decision was made to design a survey for students, representing all ages, grades, and academic levels. Students could share what made them feel comfortable at East Lyme Junior High and what changes they would like to see. Meetings with representative students from each grade level were scheduled with a group of faculty and parents to generate survey questions. Small groups of 10 students were presented with open-ended statements and encouraged to express their views. Neighborhood coffees and in-school meetings were arranged so parents could also share their perceptions of the school.

The second professional development day occurred during November. The two board representatives and three parent members of the study group participated in this activity. In the morning, five visitation teams presented their reports, and faculty discussion followed. Collaborative groups of teachers reacted to the third draft of a schoolwide mission statement. The afternoon session had members from a nearby Connecticut middle school present their concept of a middle school and their approach to schoolwide organization. There was opportunity for faculty reaction and discussion.

Three more visitations occurred in December. A fourth draft of the schoolwide mission statement and a list of five guiding principles was presented to the staff for their reaction. The faculty endorsed the fourth draft and reached consensus regarding the school mission:

"East Lyme Junior High is dedicated to lifelong learning, mutual respect, and equal opportunities for all."

Two subcommittees within the study group were formed to explore ways to gather student and parent information regarding the organizational design. Faculty members attended middle level conferences. At the second monthly study group meeting, each subcommittee presented a plan to gather student and parent input. A draft of questions was handed out and discussed. An update regarding student and parent surveys was provided to all staff at the December faculty meeting. It was decided that ninth-graders should be surveyed to gather information from students who had experienced three years at the junior high.

In January, a subcommittee of the study group designed a brochure that explained the middle school initiative to the parent community. The purpose and history of the initiative was highlighted and a timeline of teacher, parent, and student activities was presented. A news release was prepared for the local media to promote and inform the community of the middle level initiative. A series of student meetings were planned throughout January, and parent meetings were scheduled for February and March.

In February, a principal and faculty representatives from one of the visiting schools were guests at the faculty meeting. They shared their transitional experience and the benefits of the interdisciplinary team organization. Faculty members shared conference highlights with one another and school visitation reports were presented. Faculty members volunteered to attend the eighth annual New England League of Middle Schools Conference in Hyannis, Massachusetts. A prominent middle level educator was the guest for a full day in late February, visiting classrooms, presenting a two-hour faculty in-service on appropriate school culture and climate for middle school students, and offering an evening session for parents titled: The Home and School Connection: Providing an Appropriate School Program for the Young Adolescent Learner. The month concluded with study group members shadowing sixth-, seventh-, and eighth-grade students in order to experience a typical school day in the life of a student at East Lyme Junior High.

In early March, the study group met for two full days to process all of the information gathered throughout the study. They reviewed data collected from the grades 6 through 9 student surveys; reviewed all input from the three parent grade level meetings; reviewed faculty survey results; and reviewed new learning from professional in-service days, professional conferences, and school visitations. The information was analyzed and common threads were identified. The study group then began to formulate five recommendations for organizational change at East Lyme Junior High. Each of these recommendations would be presented for faculty consideration at the full-day professional in-service in March.

Members of the study group began that March meeting by reviewing all activities completed to date and highlighting the information gathered. Teacher, parent, and student survey results identified seven common issues that should be the basis for any school change. Five recommendations for organizational change were presented and the study group endorsed the formation of interdisciplinary teams for East Lyme Junior High School. The study group recommended two interdisciplinary teams for each grade level and the creation of an eight-period day.

During the morning session, the pros and cons of each recommendation were discussed. Time was reserved for each of the eight faculty collaborative groups to process and identify questions concerning each recommendation. In the afternoon, the faculty reached consensus by strongly endorsing interdisciplinary teams at all grade levels by a 46 to 8 vote. It was decided to phase in interdisciplinary teams at the junior high over a two-year period: team grade 6 and 7 during school year 1989–90 and team grade 8 and the arts during school year 1990–91.

The next task was to report to the Board of Education. The report noted the various school-community activities, discussed the process used to reach a decision, and informed the board of the faculty vote. Following this report, the parent community needed to be informed by organizing meetings to explain how the change process would be implemented.

During May, a transition team was formed to plan for interdisciplinary teams at grades 6 and 7. A parent letter was written to inform parents of the 1989–90 plans and parent meetings were conducted. Goals for year 1 of teaming were drafted and submitted to faculty for approval. In-service needs for 1989–90 were communicated to the building professional development team. A checklist of needs to be accomplished prior to the end of the school year was developed. This list included teaming assignments, room assignments, professional-development activities for teams before June 20, and school-community communications and meetings. Later in May, all grades 6 and 7 staff were assigned to teams. Room assignments were made and a plan to relocate faculty was developed and agreed upon.

Each new team was provided with two days during the month of June to begin planning for the organizational change. A consultant worked with each team for a half day in June. Teams reached consensus on their goals for the first year of teaming and developed policies and practices for their new team. They explored the potential benefits of teaming and the pitfalls to avoid. Each team agreed on a decision-making process to ensure team effectiveness and discussed the various roles each member would assume on the team. The study group transition team drafted a teaming philosophy, realistic expectations for the first year of teaming, and suggestions on ways to keep all staff members aware of team business. These recommendations were endorsed by the faculty. Teaming was underway at East Lyme Junior High!

### Year Three: Implementation

Two of the four teams met during the summer to plan for the first week of school in August. The first professional development day occurred prior to the new school year in late August. A nationally known consultant and trainer worked with the staff on team-building skills. She reviewed how to conduct a successful team meeting, explained the various roles each member would play at a team meeting, and assisted each team in formulating and adhering to a meeting agenda. Each team worked through exercises on building toward consensus when making decisions. The consultant focused on team identity and spirit. This session proved invaluable, as each member of the team had an opportunity to practice each of the roles through simulation exercises.

### Final Comment

The change process was successful at East Lyme Junior High because it involved the entire school community of students, parents, teachers, Board of Education members, and central office staff. Faculty reviewed the research, gathered its own information by attending professional conferences, and visited eleven different school sites. They also interviewed practitioners as well as parents and students, considered the needs of parents and students, remained open to change, supported one another, and were united in their desire to provide the very best for their students.

During the 1989–90 school year, eighth-grade teachers and all members of the related Arts were involved in planning for phase two of the middle school initiative. They benefitted from the learnings of grade 6 and 7 teams, and members of the Arts staff visited other schools with Arts teaming.

Change is a process. The success at East Lyme Junior High is attributed to the involvement of all concerned with the effort. Because all stakeholders were involved — teachers, parents, students, and community members — East Lyme Junior High School is on its way to designing a successful school program that best meets the needs of young adolescents in East Lyme.

During the Spring of 1990, faculty participated in a number of developmental growth assessments related to the new changes at East Lyme Junior High. They identified what worked especially well and noted what didn't work as well as they had hoped. Plans for improvement for the 1990–91 school year were developed. Conclusions drawn from these assessments were as follows: East Lyme Junior High is on its way to providing time for staff, students, and parents to communicate with one another. A supportive environment for staff and students has been established. The coordination of curriculum is taking shape on each team. Consistent academic and behavior expectations are in place. Enrichment and special activities are being offered to the entire school community.

The East Lyme Junior High School community is truly dedicated to lifelong learning, mutual respect, and equal opportunities for all.

On April 8, 1991, the name of the school was changed by the Board of Education to East Lyme Middle School in a unanimous vote. The school name now reflects its philosophy and practice.

## Conclusion

The three stages of change identified by Berman and McLaughlin (1978) have been discussed and illustrated, and it appears that effective strategies for change are known. Fullan (1982) said, "People will always misinterpret and misunderstand some aspect of the purpose or practice of something that is new to them" (p. 167). As individuals within a school organization consider moving to a middle school philosophy, various components of the change process may be more significant.

Time spent in the early stages, planning a change, assessing the obstacles to change, and developing strategies will significantly make an impact on mobilization, implementation, and institutionalization of the change effort. Critical issues include: finding time; developing an appropriate plan; and implementing a caring, sensitive method in working with professionals. "No simple or sure way can be found to effect educational change and have it persist. . . . The fate of an innovation depends on the complex interplay among characteristics of the innovative project itself and the institutional setting it seeks to change" (Berman & McLaughlin, 1978, p. 22).

As more schools move to middle school organizational structures and programs, the task will become more manageable. Many schools have now changed and others can draw on their experience. One school's successful model cannot be transplanted into another setting. However, through sharing, discussion, and study, one can learn from another's experience.

The middle school movement is a powerful force in the education of young adolescents (Johnston & Markle, 1988). It is a worthwhile investment in the future of young people and holds promise for their education, not only for the skills of learning but for the skills of life.

*Policy, practice, theory, and research in education are converging to spotlight the critical importance of the middle grades. The awareness has grown from the strong and respected literature on the characteristics of early adolescents, from an exciting and expanding collection of recommended school and classroom practices, and from a new research agenda focused on the effects of recommended practices on the quality of school programs and on the learning and development of young adolescents. (Epstein, 1990, p. 436)*

Perhaps the information in this chapter can be used to enhance the development of individualized plans and strategies for change in middle schools.

## References

Alexander, W., Arth, A. A., Cherry, C., Eichhorn, D., Toepfer, C., Vars, G., & Lounsbury, J. (1982). *This we believe*. Macon, GA: National Middle School Association.

Alexander, W. M., & George, P. S. (1981). *The exemplary middle school*. New York: Holt, Rinehart and Winston.

Alexander, W. M., & McEwin, C. K. (1989). *Schools in the middle: Status and progress*. Columbus, OH: National Middle School Association.

Belenky, M. F., Clinchy, B. M., Goldberger, N. R., & Tarule, J. M. (1986). *Women's way of knowing: The development of self, voice and mind*. New York: Basic Books.

Bennis, W., & Nanus, B. (1985). *Leaders: The strategies for taking charge*. New York: Harper and Row.

Berman, P., & McLaughlin, M. W. (1978). *Federal programs supporting educational change. Vol. VIII: Implementing and sustaining innovations*. Santa Monica, CA: Rand Corporation.

Burden, P. R. (1982, February). *Developmental supervision: Reducing teacher stress at different career stages*. Paper presented at the Association of Teacher Educators Annual Conference, Phoenix, AZ.

Burke, P. J., Christensen, J. C., Fessler, R., McDonnell, J. H., & Price, J. R.

(1987, April). *The teacher career cycle: Model development and research report.* Paper presented at the annual meeting of the American Educational Research Association, Washington, DC.

Burke, W. W. (1982). *Organizational development: Principals and practices.* Boston: Little, Brown.

Capelluti, J., & Eberson, J. (1990). *Change in education: Strategies for improving middle level schools.* Rowley, MA: New England League of Middle Schools.

Carnegie Council on Adolescent Development's Task Force on Education of Young Adolescents. (1989). *Turning points: Preparing American youth for the 21st century.* Washington, DC: Carnegie Council on Adolescent Development, a program of Carnegie Corporation of New York.

Cawelti, G. (1988, November). Middle schools a better match with early adolescent needs, ASCD survey finds. *ASCD Curriculum Update.* (Available from the Association for Supervision and Curriculum Development, Alexandria, VA: 22314-2798.)

Deal, T. E. (1990). Reframing reform. *Educational Leadership, 47*(8), 6–12.

Dorman, G. (1981). *Middle grades assessment program.* Chapel Hill, NC: Center for Early Adolescence, University of North Carolina at Chapel Hill.

Epstein, J. L. (1990). What matters in the middle grades—grade span or practice. *Phi Delta Kappan, 71*(6), 438–444.

Epstein, J. L., & Mac Iver, D. J. (1990). *Education in the middle grades: Overview of national practices and trends.* Columbus, OH: National Middle School Association.

Florida Department of Education. (1990). *Coming of age: The impact of PRIME legislation on middle level schools in Florida.* Tallahassee, FL: Author.

Fullan, M. (1982). *The meaning of educational change.* New York: Teachers College Press.

Garvin, J. P. (1990). *Sane transition to the middle school program.* Newburyport, MA: Garvin Consultant Services.

Glatthorn, A. A. (1987). Cooperative professional development: Peer-centered options for teacher growth. *Educational Leadership, 44*(3), 31–35.

Glatthorn, A. A., & Spencer, N. K. (1986). *Middle school/junior high principal's handbook: A practical guide for developing better schools.* Englewood Cliffs, NJ: Prentice-Hall.

Glickman, C. D. (1990). *Supervision of instruction: A developmental approach* (2nd ed.). Boston: Allyn and Bacon.

Goodlad, J. I. (1984). *A place called school: Prospects for the future.* New York: McGraw-Hill.

Hall, G. E., & Loucks, S. F. (1979). Teacher copncerns as a basis for facilitating and personalizing staff development. *Teachers College Record, 80*(1), 36–53.

Harvey, O. J., Hunt, D. E., & Schroeder, H. M. (1961). *Conceptual systems and personality organization.* New York: Wiley.

Hersey, P., & Blanchard, K. H. (1988). *Management of organizational behavior: Utilizing human resources.* Englewood Cliffs, NJ: Prentice Hall.

Hickman, C. R., & Silva, M. A. (1984). *Creating excellence: Managing corporate culture, strategy, and change in the new age.* New York: New American Library.

Johnston, J. H., & Markle, G. C. (1988). *What research says to the middle level practitioner.* Columbus, OH: National Middle School Association.

Joyce, B., & Showers, B. (1988). *Student achievement through staff development.* New York: Longman.

Karp, H. B. (1984). Working with resistance. *Training and Development Journal, 38*(3), 69–73.

*138    Part Two • Developing a Sense of Responsiveness*

Kasak, D. T. (1988). Changeable you — The other transition in middle school. *The Middle School Journal, 19*(2), 14–15.

Levine, S. L. (1989). *Promoting adult growth in schools.* Boston: Allyn and Bacon.

Levinson, D. J. (1977). *The seasons in a man's life.* New York: Knopf.

Little, J. W. (1982). Norms of collegiality and experimentation: Workplace conditions of school success. *American Educational Research Journal, 19*(3), 325–340.

Loevinger, J. (1976). *Ego development.* San Francisco: Jossey-Bass.

McNergney, R. F., & Carrier, C. A. (1981). *Teacher development.* New York: Macmillan.

Neugarten, B. L. (1977). Personality and aging. In J. E. Birren, & K. W. Schaie (Eds.), *Handbook of psychology of aging.* New York: Van Nostrand Reingold.

New England League of Middle Schools. (1988). *Middle school program evaluation instrument.* Rowley, MA: Author.

Oja, S. N. (1979, April). *Toward a theory of staff development.* Paper presented at the American Educational Research Association Annual Conference, San Francisco.

Rogus, J. F. (1990). Developing a vision statement — Some considerations for principals. *NASSP Bulletin, 74*(523), 6–12.

Rubin, L. (1978). *The nature of teacher growth: The inservice education of teachers.* Boston: Allyn and Bacon.

Showers, B. (1985). Teachers coaching teachers. *Educational Leadership, 42*(6), 43–48.

Sprinthall, N. A., & Thies-Sprinthall, L. (1982). Career development of teachers. *Encyclopedia of educational research* (5th ed.). New York: Free Press.

Tyler, R. W. (1989). Personal conversation, Amherst, MA.

Whitbourne, S. K. (1986). *Adult development.* New York: Praeger.

Wood, F. H., & Thompson, S. R. (1980). Guidelines for better staff development. *Educational Leadership, 37*(4), 375–377.

# CHAPTER NINE

# Interdisciplinary Teaming and the Social Bonding of Middle Level Students

JOANNE M. ARHAR
*University of South Florida*

Interdisciplinary teaming has been advocated by middle level experts as the key feature of effective middle level programs (Alexander & George, 1981; Carnegie, 1989; Epstein & Mac Iver, 1990; George & Oldaker, 1985; Johnston & Markle, 1986; Merenbloom, 1986). Although not confined exclusively to the middle school, its use in elementary schools and high schools is generally *not* central to all other programs and practices. Interdisciplinary teaming has its historical roots in the *core* curriculum of the 1930s. The core curriculum was an attempt to break down the so-called artificial barriers between subjects through curriculum integration and provide teachers with the opportunity to know their individual students. To accomplish these ends, core curriculum enthusiasts advocated block scheduling and joint planning time for teachers. The focus here is the social organization of students and teachers into teams rather than curriculum organization. In this context, *interdisciplinary teaming* is commonly defined as the organization of two or more teachers from different disciplines who share the same group of students and share the responsibility for the curriculum, instruction, and evaluation of that group of students (Alexander & George, 1981).

Reformulating assumptions about human work relationships as well as the manner in which knowledge is presented are both dimensions of school restructuring in need of reexamination. It may be argued that without reorganizaing the social dimension of middle schools, little will happen in the way of developing a curriculum unique to the personal and social developmental needs of young adolescents. Without changes in the social organization of the delivery system, the incentive to reorganize curriculum to meet the needs of young adolescents resides in individual teachers who are held accountable for teaching academic disciplines, not for developing innovative interdisciplinary designs. The efforts of individual teachers may lead to some modification of a school's curriculum, but not the kind of sweeping changes that middle level curricularists feel is necessary.

A national survey of middle grades practices and trends (Epstein & Mac Iver, 1990) reports that principals "rate their programs higher overall and expect their students to have fewer problems" (p. 74) when their school includes interdisciplinary teaming, a practice responsive to the social, personal, and academic development of early adolescents. Interdisciplinary teaming is the first recommendation of the Carnegie Council on Adolescent Development in *Turning Points: Preparing American Youth for the 21st Century* (Carnegie, 1989). As a strategy for improving the educational experience for all middle grades students, and especially for at-risk students, the report recommends that middle grades schools "create small communities for learning where stable, close, mutually respectful relationships with adults and peers are considered fundamental for intellectual development and personal growth" (p. 9). One of the key elements of these communities is *students and teachers grouped together as teams*.

Theoretically, interdisciplinary teaming allows students to identify with a small group. Students are grouped and regrouped with the same peers for the subjects taught by their team of teachers.

> *The aim is to minimize the number of students who feel that no teacher knows them, that the teachers do not know how they are doing in other classes, or that no students know them well enough to accept them as friends. . . . Interdisciplinary teaming helps students build team spirit and improves attitudes and work habits because of the closer, more coherent supervision and caring that occurs on a team. (Epstein & Mac Iver, 1990, p. 34)*

Teaming has the potential to create an environment conducive to learning by reducing the stress of anonymity and isolation (Arhar, Johnston & Markle, 1988, 1989).

Equally as important, teaming has the potential to create a more professional work environment for teachers by providing them with the time to work with colleagues for the improvement of the educational program. By providing teachers with the opportunity for joint work through a common planning time, interdisciplinary teaming also offers teachers the potential cognitive and affective benefits of collaboration: thoughtful planning and reflective practice, ongoing professional development, increased satisfaction with work, increased efficacy, improved professionalism through extended roles, enhanced decision-making rights, control, and autonomy. Under professional conditions, teachers achieve greater satisfaction and productivity (Lieberman, 1990; Lieberman & Miller, 1986; Little, 1982; Rosenholtz, 1989; Scott & Smith, 1987). Thus, the conditions of teaming may enable teachers to develop instructional practices responsive to the developmental needs of young adolescents.

Two recent national surveys of middle level practices indicate that interdisciplinary teaming is on the rise. Alexander and McEwin (1989) report that interdisciplinary team organization of the four core subjects has increased in popularity over the past 20 years at every grade level from fifth to eighth. From a 10 percent random sample of 10,857 middle/junior high schools containing grades 5 through 9, 31 percent of fifth grades were organized into teams in 1988, as opposed to 3 percent in 1968; 38 percent of sixth grades were organized into teams in 1988, as opposed to 8 percent in 1968; 38 percent of seventh grades were teamed in 1988, as opposed to 6 percent in 1968; and 28 percent of eighth grades were teamed in 1988, as opposed to 6 percent in 1968. A survey of middle grades practices and trends reported by Epstein and Mac Iver (1990) indicates that an overall increase of 10 percent or more is anticipated in the use of interdisciplinary teams over the next three years. The greatest change in use of teaming is expected to be in schools with grades 7 through 9, typically called junior high schools. Yet, little systematic research on the outcomes of teaming for students has been undertaken.

Although researchers have attempted to justify the reorganization of students and teachers into teams by studying the effects of teaming on student achievement, the results of such studies have proven inconclusive. It appears that teaming is not less adequate an organizational strategy for middle level students in terms of verbal and math skills than departmentalization or self-contained classrooms. Only a handful of studies address the questions surrounding the psychosocial outcomes of teaming, but this growing body of literature suggests that student affective outcomes are influenced by this organizational arrangement (Arhar, Johnston, & Markle, 1989).

To address the concerns of practitioners about the efficacy of teaming in light of the additional cost involved in its implementation (cost for additional staff due to reduced teaching loads when additional time is given for common as well as individual planning periods) and because of the need for research in the area of the noncognitive outcomes of school reorganization, this chapter will develop a theoretical and empirical rationale for teaming. Because of the potential benefits of teaming for at-risk student populations, the rationale is based on the adolescent need for membership. A theory of school membership, based on students' need for social bonding with peers, teachers, and school, is presented to explain the importance of social bonding for student outcomes related to achievement as well as personal and social development. Teacher membership, an outcome of professional collaboration, is viewed as an enabler of student social bonding. Finally, a review of the literature of the psychosocial outcomes of teaming for students will provide a broad picture of the implications of teaming for practice and research.

## Adolescent Alienation

The fragmentation of human experience, resulting in alienation, is a central theme in contemporary social theory. Focusing this criticism on schools, Bowers (1985) argues that the "nihilistic" quality of school environments renders human action meaningless, fosters disillusionment, and produces a sense of rootlessness and estrangement.

Adolescents are particularly vulnerable to alienation. According to Brofenbrenner (1986), to be alienated is to lack a sense of belonging, to feel cut off from family, friends, school, or work—"the four worlds of childhood." It is during this time that adolescents seek independence. But it is also a time when group identity is needed so that the individual will become socially integrated. Thus, peer acceptance is sought. The role of the adult is to provide models of adult behavior. According to Erikson (1968), it is through the integration of the many influences in their lives (personal desires, peers, families, other adults) that adolescents will develop a clear sense of identity. The failure to integrate the self with other people leaves the adolescent with a feeling of aloneness, "a feeling that no one else is quite like you, and that you are not what other people want you to be" (Mackey & Appleman, 1984).

Under current conditions of rapid social, economic, and technological change, many young people, faced with their own developmental processes, feel isolated. Social forces that contribute to adolescent alienation include changes in the family structure from two-parent to one-parent families, decreased family stability, increased mobility, population increases, depersonalization of the individual, and new standards of sexual behavior. These features of modern life tend to fragment adolescent experience. Further, technological inventions, such as the computer and home video, have drawn many adolescents away from relationships into a state of isolation (Fetro, 1985).

Because of these changes, the basic human need for caring relationships with adults and the security of belonging to constructive peer groups frequently goes unmet in this critical stage of their lives. Some students handle early adolescence more successfully than others. For those who cannot cope with all of the changes and demands they encounter, "the engagement of many youth in learning diminishes, and their rate of alienation, substance abuse, absenteeism, and dropping out of school begins to rise" (Carnegie, 1989, p. 9).

### School Organization as a Contributor
### to Student Alienation

In an extensive review of the literature on alienation, Newmann (1981) directed attention to the structural aspects of the organization of instruction and the nature of human relations in schools as contributors to student alienation. He argued that these school features can affect their sense of belonging. He suggested that recent developments in school organization, such as larger school size, increasing specialization of staff, and diversification of curriculum, have contributed to a heightening of student alienation. *Turning Points* underscores the negative aspects of current school organization: "Most adolescents attend massive, impersonal schools, learn from unconnected and seemingly irrelevant curricula, know well and trust few adults in school and lack access to . . . counseling" (Carnegie, 1989, p. 13).

Increased subject specialization has oriented many teachers toward content at the expense of attention to students. Given the fragmentation of curriculum and scheduling, most teachers do not have the opportunity to see their students in other subjects, demonstrating other skills and abilities. According to Newmann (1981), "teachers' transient relationships with students for the sole purpose of teaching a single subject . . . creates barriers to understanding one another as individuals and to developing affiliative bonds" (p. 553). McPartland (1987) found that the responsibility for large numbers of students inhibits teachers' ability to attend to individual students. Consequently, specialized teachers are more likely to adopt a subject matter orientation that emphasizes knowledge expertise rather than a student orientation that emphasizes concern for individual students.

Other school organizational features that increase student disengagement include impersonal rules and regulations, lack of involvement in decision making, and institutional control of educational goals and means. In other words, when students feel that external forces are controlling their lives, increased levels of alienation develop (Calabrese & Seldin, 1987).

## Minimizing Student Alienation

According to Newmann (1981), three fundamental human needs must be met to minimize alienation: "the need for integration, or consistency and continuity in one's experience; the need for individuality; and the need for communality" (p. 549). *Individuality* refers to such things as personal expressions of ideas and the identification with certain values that distinguish one person from the next. Individuality also requires integrating oneself with others and with social institutions (Erikson, 1968). *Communality,* according to Newmann, is "the tendency to affiliate with others, to identify oneself with human groups, organizations, and causes. Through communal experience, humans form attachments with one another and establish a sense of belonging to one or more groups" (p. 550).

Newmann (1981) stated that stronger, trusting relationships are more likely to develop if students spend longer periods of time with teachers who define their roles in terms broader than classroom instruction. Extended time together in formal and informal activities gives students and teachers the opportunity to gain a better understanding of one another. Extended contact and extended roles thus generate a greater sense of communality.

Sources of alienation extend to relationships with peers. Newmann argued that instruction is organized to isolate students from each other. He cited an emphasis on individual achievement and the neglect of cooperative group work as a violation of students' need for communality.

The adolescent need for group identification as a means of self-definition is often frustrated by the fragmentation students experience in middle level schools. The result, for many adolescents, is an increasing sense of alienation. School reform, if it is to be meaningful, must take into consideration the impediments to membership posed by the way teachers and students are organized for work. Addressing these impediments increases the likelihood that students will feel a bonding to school, to teachers, and to peers, and decreases the likelihood that students will view school as inconsequential to their development into adulthood.

On the one hand, the literature on adolescent alienation describes the lack of success, isolation, apathy, incongruence, and disengagement experienced by many students. On the other hand, successful middle level schools offer new ways of organizing school routines to enhance student success, to prevent disengagement, and to promote a sense of membership, identity, and self-esteem. Reorganizing middle level schools into interdisciplinary teams has been proposed as a way of reducing student alienation and increasing student sense of membership.

Alienation is closely tied to an increasing sense of anonymity many students experience as they leave the elementary grades. At the middle level, this feeling is intensified because adolescents are entering a new developmental stage and beginning to form their sense of individual identity in relation to the larger society. Leaving the elementary school, where students learn in self-contained classrooms with one teacher and a group of peers who get to know them well, young adolescents often enter large, impersonal junior high schools, where they meet seven different teachers from different departments and seven different sets of classmates as they move from subject to subject. Any child is likely to feel somewhat overwhelmed and lost in such a setting. Vulnerable students, those with unstable family lives and previous lack of school success, experience even more difficulty. In large impersonal schools, many students come to believe that no one cares about them.

Theoretically, when interdisciplinary teaming is implemented as it is designed, students are much more likely to feel that they belong to the school, that they are known by name, and that at least one adult cares about them. Consistency of teacher expectations and rules makes it easier for students to figure out how to interact with their teachers. Organizing teachers into teams allows teachers to share information about individual students who may need extra help and work together in practical ways to coordinate such things as homework, exams, and communication with parents and school support personnel.

Moreover, when the team focus is on students rather than subject areas, teachers are more likely to adapt curriculum to individual basic skills needs. If the team is interdisciplinary, teachers attempt to integrate disciplines rather than fragment them, thus helping adolescents see the relationships between knowledge, skill, and practical application. This interdisciplinary approach is particularly well suited to the young adolescents' need to make personal and social sense out of what they learn. In addition, opportunities to refer to knowledge and skills from different disciplines increases academic rigor because students can be held accountable for learning in multiple settings.

Finally, the organization of students into teams provides the opportunity for students to develop stronger ties with peers. The literature on cooperative learning, although a separate issue from teaming, indicates that when students get to know each other well under carefully structured circumstances that promote interdependence, there is as greater likelihood that they will form friendships with students representing a wider spectrum of social and educational backgrounds, and that they will be able to identify more closely with others, understanding their needs and motivations (Johnson, Johnson, & Holubec, 1986).

According to Paul George, "Certain programs, when present, strengthen everything else in the school. In middle schools, it's what ever gives you smallness within bigness" (Massachusetts Advocacy Center, 1986). George, like Lipsitz (1984), emphasized that it is the way that teachers and students are organized to work and to learn that is the key feature of exemplary middle schools. Others argue further that "personalization is a matter of organizational design rather than of individual teacher's values and practices" (McLaughlin, Talbert, Kahne, & Powell, 1990, p. 235).

# A Theoretical Rationale for Interdisciplinary Teaming

### Social Bonding Theory

Social bonding theory is part of a larger body of literature on student participation and identification as mediators of school outcomes. This literature views student disengagement from school as a developmental process. For some students, disengagement culminates in early school leaving (Finn, 1989). In *Causes of Delinquency,* Hirschi (1969) develops a theory of deviancy, which assumes that "delinquent acts result when an individual's bond to society is weak or broken" (p. 16). Although this chapter does not deal directly with deviancy—truancy, chronic misbehavior, and dropping out of school—it does focus on the emotional antecedents of delinquency—lack of bonding to school, teachers, and peers.

According to Hirschi (1969), deviancy is the result of an individual's weak bonds to conventional society. A person free of bonds is *more likely* to commit delinquency acts than a person strongly tied to conventional society. Hirschi assumes that social institutions, such as schools, represent middle-class values. He does not question those values but argues that the extent to which individuals value such institutions represents the extent to which they value the outcomes asociated with membership in that institution.

These bonds, according to Hirschi, have four elements that encourage conformity: *attachment,* or concern with the opinions of others; *commitment,* a rational decision to behave in acceptable ways because of gratification of immediate and long-term goals; *involvement,* the expenditure of time and energy in institutionally encouraged behaviors, which precludes involvement in delinquent behaviors; and *belief,* a view that the principles encouraged by the institution are valid. These four elements also form the basis of current theoretical work used to explain the school's role in preventing early school leaving.

### Theory of School Membership

Wehlage, Rutter, Smith, Lesko, and Fernandez (1989) build on Hirshi's work to explain dropping out of school as a function of a lack of school membership. Membership depends on social bonding, the extent to which an individual forms meaningful and satisfying links with a social group and the extent to which the group encourages the formation of those bonds. In *Reducing the Risk: Schools as Communities of Support,* Wehlage and colleagues sum up their theory of school membership:

> *The theory hypothesizes school membership as the foundation upon which educational engagement is built. Interaction between these two concepts is indicated. Engagement and membership are shown as intermediate goals that schools must promote as a way of helping students arrive at the outcomes of achievement and personal and social development. (p. 279)*

According to Wehlage and colleagues, *social bonding* is defined as "a social-psychological state or outcome in which a student is attached, committed, involved, and has belief in the norms, activities and people of an institution" (p. 168). A student is socially bonded to the extent that he or she is attached to adults and peers, committed to the norms of the school, involved in school activities, and believes in the legitimacy and efficacy of the institution. Thus, this theory builds on Hirschi's (1969) four conditions of social bonding.

*Attachment* refers to social and emotional ties to others. When an individual cares about what other people think and expect, he or she feels a personal stake in meeting the expectations of others and conforming to the norms of appropriate behavior as socially defined. If attachment to individuals is missing or weak, one can act without regard for the feelings and expectations of others. According to this theory, attachment is reciprocal. When students have low attachment to teachers and administrators, they do not care what these people think about them, especially as students. In return, students perceive that these adults do not care about them. Under these conditions, students feel disengaged from the school and may chose to leave.

Whereas attachment emphasizes the emotional, *commitment* emphasizes the rational side of participation in school. Commitment stems from a rational calculation of whether remaining in school is worth putting up with unattractive demands. For the uncommitted student, conformity to school demands does not appear to yield a worthwhile payoff.

*Involvement* means engagement in academic or nonacademic school-sponsored activities.

> *If school activities fail to engender involvement . . . students drop out psychologically, as evidenced by their passivity and boredom. . . . Thus, schools must be sensitive to the relative involvement . . . they can achieve in comparison with other attractive activities. . . . This is especially a problem if the range of activities in school is relatively small, an elite group of students appears to dominate these activities, and success is awarded to a few. (p. 170)*

Without *belief* in the legitimacy or efficacy of schools, social bonding will not occur. Students vary in their beliefs about the value of school and its potential benefits. The potential dropout may question the efficacy of schooling to fulfill his or her goals. Evidence suggests, however, that even dropouts do believe in the value of getting an education. It is the interaction between personal background variables and school that prohibit full expression of that belief.

Membership theory recognizes that schools may have policies and practices that inhibit the development of bonds. "The goal of school membership does not suggest that all students in conflict with their norms of public schooling are socially deficient and must change their ways to conform to the demands of the institution" (p. 171). Thus, the concept of school membership includes a greater degree of reciprocity between students and school than does the traditional concept of social bonding. McLaughlin and colleagues (1990) further argued that in personalized schools, authority is "interpersonal and institutional — earned and granted within social relations and defined in terms of organizational rights and obligations" (p. 235). Accountability is more a matter of a "social contract" between teachers and students than adherence to impersonal rules and regulations.

Many students, particularly students who are in danger of dropping out, fail to experience a sense of membership. According to membership theory,

> *The specific impediments to both engagement and membership are the leverage points for practitioners—adjustment, difficulty, incongruence, isolation, and lack of extrinsic and intrinsic rewards. It is this notion of impediments that makes the theory helpful to practitioners. By identifying impediments within the school, educators can focus on those conditions that block students' movement into membership and engagement. Educators can use this theory to analyze their school and to invent ways of altering the experiences of students. (Wehlage et al., 1989, p. 279)*

The four common impediments are *adjustment, difficulty, incongruence,* and *isolation.* Academic failure and alienation from the school may result if students fail to *adjust* to the new demands experienced in the transitions between elementary, middle, and high school. Students need to adjust to new peer groups, new teachers, a more impersonal environment, fragmentation in curriculum, and teaching methods. *Difficulty* in academic matters, particularly difficulty in "sustaining interest and effort," is often a precursor to academic failure. If students are to become socially bonded to school, academic success is essential. "*Incongruence* describes the personal and social match between the student and the institution" (p. 182). In the absence of opportunities for success, students, particularly nonacademically oriented students, will find school meaningless, thus increasing the feeling of alienation. *Isolation* from meaningful interaction with adults and peers impedes student membership to school. "Of great importance in student persistence is the amount and warmth of faculty-student interaction *outside* the classroom" (p. 189).

School structure, when viewed from the perspective of social bonding, imposes impediments relevant to adjustment, difficulty, incongruence, and isolation. Certain structural elements, such as grouping of students and departmentalization, may pose difficulties for students because of the problems of transition from a self-contained, student-centered environment to a more fragmented subject-centered environment. Students may find it difficult to adjust to the new set of curricular and social circumstances in middle level schools that are subject centered. They may also find it difficult to make meaningful connections between curricular areas because of the emphasis on discrete disciplines. The mismatch between the adolescent cognitive need to view knowledge as an integrated whole and the fragmentation of traditional curriculum further impedes social bonding.

Membership is important for all students, but it is of critical importance for middle level students who are also faced with developmental changes and formation of identity. Milgram (1985) goes so far as to say that middle level students actually define themselves by their group membership. For at-risk students in particular, with backgrounds of school failure and lack of support of strong homes and communities outside the school, a strong sense of membership is essential to persistence in school. When identification with social institutions outside of the school is weakened, membership in school becomes critical for adolescent development into adulthood.

Middle level advocates recommend practices that directly address the student need to belong (Alexander & George, 1981; Erb & Doda, 1989; Lipsitz, 1981). Successful middle level schools offer new ways of organizing school routines to promote school membership, as well as student success, identity, and self-esteem—conditions that not only address the antecedents of deviance (dropping out, poor attendance, retention, and discipline problems) but also meet normal adolescent needs. Relationship building is the keystone of middle school philosophy. But, as McLaughlin and colleagues (1990) argued, the resulting "personalization" is more a matter of organizational design than of individual teacher's preferences and behavior.

Underlying the model of school membership and student engagement is another set of factors cited by Wehlage and colleagues that enable schools to work more effectively with students. For educators to be in a position to help students overcome the impediments to membership, teachers must work in a professional environment that grants them the authority and resources to shape school practice and policy.

An explanation of the relationship between teacher professionalism and student membership as well as a school's structural and organizational response to student membership is the focus of the theory of teacher collaboration.

## Teacher Collaboration

A second theoretical consideration for teaming stems from the benefits of collaboration for teachers. Recent literature, both popular and empirical, has dealt with the need to make teaching a more rewarding profession. Specifically, the call has been to make teaching truly a profession — one that values intelligence and initiative rather than conformity and acquiescence. The Carnegie Forum on Education and the Economy (1986) calls for a restructuring of schools to provide for a more professional environment for teaching. More specifically, it calls for collaborative relationships in which

> *teachers work together in a school, not separately in isolated classrooms; they take mutual responsibility for the curriculum and instruction on the basis of thinking together and individually about the substance of their work — children's learning — and how to make themselves better at it. (p. 58)*

The Massachusetts Advocacy Center (1988) refers to the need for schools to create *membership* for teachers, an outcome worthy in itself, but by virtue of the personal and professional satisfaction it affords to teachers, an outcome also linked to student membership. The argument here is that teachers who value their membership in the teaching profession because of the respect and status it affords them, and likewise value their membership in a school because of the norms of support and collegiality, will be able to provide the support students need in order to feel connected to school.

Typical school organization often promotes isolation and individuality of teachers. Bureaucratic structures and norms of isolation prevent professional interaction among teachers. Teachers are thus cut off from professional growth opportunities afforded by peers. Further, teachers have few decision-making rights and suffer from low status as a profession. Fine (1986) has suggested that teachers who receive little respect in school will be unable to give students the respect they deserve, thus contributing to student alienation.

Research suggests that schools in which student learning gains are the greatest do not isolate teachers, but rather encourage professional interactions and collegial relations (Armor, Conry-Osequera, Cox, King, McDonnel, Pascal, Pauly, & Zellman, 1976; Little, 1982; Rutter, Maughan, Mortimore, Houston, & Smith, 1979). In these effective schools, teaching is defined as a collective rather than an individual responsibility. Under these conditions, professional growth is an ongoing, collective responsibility, where analysis, evaluation, and experimentation with one's colleagues set the conditions under which teachers improve (Ashton & Webb, 1986).

In collaborative settings, teacher interactions arise out of professional rather than merely social concerns. Instead of seeking sympathy from colleagues for the difficulty of dealing with misbehaving or undermotivated children and working conditions that undermine professionalism, teachers in collaborative schools seek new ideas (Cohen, 1981). Because colleagues work together to solve problems, teachers in collaborative settings feel a greater sense of efficacy. They come to believe that they can make a difference with even the most difficult children (Ashton & Webb, 1986). In collaborative settings, teaching is defined as inherently difficult work. Therefore, request for advice and giving help is viewed as a legitimate rather than esteem-threatening activity (Rosenholtz, 1989). Because colleagues in effective schools help each other improve, faculty interactions increase, whereas in isolated schools, a decrease in teacher interactions over time convinces teachers that they do not hold the answers to difficult problems of curriculum, instruction, and student learning.

Interdisciplinary teaming offers teachers the opportunities for collaborative work. Ideally, teachers on teams cross disciplinary lines to help students see how math, science, English, social studies and other subjects are integrated in real life. Teamed teachers not only coordinate content but also jointly address problems and needs of individual students, meet with parents, revise schedules for classes that need more time, group and regroup students to match lessons to abilities, and plan assemblies, trips, and other special events.

A regularly scheduled common planning time has been cited by advocates of teaming as an essential resource needed to facilitate collaborative planning (Alexander & George, 1981; Carnegie, 1989). Mac Iver (1990) indicated that the greater the amount of common planning time, the greater the amount of time the team spends coordinating content, diagnosing individual student needs, planning special events, conducting parent conferences, regrouping, and rescheduling. The satisfaction, sense of control, and efficacy associated with these conditions increases the likelihood that teachers will be able to create the conditions necessary for student social bonding to teachers as well as to school and to peers.

The theoretical premises outlined in this section provide a framework for the discussion of interdisciplinary teaming as an organizational intervention with the potential for creating a sense of community and membership for students as well as teachers. In the next section, the literature on middle level interdisciplinary teaming will be examined from the perspective of psychosocial outcomes for students. More specifically, interdisciplinary teaming will be viewed as an intervention with the potential to increase student social bonding to school, peers, and teachers, through the conditions of attachment, commitment, involvement, and belief in the efficacy of schooling.

## The Value of Interdisciplinary Teaming

From the previous sections, it is clear that teaming has important effects on the organizational climate of the school, the satisfaction and professional development of teachers, and collaboration within the workplace. It is tempting, therefore, to conclude that any practice that has such wide-reaching influences in the school must affect student learning and school adjustment in equally potent ways.

Caution must be exercised in applying this logic, however. Teaming is an organizational change that *may* affect the way instruction is delivered in the school. It is also a way of restructuring human interaction among teachers and, possibly, among students, so that the school *can* become a collection of smaller, relatively cohesive groups. In other words, teaming creates an opportunity for things to be done differently in the school; it does not assure that they will. Therein lies the first problem: No organizational practice can guarantee that its major tenets will be implemented if the implementation depends on the idiosyncratic decision of members of the organization to participate. And, while a team teaching arrangement may allow teacher collaboration to occur, it cannot compel it. Nor can it compel cross-disciplinary planning or instruction. As with all organizational concepts, teaming is at the mercy of the people who work on the teams.

Beyond the question of whether the major principles of teaming actually ever get implemented is the question of whether the implementation will affect the school's clients. Collaborative planning by teachers, a greater sense of camaraderie among staff, and greater professional development among teachers are, themselves, desirable outcomes. Whether these outcomes have an effect on the nature of student learning, though, is a very different issue. Establishing links between organizational changes and operations is fairly straightforward; when organizations change, the things the organization does change as well. The links between an organizational change and the ultimate product of the organization are much more tenuous. So, while we can be almost certain tht teaming changes how schools work, we cannot assume that those procedural changes alter the school's "product" — student learning and behavior — in the same way.

Clearly, because of its popularity, there is a strong *belief* among school people that teaming benefits the students. Is that belief rooted in empirical reality? The remainder of this review is devoted to that question.

In *Secondary School Environments and Student Outcomes* (1981), Epstein reviews the literature on school climate and its effects on students. According to Epstein, school climate is assumed to shape or motivate the achievement, behavior, and attitudes of students. Further, we cannot understand student behavior without examining the environment in which it occurs. School climate, environment, and context are used synonymously to characterize the specific processes or practices of a school or teacher's classroom. The social-emotional tone of the school, which stems from interpersonal relationships (Schmuck, 1982), determines to a large extent whether students will come to school, whether they will learn, and what they will learn in basic skills and in other skills that affect their chances for success as adults.

Epstein indicates that some aspects of school climate have been consistently identified as potentially important social organizational factors that may more directly affect psychosocial skills and indirectly affect achievement. These social climate features include small school size or "school-within-a-school" organization and programs that increase student-teacher interaction and permit flexible scheduling of time for learning.

What follows is a review of how characteristics of schools' social organization may be linked to student psychosocial outcomes. More specifically, the review focuses on the social organization of students and teachers into interdisciplinary teams and its potential for increasing student sense of affiliation with school, teachers, and peers.

Advocates of middle level education programs in general and teaming in particular have long argued that a necessary goal for the middle level school is the affective and social development of children. In the past decade, these advocates have received support for this position from much of the research on school effectiveness, notably that of Rutter and colleagues (1979).

## Interracial Relationships

Both Metz (1986) and Damico (1982) and colleagues found that teaming has an effect on interracial relationships in the school. White students reported having more black friends in team-organized schools than in traditional arrangements. Furthermore, white students' attitudes toward black students were significantly better in team arrangements. Black students' friendship patterns and attitudes were not significantly different as a result of school organization, but the trend in those data follow the same pattern as for the white students.

Metz's work on urban desegregated middle schools speculated that faculty norms, teaching practices, and student attitude toward learning are all interrelated. In the schools that employed teaming, students expressed more enthusiasm about school and their teachers than did the students at the more traditional school (with departmentalized structure). Interracial cooperation in the classroom and interracial friendships were more common in the two team-organized schools. Conversely, racial tensions were more evident in the nonteamed school in this study. The staff at one of the teamed schools felt that low levels of conflict, which they attributed to the team structure, allowed them to help students cultivate their self-control and social responsibility. By modeling cooperative behavior, teachers felt that they were encouraging similar behavior on the part of their students. In contrast, teachers in the departmentalized school emphasized coverage of content rather than the social and group development in the class.

## School Environment and Student Behavior

Sinclair (1980) found that there was a difference in student perception of school environment between teamed and departmentalized schools, with team-taught students finding the environment to be more supportive and facilitative. Gamsky (1970) found that team arrangements positively affected student attitude toward teachers, interest in subject matter, sense of personal freedom, and sense of self-reliance. George and Oldaker (1985) reported improvement in school discipline and student personal development as a result of their enrollment in middle schools, a principal component of which was team teaching. In general, they found that tardiness and truancy decreased, as well as school vandalism and theft.

> *Approximately 80% (of the sample) noted significant reduction in office referrals and suspensions, while close to 60% expelled fewer students after the transition. Almost 90% observed that teacher and staff confidence in managing disruptive students increased, diminishing administrative involvement in discipline in many schools. (p. 31)*

One-fourth of their respondents gave anecdotal evidence specifically related to team organization. These respondents claimed that this organizational arrangement enabled teachers to develop consistent procedures for handling disruptions.

George and Oldaker (1985) also offer anecdotal evidence that teaming, in combination with the resulting teacher-based guidance that grows naturally from this arrangement, facilitated productive peer relationships and reduced conflict. Student emotional health, creativity, and confidence in self-directed learning, as well as student self-concept, were also positively affected.

George (1987) studied the long-term teacher-student relationships in a Florida middle school and found that the long-term relationships that resulted from a team arrangement in which students and teachers remain together for up to three years helped to improve discipline. George says that "teachers saw themselves as being much more willing to attempt behavior management alternatives when conventional or accustomed techniques failed to achieve the necessary results" (p. 10). These teamed teachers were less likely to use formalized, routine discipline procedures and were able to match both control strategies and consequences to the individual child. Both teachers and students agreed there was a stronger sense of student pride in their group and in their school as a whole. Students felt that they were more self-confident, that they had more friends, that they "belonged" to the school, and that they could be friends with all kinds of people.

Doda (1986) found that long-term, multiage grouping, often a feature of team arrangements, prevented teachers from "writing off" students who were difficult to teach. Because teachers knew that they would be working with the student over a longer time period than just one year, they were less willing to abandon efforts to reach a difficult child, knowing that they would be "finished" with him or her at the end of the year. Middle school teachers tend to focus on long-term goals and tried to create an environment that encouraged student development and happiness.

## Dropout Prevention and Student Bonding to Teachers, Peers, and School

According to the report, *Before It's Too Late: Dropout Prevention in the Middle Grades* (Massachusetts Advocacy Center and The Center for Early Adolescence, 1988), school structures based on effective teams is key to improving the holding power of middle level schools. The report echoed the recommendations of other researchers, child advocates, and educators, which call for structural reforms aimed at "smallness-within-bigness" as a means to promote a sense of inclusion for all students, as opposed to tinkering with programs and practices.

Several studies of middle school organization found links between teaming and social bonding, adding support to the idea that teams have the potential to prevent students from dropping out. Epstein and Mac Iver (1990) analyzed data obtained from *Education in the Middle Grades,* a national survey of practices and trends using a representative sample of principals in public schools containing grade 7. The survey was designed to examine the use and effects of practices believed to be responsive to the needs of young adolescents. Epstein and Mac Iver's study hypothesized that schools with high dropout rates may adopt interdisciplinary teaming and other responsive practices (advisory groups, remediation programs, and grading practices such as progress grades, effort grades, and written comments) in an effort to "rescue potential dropouts" (p. 16).

What they found supported their hypothesis. In schools with a deeper commitment to interdisciplinary teaming, principals expected a higher dropout rate than would otherwise be predicted based on background and demographic variables. The researchers concluded that "it may be that a school's current expected dropout rate influences the openness to making a commitment to interdisciplinary teaming" (p. 15). This logic helps to explain the study's finding that schools serving lower-ability students were more likely to have a deeper commitment to interdisciplinary teaming than other schools.

School organization also has the potential to increase student sense of social bonding. When comparing nearly 5,000 seventh-graders in teamed- and nonteamed-matched schools on three measures of social bonding, Arhar (1990) found that student social bonding to teachers and to school was greater in teamed schools. Bonding to peers appeared to be influenced more by socioeconomic status than by the school intervention of teaming, suggesting that further study of peer groups from varying socioeconomic backgrounds is warranted.

Although the effect sizes on all three measures of social bonding are small, they do have implications for larger populations. Research suggests that a linear relationship exists between social bonding and dropping out of school (Finn, 1989). Research also suggests that school organization has an impact on keeping students in school (Newmann, 1981). If a linear relationship can in fact be established between social bonding and dropping out of school, small effect sizes could drastically reduce the dropout rate. Thus, interdisciplinary teaming, a low-cost intervention, has the potential for making a dramatic change in the number of students who leave school before graduation.

As might be expected, all research conclusions are not consistent with those reported above. Odetola, Erickson, Bryan, and Walker (1972) found that middle school students taught by team-teaching methods were not necessarily less alienated from the school than those in traditional settings, and the students taught by teacher teams indicated the greatest sense of powerlessness. Middle level students taught in conventional arrangements also gave the most positive responses to questions dealing with pride in or happiness with their schools. Sinclair (1980) found no significant differences between students in team-teaching arrangements and departmentalized arrangements in student attitudes toward their teachers.

Lipsitz (1984) studied four exceptionally successful middle level schools and found that they all used some variety of team arrangement. Ironically, the teachers in the school were not willing to attribute their success to any particular organizational arrangement. They were able to imagine that other, competing arrangements might be as successful, although satisfaction with the team arrangement was high. However, as Lipsitz concludes, "organizational ingenuity is possible in any school, reducing isolation by allowing for the small student focus groups and joint teacher planning time that characterize the four successful schools" (p. 200). Despite the fact that ingenuity is not confined to a given organizational type, it appears that the essential elements noted by Lipsitz seem to be characteristic of team arrangements.

## Conclusion

Does teaming make a difference in student outcomes? The answer is that it probably does, but not in direct, easily discernible ways. It appears as if teaming is a manifestation of a commitment on the part of teachers to engage in teacher-student relationships that facilitate growth and individual student development. That teaming causes the philosophical commitment is unlikely; that it gives teachers the ability to translate this commitment into action is almost certain.

More importantly, teaming creates conditions that are directly related to student social bonding. It reduces isolation and anonymity; it allows teachers to know their students quite well; and it permits teachers to "gang up" on students in positive ways to affect their learning. Lipsitz (1984) says

> *Organizational structure establishes continuity in adult-child relationships and opportunities for the lives of students and adults to cross in mutually meaningful ways. In each school, students express their appreciation for being cared about and known. Students seem to be actively aware of being liked, which is notable only because, in most schools, young adolescents are generally disliked. (p. 181)*

It is the ability of teams to create a sense of smallness within largeness, a sense of community within a more impersonal environment, that makes it an intermediary between students and academic and social outcomes. Teaming has the potential, if implemented in the spirit of student centeredness, to help young adolescents become academically involved in school work as well as to become more bonded to an intimate group of teachers and peers. Through coordination of curriculum, emphasis on the individual, social and educational needs of the learner, flexibility of scheduling to provide extended time for classes that need it, special events that enhance the group identity of the team, and close relationships with parents to solve problems and provide assistance, students may come to reap the benefits of a school commitment to their welfare.

### Recommendations for Further Research

Historically, research on dropout prevention has focused on either the unalterable characteristics students bring to school with them *or* school impediments to successful completion of school. The contribution made by Wehlage and colleagues (1989) is the recognition of the interaction of these two variables. Although the work of Wehlage and others suggests a link between social bonding and student dropping out of school, further research is needed to establish such a liner relationship. Such research would lay the groundwork for study of the relationship between interdisciplinary teaming and dropping out of school, as well as other student outcomes such as attendance and discipline.

Another area of study is the potential of interdisciplinary teams to minimize the negative impact of poverty on student social bonding. How can teachers and students interact on teams in ways that will help to overcome the adjustment difficulties students from low SES families bring to school? Because of extended roles assumed by teamed teachers, teams are an ideal place to help students develop the social and academic skills necessary to school success.

How does variation in the way teams are implemented affect student outcomes? Do factors such as multiage grouping, teacher preparation and certification, ability grouping, and school grade span influence the extent to which students bond to the school, to their teachers, and to their peers? What about the implementation process and its effect on student bonding?

Finally, further research on the collaborative behaviors of teachers and students in teamed and nonteamed schools may enable researchers to link specific behaviors and conditions to the bonding of students as well as to specific information about the elements of collaboration that promote bonding. Such research may ultimately prove beneficial to practitioners concerned with promoting the bonding of at-risk students.

Many factors that affect students and their membership in schools are outside of the influence of the school. Poverty, family background, language, and personal problems are among the factors that impact the success of young adolescents in school. But the concern here is with the things that *schools* can do to increase student sense of social bonding. Interdisciplinary teaming offers schools the opportunity to positively influence student bonding to school, to teachers, and to peers. Qualitative research needs to be conducted to find out more about the process of building membership through social bonds. Researchers need to get into teams and team-planning sessions to observe teacher interactions during planning time, teacher performances in the classroom, and the processes by which students become socially bonded.

## References

Alexander, W. M., & George, P. S. (1981). *The exemplary middle school.* Chicago: Holt, Rinehart and Winston.

Alexander, W. M., & McEwin, C. K. (1989). *Schools in the middle: Status and progress.* Columbus, OH: National Middle School Association.

Arhar, J. M. (1990). The effects of interdisciplinary teaming on social bonding of middle level students. In J. L. Irvin (Ed.), *Research in middle level education:*

Selected studies (pp. 1–10). Columbus, OH: National Middle School Association.

Arhar, J. M., Johnston, J. J., & Markle, G. C. (1988). The effects of teaming and other collaborative arrangements. *Middle School Journal, 19*(4), 22–25.

Arhar, J. M., Johnston, J. H., & Markle, G. C. (1989). The effects of teaming on students. *Middle School Journal, 20*(3), 24–27.

Armor, D., Conry-Osequera, P., Cox, M., King, N., McDonnel, L., Pascal, A., Pauly, E., & Zellman, G. (1976). *Analysis of the school preferred reading program in selected Los Angeles minority schools.* Santa Monica, CA: Rand Corporation.

Ashton, P. T., & Webb, R. B. (1986). *Making a difference: Teacher's sense of efficacy and student achievement.* New York: Longman.

Bowers, C. A. (1985). Culture against itself: Nihilism as an element in recent educational thought. *American Journal of Education, 93*(4), 465–490.

Brofenbrenner, U. (1986). Alienation and the four worlds of childhood. *Phi Delta Kappan, 67*(6), 430–436.

Calabrese, R. L., & Seldin, C. A. (1987). A contextual analysis of alienation among school constituencies. *Urban Education, 22*(2), 1–7.

Carnegie Council on Adolescent Development's Task Force on Education of Young Adolescents. (1989). *Turning points: Preparing American youth for the 21st century.* Washington, DC: Carnegie Council on Adolescent Development, a program of Carnegie Corporation of New York.

Carnegie Forum on Education and the Economy. (1986). *A nation prepared: Teachers for the 21st century.* New York: The Carnegie Foundation.

Cohen, E. (1981). Sociology looks at team teaching. *Research in Sociology of Education and Educational Socialization, 2,* 163–193.

Damico, S. (1982). The impact of school organization on interracial contact among students. *Journal of Educational Equity and Leadership, 2*(3), 238–252.

Doda, N. M. (1986). School organization and teachers' sense of efficacy. In P. T. Ashton & R. B. Webb (Eds.), *Making a difference: Teachers sense of efficacy and student achievement* (pp. 91–123). New York: Longman.

Epstein, J. (1981). *Secondary school environments and student outcomes: A review and annotated bibliography.* (Report No. 315). Baltimore, MD: Center for Social Organization of Schools, The Johns Hopkins University.

Epstein, J. L., & Mac Iver, D. J. (1990). *Education in the middle grades: Overview of national practices and trends.* Columbus, OH: National Middle School Association.

Epstein, J. L., & McPartland, J. M. (1988). *Education in the middle grades: A national survey of practices and trends.* Baltimore: Johns Hopkins University Center for Research on Elementary and Middle Schools.

Erb, T. O., & Doda, N. A. (1989). *Team organization: Promise—Practices and possibilities.* Washington, DC: National Education Association.

Erikson, E. (1968). *Identity, youth and crisis.* New York: Norton.

Fetro, J. V. (1985). *Adolescent alienation: Assessment and application.* Paper presented at the Annual Meeting of the American Public Health Association, Washington, DC.

Fine, M. (1986). Why urban adolescents drop into and out of public high school. *Teachers College Record, 87*(3), 393–409.

Finn, J. D. (1989). Withdrawing from school. *Review of Educational Research, 59*(2), 117–142.

Gamsky, N. (1970). Team teaching, student achievement and attitudes. *Journal of Experimental Education, 39*(1), 42–45.

George P. (1987). *Long-term teacher-student relationships: A middle school case study.* Columbus, OH: National Middle School Association.

George, P., & Oldaker, L. (1985). *Evidence for the middle school.* Columbus, OH: National Middle School Association.

Hirschi, T. (1969). *Causes of delinquency.* Los Angeles: University of California Press.

Johnson, D. W., Johnson, R. T., & Holubec, E. J. (1986). *Circles of learning: Cooperation in the classroom.* Edina, MN: Interaction.

Johnston, J. H., & Markle, G. C. (1986). *What research says to the middle level practitioner.* Columbus, OH: National Middle School Association.

Lieberman, A. (Ed.). (1990). *Schools as collaborative cultures: Creating the future now.* New York: Falmer Press.

Lieberman, A., & Miller, L. (1986). *Teachers, their world and their work: Implications for school improvement.* Washington, DC: Association for Supervision and Curriculum Development.

Lipsitz, J. (1981, March). *Early adolescence: Social-psychological issues.* Paper presented at the Association for Supervision and Curriculum Development Annual Convention, St. Louis.

Lipsitz, J. (1984). *Successful schools for young adolescents.* New Brunswick, NJ: Transaction Books.

Little, J. W. (1982). Norms of collegiality and experimentation: Workplace conditions of school success. *American Educational Research Journal, 19*(3), 325–340.

Mac Iver, D. J. (1990). Meeting the needs of young adolescents: Advisory groups, interdisciplinary teaching teams, and school transition programs. *Phi Delta Kappan, 71*(6), 458–464.

Mac Iver, D. J., & Epstein, J. L. (1989). *Responsive education in the middle grades: Teacher teams, advisory groups, remedial instruction, school transition programs, and report card entries.* (Report No. 46). Baltimore: Johns Hopkins University Center for Research on Elementary and Middle School.

Mackey, J., & Appleman, D. (1984). Broken connections: The alienated adolescent in the 80's. *Curriculum Review, 24*(5), 14–20.

Massachusetts Advocacy Center. (1986). *The way out: Student exclusion practices in Boston middle schools.* Boston: Author.

Massachusetts Advocacy Center. (1988). *Before it's too late: Dropout prevention in the middle grades.* Boston: Author.

McLaughlin, M., Talbert, J., Kahne, J., & Powell, J. (1990). Constructing a personalized school environment. *Phi Delta Kappan, 72*(3), 230–235.

McPartland, J. M. (1987). *Balancing high quality subject-matter instruction with positive student-teacher relations in the middle grades.* (Report No. 15). Baltimore: Johns Hopkins University Center for Research on Elementary and Middle School.

Merenbloom, E. Y. (1986). *The team process in the middle school: A handbook for teachers* (2nd ed.). Columbus, OH: National Middle School Association.

Metz, M. H. (1986). *Different by design: The context and character of three magnet schools.* New York: Routlage and Keegan Paul.

Milgram, J. I. (1985). The development of young adolescents. In J. H. Johnston & J. H. Lounsbury (Eds.), *How fares the ninth grade?* (pp. 5–9). Reston, VA: National Association of Secondary School Principals.

Newmann, F. M. (1981). Reducing student alienation in high schools: Implications of theory. *Harvard Educational Review, 51*(4), 546–564.

Odetola, T., Erickson, E. L., Bryan, C. L., & Walker, L. (1972). Organizational structure and student alienation. *Educational Administration Quarterly, 8,* 15–25.

Rosenholtz, S. (1989). *Teachers workplace: A study of social organizations.* New York: Longman.

Rutter, M., Maughan, B., Mortimore, P., Houston, J., & Smith, A. (1979). *Fifteen thousand hours: Secondary schools and their effects on children.* Cambridge, MA: Harvard University Press.

Schmuck, R. A. (1982, April). *The school organization and classroom interaction once again: School climate.* Paper presented at the 1982 Annual Meeting of the American Educational Research Association, New York.

Scott, J. J., & Smith, S. C. (1987). *From isolation to collaboration: Improving the work environment of teaching.* Prepared for the North Central Regional Educational Laboratory by the ERIC Clearinghouse on Educational Management, University of Oregon.

Sinclair, R. (1980). *The effect of middle school staff organizational patterns on student perceptions of teacher performances, student perceptions of school environment and student academic achievement.* Unpublished Doctoral Dissertation, Miami University.

Wehlage, G. G., Rutter, R. A., Smith, G. A., Lesko, N., & Fernandez, R. R. (1989). *Reducing the risk: Schools as communities of support.* Philadelphia: Falmer Press.

# CHAPTER TEN

# Teacher Advisory: The Fourth R

NEILA A. CONNORS
*Valdosta State College*

Early adolescence is a crucial stage in human development.

*In their struggle for identity, many adolescents come to view themselves as creatures apart from humanity, alienated from the mainstream. They perpetuate such thoughts as "no one feels the way I do about anything — my problems are larger than life, unlike those of anyone else" and "no one cares about me." In short, the search for identity, one of the principle tasks of adolescence, leaves many young people feeling alone and without hope. (Gerler, 1986, p. 36)*

These feelings of uncertainty and confusion in students demand that all aspects of the middle school program contribute to every student's personal growth and development. The core of this effort lies in the teacher advisory program based on the "Fourth *R*" — relationships.

In this chapter, I will (1) define *teacher advisory programs,* (2) discuss the role of the teacher as an advisor, (3) present some advisory topics and scheduling options, (4) present a rationale for teacher advisory programs in middle level schools, (5) present a review of relevant literature and implications for sustaining advisory programs, and (6) present recommendations for needed research.

## Teacher Advisory Programs Defined

The major focus of a successful teacher advisory program is emphasis on the social and emotional development of every young adolescent in a middle level school. To assist students in this development, teachers are assigned as facilitators and meet with small groups of students. Their primary goal is to help students feel significant — as though they belong to a valued and meaningful group. This "belonging" enhances the promotion of *relationships* (the fourth *R*), while allowing teachers to communicate with a manageable number of students. Significant teacher-to-student and student-to-student communication can be an integral component of the development of positive relationships. Through the advisory program, teachers and students have a time and a place to get to know one another as a group and to develop caring attitudes. When students are a part of a group in which each member contributes, students feel significant and important (Bergman, 1986).

Teacher and advisory programs provide an adult for students to turn to and trust, and these programs also allow students to see the teacher as a "real person" with likes and dislikes, hobbies, and interests. Too often, our schools become similar to factories run by professionals concerned only with the "end product," usually reported through test results. The coverage of subject matter can unfortunately become more important than the students' personal and emotional development. Without an advisory program, teachers have little or no time to develop relationships and share personal interests with students. Conversely, through the advisory program, students can recognize the many similarities between themselves and teachers and can formulate more positive attitudes toward authority figures.

Young adolescents, faced with dilemmas and pressures on a daily basis, need positive relationships. Hopefully, through advisory sessions, students can meet with caring, sensitive, and informed adults who are prepared to help students learn how to make decisions and deal with their own personal development and self-concept.

> *Every student needs to have a relationship with at least one adult in the school which is characterized by warmth, concern, openness, and understanding. Such a program focuses on the "fourth R," relationships: interpersonal relationships which produce growth for both people involved. Good middle schools cannot be places where teachers and students pass by each other without recognition or attachment, like the stereotypical ships in the night. (Alexander & George, 1981, p. 90)*

Effective middle level schools contain the teacher advisory program because the staff involved realize their commitment to the personal and social growth of young adolescents, many of whom lack home support. Educators who understand the importance of students feeling significant and having a high self-esteem are essential in middle schools. Students who do not feel good about themselves and who are extremely stressful are unlikely to get excited about learning. Successful schools are built on the premise of students and teachers becoming partners in the learning process.

### The Teacher as Advisor

The teacher/advisor assists the effective channeling of counseling services by providing every student with at least one caring adult to turn to for support and trust. Clearly, the intent of an active advisory program is to supplement, *not supplant,* the guidance program in the middle school.

Teachers as advisors do not have to master the counseling skills necessary to obtain a degree in counseling nor to deal personally with issues or topics causing discomfort. Their main role is that of facilitator — encouraging positive relationships with students and assisting them in dealing with the many dilemmas of the 1990s. The school counselors and teacher advisors should work together to determine the special needs of the students. Special cases involving threat of suicide or drug use should, of course, be referred to a counselor immediately.

James (1986) stated that the advisor must emphasize consistence, support, and advocacy for the student during this period of rapid change. Vars (1989) supported the importance of the teacher/advisor when he reported "small groups provide a more intimate environment in which to help young people deal with the many decisions and concerns that accompany the 'in-between years.' In the hands of a skillful adviser, advisory groups reach a high level of trust and function as effective groups" (p. 2). This skillful teacher/advisor must recognize that helping students to improve their self-concept will naturally improve students' ability to perform academically. Successful teachers recognize that serving as advisors to young adolescents is an important responsibility and extremely necessary in this time and at this age.

Another important decision teachers must face in their role as advisor during the planning and piloting stages is whether they will remain with the same group of students for their entire stay in the school. Many advisors interviewed prefer maintaining the same group for the two- or three-year period because of the bonding that occurs. Also, a sixth-grade advisor recognizes the difference of concerns and sees growth as the students move to the seventh and eighth grades. The eighth-grade advisors also appreciate the characteristics of a sixth-grade student when they receive their new group of advisees. This three-year commitment also generates a respect between teachers at different grade levels.

The most competent advisors do not label or abandon students because of previous academic records, interests, behavior, or attitudes. All students experience a fair chance. Hence, the existence of caring advisors is an integral part of the teacher advisory program.

### Advisory Topics

The content of the teacher advisory program differs from one school to another. The topics, based on teacher and student input, should address needs of the specific school and community. Examples of general themes can include, but must not be limited to, the following:

- Establishing an orientation program that familiarizes students with the procedures and rules of the school
- Developing group, team, and school spirit
- Accepting responsibility for education and actions
- Establishing and maintaining positive, interpersonal relationships
- Making career choices and planning for the future
- Learning the decision-making process
- Setting and obtaining goals
- Organizing time
- Establishing coping skills
- Developing positive problem-solving skills
- Discussing current adolescent issues and concerns
- Understanding and making commitments
- Appreciating talents, health, and potential
- Transitioning from one grade to the next
- Improving study, test-taking, and note-taking skills

Many schools have different topics for each grade level, other schools maintain the same topics for each grade. If the themes remain the same, however, it is *imperative* that each grade level plans different activities, taking into consideration maturation levels, to avoid student burnout and hearing students remark, "We did that last year."

Each theme or topic includes a variety of activities to support the predetermined goals and purposes. Activities, designed on the characteristics of young adolescents (diverse, concrete, relevant, interesting, flexible, creative, positive, nongraded) allow for movement and permit positive social interactions provide successful experiences. If the activities become boring, childish, and continually involve "complete the ditto and discuss," students and advisors quickly lose interest.

Activities based on the affective domain lead to the development of positive attitudes, values, and emotional control. Many advisors have found

Krathwohl's (Krathwohl, Bloom, & Masia, 1964) taxonomy of educational objectives for the affective domain (receiving, attending, responding, valuing, organization, and characterization) helpful in planning activities. If students experience each level of the taxonomy in a given theme, the possibility is improved that they will internalize the belief and change their behavior or attitudes about themselves or others.

Many successful schools that schedule the program during the same time every day of the week plan additional activities. The activities can include silent reading, free writing, club activities, games, or attitude adjustment days. Additionally, it is important that student and teacher interest is high through variety and flexibility in planning activities. Too much of the same thing can contribute to boredom and a breakdown of the program's main focus — establishing positive relationships.

### Scheduling a Program

The scheduled program can meet from once a week to five times a week, depending on the needs of the staff and students. A scheduled, weekly meeting offers young adolescents opportunities for interaction, leading to increased self-awareness, a consideration of values, and the development of decision-making and coping skills in dealing with school-, home-, or peer-related problems.

The assigned time for each session also depends on the input from staff members. Some scheduled advisory programs meet for 15 minutes a session, others last an entire 45- to 55-minute period. Most experts agree that flexibility is the key to a successful session, with the time determined by the teachers based on the purpose of the program. Teachers who serve as advisors generally agree that 20 to 30 minutes provides ample time for each session. Epstein and Mac Iver (1990) reported, "When schools have one period, they schedule it daily for 20–25 minutes, on an average. When two periods are scheduled, the second one is often added once or twice a week, and the average combined length of time scheduled daily for advisory and homeroom activities is between 30–35 minutes" (p. 18). The most important factor in scheduling the program is to provide for continued teacher/team input and revision.

Another consideration in scheduling a program is the time during the day to conduct the sessions. Most agree that in scheduling a slot of time during the beginning hours of the day, advisors can quickly identify any students arriving at school with concerns or negative attitudes, thus allowing the advisor time to inform all teachers of troubled students. Some schools to implement the program immediately following the lunch period or even the last period of the day. Again, the key for success is to allow teachers to pilot different schedules and then determine the most beneficial time for the program in their school.

One caveat is in order: The program can be successful only after careful organizing, planning, and preparing prior to the actual implementation. The same detailed planning necessary for any major curricular change is required in designing the teacher advisory program (Sizemore & Travis, 1986). The involvement of everyone in the school throughout all stages of the program and training affects the outcome of the program. Effective advisory programs require a commitment on the part of the teachers, enhanced by the willingness of administrators to allow teachers to make changes as needed. An unfocused or unplanned advisory program that lacks administrative and district level support or teacher, parent, and student input and involvement can be a disaster.

## Rationale for Teacher Advisory Programs

When asked why we need teacher advisory programs in middle schools, it is evident that during these turbulent young adolescent years, students most need assistance in growing up. According to Simmons and Klarich,

> *Advisory programs are an integral part of the middle school curriculum because they provide opportunities for social development within a structured environment. Often students' only social contact with others occurs in a haphazard manner. They sometimes learn inappropriate behaviors in the school hallway, locker room, playground, or cafeteria. (1989, p. 12)*

Advisory programs facilitate the development of decision-making skills focusing on school, personal, and home issues. At the same time, the program serves to help students build strong bonds of friendship, acquire school pride, and discover an appreciation for life and learning (Bergman & Baxter, 1983).

By combining what we know about self-esteem and the characteristics of young adolescents, middle level educators can easily provide a rationale for the teacher advisory program. Students at this stage of life need guidance and they need adults who will give them individual attention and support. The "fundamental purpose of the advisor-advisee program regardless of its design in any school is to promote involvement between a teacher and the students involved in the advisory group" (Alexander & George, 1981, p. 90). Promoting involvement of students and teachers in advisory programs is promoting the fourth *R* in the mission of the school.

Ideally, every middle school should be staffed with highly effective and trained guidance counselors prepared to meet the ever-changing needs of *all* students. Realistically, however, funding for an adequately staffed guidance department in middle schools does not seem to be a top priority to state decision makers. Consequently, most middle schools, if they are fortunate enough to have a counselor, work with an unrealistic counselor-student ratio of 1:400 or higher. No one person could even ensure a degree of success for every student operating under those conditions. This impractical ratio makes it difficult to practice effective guidance counseling in the middle schools, thus requiring additional alternatives such as an advisory program.

### Our Changing Society

Increasingly, this period of life for many middle level students is the first time they become aware of their emotions and question why they feel certain ways. This is a period when students begin to try to understand who they are, who their teachers are, and the significance of education, school, peers, and adults as they relate to life. "Too many young people turn to drugs, delinquency, and procreation in an effort to satisfy whatever it is they want" (Glasser, 1986, p. 3). It is precisely these concerns, along with the changes in the family structure, that contribute to the stress of our students.

Johnston (1990) summarized some of the conditions that schools must deal with on a daily basis. He stated, "Two working parents has become the norm rather than the exception in most intact families" (p. 3), meaning that our students are returning to homes lacking in adult supervision and support. He further indicated, "At present, nearly fifteen percent of our children are born out of wedlock, fifty percent of those to teenage mothers" (p. 4), supporting the fact that the adolescent pregnancy rate continues to rise. Johnston reported that "everyday in the United States, forty teenage girls — a school bus full — give birth to their third child" (p. 5).

Family structure is continually changing. Some of our students arrive at school each day without the feeling of family that many of their teachers experienced when they were in the middle grades. Public schools are losing the family-motivated students. "As many as one-third of all children born in the 1980's will live in a step family or 'reconstituted' or 'blended' family before they reach the age of 18. Nearly 9 million children, or about 15% of all school-age children, currently live in such a family" (Johnston, 1990, p. 6). As Beane and Lipka (1987) expressed, "Transescents have the best chance at positive mental health when both peers and parents are supportive. They are at risk when one or the other, or both, are lacking in support" (p. 23).

It is important to recognize, nonetheless, that we cannot give up on our students, using the excuse that their homes are "debilitating to their sense of self," as noted by Beane and Lipka (1987, p. 25). "It may well be true that there are some parents and guardians who are beyond our reach. However, the school is within our reach and it is important that for at least that period of time each day, these young people be treated with dignity and respect" (p. 25).

Furthermore, the 1990s will experience a population of stressful young adolescents. Elkind (1986) found,

> *Middle schoolers experience more stress today than in the past. They are experiencing these stressors at a time when they are more vulnerable to stress. Security and self-esteem, so important in coping with stress, have been diminished by changing family styles and the absorption of society in a self-fulfillment philosophy. (p. 33)*

Students at risk have stresses at home, in school, with peers, or somewhere else in their lives. Programs focusing on developing positive relationships can give young adolescents a resilience to stress, emphasizing that stress is a part of life and teaching them how to cope. According to the authors of *Turning Points* (Carnegie, 1989),

> *Caring is crucial to the development of young adolescents into healthy adults. Young adolescents need to see themselves as valued members of a group that offers mutual support and trusting relationships. They need to be able to succeed at something, and to be praised and rewarded for that success. They need to become socially competent individuals who have the skills to cope successfully with the exigencies of everyday life. They need to believe that they have a promising future, and they need the competence to take advantage of real opportunities in a society in which they have a stake. (p. 33)*

The students in our present middle level classrooms are our hope for the future and we, as educators, owe it to them to provide them with the appropriate tools to build their future. As summarized by Lipsitz (1984),

> *Because of their changing relationships with adults, especially parents, and the increasing importance of peers, positive social interaction with these groups is extremely important to young adolescents. Schools can encourage peer interaction by offering small-group learning activities and by providing space for small groups of students to informally congregate. Positive social interactions between adults and students are facilitated by adviser-advisee relationships, staff participation in activities, and informal contact outside the class. (p. 181)*

Students at this age need to experience opportunities to develop positive relationships with adults.

The authors of *Turning Points* (Carnegie, 1989) further stated,

> *By age 15, millions of American youth are at risk of reaching adulthood unable to meet adequately the requirements of the workplace, the commitments of relationships in families and with peers, and the responsibilities of participation in a multicultural society and of citizenship in a democracy. These young people often suffer from underdeveloped intellectual abilities, indifference to good health, and cynicism about the values that American society embodies. (p. 21)*

These "at-risk" students enter classrooms each day, frustrated and in search of answers to important questions in their lives.

Presently, the number of at-risk students is alarmingly high. These students have mentally dropped out of school and are likely to drop out of school physically when they reach age 16. They have difficulty succeeding during this period of development, as indicated by a noticeable increase in pregnancy, runaways, anorexia nervosa, drug abuse, venereal disease, truancy, and delinquency.

### The Role of the School

It is the responsibility of middle level educators to guide students through these difficult years.

> *Middle school students gain a healthy sense of self-esteem and security from deep interactions, from talking to and being with people to whom they are attached and who are attached to them. The advisor/advisee program in the middle school concept enhances positive self-esteem. This positive feeling of one's worth enables the transescent to cope with stresses that invade this age child. (Elkind, 1986, p. 34)*

The authors of *An Agenda for Excellence* (National Association of Secondary School Principals, 1984) encouraged educators to

> *institute student advisement programs that assure each student regular, compassionate, and supportive counsel from a concerned adult about his or her academic progress, adjustment to school, and personal adjustment. While this does not replace professional counseling, it provides a consultation system to give students immediate assistance with their problems. (p. 4)*

It is important to help students deal with problems, find answers to questions, and learn to communicate their feelings and beliefs while learning how to appreciate themselves, their lives, and their education. Obviously, for this to occur, the advisor must be a dedicated, positive, and supportive teacher.

Vars (1989) further indicated, "An adviser-advisee program makes it clear that guidance is everybody's job. Having a regularly-scheduled advisory group period in the schedule demonstrates that guidance is part of the curriculum and also protects the guidance function from encroachment" (p. 2). Middle level schools that maintain personal development, along with the acquisition of the learning process and the acquisition of content knowledge, provide students with the appropriate tools for living and growing.

## Review of Relevant Literature

Although the literature is replete with the relationship of students' self-concept to their attitude toward school, little research exists on the specific effectiveness of the teacher advisory program. Most evidence supported by teachers' perceptions and success stories advocate the program. In a very real sense, however, individuals involved in the program agree, without hesitation, that the teacher advisory program contributes to the academic and personal success of students. Students who are listened to and recognized by adults and peers feel a sense of belonging and are apt to demonstrate more appropriate behaviors.

A study by Connors (1986) found the benefits and overall effects of an advisory program (PRIME TIME) in Sarasota, Florida, reinforced what middle level educators already suspected. The results of the study, determined through surveying and interviewing students, teachers, administrators, guidance counselors, and parents, evidenced that the program:

1. Helped students in their social growth
2. Contributed to a positive school environment
3. Helped students learn about the school
4. Helped students learn to make friends
5. Helped students learn how to get along with others
6. Enhanced the teacher-student relationship
7. Provided the advisors the opportunity to know students on a one-to-one basis
8. Helped students develop a sense of positive self-worth
9. Helped students acquire and improve the habits and attitudes necessary for responsible citizenship

The study also found that after implementing many components of the middle school concept, including the teacher advisory program, the average daily school attendance increased, along with standardized test scores. Through personal interviews, many positive statements supporting the program evolved. The results proved that

> *overall, the administrative staff and faculty have also seen a remarkable decrease in discipline problems, office referrals, and truancy. One teacher stated, "In the past, on the last day of school, students would leave yelling obscenities from the busses, but now the students are sad that school has ended and leave with tears in their eyes and positive remarks" proving the program can make a difference. (Connors, 1986, p. 46)*

An additional benefit of the program is the development of a "positive attitude" climate where every student is a winner and expectations are high. "Apart from channeling, teacher expectations, both reasonable and unrealistic, have a significant effect on student self-concept" (Johnston & Markle, 1986, p. 83). When teachers see students as functioning human beings and do not condemn or criticize but expect the best—the results are rewarding. Beane and Lipka (1987) noted,

> *Learning is not confined to the classroom nor is it limited to the intentions described in curriculum documents such as course syllabi. Young people learn in hallways, on buses, on playgrounds, and in the principal's office. They learn from the expectations of teachers, from interactions with peers, and from ways in which they are treated as people and as students. (p. 17)*

Added evidence supports the importance of the role of the teacher as advisor. Effective advisors can positively impact the success of the program. When students feel as though someone cares about their existence, they tend to become more involved and take an interest in their environment. According to Chase (1975), "The critical question for practicing teachers, therefore, is not *whether* affective education should occur, but *how* affective education is to occur" (p. ix). Basically, the advisory program assists teachers in developing personal relationships with each student, while serving as a positive role model for students who often view adults as opponents rather than advocates (Simmons & Klarich, 1989).

## Implications for Sustaining Advisory Programs

Connors (1986) made recommendations that would apply to all systems presently involved in the teacher advisory program or preparing to begin a program. The following summarizes the recommendations:

1. The program is successful when it is continually monitored and visibly supported by the administration and guidance department of the school. This support must be a collaborative effort, with all parties acting as resource persons. It should never be assumed that the program is running smoothly; the administration must reevaluate its effectiveness on a continual basis, encouraging teachers to openly assess the activities and discuss feelings. An advisory committee comprised of schoolwide representation should meet on a monthly basis to discuss the program.

2. A parental awareness program included in the planning stages of the program contributes to the acceptance of the program. With parents involved throughout, especially parents of students entering the middle school each year, a support base is established. When parents understand the purpose and realize their children will have an assigned adult to help them through these impetuous years, the program prospers.

3. The purpose, goals, and objectives of the program should be reevaluated annually. Teachers should be reminded of the nature and needs of young adolescents and current research supporting affective education—reinforcing their role as an advisor and its importance.

4. New and first-year teachers must receive individual in-service each year to explain the program in preparation for their role as a facilitator. Uninformed teachers can have a negative impact on the intent of the program.

5. The guidance program must be actively involved in the program. Guidance counselors should serve as resources and be available to deal with serious situations requiring sophisticated counseling (e.g., suicide attempts, sexual abuse, delinquency).

6. The teacher-student ratio should remain workable. All advisors interviewed indicated that the ideal size was 15, but 20 was still manageable. They did state, however, when the group began to increase from 20, many of the small group activities involving discussions, roleplays, and simulations were ineffective.

7. Administrators and personnel involved in overseeing the teacher advisory program must take measures to avoid advisor burnout. These measures include providing advisors with:

   a. A variety of activities relating to the needs of their specific group of advisees;
   b. Released time to observe other advisors or visit schools to obtain new ideas;
   c. An active role in the decision-making process concerning activities, evaluation, and responsibilities;
   d. The inclusion of field trips, guest speakers, principal as advisor, and other creative activities that maintain the flow of enthusiasm;
   e. Flexibility within the program so all advisors can tap their own

potential and feel comfortable with the activities and overall program;

    f. An opportunity to discuss the program and some innovative activities at faculty and parent meetings; and

    g. The opportunity to attend state and national meetings to present the specifics of the school's advisory program.

    8. Staff development must be provided to all advisors for a continual rejuvenation of the program.

    9. The school's entire faculty, staff, administration, and guidance personnel should model the purpose of the teacher advisory program — team spirit, positive attitudes, a place to belong, and a positive school climate. A faculty committed to the program must represent a team effort, demonstrating this commitment together by building a "family environment" where everyone feels like a contributing and important member.

    10. Opportunities for advisors to discuss their concerns, frustrations, achievements, and overall program operations on a regular basis are essential. Student input is necessary for improvements.

    11. District level administrators and school board members involved throughout all planning and implementing stages ensures support and understanding of the program. If school board members and superintendents do not understand the program, community criticism can emerge.

    12. The program must have someone responsible for overseeing its operation, preferably a guidance counselor. The program is not self-sustaining.

    13. Most importantly, the program must be a teacher-developed and teacher-designed program based on the needs of the staff, students, and parents of the school. Self-esteem cannot be bought; consequently, the purchase and implementation of already developed programs may have negative ramifications, causing discomfort to advisors due to inflexibility and misrepresentations.

Middle school teachers who are concerned with each student's growth have found

> *Their students turn to them for guidance in increasing increments under circumstances fed by an effective advisor-advisee program if, for no other reason, because the student's needs for guidance are often immediate and situation specific. Such needs must be dealt with at the time they occur. Waiting for an appointment with a counselor who may have more than 500 other students to deal with or for a small group counseling session is often ineffective and counterproductive. Teachers can provide on the spot assistance. (Alexander & George, 1981, p. 91)*

Students feel accepted, a sense of security, and an important part of the school. Fenwick (1986) agreed that

> *there is no other single technique which is more powerful in breaking down the generational walls than for adolescents to find adults who affirm them as persons. To have another individual express belief in you as a worthy human being in spite of your acne, awkwardness, and inexperience can be overwhelming. (p. 82)*

Programs often fail to fulfill the potential they possess. Today's advisory programs, designed to provide guidance to students from teachers who have had little or no training in the skills required, can be ineffective. The programs are sometimes portrayed to parents and the community in a manner that arouses suspicion and concern about the moral or spiritual values and beliefs that might be involved. Too often, in districts that are uncertain of or uneducated about the middle school program, advisory programs are introduced in schools where teachers are still organized into departments. Almost always, such efforts fail.

Properly understood as an important building block for group membership, advisory programs can be extremely successful. When administrators and teachers approach the program in a way that permits the advisory group to be a part of an interdisciplinary team, it is almost always a more effective experience for everyone involved (George, 1983, p. 47). Educators concerned with young adolescents and knowledgeable of the developmental characteristics of this age group recognize the importance of advisory programs in middle schools; they can make a difference.

## Recommendations for Needed Research

Perhaps one reason for the limited quantitative data on the effectiveness of advisory programs is the difficulty in measuring the success or failure of the intended outcomes of the program. Qualitative evidence suggests that advisory programs are necessary and can be effective. At the present, there is still a need to validate teacher advisory programs. Additional research is necessary to identify specific areas of the program that are most effective and those areas needing improvement. Recommended areas to investigate include the following:

1. Identify the necessary components required to prepare teachers adequately for their role as an advisor—during preservice and in-service.
2. Evaluate the significant competencies of effective advisors and their relationship to other areas of the school and curriculum.

3. Study the effects on students who remain with their advisor for their entire middle level experience as compared to students who change advisors each year.

4. Identify the necessary elements in sustaining an effective advisory program while avoiding advisor burnout—improving the program annually.

More states and schools are funding and implementing advisory programs. For example, a recent report in Florida, *Coming of Age* (Florida Department of Education, 1990), stated, "In Florida, the presence of guidance or advisory programs has increased from 18% in 1984 to 80% in 1989" (p. 13). This growth is encouraging, but it brings to mind some important questions: How effective are these programs and how long will they be sustained? The teacher advisory program is a difficult program to implement and more difficult to sustain. But when it comes to doing what is best for our energetic, enlightening young adolescents, it is worth all of the effort.

## Conclusion

The importance of advisory programs in middle level schools cannot be overstated. Research indicates that our society has been failing our young adolescents, evidenced by their rejection of school, parents, peers, and community. Making schools work for young adolescents, as cited by Dorman, Lipsitz, and Verner (1985), "is one of public education's greatest challenges. By combining what we know about academically effective schools, and ten to fifteen year olds in particular, we can define the outcomes we want from middle-grade schools and work to improve them" (p. 44).

Glasser (1969) stated, "If teachers would get personally involved with students, teach things that were relevant and promote thinking rather than memorizing, most school failure could be eliminated" (p. 16). Given that Glasser made this statement in 1969, it appears that the concern for a personal relationship with students remains an interest for educators. James (1986) noted,

> *If it is true, as many middle school authorities suggest, that these middle grade years may be the last chance to significantly intervene in the positive development of youth, both cognitively and affectively, then everyone involved with youth from family, to social agencies, to administrator-staff support personnel in schools, to youth itself needs to recommit available energies to the further continuance and enhancement of school programs which promote affective growth. (p. 4)*

This affective growth is sought through the teacher advisory program.

Beane and Lipka (1987) succinctly summarized the need for the fourth R in middle schools when they stated,

> *Middle level professionals who advocate these programs understand one of the odd ironies in schooling: we want young people to read, so we teach them directly to read; we want young people to write, so we teach them directly to write; we want young people to have positive mental health, but we expect that it will emanate out of some indirect part of the school program. To top things off, we are then surprised when it doesn't. The fact is that if you really want someone to learn something, you have to "teach" it to him/her. With regard to affective education in general and self-concept/esteem in particular, this is just what advisory programs are meant to do. (p. 40)*

Middle level educators in schools that implement an advisory program report a significant difference in the overall attitude of students. Students feel as though someone cares about them and they are an important element in the school. The program is education's response to the needs and characteristics of young adolescents by dealing with the full range of their intellectual and social development. Clearly, the program helps make the time students spend in school more meaningful.

We, as educators and caring adults, have a responsibility to help young adolescents prepare for and reach adulthood successfully—no matter what it takes. As mentioned previously, students in middle level schools greeted by sensitive and caring teachers who take the time to treat students as people seem to enjoy their middle level years more. Time scheduled into the regular school day for an advisory session makes a statement: "In this school, the students really do come first and the fourth R is as important, if not more so, than the other three Rs."

The process of growing up is the process of trying things out, of making mistakes, and of finding successes (Beane & Lipka, 1987). Thus, the effective advisory program is based on the premise that school should be an exciting, student-oriented place where the kids *do come first.*

## References

Alexander, W., & George, P. (1981). *The exemplary middle school.* New York: CBS College Publishing.

Beane, J., & Lipka, R. (1987). *When the kids come first: Enhancing self esteem.* Columbus, OH: National Middle School Association.

Bergman, S. (1986). Making decisions about the tough topics. *Clearing House, 60*(1), 24–26.

Bergman, S., & Baxter, J. (1983). Building a guidance program and advisory concept for early adolescents. *NASSP Bulletin, 67*(463), 49–55.

Carnegie Council on Adolescent Development's Task Force on Education of Young Adolescents. (1989). *Turning points: Preparing American youth for the 21st century.* Washington, DC: Carnegie Council on Adolescent Development, a program of Carnegie Corporation of New York.

Chase, L. (1975). *The other side of the report card: A how to do it program for affective education.* Glenview, IL: Scott, Foresman.

Connors, N. A. (1986). *A case study to determine the essential components and effects of an advisor/advisee program in an exemplary middle school.* Unpublished doctoral dissertation, Florida State University, Tallahassee, FL.

Dorman, G., Lipsitz, J., & Verner, P. (1985). Improving schools for young adolescents. *Educational Leadership, 42*(6), 44–49.

Elkind, D. (1986). Stress and the middle-grader. *School Counselor, 33*(3), 196–206.

Epstein, J. L., & Mac Iver, D. J. (1990). *Education in the middle grades: Overview of national practices and trends.* Columbus, OH: National Middle School Association.

Fenwick, J. J. (1986). *The middle school years.* San Diego, CA: Fenwick Associates.

Florida Department of Education. (1990). *Coming of age: The impact of PRIME legislation on middle level schools in Florida.* Tallahassee, FL: Author.

George, P. S. (1983). *Theory Z school: Beyond effectiveness.* Columbus, OH: National Middle School Association.

Gerler, R. (1986). Teaching teenagers skills for adolescence. *Education Digest, 52*(2), 36–38.

Glasser, W. (1969). *Schools without failure.* New York: Harper and Row.

Glasser, W. (1986). *Control theory in the classroom.* New York: Harper and Row.

James, M. (1986). *Advisor/Advisee: Why, what and how.* Columbus, OH: National Middle School Association.

Johnston, J. H. (1990). *The new American family and the school.* Columbus, OH: National Middle School Association.

Johnston, J. H., & Markle, G. C. (1986). *What research says to the middle level practitioner.* Columbus, OH: National Middle School Association.

Krathwohl, D. R., Bloom, B. S., & Masia, B. B. (1964). *Taxonomy of educational objectives: Affective domain.* New York: David McKay.

Lipsitz, J. (1984). *Successful schools for young adolescents.* New Brunswick, NJ: Transaction Books.

National Association of Secondary School Principals. (1984). *An agenda for excellence at the middle level.* Reston, VA: Author.

Simmons, L., & Klarich, J. (1989). The advisory curriculum: Why and how. *NELMS Journal, 2*(2), 12–13.

Sizemore, J., & Travis, S. (1986). Teacher based guidance. *Dissemination Services on Middle Grades, 17*(8), 1–6.

Vars, G. E. (1989). Getting closer to middle level students: Options for teacher-advisor guidance programs. *Schools in the middle: A report on trends and practices.* Reston, VA: National Association of Secondary School Principals.

# CHAPTER ELEVEN

# Exploratory Programs in the Middle Level School: A Responsive Idea

SHERREL BERGMAN
*National Louis University*

Every year, middle level teachers, principals, and school boards are faced with curricular questions that involve strategic planning for future courses. The area of concern that is least defined in many schools is their exploratory offerings. Frequently, committees are charged with designing and implementing a program for young adolescents that is often based on what is available rather than what students actually need.

*Exploration,* as it is frequently defined, includes those offerings in the middle level school that encourage and allow students to explore new arenas of interest, both as specific courses and as methodology within courses. A variety of titles have been given to this process: some schools call it *unified arts,* others call it *specials,* and some call it *exploratory.* The concept, not the name, is important. Later in this chapter, a variety of definitions will be given. These definitions all have a philosophical base that considers the developmental needs of young adolescents.

It is obvious to most who work in middle level schools that students need the opportunity to explore a wide variety of subjects and group processes. The middle school may be the students' first and last chance to see if they can create a piece of artwork, play the trombone, spike a volleyball, play the role of someone else, use a computer program, cook a meal, experiment with new designs in industrial technology, converse in another language, complete a community project, or find ways to use their leisure time productively and safely.

To make effective decisions in the future about exploratory experiences, it is helpful for curriculum designers to study the history of the concept and the rationale for including it in the schooling experience of young adolescents. In this chapter I will discuss (1) the history and the philosophical basis for program development, (2) research findings on the current status of the concept, and (3) issues in exploration that schools may face in the future.

## The Concept and History of Exploration

Exploration is not a new concept for schools. In fact, there is evidence that the Academy founded by Benjamin Franklin in 1751 recommended a more practical curriculum to prepare students for business and industrial needs (Curtis & Bidwell, 1977). Extracurricular activities were a common feature in early boarding schools and high schools. In the early 1920s, the National Education Association's Department of Superintendence listed 15 purposes of the junior high school. Second only to meeting individual differences in pupils was prevocational training and exploration (Van Til, Vars, & Lounsbury, 1967).

During its formative period, one of the five major functions of the junior high was

> *to provide for exploration by (1) offering short-term or try-out courses which would acquaint students with various subjects and interest areas, (2) testing, counseling, and exploratory work to discover the interests, abilities, and capacities of individual pupils, and (3) by offering prevocational exploratory and orientation experiences. (Van Til, Vars, & Lounsbury, 1967, p. 27)*

As the junior high was more widely implemented, exploratory programs became one of the distinguishing features, but prevocational programs were deferred to the high school. Studies in the 1940s by Gruhn and Douglass, and in the 1950s by Lounsbury, again reiterated the need for and acceptance of exploratory courses as a primary function of the junior high.

Between 1950 and 1960, health, industrial arts, homemaking, music, and physical education were required courses in over 50 percent of the junior high schools. Although those courses were taken by every student, some junior high schools offered exploratory programs in an elective format with some element of student choice in areas of study. The most commonly offered electives were music, foreign language, art, industrial arts, homemaking, business education, and science. In 1964, 52 percent of the 202 schools studied offered foreign language in grades 7 and 8 (Van Til, Vars, & Lounsbury, 1967).

Some educators looked beyond the concept of exploratory courses and broadened the definition to include methodology. Faunce and Clute (1961), for example, offered a clarifying definition of when courses were and were not exploratory in nature. They warned against considering a subject field as exclusively general or exploratory. They looked at student experiences as becoming exploratory when they required special facilities, a specialized teacher for depth of knowledge, and specialized grouping to facilitate the experience. Faunce and Clute also stated that they had "no intention of separating children into groups composed of explorers and nonexplorers" (p. 105). Finally, they strongly urged that all learning be regarded as exploratory.

Perhaps today's middle level schools are still trying to force a natural developmental characteristic of the student into a contrived separation within the curriculum. The characteristics upon which the exploration programs were founded are the same needs expressed by students in all areas of the middle school curriculum. Students cannot separate their need to explore social studies concepts from their need to explore art or music. We have moved far afield from the warnings of Faunce and Clute by designating some courses for exploration and others as academics. There is little evidence that integration of the two curricular areas takes place in middle schools today. Some schools may choose to do a whole-school unit that incorporates everyone in the building, but those instances are rare.

The authors of *An Agenda for Excellence at the Middle Level* (NASSP, 1984) make two recommendations related to future planning in exploratory programs:

1. Provide opportunities for students to achieve and demonstrate excellence in a number of domains (i.e., the arts, asthletics, academics, crafts). Make certain that every student in the school has a reasonable opportunity to excel at something (p. 3).
2. Recognize that the young adolescent is interested in virtually everything, but nothing very much, by providing adequate exploratory programs that introduce students to a variety of topics, skills, and content fields without requiring mastery. This can be accomplished through a series of short courses or elective units that give the student some sense of control over the kind of learning he or she undertakes (p. 7).

These recommendations broaden the definition of exploration to include not only coursework but participation in extracurricular activities. The concept of provision of experiences to meet student needs is the glue that should hold the purpose and the program design together.

Because the needs and characteristics of young adolescents are the focus of middle school education, exploration continues to be a necessary component of young adolescents' schooling experience. Students now experience a variety of models of courses, scheduling, and activities. As the current movement toward minimum competency testing takes more and more time from the school schedule, it becomes increasingly difficult for schools to provide programs of exploration to each student. The questions become ones of justification of time and money spent for courses not directly related to science, math, language arts, and social studies.

A collection of reports issued in the late 80s have all made suggestions for new required courses that have traditionally been exploratory. For example, in *A Nation at Risk* (National Commission on Excellence in Education, 1983), the Commission recommended that foreign language study begin in the elementary school and that in the arts, vocational, and other areas, the same level of performance as in the basics be demanded. It is still not clear whether the recommendations should be interpreted as courses, standards for existing courses, or time of introduction of exploratory concepts. To develop and sustain responsive programs for exploration in the future, we must again consider the psychological developmental characteristics of the young adolescent.

## The Need for Exploration for the Young Adolescent

Exploratory program designers must realize that the nature of early adolescence causes students to explore, whether schools provide opportunities or not. Exploration is one visible behavior of the young adolescents' attempt to meet their five basic needs. According to Mitchell (1974), young adolescents need:

1. Status and acceptance
2. Independence
3. Achievement
4. Role experimentation
5. Positive self-regard

Typically, young adolescents need more time to explore because they are more aware and curious about the ideas they encounter. This is the age of endless discovery, and young adolescents discover themselves, their intellect, their sexuality, and the opposite sex (Mitchell, 1974).

Even a casual observer will notice the constant aura of discovery that surrounds a group of 10- to 14-year-olds. They want to do everything they have never done before, be someone else for a while, and search for their own talents and skills. Recognition of this exploratory nature of young adolescents has led middle level schools to provide exploratory programs that attempt to meet the needs of discovery, group participation, and exposure to a wide range of talents and skills. Unfortunately, the purpose and goals of these programs and how exploratory programs should be implemented has never been consistently defined and clarified.

The research of Erikson (1963) has been helpful to many program designers. His model of personality development is divided into the developmental stages of trust, autonomy, initiative, industry, identity, generativity, and integrity. Middle school students, for the most part, are functioning between the stages of industry and identity. They take pleasure in real-work projects that have a visible result. They enjoy seeing the completion of their tasks and the recognition for that task completion. Successful experiences at the industry stage lead a student to the development of a positive identity. The inability to experience real-work projects may lead a student to a sense of inferiority and the resulting identity confusion. Erikson (1968) lists the elements that young adolescents need in order to develop a positive identity:

1. People and ideas to have faith in
2. An opportunity to decide for oneself on the types of activities one wishes to pursue.
3. A variety of self-images from which to choose and opportunities through which they can be expressed.
4. To be affirmed by peers, confirmed by teachers, and inspired by worthwhile ways of life

Identity confusion for the young adolescent may come from not having a protected environment in which to have some free experimentation with several roles. The most serious outcome of identity confusion may be a negative identity.

When programs are not provided in the schools or other social institutions, young adolescents explore randomly, with peer pressure being the common variable for achievement. Status and acceptance may be gained through exploration in socially unacceptable or dangerous encounters. Role experimentation often occurs, using media role models without the benefit of balance from parents or teachers.

## Program Models for Exploration

When examining the writings on middle level curriculum, a variety of definitions and program models are given. Although there are many differences, the similarities include the need for the programs and the philosophical basis of young adolescent development.

Alexander and George (1981) stated, "The original intent of the exploratory program was to have relatively brief introductory courses for beginners, with longer, more intensive courses available another year for those interested" (p. 61). These courses might include art, music, home economics, industrial arts, drama, business, typing, health, and physical education. Alexander and George classify exploratory activities into three categories:

1. Exploratory courses
2. Special interest activities
3. Seminars and independent study

Lounsbury and Vars (1978) call exploration the "variable component" of the curriculum. Within their definition, they include elective mini-courses, skill development in music and art, activities, clubs, and independent study opportunities. "Perhaps it is this component of the curriculum that comes closest to mirroring the bewildering transcience and diversity of the transescent student" (p. 83). Vars and Lounsbury contend that "every student should have access to a rich variety of exploratory experiences, both required and elective" (p. 41). They cite the following as typical components of an exploratory program:

Health and physical education
Intramural programs
Interscholastic athletics
Outdoor education
Music
Art
Home economics
Industrial arts
Electives (such as general business, band, chorus, foreign language, typing, and algebra)
Interest and enrichment courses
Independent study
Study activities
Student government (p. 98)

These experiences may vary widely in structure, time allotment, and student grouping. Curricular decisions must be based on what we know about students, what society demands, and the nature of knowledge in each subject or activity.

Eichhorn (1966) defined exploration within the physical-cultural curriculum and divided it into four content areas: fine arts, physical education, practical arts, and cultural studies (p. 66). He urged that all of these areas be interrelated. He also separated interest clubs, activities, and student government as guidance rather than exploratory functions.

## Research on Models of Exploration

To conduct research on the current status of exploratory programs, Alexander and McEwin (1989) have divided exploration into the following areas:

1. Traditional exploratory programs that were evident in the early junior highs and were maintained in middle schools, such as art, music, industrial arts, and home economics, plus those added to early middle school curricular offerings, introductory foreign language, and special reading classes.
2. Newer exploratory subjects such as activities, clubs, and special-interest activities.

How these programs have been implemented to meet the needs of students has been determined by looking at frequency of offerings rather than student attitude or response to the programs or lack of programs. Student learnings in the programs are rarely tested or researched. Perhaps it is the lack of agreement on what is included in exploration that has kept it vulnerable to frequent curricular change.

The issue of purpose, offerings, structure, grouping, and scheduling becomes hazy as all of these elements are studied and compared. In a national survey, Epstein and Mac Iver (1990) found that the following exploratory programs are currently being offered: physical education (80 percent of middle schools offer two years to all or almost all of their students); art (offered to seventh- and eighth-graders in seven out of eight schools); industrial arts, home economics, and computer education (offered in two-thirds of all middle schools); and typing or keyboarding (40 percent of middle schools offer some exposure to typing or keyboarding to their seventh- or eighth-graders).

This study also documented the incidence of mini-courses and found that only 30 percent of the students in the seventh or eighth grade in the schools in this study have taken a mini-course. Some of the courses listed included study skills, foreign language, and family life.

Lounsbury and Johnston (1988) concluded after studying sixth-grade students that "the curriculum provided by the middle level school, or schools with teamed or partially teamed organizations, tend to offer more exploratory opportunities for students than do elementary organizations" (p. 39). Alexander and McEwin (1989) found that foreign language has become less widely required between 1968 and 1988 without a corresponding increase as an elective. They saw a corresponding decrease in home economics and industrial arts as required courses and more schools offering these as electives. General music decreased in offering, both as a required course and as an elective, but the percentage of schools offering instrumental music increased sharply in all grades from 1968 to 1988.

Significant increases in offerings of computers, health, careers, and sex education were found in the middle schools studied by Alexander and McEwin (1989). An analysis of their data on newer exploratory activities found a significant increase in the number of schools that offer intramural programs for both boys and girls, arts and crafts, photography, publications, school parties, social dancing, student council, and interscholastic athletics.

They concluded that "there are few consistent differences between the different grade organizations as to the offering of these traditional exploratory subjects, although their required status tends to be greater in the middle school organization" (p. 54).

A number of studies have been conducted on what is offered, how often exploratory courses are offered, who takes them, whether they are required or electives, and trends in curricular offerings. What is missing from all of the studies is impact data. Unanswered research questions remain. We must ask students: (1) How do you feel that you can best learn the skills, concepts, and attitudes that are taught in exploratory courses? and (2) What would you like to explore and how would you like to be taught? Further research questions involve the training of teachers for middle level exploratory experiences.

A review of the literature on middle school exploration reveals consensus on the following characteristics that should be included in an exploratory program. When an exploratory component curriculum is based on the needs of the students it serves, it will have the following components:

1. It will not be competitive in nature. It will not pit one student against another during the exploratory process.
2. It will have teachers who understand the process of exploration and the needs of the students.
3. It will be a safe time and place for students to explore individual talents and ideas as a member of structured peer group.
4. It will allow students to begin or continue to develop their own ideas and talents.
5. It will include a series of courses or experiences that enable students to:
   a. gather information and strategies
   b. take risks without fear of failure
   c. use their bodies and minds to create both products and processes
   d. look at alternative ways of doing things
   e. interact with peers in a productive nonthreatening environment.

If exploratory programs are to survive the current emphasis on state mandates and competency requirements, middle school proponents must be willing to confront the major issues involved in the design, implementation, and evaluation of exploratory programs. They must examine the concept of exploration rather than specific courses and programs.

## Issues in Exploratory Programs

### Issue One: Offerings

Goodlad, in *A Place Called School: Prospects for the Future* (1983), suggested an emphasis on general education that included five domains of human knowledge offered in the following percentages of time: 18 percent literature and language; 18 percent math and science; 15 percent each social studies, the arts, and vocations; up to 10 percent physical education; and the remaining 10 percent guided individual choice. His sixth domain of individual choice stated that all students be afforded the chance to develop their special interests and skills. This may well be the best supported argument for exploratory courses in the middle school. It also offers flexibility in definition of what is offered and when. It also implies articulation of programming between the elementary, middle, and high school.

What should a yong adolescent of this decade explore? The Carnegie Council on Adolescent Development (Carnegie, 1989) recommends a core of common knowledge that includes critical thinking skills, development of healthy lifestyles, active citizenship, integration of subject matter, and teaching students to learn. Although they do not endorse any specific courses in the exploratory areas, they insist that schools attempt to ensure success for all students. The authors of the report state for many young people, mastering the core academic program will provide the opportunities to gain the confidence and personal satisfaction of becoming expert or very good at something. For others, opportunities to exhibit excellence may be found in exploratory courses or athletics (p. 49).

Middle level schools will need to examine carefully the vehicles by which students currently arrive at a common core of knowledge. Perhaps this core knowledge is not most effectively transmitted when divided into separate subjects within the exploratory areas. For example, schools may need to begin by placing all of their exploratory teachers on their own team so that they can communicate about ways to integrate the content and discuss students that they have in common. The more important question, however, may be whether schools should limit the offerings and expand the experiences within them or expand the offerings and limit student experiences. Each school must answer this question in response to the needs of its young adolescents and

and its community. Schools must also determine how extracurricular offerings can meet the needs of the majority of the students rather than a selected few.

### Issue Two: Elective vs. Required Courses

Van Hoose and Strahan (1988) considered the element of student choice in exploration activities. In successful schools, students participate in a variety of exploratory learning opportunities in enrichment programs and in their content classes. They have opportunities to select projects and to discuss ideas.

Curtis and Bidwell (1977) stated that exploration should be possible in all areas of the curriculum, and include the classroom, innovative courses, extra-class activities, media, and homeroom. Exploration in the classroom can provide for enrichment, acceleration, classroom leadership, and the use of the unit approach. Innovative courses can be derived from any of the regularly taught curricular areas or subjects normally outside of the general course offerings. For example, whereas astronomy might be an exploratory course within science, a mini-course in operetta production could be considered an innovative course stressing interrelationships between disciplines.

Most middle level educators agree that a variety of models for implementing an exploratory program exist. While each educator generally has a preferred implementation design, most would agree that the program should be offered and should be designed on the basis of student needs. Individual school districts have completed attitude questionnaires, but little hard data are available on the impact of these courses on students' attitudes, learning, and abilities.

One school district in Illinois recently completed a survey of all parents, students, and faculty in middle schools. District personnel were attempting to determine desired course offerings of each of these groups in the next 10 years. The committee discovered that most respondents wanted a return of the industrial arts and home economics program that had been dropped eight years earlier for lack of funding. Also requested was keyboarding and foreign language. Students, in particular, wanted these courses returned because they could make things and work with friends on projects.

Districts must grapple with the cost of developing, reinstituting, or maintaining programs that require extensive labs or equipment. They must look at the relevance of the offerings to the total curriculum. They must assess local public attitudes toward the arts, music, applied arts, and other exploratory offerings. They must think in terms of conceptual and attitude development of students rather than a series of courses.

When exploration is a series of courses, an unhealthy dichotomy evolves in a middle level school. Teachers are labeled as academic and special or academic and exploratory. They are not seen as equal in the eyes of students, faculty, or administrators. This dichotomy causes a serious negative role model to students when teachers feel inferior or unimportant. All teachers should be charged and held accountable for providing opportunities for exploration within their classrooms.

### Issue Three: Scheduling, Organization, and Integration of Exploratory Experiences

In scheduling the exploratory programs in the middle school, Lounsbury (1981) suggested that one-fourth to one-third of the day should be for exploratory courses and that physical education should be offered every day. In addition to physical education and health, Lounsbury suggested an intramural program. He stated that the "exploratory area offers the most flexibility in scheduling and provides the most creative activities for students" (p. 17).

Placing students in a schedule of exploratory courses frequently causes teacher communication problems. Tuttle (1985) examined the issue of the arts as a curricular caboose. He realistically projects that fine arts classes are valued for the time they give other teachers to plan, as electives, and as frill courses squeezed in between the "real courses" (p. 7).

Middle schools that do have common planning time for interdisciplinary teams send the students to exploratory classes during the team planning time. Infrequently is it possible to schedule the exploratory teachers to enable them to share a common planning time with interdisciplinary teams. It is not impossible, however. Indian Prairie School District in Naperville, Illinois, has confronted the issue by calling one group of teams the core teams and the other team the encore team. In this district, all teams have common planning time and this facilitates interaction among the core and encore teams.

Many excellent middle schools have attempted to overcome the lack of communication between the exploratory teams and other teams by designating a team leader from the exploratory teachers who meets with the other team leaders in the building on a weekly basis. The most commonly used excuse for lack of attention to the exploratory teachers is that integration of that group with the other teams is difficult to schedule. It may be difficult, it may require a new look at staff assignments, it may require a change in the way we "have always done things," but it can be done.

When middle schools offer mini-courses or activities, they appear to be scheduled in a variety of ways. Some are offered on alternate days with advisor/advisee programs, some are offered during lunch, and some are offered one Friday afternoon each month for at least an hour. Other mini-courses are offered after school or as special interdisciplinary unit projects.

Only 39 percent of the middle school principals surveyed by Becker (1990) reported that their schools offered mini-courses. Many of the mini-courses were shorter offerings of what might have been lengthier courses in the past. Becker also found that exploratory mini-courses exist for seventh- or eighth-graders in about half of all schools of 600 or more students, but in only about a fourth of the schools with 250 or fewer students.

Becker also found that students in suburbs of large cities generally take more exploratory courses than students in large cities or rural towns. Becker identified six noncore courses: industrial arts, home economics, physical education, art, science, and mini-courses for his study and found that eighth-graders in large cities are less likely to experience these courses than other students. He did find that students in large city schools and their suburbs offer more foreign language courses than schools in other areas and as much or more opportunity in computers.

Ethnicity seems to be a factor in whether or not a student is offered exploratory courses. Becker found that middle school students in mixed/minority schools have fewer mini-course experiences than do students in schools that have less than 10 percent minorities. Obviously, the middle school tenet of offering exploration to everyone as a regular part of the curriculum still has a long way to go.

## Conclusion

Historically, students have experienced a variety of special courses to provide them with exploration opportunities. Traditionally, these courses have included physical education, home economics, industrial arts, art, music, and foreign language. Recently, health, computers, and mini-courses have been added to the list of regular exploratory courses. Most middle level educators recommend a continuation of exploratory courses. What to offer, when to offer it, and how to schedule it during the school day are all issues that have been researched. What appears to be lacking in the literature, however, is student feedback on the worth of these experiences to them.

A two-level system has evolved in many schools, causing teachers who teach exploratory courses to feel less important than their peers who teach what many schools call academic courses. This labeling practice has caused a lack of cooperation on the part of many teachers to involve themselves in interdisciplinary units that would have been enriched by their participation.

Although the characteristics of young adolescents may not have changed since the inception of exploration programs, the experiences outside of school have increased and in many cases competed with school programs. A reexamination of exploratory experiences in light of the demands of the twenty-first century we will enter shortly seems appropriate at this time. It is possible that student needs for the future may not be served by the courses and schedules we have been offering in the past.

Questions that remain for curriculum designers in middle level schools include:

1. What type of exploratory opportunities do we currently offer?
2. What types of exploratory opportunities can we offer in the future?
3. Who should teach these courses?
4. How can teams be used more effectively in the exploratory process?
5. How can educators evaluate student participation in these activities?
6. How can educators increase community awareness of the need for exploration during early adolescence?
7. How can educators determine what these opportunities provide for students?
8. How can educators provide program consistency?
9. How can educators provide exploratory opportunities that will ensure student success?
10. How can educators integrate all students and curricular activities into a comprehensive program that meets the needs of the students?

## References

Alexander, W., & George, P. S. (1981). *The exemplary middle school.* New York: Holt, Rinehart and Winston.

Alexander, W., & McEwin, K. (1989). *Schools in the middle: Status and progress.* Columbus, OH: National Middle School Association.

Becker, H. J. (1990). Curriculum and instruction in middle-grade schools. *Phi Delta Kappan, 71*(6), 450–457.

Carnegie Council on Adolescent Development's Task Force on Education of Young Adolescents. (1989). *Turning points: Preparing American youth for the 21st century.* Washington, DC: Carnegie Council on Adolescent Development, a program of Carnegie Corporation of New York.

Curtis, T., & Bidwell, W. (1977). *Curriculum and instruction for emerging adolescents.* Reading, MA: Addison-Wesley.

Eichhorn, D. (1966). *The middle school.* New York: Center for Applied Research in Education.

Epstein, J., & Mac Iver, D. (1990). *Education in the middle grades: An overview of national practices and trends.* Columbus, OH: National Middle School Association.

Erikson, E. (1963). *Childhood and society.* New York: Norton.

Erikson, E. (1968). *Identity: Youth and crisis.* New York: Norton.

Faunce, R., & Clute, M. (1961). *Teaching and learning in the junior high school.* Belmont, CA: Wadsworth.

Goodlad, J. (1983). *A place called school: Prospects for the future.* New York: McGraw-Hill.

Lounsbury, J. H. (1981). Less is more in middle school scheduling. *The Principal,* *60*(3), 24.

Lounsbury, J. H., & Johnston, J. H. (1988). *Life in the three sixth grades.* Reston, VA: National Association of Secondary School Principals.

Lounsbury, J., & Vars, G. (1978). *A curriculum for the middle school years.* New York: Harper and Row.

Mitchell, J. (1974). *Human life: The early adolescent years.* Toronto: Holt, Rinehart, and Winston of Canada.

National Association of Secondary School Principals Council on Middle Level Education. (1984). *An agenda for excellence at the middle level.* Reston, VA: National Association of Secondary School Principals.

National Commission on Excellence in Education. (1983). *A nation at risk: The imperative for educational reform.* Washington, DC: U.S. Government Printing Office.

Schneider, G. (1986). Exploratory programs and educational reform: A second look. *Middle School Journal, 17*(2), 3, 23–24.

Tuttle, F. B. (1985). *Fine arts in the curriculum.* Washington, DC: National Education Association.

Van Hoose, J., & Strahan, D. (1988). *Young adolescent development and school practices: Promoting harmony.* Columbus, OH: National Middle School Association.

Van Til, C., Vars, G., & Lounsbury, J. (1967). *Modern education for the junior high school* (2nd ed.). Indianapolis, IN: Bobbs-Merrill.

# CHAPTER TWELVE

# Maintaining Middle Schools

JAMES P. GARVIN
*New England League*
*of Middle Schools*
*Rowley, Massachusetts*

Middle school educators cannot expect to gain credibility unless they produce practices that work. Educators in effective middle schools set realistic goals that match the age/learner characteristics of young adolescents and they believe in a collaborative organization, placing teachers together on interdisciplinary teams with a common group of students. Building student self-esteem is central to practices within effective middle schools. They understand that their unique mission requires continual professional growth to sustain a level of credibility with the communities they serve.

Starting a middle school is easier than sustaining one. Starting one often carries strong administrative support. Sustaining a middle school depends on how well a staff understands the process of change and how well they implement their transitional program. The process of changing a school organization takes time and input from all participants. Sustaining the change requires continuing incentives, leadership, and training until the new organization becomes the integral part of the climate of the school (Christ, 1982; Merenbloom, 1983).

Information is abundant for those looking for transitional techniques to change school organization (Bondi, 1982; Eichhorn, 1980; George, 1986). These earlier works treated lightly the magnitude of individual change for those within a middle school. Most educators who have been through a transition to a middle school concept will testify that the most important obstacle to overcome is that of changing the attitudes of individuals, not organizational programs. Sustaining middle level schools effectively is based on how well change agents resolve the initial human anxiety. It may take five or more years of careful planning to make the organizational change accepted as part of the total personality of school life. Sustaining individual attitudes have been altered in the initial phase of the change process. Maintaining organizational change requires that the following components are in place.

1. *Philosophical commitment from the school board and superinten-dent:* When difficult decisions are necessary, principals must be assured that policy makers are philosophically committed to the concept (George, 1986).

2. *Leadership with effective interpersonal abilities that is informed, committed, courageous, and energetic:* Transition to middle school and maintaining schools require strong leadership. Schools cannot expect to experience success if they do not select a principal based on his or her ability to facilitate change. The transition process needs informed leadership with vision and experience. At least two leadership types seem to be present in middle level schools: those who manage and those with vision. Managers spend a lot of time managing someone else's program. These are people who spend most of their time preserving the status quo or insuring that no one is "rocking the boat." Second, the principal with vision is motivated by ideas to effect change, able to keep and implement a plan, and able to keep others involved in the development process. These leaders are confident in themselves and believe they can bring about change (Johnston, 1988).

3. *A strong faculty:* Research is clear concerning the effect of faculty commitment and skill in restructuring schools (Boyer, 1986; Brophy & Good, 1974). Once a faculty is committed to a set of beliefs, they can produce just about any type of school they desire. Restructuring teacher organization to interdisciplinary teams requires the highest level of professional maturity. Schools that resist organizational change because they suspect it might affect their professional maturity should be reminded that professional maturity values interdisciplinary work. In fact, Eichhorn (1981) believed that inter-disciplinary work between teachers was the highest level of professional maturity. Professionally mature teachers naturally desire collaboration with colleagues. Teachers who prefer the isolation of their classrooms can change, if slowly, during the collaboration process (Erb & Doda, 1989).

4. *A mission statement:* Effective middle schools have a set of beliefs from which all decisions are made. This mission statement serves as a framework from which all programs are evaluated, organizational structure is developed, curriculum and instructional practices are justified, and disputes settled. Schools without a mission are like boats without a rudder; they drift wherever the wind blows (Melton, 1988). Effective mission statements grow from faculties and staff articulating their beliefs about the unique needs of young adolescents and accommodating the school program to meet these needs. These schools know what they seek in student behavior. Unless the

faculty and staff have agreed to a set of basic beliefs, the school community will not develop; rather, vested interest will prevail.

When educators within a school agree on a content from which to make decisions, collaboration naturally develops. If a mission statement is not in place, teachers tend to refer to students as *my* students, not *our* students; courses will be considered *my* course, not *our* course; and emphasis on what is going on in *my* class will be more important than what faculty is doing together in *our* school. Individual concerns will circumvent team concerns (Eichhorn, 1981).

5. *Sufficient transition time:* Success requires that enough time is planned to educate constituent groups who are expected to make the change (Merenbloom, 1983). Schools sometimes expect that they can announce a change in June and expect it to be functioning by the following September. Once leadership announces change, it may take two years to establish the awareness level before the staff feels comfortable operationalizing the model. Understanding the intended change develops from making visitations, reading professional literature, attending conferences, and developing planning committees to shape and fashion a program that fits the community. Constant dialogue between all parties is also important (Erb & Doda, 1989). These activities are designed to produce new thinking, a new environment, and a new vision for schooling. A new level of professional satisfaction will eventually change the behavior of faculty and staff to do things differently and more effectively.

6. *Realistic expectations:* Maintaining an effective middle level school requires a transitional plan that allows time for consumption and practice before expecting advanced levels of performance (Garvin, 1989). Middle school change will be thwarted if ambitious leaders expect change too quickly. Collaboration is predicated on teachers learning to talk with each other. Helping teachers feel "psychologically safe" with each other may take longer than most ambitious principals want to take time to develop.

Sustaining change requires a plan of transition where teachers have common planning time and the opportunities to develop mutual respect for one another. This mutual respect is basic to sophisticated decision making. Agendas during team meetings begin by dealing with common concerns. Coordinating homework and testing assignments, developing disciplinary policies, setting parent conferences, and developing team goals are nonthreatening issues to professional autonomy. Teachers who are expected to develop interdisciplinary units, adjust to more heterogeneously grouped students, and implement more developmentally appropriate practices are more likely to produce resistance to change due to these professionally threatening activities. In this case, teachers sometimes use common planning time to subvert the intended outcomes (Garvin, 1989).

7. *In-service:* Learning how to function effectively as a team will occur

when teachers learn how to coordinate teaching time, schedules, advisee/advisor activities, instructional practices, and curriculum. The evolution of effective teaming requires moving through levels of maturity and practice (George, 1986). Initial in-service activities should center around needs of young adolescents and the value of collaborative teaching efforts. As a school opens communication between staff, in-service should focus on teams developing operational goals.

Knowing how to take advantage of block schedules to bring about effective small and large group instruction, making the length of classes more flexible, rotating classes, and changing grouping patterns are possibilities for teachers, but will require in-service and practice under the guidance of an informed principal or team leader. Learning how to deal with student concerns through a collaborative approach will require education. Using the common planning time to work effectively with parents needs attention. The role of support staff in the collaborative model is important for in-service. Assuring the related arts people that they are important and showing how they can collaborate with core teachers will require new learning.

Teams need to learn how to evaluate their performance and administrators need to learn how to develop criteria for effective teaming from which to conduct teacher evaluation. The role of student evaluation as a team effort will be new to most teachers. Learning to work with mixed ability classes or with classes grouped by other factors, such as interest or topic, will need to be addressed. Developing teams that work harmoniously rather than in isolation of each other will need attention. Working transition into and out of the school will require emphasis on blending curriculums and instructional practices with the elementary and high schools.

8. *Team issues:* Teams make middle schools work. The following elements should be considered in maintaining successful teams.

a. *Leadership:* The anxiety of working together collaboratively can be relieved considerably by a team leader who is trained to give direction and instill confidence in team members. During the first year of implementation, it is important to have success, which in turn, breeds success. Team leadership can assist in developing realistic goal setting, team-meeting climate, diffusing resistance, informing administrators of progress, identifying professional growth needs, and keeping teams on task. These key people meet with leaders from other teams to insure continuity and maintain a sense of community. This focused leadership facilitates a high probability of success over the important formal years of team growth (Erb & Doda, 1989). Team leaders need to see their role as helping team members become a cohesive group, blending efforts to maximize effectiveness as a facilitator, not an indoctrinator.

Good team leaders share responsibilities and, if effective, eventually work themselves out of a job!

b. *Sharing:* Middle level schools need to be aware that teams periodically become "islands unto themselves," forming cliques. Some schools allow teams to become isolated, which often results in lack of connectiveness and transition between grade levels. Students run the risk of having a warm sixth-grade team, a tyrannical seventh-grade team, and a content-centered eighth-grade team. The lack of communication between teams generates three transitions for students—the very thing the middle school is designed to eliminate. Teams need to have opportunities to share with each other. Early release days allow for teams to be free at the same time. This time also allows the related arts teachers to join team meetings. Team members should consider taking a leave of absence from their team periodically to become acquainted with other grade levels and another team. Schools may want to consider more multilevel teams to insure transition between grades. Schools that maintain excellence do not allow splinter groups to plan and act apart from the school mission (Erb & Doda, 1989; Garvin, 1989).

c. *Record keeping:* Sustained successful schools requires keeping a record of the events that contribute to the outcomes of established goals. Records of team meetings are helpful in charting team growth and reviewing effectiveness. Written records are helpful in explaining to outside groups how teams work, especially those who think it is "fun and games." Records serve as a historical chronicle of team effectiveness (Erb & Doda, 1989). When school boards/committees need to cut budgets, teaming is often at the cutting edge. Sustaining middle level programs may well depend on keeping a record of effectiveness when "hard data" are required to justify expenditures to keep the programs they worked hard to develop.

d. *Unified arts:* Unified arts teachers (industrial arts, music, art, and so forth) often feel disenfranchised when schools move toward a different organizational structure. These teachers are seldom included as members of a team. Consequently, they often feel like "babysitters," watching students so that core teachers can be free for common planning time. In effective schools, this mentality does not exist when the importance of unified arts is reinforced within the school mission. The "arts" are essential in the educational program of young adolescents. The leadership of the school must find ways to insure that unified arts teachers are valued and that opportunities exist to include them in team activities.

Schools that restructure and leave out unified arts teachers in the teaming process prevent the community purpose of collaborative involvement from existing in the growth of the school. Teams can do many things to insure better working relationships with the unified arts teachers. For example, team members can send them copies of team minutes, offer to exchange classes with them to provide release time to attend occasional team meetings. Team members can spend portions of common planning time visiting their classrooms, enabling core teachers to see their students in another environment, watch what they are doing, talk with the arts teacher, and discuss ways of working together on a project.

Healthy middle level schools understand that the unified arts people are very important in advisee/advisor relationships with students. Unified arts teachers are respected because they are able to motivate students in ways often not possible in the core classes. Effective schools continually brainstorm activities to use this valuable resource in the total mission of the school (Garvin, 1989).

e. *Incentives:* Individual faculty members and teams need to be professionally recognized on a regular basis (Erb & Doda, 1989). Recognition at special assemblies, team of the week awards, courtesy notes, early release time for special projects, and media recognition are a few of the activities schools can use to recognize individual faculty members and teams to sustain the professional life and maintain the momentum of healthy schools.

f. *Periodic evaluation:* Assessment of effectiveness ought to be an ongoing process throughout the school. Professional growth seldom occurs without it. It is especially important for the effectiveness of teaming. Developing a technique to assess team effectiveness should include team members. One of the outcomes of team assessment should be to assist team members to grow together and become more and more effective with students. Another outcome should determine the degree to which the team is consistent with the goals of the school. Principals who strive to maintain and improve the restructuring effort should suggest tying effectiveness as a team member to the annual evaluation. Leadership should develop and promote criteria on effective teaming from which to conduct faculty assessment.

g. *A mindset that people helping people develops a healthy community:* Effective middle level schools are identified by a prevailing attitude of caring for one another. The mission projects an ethic that if one person in the community fails, we all fail. People helping people is the norm for building productive relationships and collaborative outcomes. Schools that foster the notion that students need to learn the importance of helping others make it an important part of the school experience. This value is evidenced when schools spotlight cooperative learning, peer tutoring, mixed ability grouping, student support groups, and other activities designed to build cooperative rather than competitive relationships. Gifted and talented programs become the norm for every student. Students are not seen as part of a pecking order; they are perceived as people with human potential released best through community effort. It is this ethic that blends a school into a community. Effective middle level schools hold a system of beliefs in one another and demonstrate it by respecting the right to learn as common to everyone (Epstein & Mac Iver, 1990; Lounsbury, 1986; Toepfer, 1988).

## Conclusion

People who are closest to instruction generally make the best decisions (George, 1986). Administrators should view teachers as important in the decision-making process. Teachers need to know that their decisions will affect school policy. When teachers are empowered, they generally become creative, energized, and productive (George, 1986). Administrators who develop a teacher centeredness produce teachers who become student centered.

Recognizing teachers for their professional worth and professional accomplishments is essential in building a climate of self-esteem among teachers and students. When teachers know they are valued, they tend to value the system — they give to it, protect it, and direct energies into its preservation (Johnston & Markle, 1986). Empowering teachers to make decisions through the shared teaming model generates this value into an even more powerful force where teachers can create and dream together ways to bring students into an exciting set of experiences they themselves generated. Empowering teachers allows them to dream today and act tomorrow with an ownership in design for learning that develops an obligation to succeed. It is this feeling of professional importance that maintains effectiveness in middle level schools.

## References

Alexander, W. M., & George, P. S. (1981). *The exemplary middle school.* New York: Holt, Rinehart and Winston.

Blum, R. E., Butler, J. A., & Olson, N. L. (1987). Leadership for excellence: Research based training for principals. *Educational Leadership, 45*(1), 25–29.

Bondi, J. (1982, October). *Tips for successful transition to the middle school.* Paper presented at Florida League of Middle Schools Conference, Gainesville, FL.

Boyer, E. (1986). *Values in effecting personal growth.* Paper presented at Gordon College Commencement, Wenham, MA.

Brophy, J. E., & Good, T. L. (1974). *Teacher-student relationships: Causes and considerations.* New York: Holt, Rinehart & Winston.

Christ, H. (1982, March). *Moving to a middle school.* Paper presented at New England League of Middle Schools Conference, Peabody, MA.

Eichhorn, D. H. (1968). *The middle school.* New York: National Association of Secondary School Principals and National Middle School Association.

Eichhorn, D. H. (1980). *The Boyce medical study.* Paper presented at Massachusetts Superintendents Meeting, Acton, MA.

Eichhorn, D. H. (1981, March). *Essentials in effective middle schools.* Paper presented at the New England League of Middle Schools Conference, Sharon, MA.

Eisner, E. W. (1989). The ecology of school improvement. *Educational Leadership, 45*(5), 5–24.

Epstein, J. C., & Mac Iver, D. J. (1990). *Education in the middle grades: Overview of national practices and trends.* Columbus, OH: National Middle School Association.

Erb, T. O., & Doda, N. M. (1989). *Team organization: Practices and possibilities.* Washington, DC: National Education Association.

Garvin, J. P. (1985). *Common denominators in effective middle level schools.* Reston, VA: National Association of Secondary School Principals.

Garvin, J. P. (1989). *Merging the exploratory and basic subjects in the middle school.* Rowley, MA: New England League of Middle Schools.

George, P. S. (1977). *The middle school: A look ahead.* Columbus, OH: National Middle School Association.

George, P. S. (1986, March). *A nation at risk.* Address to the New England League of Middle Schools Conference, Hyannis, MA.

George, P. S., & Oldaker, L. L. (1985). *A national survey of middle school effectiveness.* Alexandria, VA: Association of Supervision and Curriculum Development.

Johnston, H. J. (1988, November). *What research says on leadership.* Paper presented at the Annual Conference of the National Middle School Association.

Johnston, H. J., & Markle, G. C. (1986). *What research says to the middle level practitioner.* Columbus, OH: National Middle School Association.

Lezotte, L. W. (1985). Growing use of the effective schools model for school improvement. *Educational Leadership, 42*(5), 6–23.

Lieberman, A. E. (1986). Collaborative research working with, not working on. *Educational Leadership, 43*(5), 5–28.

Lipsitz, J. (1984). *Successful schools for young adolescents.* New Brunswick, NJ: Transaction Books.

Lounsbury, J. H. (1986). *Perspectives: Middle school education.* Columbus, OH: National Middle School Association.

Martinez, M. E. (1989). Assessment for Learning. *Educational Leadership, 46*(7), 6–23.

Melton, G. (1988). *A nation at risk.* Address to the New England League of Middle Schools, Hyannis, MA.

Mendez, R. E. (1986). Can principals improve their instructional leadership? *NASSP Bulletin, 70*(488), 1–6.

Merenbloom, E. Y. (1983). *The team process in the middle school: A handbook for teachers.* Columbus, OH: National Middle School Association.

Morrison, W. L. (1975). *Good schools for middle grade youngsters: Characteristics, practices, recommendations.* Columbus, OH: National Middle School Association.

Toepfer, C. Jr. (1988, November). *Allowing for cultural diversity throughout the curriculum.* Paper presented at the Annual Conference of the National Middle School Association, St. Louis, MO.

Wiles, J., & Bondi, J. (1986). *The essential middle school.* Tampa, FL: Wiles and Bondi Associates.

PART THREE

# *Developing a Sense of Relevance*

A recent report, Coming of Age: The Impact of PRIME Legislation on Middle Level Schools in Florida *(1990), documents the progress of implementing middle school organization in that state. This report included a recommendation to develop curriculum and instruction that are consistent with the nature and needs of young adolescents. The report concluded that "while Florida is making significant progress in the restructuring of middle level schools, much remains to be done to improve the heart of the middle school—the classroom" (p. 16). This recommendation is from a state that has already invested millions of dollars and long hours of in-service efforts to improve middle level education. In some areas of Florida, significant changes in curriculum, instruction, and grouping practices have occurred. In many others, however, the school is reorganized—name, grades, and structure are changed—but the individual classroom is left unchanged.*

*Recent "shadow studies" indicate that Florida is not unique in this respect (Lounsbury & Johnston, 1988; Lounsbury & Clark, 1990). Prevailing practices seem to indicate that middle grades students (1) are not provided a curriculum that is relevant or integrated; (2) are bored with the endless worksheets, tests, and copying from the chalkboard; (3) are not challenged to think critically or become involved in the decisions of learning; (4) are often "tracked" with the same students all day and all year; and (5) are not given time to interact with peers, especially within a learning context. It is little wonder that young adolescents today do not seem motivated to learn.*

*Part Three of this book deals with the relevancy of student learning. In Chapter Thirteen, Conrad Toepfer, Jr., addresses curriculum from an historical and definitional perspective, presents related curriculum models, and makes a plea for more interdisciplinary and relevant curriculum. In Chapter Fourteen, Robert Spear introduces and closes his thorough review* of literature on appropriate grouping practices by presenting an interview with a teacher, Mike, who reveals the amount of personal change required to move from teaching homogeneously grouped students toward teaching more heterogeneously grouped students. Bob also discusses the impact that rigid ability grouping has on young adolescents. Julia Thomason and Max Thompson, in Chapter Fifteen, summarize the literature on student motivation and provide practical suggestions for increasing student motivation in the middle grades.

In Chapter Sixteen, Judith Irvin (your editor) discusses the reasons why middle level students generally have difficulty with learning and presents the concepts of schema, metacognition, and strategic learning. Interdisciplinary team organization is advocated and two strategies for learning and presenting the components of a successful instructional program are suggested.

Many of the chapters in this book mention cooperative learning as an appropriate method for creating an environment more conducive to meaningful student learning. Karen Wood, in Chapter Seventeen, discusses how cooperative learning helps to meet the social, emotional, intellectual, and physical needs of young adolescents and offers numerous strategies for implementing cooperative learning. In the closing chapter of this section (Chapter Eighteen), Gordon Vars presents research on evaluation and reporting, identifies issues in marking and reporting procedures used, and makes suggestions for making this key aspect of education more age appropriate.

Middle school practices such as interdisciplinary teaming, advisory programs, and expanded exploration programs lend themselves to providing learning experiences that are more integrated and relevant. Some middle level educators refer to this school reform as "Phase One." Making the leap into a true transformation of curriculum, instruction, learning environments, and evaluation procedures will most assuredly lead to improved student achievement and behavior. That is "Phase Two."

## References

Florida Department of Education (1990). Coming of age: Impact of PRIME legislation on middle level schools in Florida. Tallahassee, FL: Author.

Lounsbury, J. H., & Clark, D. C. (1990). Inside grade eight: From apathy to excitement. Reston, VA: National Association of Secondary School Principals.

Lounsbury, J. H., & Johnston, J. H. (1988). Life in the three sixth grades. Reston, VA: National Association of Secondary School Principals.

# CHAPTER THIRTEEN

# Middle Level School Curriculum: Defining the Elusive

CONRAD F. TOEPFER, JR.
*State University of New York at Buffalo*

American school-communities reflect the increasing growth of a three-level school system. As middle level schools focus increasingly on young adolescent concerns, their identity separates from the shadow of the high school that long encompassed it. Those of us long involved with middle level education delight in this growing recognition of the critical mass of educational needs during the years between the elementary and the high school.

The successful move of states and their communities to specify this separate identity is seen in such achievements as California's report *Caught in the Middle* (1987), the *New York State Board of Regents Policy on Middle-Level Eduction and Schools with Middle-Level Grades* (1989), and *Coming of Age: The Impact of PRIME Legislation on Middle Level Schools in Florida* (Florida Department of Education, 1990). Such efforts are increasing public and professional recognition of the need to implement programmatic components that effectively deal with educational differences at the middle level of schools.

There is increasing professional agreement about the *how* issues of middle level school level organization. However, I am alarmed that parallel attention has not been devoted to the *what* of the middle level school—the curriculum itself. In his poem, "The Rubiyat," Omar Khayyam asks a fascinating rhetorical question about the activities of the vintner, or winemaker: "What can it be the vintner buys that is half as precious as what

205

he sells?" While the answer would seem to be grapes, the question of the *what* dimension of the curriculum is a more perplexing issue.

It seems to me that the curriculum should be the substance that organizational and methodological efforts attempt to implement in middle level schools. This view does not deemphasize the achievements that organizational features have contributed to improving middle level school programs. Structures such as interdisciplinary team teaching, block schedules, advisory programs, and activity programs have certainly responded to young adolescent developmental educational needs. Beane (1990a, 1990b), however, sees the continuing need to devote attention to the middle level school curriculum question. The centrality of his argument is worthy of serious attention.

> *What should be the planned curriculum of the middle school? The importance of the "curriculum" question cannot be overestimated since it opens up the way to several key factors that are partially addressed by structural reform. For example, if the middle school is to be based upon the characteristics of early adolescence, then the curriculum ought to be redesigned along developmentally appropriate lines rather than simply a slightly revised version of the traditional high school curriculum.*
>
> *Furthermore, if "reform" means that relations among schools, teachers, and young people are to be reconstructed, then the planned curriculum itself, as one of the powerful mediating forces in that relationship, must also change. In other words, being sensitive to early adolescent characteristics is only part of "reform." The "how to teach" question must be accompanied by a "What do we teach and learn question." (Beane, 1990a, p. 1)*

It is inappropriate to focus myopically on the *how* of middle level school organizational features while virtually bypassing the *what* of the curriculum. This limited view weakens the inextricable relationship that should exist between the form and function of middle level school curriculum and program features. Yet, with the best of intentions, some national spokespersons suggest that what we teach in the middle level school is not as important as how we teach it. I believe that position to be a misleadingly dangerous one. However, it remains for both the reader and middle level curriculum scholars to focus and resolve this issue.

In this chapter, I will focus on areas that should be addressed in defining the *what* of middle level school curricula and school programs. Following a discussion of curriculum definition concerns, I will present an historical perspective on organizational changes that framed junior high curriculum issues and discuss the stages of curricular concerns in the subsequent middle school movement. I will then present middle level curricular functions and specific curriculum issues as they have prompted the development of models to deal with the *what* issues of middle level curriculum. A treatment of how curriculum approaches have been used to structure middle level school curricula leads to a consideration of learning focuses that middle level school curriculum ought to consider.

## *Curriculum* Defined

Curriculum has been defined in a number of ways. The following definition of curriculum, made by Hass (1980), seems sufficiently open to allow educators to deal appropriately with middle level school curriculum issues.

> *Curriculum is all the experiences that individual learners have in a program of education whose purpose is to achieve broad goals and related specific objectives, which is planned in terms of a framework of theory and research or past and present professional practice. (p. 37)*

Developers of middle level school programs at the local school level need to focus on how best to frame the *what* of the curriculum as reflected in the all-school program. Beane, Toepfer, and Alessi (1986) offer four classifications of how curriculum may be considered in planning and developing the *what* of the local school program.

1. *Curriculum as product* derives from the idea that such documents as listing of middle level school courses, syllabi for various courses, curriculum guides, lists of skills, and so on are the results of curriculum planning or curriculum development. In other words, if these documents are the results of curriculum planning and development, they must be the curriculum.

Curriculum as product is useful in developing materials based on state and other requirements that must be accommodated in district middle level schools. Such materials manifest efforts to codify curriculum as program.

2. *Curriculum as program* derives from the use of curriculum in reference to the program of the school. If the purpose of the school is learning, curriculum is the program for carrying out that purpose. Curriculum as program must consider that students learn from aspects of the middle level school program other than just the courses of study or classroom activities. This leads to the recognition that learning takes place in many different settings in the middle level school.

Curriculum program provides the focus for local staff organizing curriculum as product into a program that can be delivered within the logistics of the local middle school community. How middle level schools in different districts develop programs dealing with curriculum as product creates programs that respond to local realities and needs.

3. *Curriculum as intended learnings* refers to curriculum used as the learnings that are intended for students. Curriculum as intended learning outcomes considers that curriculum becomes a concept or idea rather than a product. It also defines curriculum in a more manageable focus by limiting its scope.

Defining the *what* of curriculum requires goals and objectives that specify the purposes and intended learnings of middle level school programs. Specification of local issues and needs through curriculum as intended learnings can identify directions that local middle level school curricula and school programs need to pursue.

4. *Curriculum as the experience of the learner* represents a major departure from the previous three categories. here, curriculum refers to the experiences of the learner that are outcomes of the planned situations. Thus, the courses of actual events or the curriculum can only be found in the learnings that students take away from the various experiences provided by the school. This definition takes its focus primarily on learning and the learner rather than teaching in itself.

Curriculum as experience of the learner is infrequently used. It is most often utilized in nonrequired exploratory and electives course areas. Teachers recognize the value of student learning experiences organized in this manner. Middle level school curriculum planning should pursue this dimension in required areas of curriculum program and curriculum as product.

Specific aspects of the middle level school program can be categorized under the four classifications just described. As local middle level educators develop that frame of reference, the task of planning the middle level school curriculum to develop programs that respond to the critical mass of characteristics of young adolescents in that school must be undertaken. The following statement focuses on defining the process to organize the *what* of the curriculum.

> *Curriculum planning is a process in which participants at many levels make decisions about what the purposes of learning ought to be, how those purposes might be carried out through teaching-learning situations, and whether the purposes and means are both appropriate and effective. (Beane, Toepfer, & Alessi, 1986, p. 56)*

Curriculum planning activities range from identification of broad goals to description of possibilities for specific teaching-learning situations. Curriculum development and instruction are elements within the total curriculum planning process. They are defined to help middle level educators specify how to best approach curriculum-related tasks.

> *Curriculum development is mainly concerned with the design of plans for actual teaching-learning situtions. It is based upon the broad goals and related program of learning activities identified in curriculum planning activities.*
>
> *Instruction is developed from broad goals and curriculum plans and focuses on methodological questions, resources, and teaching techniques. Individual teachers or teams of teachers develop specific teaching learning situations such as units or lessons. They work to decide the most appropriate implementation of activities, resources, and measuring devices used in those specific teaching-learning situations. (Beane, Toepfer, & Alessi, 1986, p. 57)*

Efforts to define the *what* of middle level curriculum need to deal first with the planning and development of curriculum and then the instructional implications of the curriculum. The history of the establishment of a separate middle level school unit also needs consideration in reviewing how things have come to be as we approach the twenty-first century.

## Middle Grades Organizational Changes: A Historical Perspective

It is incorrect to asume that the junior high movement was a distinct attempt to improve curriculum and instruction in the middle grades. The organizational changes that established junior high schools did not seek to establish a separate program unit between elementary and high schools. In tracing those changes, it is clear they were not made for curricular reasons. There were major conceptual differences in the development in the contemporary middle school movement from the earlier establishment of junior high schools. The latter began as an effort to reorganize the balance of elementary and secondary from its 8-4 pattern of grades (Toepfer, 1982a).

In 1898, influential Harvard University president Charles Eliot began a campaign to reorganize the structure of U.S. elementary and secondary education. That February, he addressed the National Education Association on the topic "Can School Programs be Shortened and Enriched?" He stated that the last two years of elementary school be removed to create a six-year elementary program. Over the next five years, his campaign across the country gained increasing support. He contended that students and the nation would be better served by a grade 7 through 12 secondary program (Eliot, 1898).

The National Education Association established their *Committee of Ten on Secondary Education* (NEA, 1894), which endorsed Eliot's recommendation. This endorsement resulted in a national movement toward a pattern of six elementary and six secondary grades in U.S. public schools. This movement was monitored for the next 15 years by another NEA committee. The Committee on the Equal Division of the Twelve Years in the Public Schools between the District and the High School (NEA, 1907) continued to support that change.

The extended NEA Committee on the Culture Element and Economy of Time in Education (NEA, 1909) also endorsed creation of a six-year secondary school program: "In the entire period of general education, two years can be saved, without loss of anything essential in culture, efficiency, or character-making, this thesis to be proved or disproved" (p. 374).

This move focused on lowering the grade in which the shift from self-contained classroom teaching to departmentalized instruction was made. The beginnings of middle level education arose from the subsequent movement to subdivide the scope of the new six-year secondary school program into two segments. The consideration in this move was organizational. There was no substantive curricular rationale behind that decision. In this subdivision of the grade 7 through 12 pattern development, an issue arose that continues to hound efforts to improve middle level curricula and school programs. Growing needs to relieve classroom space shortage at the secondary school level were a major concern even during the birth pangs of separate middle level schools. Hartwell (1905) was one of the first to focus on this issue.

> *When the seventh and eighth year pupils are placed under departmental teaching in separate buildings, the first year of the high school will soon be added to their course, making an intermediate course of three years. This will relieve the high school and save the immense expense of more high school buildings. The first year of high school is preparatory to selection of the regular courses, and may as well and better be taken with the last two years of the grammar school. (pp. 162–163)*

Yet, an earlier innovtion largely escaped attention. In 1885, Richmond, Indiana, developed the Garfield School for all of Richmond's seventh- and eighth-grade students (Toepfer, 1962a). This was the first attempt to develop a separate middle level school based on educational reasons alone. The Garfield School preceded the movement to subdivide the high school into junior and senior high units. However, the national movement to establish separate school units between elementary and high schools responded primarily to logistical and economic needs.

The publicized establishment of the Indianola Junior High School in Columbus, Ohio, in 1909 and the Berkeley, (California) Intermediate School the following year initiated this movement. Examination of local school records (Toepfer, 1962a) revealed that classroom space shortage was the primary motivation in spite of educational advantages cited in both communities. Movement from a two-level (elementary and high school) to three-level (elementary, junior high, and high school) system did not initially recognize students in the middle grades as significantly different from high school learners.

The early establishment of separate junior high schools sought to increase the numbers of students who completed high school. The United States Bureau of Education convened its own committee to examine these issues. Reporting in 1913, the National Council of Education on Economy of Time in Education (Baker, 1913) made the following statement about the grade 7 through 12 secondary school.

> *No matter how varied the offering of studies is, or how adjustable the privilege of election, the six-year course is not an attractive or practical scheme for all those who might be able to pursue their general course beyond the primary school. It ought to be subdivided into two administrative sections: (1) a junior high school of three years, extending from the twelfth to the fifteenth year; and, (2) a senior high school, also of three years, covering the period from the fifteenth to the eighteenth year.*
>
> *Such a subdivision and point of articulation is necessary upon social as well as individual grounds. A three year junior high school will assure a larger number of citizens possessing some cultural training of a secondary grade than the six-year school. A point of articulation in the middle of such a high school system would afford an appropriate position for the establishment of vocational school of a type now largely missing in the proposals for vocational schools. (pp. 26–27)*

The contention that a three-year junior high school would provide some general education for more citizens in the foregoing statement is noteworthy. It was the first such statement of a curricular concern to appear in commentaries about the subdivision of the six-year high school. Primary sources, including reports and school district minutes (Toepfer, 1962a, pp. 10–96), confirm the foregoing statement was the emphasis as junior high schools were established. Attempts to differentiate curriculum and program in the two school levels did not arise until the 1920s.

Introduction of the Carnegie Unit in 1910 established time and unit requirements in grades 9 through 12. To earn Carnegie Unit credits toward graduation, students had to spend specified minutes in daily classes in English, history, science, and mathematics. This action ushered in quantitative measurement of time spent in class with no qualitative stipulations of what should be done during a particular class in the subjects. Carnegie Unit accreditation was based on "time served," rather than the learning that transpired during class (Tompkins & Gaumlitz, 1954).

Carnegie Unit designation did not recognize curriculum and program differentiation in junior high from senior high schools. Although there were no seventh- or eighth-grade Carnegie Unit requirements, ninth-grade Carnegie Unit requirements often limited seventh- and eighth-grade initiatives to preparing students for the rigors of those ninth-grade requirements (Tompkins & Gaumlitz, 1954). As a result, ninth-grade Carnegie Unit requirements served to reduce curricular initiatives in earlier junior high grades (Toepfer, 1962a).

G. Stanley Hall, the leading adolescent psychologist of the day, made this observation about adolescence in 1904:

*Adolescence is a new birth, for the higher and more completely human traits are now born. The qualities of body and soul that now emerge are far newer. The child comes from and harks back to a remoter past; the adolescent is neo-atavistic, and in him the later acquisitions of the race slowly become proponent. (p. 13)*

While Hall spoke of the emergence of new qualities, at the dawn of the junior high school they were not spelled out into guidelines that might influence curriculum practices. Early junior high schools did not recognize that young adolescents might learn differently from later adolescents. Scholarly and school-based junior high educational writings during that interval were largely focused on organizational issues.

It was another two decades before adolescent psychology identified differing developmental and learning characteristics of young adolescents from later and maturing adolescents. This is reflected in the shift from organizational to student-based concerns in the junior high literature after 1940. Differentiation of junior high from senior high curriculum emphases emerged and flourished from 1940 through 1960, on a growing base of young adolescent psychological information.

Early secondary education scholars increasingly identified the developmental and programmatic inappropriateness of junior high schools as "junior editions" of senior high schools. These differences of junior high from senior high learners served to identify appropriate junior high curriculum and school program needs.

## The Middle School Concept

During the early 1960s, another shift ushered in the beginnings of the so-called middle school movement. Eichhorn, Alexander, and other scholars began to see the need to reconstitute the scope in elementary, middle level, and high schools. Shifts from grades 7 and 8 and 7 through 9 junior schools to newer middle grades patterns responded to pediatrics and medical data confirming the increasingly earlier emergence of pubescence in that era (Toepfer, 1982a).

The recognition of the developmental needs and shared learning characteristics of students in the later junior high school era had focused efforts to unify school program needs. The beginning middle school movement primarily responded to earlier maturational development in young adolescents. This led to increasing recognition of learning differences of young adolescents from both elementary and high school learners.

After 1960, the increasingly earlier maturational development of young adolescents began to divide the developmental sameness and school program needs of students in grades 7 and 8 and 7 through 9 schools. In the 1890s, advocates had recommended movement of seventh- and eighth-graders out of elementary school (Toepfer, 1962b). By the 1960s, more sixth-graders, and even fifth-graders, were demonstrating readiness for something other than self-contained instruction along with younger children in elementary schools. At the same time, ninth-graders were becoming more like high school than middle grades students. Developmental and learning sameness of ninth-graders with tenth- through twelfth-graders was replacing the sameness ninth-graders formerly had with seventh- and eighth-graders.

Initially, this was viewed by some as a "turf battle," threatening the grades 7 and 8 or 7 through 9 junior high school pattern that had grown and flourished until then. The advantages in shifting to grades 5 through 8, 6 through 8, and other patterns between 1960 and 1980 was sometimes lost in adversarial conflicts. Even amidst "junior high versus middle school harangues," the programmatic elements refined during the later junior high school era well served middle level schools with reconstituted school grade populations. Since 1960, excellent progress was realized in defining the critical mass of young adolescent physical, social, emotional, and intellectual characteristics and needs.

### Developmental Issues

The term *middle level education* is now used to describe schools and programs involving all combinations of grades 5 through 9 for youngsters from 10 to 14 years of age. Programs, not grades, make a school. Middle level school program effectiveness is reflected in how realistically the curriculum answers the following question: To what degree does the school's program meet the developmental characteristics and learning needs of students in that school? Eichhorn (1966) defined the developmental epoch experienced by young adolescents during their middle level school years as "transescence." His definition deals with the nature of the tasks students need to master during their metamorphosis in that period. Eichhorn observed that *transescence* is

> *the stage of development which begins prior to the onset of puberty and extends through the early stages of adolescence. Since puberty does not occur for all precisely at the same chronological age in human development, the transescent designation is based upon the many physical, social, emotional, and intellectual changes that appear prior to the puberty cycle to the time when the body gains a practical degree of stabilization over these complex pubescent changes. (p. 3)*

*Transescence* (roots are *trans* from transition and *escence* from adolescence) cogently describes the growth, development, and transition tasks of the human developmental stage previously called *young adolescence, early adolescence,* or *emerging adolescence,* experienced during the middle level school years. Transescence occurs for most people during ages 10 to 14, although it may occur earlier or later for particular individuals. The ages during which students manifest transescent characteristics in the local school-community should help define which grades best belong in local middle level schools.

The chronological age at which pubescence begins has continued to decline, approximately a four-month decline per decade, since 1900 (Kramer, 1985). This is bringing more of the tasks formerly experienced during the age of 14 to 18 years into the transescent lifetime. Whereas the onset of fertility occurred at 17.6 years in our grandmothers' lives, it now occurs, on the average, during the eleventh year for transescent girls. Transescents today are also more socially aware and sophisticated than their agemates of a decade ago. However, in most cases, their social-emotional maturity has not really increased.

When struck by the physically more mature appearance of many transescents today, we should not asume that those students also possess equally precocious social-emotional maturity. In fact, the adjustment problems of physically precocious transescents may signal their need for special understanding and help by adults. We cannot assume that all of these "bigger" individuals are ready to take on physical, social, emotional, and intellectual tasks appropriate for maturing adolescents who are older and more mature than these precocious transescents.

### Diversity Issues

Widening diversity remains the hallmark of development during the middle school years. The ranges of physical, social, emotional, and intellectual development demonstrated by youngsters during their middle level school years are wider than those in either elementary or high schools. For example, we can easily see the problems created by single-size school furniture for physical diversity in transescent student populations. However, we often fail to see even more critical limitations imposed by middle level school curricula that are still largely miniaturized versions of the high school model.

Young children have relative physical, social, emotional, and intellectual similarities when they enter elementary school. They diversify as their abilities and capacities for growth allow. The range of that diversity peaks between grades 5 and 9. During their high school years, students approach the maturity of their physical, social, emotional, and intellectual potentials. The range of difference in those developmental domains begins to narrow. Some "late bloomers" now catch up with some who were precocious in reaching the fullness of their potentials. In high school, maturing adolescents and young adults demonstrate increasing abilities to integrate information learned in separate settings. However, the vast majority of students cannot make those connections during their middle level school years.

The diversity among middle level school students is complex. Some female middle level students have given birth to one or more children, whereas other agemates may still be a year away from achieving orgastic potency. Thinking levels among middle school populations range from beginning concrete operational thinkers to mature adult abstract thinkers. The national range of reading levels between sixth and eighth grades is from grade 2 through grade 13, usually with about four boys left over who don't seem to fit anywhere in that range. This diversity creates different challenges to middle level educators who need a focus different from that required in either elementary or high schools. Effective middle level educational practice requires much more than a less rigorous version of things that work well with maturing adolescents and young adults in high school. By the same token, neither is the extension of procedures appropriate for young children in elementary school appropriate or effective in meeting transescent learning needs.

Transescents learn best when they can see how facts, skills, and concepts relate to important issues in their young lives. Successful middle school teachers relate what they try to teach to student experience and the information taught in other content areas. Effective middle level school practice over the past decade has increasingly confirmed that facts, skills, and information are best learned when students can recall and apply them to their experience and knowledge. An experiential context for applying learning develops when students learn content and skills in relation to one another. Interdisciplinary teaching and learning should facilitate that for students.

## Middle Level Curricular Functions

Persisting middle level curricular functions provide the framework for organizing curriculum planning activities to develop school programs that respond to transescent educational needs. Initially, stated by Gruhn and Douglas (1947), these functions are integration, exploration, guidance, differentiation, socialization, and articulation. They remain effective reference points for determining the appropriateness of middle level curricular changes.

### Integration

Integration responds to the need for middle level schools to identify learner abilities and help individual students progress. Transescents are no longer young children. Middle level school experiences must help them grow and ease their transition from the elementary school. At the same time, middle level schools should not assume that students have high school adolescent learning capacities.

Middle level school programs are most effective when they offer skill development challenges that build carefully on how learners can and do think during transescence. At no time in their lives can students leap beyond their developmental capacities. Although some may look physically like 16-year-olds, we cannot assume that they can also think as maturely as the age they appear to be. In fact, very few transescents can be expected to perform consistently at the higher intellectual levels that normally develop when they are in high school. Schools must offer learning experiences that do not frustrate students but that still provide growth and success during early adolescence. This success is critical to continued achievement in high school.

Middle level school programs should help students develop a broad knowledge base and the skills necessary for subsequent learning. In middle level schools, the curriculum should help students learn how to learn and facilitate their becoming independent, confident students. When students take those fulfilled capacities with them to high school, they can build on the solid foundation they have successfully established in their middle level school experience.

Realistic and effective integration of learning in the middle level school combines a solid developmental program in all skill and content areas with opportunities for remediation as needed. In effective middle level schools, one can readily see the successful integration of intellectual and social skills into the students' repertoire of learning behavior. This can happen only when the program accommodates the unique needs, interests, and abilities of students between the ages 10 to 14 years.

### Exploration

Between the ages of 10 to 14 years, students live through the most serious and traumatic changes that we humans ever experience. The physiological, biological, social, emotional, and intellectual dimensions of these changes must be reflected in the school's exploratory program. Exploratory subjects such as art, music, home economics, and industrial arts are importnt to the students' personal and educational exploration. They allow students to explore their needs, interests, talents, and skills in these areas as a basis for considering educational goals in their high school programs.

Exploratory programs also assist students in using the facts, skills, and information learned in other classes (such as mathematics, science, social studies and English language arts) in the projects and activities in their exploratory courses. At this age, information learned in the academic areas is often best understood when students apply it to learning activities in the exploratory course areas. Applications such as time in music, mathematical formulas and scientific processes in industrial arts and home economics, and lines and angles in art make these exploratory courses vital learning experiences. These areas are far more than mere educational frills. They are an integral part of middle school curriculum.

Another important, but often unrecognized, aspect of exploration is the need for its emphasis in academic area courses. Exploratory learning in subjects such as English, mathematics, science, and social studies can help students define their personal interests in those subjects. Teachers need to help students relate particular facts, skills, and concepts to their areas of interest. This linking of student concerns and questions encourages their exploration.

For example, the altruism of transescents over issues of ecology and the environment is an excellent channel to stimulate individual exploration of science. Similar concern over justice issues, human hunger, and health issues in the world lead to exploration in areas such as health and the social studies. In addition, exploratory activities in the academic areas help students make reasonable career choices and understand the vast diversity of our world.

Middle level schools should help students examine the usefulness of subjects in their lives. Organized in this fashion, exploration provides students with solid content learning as well as an understanding of each subject area's relevance to success in school as well as out-of-school circumstances. Exploratory learning helps students more fully understand their emerging capacities and interests during this time of great change in their lives.

In this way, exploration can help students apply what they learn in school to current issues in their lives. It also prepares for success in high school. Time is wasted and students in middle level schools are frustrated by exploring high school kinds of experiences before they can understand and appreciate them.

### Guidance/Advisement

Guidance activities should assist students in making appropriate decisions regarding immediate and future educational and prevocational choices. Emotional aspects of adjusting to the physiological, social, emotional, and intellectual changes during transescence have middle level school program implications.

Guidance programs should help resolve educational and personal difficulties learners experience during those middle years. The services of trained guidance counselors and access to specialized personnel, including school psychologists and social workers, are necessary to these program concerns.

Decisions on the selection of course and activity offerings for individuals in their middle level school experience must be carefully considered. The functions of integration and exploration previously discussed are important as guidance personnel work with teachers and parents to plan the most appropriate programs for students.

Middle level schools need to define curriculum and school program dimensions of guidance/advisement functions. This can include such critical areas as providing appropriate information in drug, alcohol, and sex education. Participation of guidance personnel in planning and presenting such offerings is recommended.

Advisor/advisee programs provide a further means for each student to have a regular interaction with a classroom teacher to discuss school-related concerns in a noninstructional setting. Students assigned to small groups should meet on a regular basis to discuss problems of school adjustment with teachers and identify ways to gain more from the school program.

### Differentiation

The function of differentiation provides middle level programs and activities responsive to the wide range of development in middle level school populations. Differentiation of the middle level school program is essential if individual students are to fulfill their potential. Areas of consideration include reading level, level of thinking, spans of attention and concentration, frequently changing interests, and physical ability.

Developing curricula and school programs for this age group requires alternative learning arrangements, materials, times, and approaches to management and control. What works for one student may not work with another. Between the ages of 10 and 14 years, some individuals will begin to progress more slowly than they did during early childhood, while other agemates will demonstrate abilities more like high school students. This pattern of development in each individual cannot be substantially accelerated but it can be retarded. Both patterns are normal for different youngsters. Responsive middle level programs must provide means to deal with different abilities among individuals and groups of learners.

Middle level schools should present content and information in many different ways to accommodate the differences in students. Many problems between adults and transescents stem from the fact that adults do not generally understand what is "normal" in this developmental phase of life. In some cases, they may understand normalcy intellectually but not accept it in their own child. Effective middle level curricula and school programs must be planned and developed upon adequate understanding of those realities.

### Socialization

The ways in which youngsters deal with social development needs reflect the dynamic changes that occur during pubescence. Pubescence is a biological inevitability that occurs at different rates within individuals. On the other hand, transescence (early adolescence) is a developmental epoch. The social maturation and socialization implications of this developmental epoch need to be specified into middle level curricular goals and program dimensions. Traditional emphasis on schooling over socialization tasks has resulted in middle level school programs reflecting less understanding of the socialization function than the other middle level education functions discussed here.

Middle level school programs need to assist learners in understanding their rate of achieving the skills, rights, and responsibilities of adulthood. Social maturation during transescence depends on how realistically youngsters can deal with their physical growth and transformation toward biological adulthood. Social maturity comes from successful social interaction, whereas early physical growth in itself does not indicate a potential for earlier social maturation.

As life outside the home takes on greater importance, the school becomes the major structured arena for transescent social interaction. Middle level school programs afford students with opportunities for social interaction with agemates, peers, and significant adults. At times during their middle level school years, transescents will prioritize their social development needs above all else in school. School programs should allow teachers to accommodate student social needs as best they can. If not, individual students will find ways to fulfill those needs, including the disruption of the learning agenda of teachers and peers.

In developing middle level school programs, educators must be mindful not to overlook that transescents spend a major portion of their waking hours in the school. Therefore, middle level school programs should help transescents learn social skills to communicate and to interact effectively, especially considering wide developmental range among their agemates.

### Articulation

As the link between the elementary and high school, the middle level school program should be planned as part of the entire kindergarten through twelfth-grade experience. Middle level curriculum expectations should be firmly rooted in how school programs help students bridge the gap between elementary and high school.

Curriculum articulation seeks to minimize gaps and overlap in programs and learning expectations as students move from one school unit or program to the next. Thus, the middle level school program must be planned in cooperation with the elementary school if successful articulation with middle level school experience is to be achieved. The planning should encompass both academic matters and human developmental concerns.

Likewise, the planning of the high school program must start from what students have been able to develop and master in their middle level years. We must accept the reality of differentiation in rates of growth and maturation among students in their early adolescence. All students cannot be expected to be ready to learn as mature adolescents upon their entrance into the high school.

High school programs should offer their subject matter and skills using a wider range of instructional alternatives for students entering its domain. Middle level schools must count as a measure of the preparation of students to succeed when they enter high school. Articulation of middle level with high school programs requires cooperative planning between staff from both levels.

An agenda for Excellence at the Middle Level (NASSP, 1984) suggested ways to articulate middle level with elementary and high school programs. The reported recommended establishing transition panels to define and deal with program articulation between both elementary to middle level and middle level to high schools. A representative group of teachers both from the terminal elementary school grade and the entry middle level school grade works with principals and parents to deal with articulation. A similar group from the terminal middle level school grade and the entry high school grade deals with concerns at that interval.

The issues of transition from elementary to middle level and middle level to high school require local identification and examination. The need to develop means to articulate programs from elementary to middle level and middle level to high school persists (Toepfer, 1986). Regardless of the school unit pattern in the district, transition panels can identify program articulation needs and deal with those issues among the units in the school system.

The curriculum functions discussed here deal with the needs of transescents to discover who they are, and who and what they would like to and can become. This is not a new perception. Earlier scholars saw the junior high school's need to focus on self-definition and exploratory functions, not preparation for college: "There can be only one college-preparatory unit in the public school system. This has been the senior high school and this school must continue to be the sole agency responsible for accrediting pupils to the higher institutions" (Glass, 1923, p. 519).

Most transescents are still concrete operational learners. Therefore, college preparation must remain a high school function. Middle level school curricula and programs should offer challenges that allow all learners to perform successfully at their developmental levels. That will enhance later success for those youngsters ready for college preparatory experiences in the high school.

By the same token, programs for the noncollege-bound must also be grounded in challenges based on what students can, rather than what they cannot, do yet. Middle level curricula and school programs should focus on general educational development. Preparation for the world of work and definition of one's postsecondary education cannot precede general educational interests. Life in our increasingly informational society is increasing the need for middle level school programs to focus on general educational needs. The high school is the appropriate place for maturing adolescents to consider their interests and their possibilities in postsecondary school life.

## Readiness to Learn

Elkind (1981) observed that it is extremely difficult for adults to understand children's thinking levels when adults can function at cognitive levels above those of the child. He described this ability of adults to process information using their personal, full range of thinking skills as "automatization." Elkind concluded that it is almost impossible for adults to understand how a learner processes information when the adult is automatically functioning above the learner's maximum cognitive level at that age.

Elkind described the state of a learner who has not yet reached the adult's thinking levels as "the intellectual unconscious." He noted that "getting at the intellectual unconscious, . . . presents a very special problem. Once a person becomes truly skilled in a particular action, there is no way to get back to the intellectual unconscious" (p. 19). Piaget (1967) and Piaget and Inhelder (1958) suggested that the learner must construct the environment in which he or she develops new skills and then use those skills to learn new information. This notion is important in developing middle level curriculum that facilitates rather than frustrates learner readiness.

For example, let us assume that Julian, a seventh-grade learner, has not yet progressed beyond the concrete operational thinking level. When thinking at that level, Julian is using his highest "intellectual gear." Let us also assume that this transescent's teacher is a formal operational thinker who has developed skills in cognitive levels matching. Thus, the teacher can communicate with him at his concrete operational levels. However, the teacher must "shift down" from the "high (formal) thinking gear" to concrete operations while Julian is using his "highest thinking gear."

The curriculum must allow the learner to construct the intellectual environment in which he or she can function. However, the teacher who must "downshift" to match the concrete operational level will automatically think about formal operational applications of those concrete level skills in dealing with the concrete operational student. Also, a student cannot and does not perceive these formal relationships as long as concrete operations remain her or his highest achieved thinking level. Thus, this teacher cannot fully recall how one thinks when the concrete operational level is the limit of one's thinking abilities. The implications of Piaget's ideas on constructivism will be discussed further in a later section.

To deal with how learners can and do think at a particular age, adults must likewise identify the components of the stages and levels of learning that the child has achieved. Without this knowledge, the teacher may plan new instruction that is beyond the child's actual readiness and create problems that frustrate the learner's attempts to understand things beyond her or his readiness at that time.

Consider the case of overchallenge. If a transescent attempts to learn and understand overchallenging content and skills beyond her or his readiness, learning may be deterred by frustration, confusion, and strict rote memorization. In the case of underchallenge, a transescent may not fully challenge and develop her or his abilities at that time. As a result, the student may become bored and develop less positive attitudes about learning than if he or she were being challenged to use those abilities fully. Implications for planning middle level school learning activities are discussed later in the section dealing with cognitive levels matching.

### Adelson's Findings

William James observed (1890) that "to identify the moment of the instinctive readiness for the subject is, then, the first duty of educators." Adelson (1983) felt that cognitive readiness is the level of intellectual growth that allows the student to grasp the knowledge offered by the teacher. He was concerned with identifying how soon young adolescents (ages 11 to 14 years) actually developed full formal reasoning skills. He identified that the 12-year-old normally does not have the conceptual framework by which to organize and to order the information that an educator provides.

On the basis of his investigations with transescents and maturing adolescents, Adelson (1983) concluded that "the major difference between younger and older adolescents was the capacity of the latter to think abstractly when the occasion demanded it" (p. 157). Figure 13-1 presents some of Adelson's tables displaying these data.

Adelson found that transescents do not move as rapidly into formal operations as Piaget's original data might cause one to expect. The works of both Elkind and Adelson help establish that most transescents do not move rapidly into formal operations at the beginning of the Piagetian formal

**FIGURE 13–1** • *Differences in Abstraction Between Young and Older Adolescents*

Percent Demonstrating Different Levels of Abstraction in the Conceptualization of Government (*N* = 326)

| | By Age: 11 | 13 | 15 | 18 |
|---|---|---|---|---|
| Concrete | 57 | 27 | 07 | 00 |
| Low-Level Abstraction | 28 | 64 | 51 | 16 |
| High-Level Abstraction | 00 | 07 | 42 | 71 |
| Don't Know or Not Ascertained | 15 | 05 | 00 | 13 |

Percent Offering Different Opinions on the Purpose of Laws (*N* = 433)

| | By Age: 12 | 14 | 16 | 18 |
|---|---|---|---|---|
| Restriction | 37 | 35 | 29 | 19 |
| Setting Standards | 16 | 22 | 34 | 34 |
| Sense of Community | 02 | 09 | 14 | 18 |
| Other | 45 | 34 | 23 | 19 |

Percent Offering Different Opinions on the Purpose of Government (*N* = 336)

| | By Age: 11 | 13 | 15 | 18 |
|---|---|---|---|---|
| Restriction | 73 | 68 | 44 | 20 |
| Restriction and Benefit | 12 | 18 | 33 | 38 |
| Benefit | 07 | 08 | 20 | 41 |
| Other | 08 | 05 | 03 | 01 |

*Source:* Tables from Adelson, J. (1983). The growth of thought in adolescence. *Educational Horizons, 61*(4), 156–162. Reprinted with permission from *Educational Horizons,* the journal of Pi Lambda Theta national honor and professional association, Bloomington, IN 47407-6626.

operational learning stage. It also appears that consolidation of concrete skills initiated in the prior concrete operational stage continues and establishes the basis for gradual development of beginning formal operational capabilities by transescents.

Adelson's work suggests major frontier issues as middle level education attempts to deal with transescent intellectual development during the formal operational age frame. Arlin (1984a) developed a test that measures the thinking level abilities of students. Written with fifth-grade readability, the test identifies whether the transescent has achieved onset or mature concrete, or onset or mature formal operational abilities at that time. The *Arlin Test of Formal Reasoning* can identify learning stage readiness for appropriate curriculum and content challenges in middle level school programs.

### Cognitive Levels Matching

Cognitive Levels Matching (CLM), which provides a paradigm for matching instruction with student cognitive readiness, deserves increased usage. Let us assume that a particular seventh-grader has not yet progressed beyond concrete operational level thinking; that represents her highest "intellectual gear" at this particular time. Let us further assume that this student's teachers are formal operational (abstract) thinkers. Teacher communication with that student will be most effective at the concrete operational level. If teachers have developed CLM skills, they can "shift down" and communicate at the student's highest manifested thinking level.

To deal with how individuals can and do think, teachers have to know and identify the components of student thinking levels. Otherwise, teachers may propose inappropriate learnings. Epstein (1981) described CLM as providing teachers with the ability to:

- Identify and diagnose student cognitive levels
- Organize learning activities that match student readiness to learn information
- Help students consolidate and mature previously initiated thinking skills
- Introduce new and higher level thinking skills as students demonstrate their readiness.

The purpose of CLM is to help teachers minimize both over- and underchallenge in the learning experiences they develop for their students. CLM has demonstrated that it can assist teachers in identifying the most appropriate levels to challenge student variance in cognitive abilities. Brooks (1984) reported the following:

*1. The CLM experience has significantly touched most participants: "I never realized nor understood this concept"; "The problem I presented to the class was not the same problem most of the children perceived."*

*2. It gives teachers a common focus for communicating about children: "Missing addends is a tough concept for John because he is unable to conserve numbers."*

*3. It gives teachers a way to assess the appropriateness of curriculum materials: "The metaphors in this book may be too complex for my class." (p. 27)*

Fusco (1987) described the success of colleagues using this approach in a number of subject areas at the middle school level. The Arlin test, discussed earlier, makes it possible for middle level teachers to identify manifested student cognitive levels. Arlin also developed a model (1984b) to help teachers deal with this intellectual dimension in organizing their assessment and planning of instruction.

It is not wise to develop curricula and learning activities on the basis of ascending intelligence alone. We were alerted to this many years ago (Gesell, Ilg, & Ames, 1956).

*Indeed, intellectual growth itself has sometimes been considered to be "the" course of development, with mental age as its main measure. The limitations of such an approach are all too often demonstrated in a real-life situation. "Mental age," as the term is generally used, is actually a score obtained on a test; it is a valuable index of brightness. But a normal 10-year-old with a mental age of fourteen does not necessarily act like a 14-year-old; he tends to act more like a "bright" ten-year-old. (p. 30)*

Transescent intellectual development is influenced by the wholeness of the individual's growth and development (Ames, Ilg, & Baker, 1988).

### Curriculum Issues

Since *A Nation at Risk* (Gardner, 1983) was published, many states have legislated high school program requirements down into middle level schools. By assuming that earlier is better, the desire to legislate earlier learning erroneously assumes that large numbers of students possess the capacity to perform earlier. Such perceptions reflect inaccurate understanding of the differences between the intellectual and social-emotional readiness of most transescents from those of more intellectually mature high school adolescents.

"Earlier is better" is appropriate only for those students whose earlier intellectual readiness for such challenges has been confirmed.

Middle level schools ought to provide earlier intellectual challenges to students identified as intellectually precocious who are actually ready sooner for advanced challenges. However, students should not be placed in those classes if they cannot yet think at the levels required for advanced work. Lack of that clarification in state educational regulations, combined with parental expectations, has placed substantial numbers of middle level school students in situations of overchallenge. In itself, this can put students at risk of poorer school achievement.

Although well-intentioned, mandated acceleration in specific eighth-grade subject areas, such as algebra, in many states has been a developmentally unsound attempt to legislate earlier learning for large numbers of transescents. The resulting poor achievement of many overchallenged students could have been avoided had they been allowed an additional year to develop the intellectual maturity required for success in those subject areas. Moreover, students who fare poorly from such overchallenge often demonstrate lowered self-concept and self-esteem. That failure is accompanied by loss of confidence in their abilities and less willingness to extend one's abilities to meet subsequent learning challenges in their remaining school experiences (Beane & Lipka, 1987).

For example, students require formal operational thinking capacity to comprehend metaphor and imagery in language arts. In science, students must also have achieved formal operational thinking to consistently be able to solve experiments that have more than one independent variable. In mathematics, students at concrete operational thinking levels can memorize sine, cosine, tangent, and other algebraic information. However, to understand and process algebra fully, a student must also be at formal operational thinking.

Thus, it is critical that middle level educators be certain that students given such earlier challenges have manifested the thinking level capacities required to develop those skills and learn that information. Middle level schools can use the Arlin Test of Formal Reasoning (Arlin, 1984a) to identify whether a student is a concrete or an abstract thinker.

Policy regulations err when they assume that the norm of learning that is appropriate for intellectually precocious transescents can become the expected norm for large numbers of middle level school-aged students. Mass acceleration of students should not be proposed until research identifies how much those strategies actually work.

In many states, mathematics is an area of required acceleration in eighth grade. Review of such decisions should be made in light of Prevost's findings (1988a, 1988b). Eighth-grade students accelerated into algebra typically are the brightest and most able mathematics students in that grade. Prevost's data identified that, nationally, a much higher percentage of students who begin algebra in ninth grade complete the full high school sequence than do students who take it in eighth grade. Prevost's findings further revealed that most students who complete algebra in eighth grade perform at significantly lower levels than their presumed high math abilities would predict. The findings of Provost's research support developing eighth-grade mathematics programs as an alternative to accelerating eighth-graders into algebra.

Competent educators agree that middle level schools should provide early challenges to students found to be intellectually precocious. We must not, however, place youngsters in advanced challenges who lack thinking skills at levels required to succeed at such learning. Unfortunately, the pressures of legal regulations can be oppressive. Regulatory changes that violate the intellectual readiness of students for higher learning challenges only erode effective learning in middle level school programs. Present data do not substantiate that challenge alone can facilitate learning of skills or information by students who lack the skill levels to do so. Trying harder is not the simple solution many wish it to be. Research as to why some individuals delay in developing and manifesting higher intellectual abilities until they are into their adult years is still incomplete.

Could these serious concerns have been avoided if the *what* of the middle level school curriculum had been defined and communicated? Middle level schools must develop curricula and school programs that assist today's transescents in preparing to deal with these learning issues in their adolescent and adult futures (Toepfer, Arth, Bergman, Johnston, & Lounsbury, 1989).

## Toward a Middle Level Curricular Focus

Effective middle level instructional practice should grow from the characteristics of young adolescents. Their differences from elementary and high school students are documented in the uniqueness that becomes increasingly common during the middle level school years. Those differences burgeon at the close of childhood and decrease as adolescents mature into young adulthood in the high school.

During the high school years, students demonstrate increasing ability to integrate information learned in separate settings. On the other hand, the vast majority of transescents cannot make those connections so readily. Developing instructional strategies that facilitate integration of learning is a persisting challenge to middle level school educational organization.

Television programs like NOVA and the National Geographic Specials provide effective integrated learning. Those programs do not, for example, offer isolated segments on geology, followed by other detached segments in archaeology, biology, history, or anthropology on the theme of that particular program. Middle level school programs that integrate learning facilitate better student intellectual achievement.

Such integrated approaches better prepare transescents to understand our increasingly science-oriented world than departmentalized high school approaches in the middle level grades. Facts, skills, and concepts are best learned when students can recall and use information as needed. An experiential context for applying learning develops when students learn content and skills in relation to one another.

Instead of extending self-contained organization from elementary school, entry grade programs in middle level schools are increasingly moving to teaming arrangements. How teaming in the middle level school's entry grade should differ from procedures in later grades requires considerable study.

One possible approach begins with an introductory team program in sixth grade, for instance, followed by a seventh- and eighth-grade team experience continued over a two-year, 80-week cycle. This requires that seventh-grade teams remain with their students through seventh and eighth grades. Following this cycle, students matriculate to the high school while the teacher teams pick up new seventh-graders for another two-year experience.

In this way, students have a group of teachers who know and work with them for 80 rather than 40 weeks over two years. Transescent identity development is enhanced when classes and teaching teams stay and move together through these two years. Teachers gain a personalized understanding of the growth and development that young adolescents experience during those two years.

Toepfer (1982b) described a procedure for organizing two-grade middle level schools in such a manner. Middle level school programs with sufficient numbers of students and staff might find this an attractive possibility. George, Spreul, and Moorefield (1987) strongly recommend the extension of student teacher relationships beyond one year. This finding supports another contention Beane (1990a) makes regarding the middle level school curriculum question.

> *This description of a desirable curriculum also suggests that teachers be repositioned in relation to the themes rather than separate subjects. A small group of teachers might stay with a particular group of early adolescents for all three or four years of the middle school and work through a series of units with them. Some teachers might work with particular units with different groups of students in a self-contained setting. Again such matters must be decided locally and would likely differ from school to school. (p. 5)*

Agreeing on the *what* of middle school curriculum should precede the development of program organizational structures. Attending to the organization prior to identifying the curriculum itself often leads to "hardening of the categories" in scheduling that could be counterproductive to curriculum and school program needs.

## Curriculum Organization

All curriculum areas make significant contributions to young adolescent intellectual development. The classification of specific courses as either *academic* or *nonacademic* has been counterproductive in middle level schools. Such an insidious hierarchy is contrary to the goals of effective learning. Too often, concerns about academic achievement have created divisive arguments over the relative importance of "essential" versus "frill" curriculum areas.

Middle level schools need to establish a level of respect for all curriculum areas. A middle level school should be a general education institution with an exploratory approach. The importance each subject has for various students requires equity of support for all curriculum areas. Effective articulation of learning cannot discriminate against any subject area. Practices that make such distinctions are actually prejudicial against students with high abilities in what is demeaned as "nonacademic" subject areas.

Separation of academic core areas from others can result in a public and even a professional mentality that prioritizes academic learning above exploratory and other areas. Teachers in areas designated as "nonacademic" often feel that their contributions are less important than teachers in academic areas, which is an incorrect perception.

A student may acquire a rudimentary understanding of a fact or concept taught in an "academic" class. However, the conceptualization and full understanding of those data can occur from learning experiences in other content areas. Hands-on experiential and other activities in "nonacademic" areas, such as industrial arts or home economics, often develop a student's full understanding of learnings initiated in an academic content area.

For instance, the concept of assembly line production taught in social studies can be viscerally experienced by participating in such processes in technology or industrial arts classes. A science lab experiment can help some students understand differences in density among liquids. For others, a foods lesson in home economics working with different cooking oils may better personalize that understanding.

Reverse instances also occur. However, the divisiveness often felt between the relative merits of "academic" and "nonacademic" areas can create self-esteem problems for both students and teachers. Resolution of such concerns can be facilitated by designating academic subjects as "core" and other areas as "encore" can work toward eliminating separation among content areas and staff.

Attention needs to be given to the following in developing effective middle level interdisciplinary working groups.

- Make certain that concerns to integrate learning are present in all areas in the school program.
- Identify opportunities to integrate learning within each subject area.
- Identify approaches especially appropriate for integrating learning among subject areas.
- Develop middle level school teaching strategies particularly suited for integrating learning among subject areas.

### Advantages of Interdisciplinary Learning

Departmentalization does not provide the capacity for cooperative planning needed to achieve such integration of learning. Research (Feldlaufer, Midgley, & Eccles, 1987) has shown departmentalization to be the least desirable organizational pattern in middle level schools. That study shows that self-contained classrooms provide more correlation of learning and learning opportunities than departmentalization in grades 5 through 8. The advantage of self-contained overdepartmentalized classrooms at the middle level seems clear. No case has been made for the advantages of self-contained classrooms over ones organized through interdisciplinary approaches (Vars, 1987).

Those efforts also need to consider alternative means to integrate middle school curriculum. Core curriculum programs and methodology should be included in those efforts. Glass (1924) identified the "core of the curriculum" as those courses that contained the facts, skills, and information needed to deal with the central problems youth experience in growing to maturity. Subsequently, core curriculum methodology and programs (Faunce & Bossing, 1958; Vars, 1969; Wright, 1952) developed ways to integrate learning in language arts, mathematics, science, the social studies, and the general education portion of school curriculum.

Many educators still view subject matter areas, not the core methodology, as the "core curriculum." As discussed, all content areas in middle level school programs are important in developing effective interdisciplinary learning activities. Core uses major social issues, persisting life situations, and problems of living as unifying centers for learning (Stratemeyer, Forkner, McKim, & Passow, 1947). Core remains an effective means for integrating subject matter learning for young adolescent learners.

Core curriculum involves individual teachers using multiple subject disciplines in working with students. Teaming, on the other hand, brings groups of teachers together to work with groups of students. Teaming should not necessarily be construed as team teaching. The teaming of teachers to plan and develop programs for those whom they commonly teach should be the initial concern. The "gestalt" of integrated learning in middle level programs requires cooperative instructional planning. Such conjoint planning can define a solid foundation for real classroom "team" teaching rather than "turn" teaching. The former can integrate learning with content areas, whereas the latter extends the isolation of subject departmentalized teaching and learning.

Interdisciplinary teaming requires that teachers have regular opportunities to plan, develop, and deliver the instructional programs through the integration of multiple subjects and learning areas. Local definition of the *what* of these subject area enclaves and the *how* of methodological correlation needs to go beyond both academic area and single discipline concerns. Yet, Becker (1990) did not find widespread instances of this in his report of middle level curriculum and instructional practice.

To integrate all middle level curriculum areas, teaming will require a broader application than it typically is given. For example, if teaming is important for organizing instruction in academic areas, it should be equally important for all areas. Experiences in art, music, health, physical education, and the like can be powerful sources of intellectual growth. Transescent intellectual development is facilitated through the interrelationship of all curriculum areas in the middle level school. Beane (1990b) raises a number of issues that must be resolved in attempting this issue.

1. *The persistent organization around a collection of academic and separate special courses is not developmentally appropriate. (p. 2)*
2. *The middle school curriculum is not really a "curriculum" in the sense of having some clearly identified purpose or theme. (p. 12)*
3. *Interdisciplinary teaming does not necessarily lead to interdisciplinary curriculum organization. (p. 21)*
4. *The subject approach presents numerous problems to schools in general and the middle school in particular . . . it is alien to life itself. (p. 29)*
5. *The academic subject approach has helped to create the incorrect belief that cognition and affect can and ought to be separated in the curriculum. (p. 30)*

Beane's bold statements underscore our need to extend interdisciplinary teaching and learning procedures in middle level schools. How can we judge the success of middle level school interdisciplinary planning, teaching, and learning? That answer is best reflected in the accomplishments of students.

The eagerness of happy and excited learners is usually validated by their success in classroom performance.

### Grouping and Cooperative Learning

Other chapters in this volume focus on grouping and coopertive learning in middle level schools. However, a few connections of those areas to curriculum concerns need to be made here. Student learning capacities change more rapidly and more often during their middle level school years than in either elementary or high school. To improve intellectual development and achievement, middle level schools need to identify the kinds and degrees of diversity in ability, achievement, interest, and social development that will create the most effective learning environments. No single pattern will fit all situations.

Success in interdisciplinary instruction parallels that found in cooperative learning activities with transescents. The invitational climate in such environments reinforces confidence that students can grow and succeed. Diversity in ability, achievement, interest, and social development creates the most effective learning environments. No single pattern will fit all situations.

The challenge to middle level curriculum is to move away from set patterns that lock students into fixed homogeneous arrangements for the semester or the school year. To that end, Slavin (1989) concluded that "at the middle school level there is still no known benefit to ability grouping" (p. 5). The Carnegie (1989) Report also endorses the need to move away from tracking and homogeneous grouping by ability in developing more effective middle level school learning opportunities.

> *Tracking has proven to be one of the most divisive and damaging school practices in existence. Time and time again, young people placed in lower academic tracks or classes, often during the middle grades are locked into dull, repetitive instructional programs leading at best to minimum competencies. The psychic numbing these youth experience from a "dumbed-down" curriculum contrasts sharply with the exciting opportunities for learning and critical thinking that students placed in higher tracks or classes may experience. (pp. 49–59)*

In a recent interview, Hornbeck (Koerner, 1989) responded to the question "How about tracking? What would schools replace it with?"

> *One of the generally best strategies is what has come to be called cooperative learning. There are various versions of that but it basically*

> *revolves around high achieving youngsters helping those youngsters who are not achieving as well. One of the most popular forms of it is peer tutoring. An essential component to any effort to eliminate tracking depends upon staff development activities where teachers learn how to use alternative strategies. (p. 60)*

Cooperative learning approaches in more heterogeneously grouped classes allow students across the ability spectrum to learn better in terms of their own rates. The curriculum goal of middle level schools is to send forth the greatest pool of students confident in their capacities to continue and to learn as best as they can in school. Tracking and homogeneous grouping by ability approaches, on the other hand, are based in the belief that all students cannot learn adequately.

The curriculum organization issues considered in this section have developed responsively effective middle level educational practices. Those practices and their accomplishments deserve study in efforts to define the *what* of middle level school curriculum. Middle level educational effectiveness will further improve as the curriculum is increasingly based on transescent learning characteristics and needs. To begin, a curriculum focus must be defined to frame efforts to deal with the middle level school curriculum question.

## Defining a Curriculum Focus

The range of middle level curriculum issues and organizational features presented here must be focused in answering the *what* of the curriculum question introduced at the beginning of this chapter. Again, the development of middle level education in our nation's schools must be considered. The junior high school movement was primarily grounded in school reorganization and did not initially develop a curricular rationale.

The later junior high school movement began to specify the differences of developmental and learning needs of transescents from maturing adolescents. The middle school movement pursued that and extended bases for program differentiation through refined program organizational features. Thus, middle level schools developed the potential to achieve curricular ends firmly grounded in transescent developmental and learning characteristics.

The major problem overlooked in defining the *what* of the middle level school curriculum may be one of position. The focus on the beginning and end of anything usually is greater than that devoted to its midpoint. Extremes in differences of kind are more readily seen than those of degree and mediation. In addition to the position issue, another problem has grown from the sequence of when school levels emerged. The identity issue would have been more easily resolved had middle level schools emerged after elementary but before high schools. However, middle level schools emerged long after the establishment of elementary and secondary schools. By then, elementary and high schools each had a curriculum identity that clearly differentiated one from the other.

Initially construed as "early secondary education," the junior high school began in the shadow between two established units. The seedling junior high unit took some years to root but eventually began to define its purposes as something other than a "junior edition of the high school." The middle school era has brought efforts to establish a free-standing identity for middle level schools. But has that effort really succeeded?

To what degree does conventional wisdom still consider middle level schools as easier versions of the high school? Educators and laypersons recognize the differences between the pedagogic purposes, curriculum, and programs of elementary and high schools. Despite the progress made during the past half century, public and professional understanding of the differences between elementary-middle level and middle level-high school is still lacking.

Middle level schools must develop an identity focused on those differences. That is, articulation plans with both the elementary and the high school programs are needed (Toepfer, 1986). More educators and laypersons now understand the "characteristics-of-learners piece" of a middle level school. However, the "curriculum-pedagogic purposes piece" needs considerable attention. Middle level school identity must be based upon what youngsters *can* do and achieve as they pass through their middle level school years.

Education is a journey, not a destination. That perspective is vital as schools and communities attempt to articulate educational experiences across the school years. Defining and differentiating the *what* of the middle level school curriculum is central in that effort. The middle level curriculum link needs to interface vertical articulation with elementary and high schools.

### Curriculum Decision Making

When the cause of the allies was faring poorly early in World War I, French Premier Georges Clemenceau proclaimed, "War is too serious a business to be left to the generals." Who, then, should be involved in defining the *what* of the middle level school curriculum? Defined roles exist for both professionals and laypersons (Beane, Toepfer, & Alessi, 1986) in approaching that task.

The primary responsibility of professional educators should be in program design and decisions, with a supportive role in advising on goals. Assume that laypersons are planning local goals for a middle level school alcohol education program required by the state department of public instruction.

Local middle level school science staff have information on the effect of alcohol consumption on bodily functions. Driver education and health faculty have more specific data about the effect of alcohol on driving. These data could help personnel plan goals for the program in question. Although staff are primarily responsible to plan and deliver instruction, their expertise would be helpful to this planning group.

On the other hand, laypersons should be primarily concerned with defining goals with supportive involvement in advising on program decisions. In this case, assume that local middle level educators are developing an environmental education program based on locally formulated goals. The educators were selected to develop the program because of their expertise in the subject areas involved in the environmental education program. Yet, they also can be assisted on this project through periodic meetings with the laypersons who established the program's goals. This affords laypersons the opportunity to advise the staff and reconcile goal concerns with the program as the staff develops it.

Clearly, the *what* of middle level school curriculum has not been defined by such interaction. We have seen a growing move to legislate curriculum requirements by state legislatures. The National Conference of Governors has undertaken what some see as an effort to establish a national curriculum. There appears to be no understanding of a middle level educational agenda in those efforts. The degree of participation by and interaction with professionals in those deliberations is likewise difficult to find. It would seem that the definition of lay and professional responsibilities in those efforts has gone amiss.

I suggest that our nation would be far better off were the National Conference of Governors to concentrate instead of deciding how the medical profession should cure AIDS and cancer. After consultation with medical professionals, they would probably abandon that venture. Unfortunately, the ego of governors and legislators does not pale to a similar degree in the face of professional educator opinion. In fact, governmental personnel seldom recognize or seek educator's opinions, even in educational matters.

However, educators have not worked at establishing or keeping control of their professional decision-making prerogatives. This "abandonment of turf" has resulted in the turf being taken over by a range of nonprofessional constituencies. Their "squatter's rights" now seem to have given them title to such decision making. As a result, educators have been planning curriculum by default. This critical reality must be recognized in organizing efforts to define the *what* of middle level school curriculum.

The differences of transescent learners from younger elementary school children and maturing adolescents and adults in high school seems clearly established. Yet, almost 30 years later, the initiatives of the middle school concept as a curriculum planning phenomenon have not been realized.

Significant movement toward defining a middle level curricular identity is lacking. Clearly, the task for defining the *what* and *how* of middle level curricula and school programs that respond to these developmental realities is a complex one.

Pursuing that complicated task requires finding the handle on how to move it along. Initially it must be recognized that few middle level scholars have expertise in curriculum planning. The central credentials of most are either in transescent development or school organizational and instructional features. The truth of Alexander's (1973) comment persists as a serious impediment in efforts to move the curriculum question along.

> So many educators know so little about curriculum planning, but keep trying to re-invent the "curriculum" wheel. These efforts by people poorly informed of the history and practice in the curriculum field really end up only re-discovering the same old ruts in the road. (p. 3)

The framing of the middle school curriculum question should be done by those middle level educators with such curriculum expertise. Once properly addressed, dealing with the curriculum question must necessarily involve interaction with a broader range of middle level educators. Let us consider previous efforts to move this task ahead.

## Middle Level School Curriculum Models

The curriculum question was addressed by a few in the early years of the middle school movement. The first of these was by Eichhorn (1966). He developed a curriculum model in response to the characteristics of transescents he had researched and defined. His socioanalytical curriculum model was based upon the physical, mental, social, and cultural characteristics of middle level school learners. It organized language, mathematics, science, and social studies under an analytical-unifying center. Cultural arts, fine arts, physical education, and practical arts were interrelated under a physical-cultural unifying center. Eichhorn's model was based on successful integrative inter- and cross-disciplinary teaching and learning procedures and activities consistent with the developmental characteristics of transescents.

Next, Alexander, Williams, Compton, and Prescott (1968) developed a model to address the middle level school curriculum question. They had three unifying centers in their model: (1) personal development-integrated curriculum issues related to values, health, and physical development, and to individual interests; (2) skills for continued learning dealt with curriculum issues related to communications and problem-solving skills; and (3) organized knowledge dealt with the traditional range of middle level school subject/content areas.

The following year, Moss (1969) published his model for organizing a largely subject-centered middle level school curriculum framework. Academic subjects encompassed traditional middle level school academic subject areas. The arts did the same for art, health, home economics, industrial arts, and music. The final organizing center focused on health, recreation, and physical fitness. The academic subject areas described a core program centered on transescent problems of living.

Lounsbury and Vars (1978) proposed a middle level school curriculum organized around a core based on personal-social problems of transescents. It provided a continuous personal-social component to address sequential skill needs of learners in various content areas in the curriculum. It also provided a variable component that included exploratory areas, elective course opportunities, independent study options, enrichment opportunities, and a student activity program. Their proposal called for rethinking middle level school curriculum and its reorganization, something that continues to elude our educational awareness.

The models developed by Eichhorn and by Lounsbury and Vars were well-conceived attempts to deal with serious curriculum issues. Beane (1990b) has developed a model centered in the need to define and to focus the *what* issue of middle level curriculum. Because it is so recent, his model is presented in a bit more detail here. He stated, "Early adolescents do not live in isolation within that stage of development or apart from larger realities of the world" (1990b, p. 38).

Beane's model identifies middle level curriculum themes (e.g., transition, identities, interdependence, wellness, social structures, independence, conflict resolution, commercialism, justice, caring, institutions) within the intersection of categories called Early Adolescent Concerns (understanding personal changes, developing a personal identity, finding a place in the group, personal fitness, social status, dealing with adults, peer conflict and gangs, commercial pressures, questioning authority, personal friendships, living in the school) and Social Concerns (living in a changing world, cultural diversity, global interdependence, environmental protection, class systems, human rights, global conflict, effects of media, laws and social classrooms, social welfare, social institutions) (see Beane, 1990b). This carries out the thrust of the model that "the centerpiece of the curriculum would consist of thematic units whose organizing centers are drawn from the interacting concerns of early adolescents" (p. 45). This reflects the belief that "the middle school curriculum ought to be a general education school with a coherent, unified, and complete curriculum" (p. 47).

Beane's model reflects the concerns of others (Toepfer, 1990) regarding the folly of merely restructuring middle level school programs without reconceptualizing the curriculum. In that regard, Beane is hopeful that the following may occur: "As more and more middle school educators work out the organizational reforms and think about early adolescents, they will eventually see that organizational 'restructuring' is an incomplete version of reform" (p. 64).

Agreement on the need to deal with the curriculum question should consider architect Frank Lloyd Wright's observation that "form must follow function." Middle level education has dealt with defining the form of its organizational features well beyond agreement on the *what* of its curriculum function. There are curriculum planning means to correct that imbalance.

### Curriculum Approaches

The theory and practice of curriculum planning offer a range of curriculum planning. However, these cluster into four major categories (Beane, Toepfer, & Alessi, 1986): Subject Areas, Broad Fields, Social Problems, and Emerging Needs of Learners. None of these approaches should be used exclusively at any school level. However, appropriate use of all four curriculum approach categories would help define middle school curricula deal with many accepted middle level school organizational features.

For example, the Broad Fields approach lends itself well to the correlation of content and subject matter from multiple subject areas. It is well suited for organizing the *what* of the curriculum for core curriculum, teaming, and interdisciplinary teaching and learning purposes. Yet the Broad Fields curriculum approach still is seldom used in planning and developing middle level school curricula and school programs.

The Social-Problems approach can be used to develop units of work that use subject matter in studying and learning about ecological, environmental, global interdependence, and technologically based concerns. This approach is well suited to help transescents develop skills and prioritize their need to continue to work toward solving these problems in their futures. Again, it is infrequently used in planning middle level school curricula and school programs.

The Emerging Needs approach can be used to organize the curriculum to respond to emerging transescent concerns during the middle level school years. Issues to be studied can be related to interests pertinent to the transescent developmental stage and can draw upon information and skills from various subject areas.

The Subject Area approach is appropriate for dealing with focused learning in content areas restricted to content specific skills and information. It is valid for use with all age levels in appropriate circumstances. It remains the dominant approach used in postsecondary educational settings.

Consider the following historical vignette. After mimicking collegiate approaches, the high school's subject-area mode transferred to the junior high school as it subdivided from the six-year high school. The almost exclusive use of the Subject Area approach inherited by early junior high schools in the subdivision of the secondary school into a junior and senior unit persists.

Why? One can easily fall prey to any paranoid tendencies in realizing there is a dimension of the child's story of "The Emperor's New Clothes" in all this! In light of that conundrum, another question posed by Beane (1990a) must be seriously studied: "How then, we might ask, has the subject-area approach to the curriculum held up so long?" (p. 4)

There also is the reality that beginning with the conclusions of the Eight Year Study (Aiken, 1941), the Subject Area approach has not measured up well with other curriculum approaches. Contemporary support of the Subject Area approach from curriculum scholars (Apple, 1986; Kliebard, 1986; Popkewitz, 1987) is tenuous, at best.

There certainly is the need to identify the political considerations in this dimension of school practice. However, and more importantly from this writer's perspective, it remains for middle level educators, particularly curriculum planners, to become more knowledgeable in the area of curriculum planning and development procedures. Tinkering with the *what* of middle level school curriculum will be of no help. In fact, it probably would confound matters.

## Conclusion

In a contemporary cereal advertisement, actor Wilfred Brimley concluded, "It's the right thing to do!" Developing middle level school programs that help transescents initiate and develop skills to function successfully in our changing world is also "the right thing to do." Revisioning this challenge through curriculum planning in middle level schools must precede restructuring of those school programs (Toepfer, 1990).

Our task of planning middle level curricula and developing school programs that appropriately challenge transescents is extremely complex. The goal is to deliver transescents to the threshold of maturing adolescence and beginning adulthood who can continue to learn into their adult futures. That requires developing middle level programs that deal with the reality of transescents' diverse developmental levels. The duality to provide high expectations and appropriate options is a difficult challenge (Toepfer et al., 1989).

*Instead of trying to force the masses of early adolescents to higher-level thinking, ready or not, perhaps we should help each student become the best thinker she or he can be at the rate and pace that her or his capacities and developmental readiness will allow. Such an approach will help ensure a better attitude toward learning and prepare youth for a long-term learning effort that extends far beyond the middle grades (p. 42).*

This requires organizing the *what* of the middle level school curriculum to provide the broadest possible range of appropriate middle level school learning options. Middle level school programs must allow some transescents to learn as fast as they can while insuring that others will be allowed to learn as slow as they must. The Carnegie Council on Adolescent Development's Task Force on Education of Young Adolescents (1989) identified the critical nature issues facing contemporary middle level schools: "For many youth 10 to 15 years old, early adolescence offers opportunities to choose a path toward a productive and fulfilling life. For many others, it represents their last best chance to avoid a diminished future" (p. 8).

The report discussed how changes in life and society are making one's experiences during the middle level school years more critical to the success in later life.

*The conditions of early adolescence have changed dramatically from previous generations. . . . In these changed times when young people face unprecedented choices and pressures, all too often the guidance they needed as children and no less as adolescents is withdrawn. Freed from the dependence of childhood, but not yet able to find their own path to adulthood, many young people feel a desperate sense of isolation. Surrounded only by their equally confused peers, too many dependence of childhood, but not yet able to find their own path to adulthood, many young people feel a desperate sense of isolation. Surrounded only by their equally confused peers, too many make poor decisions with harmful or lethal consequences. Middle grade school — junior high, intermediate, and middle schools — are potentially society's most powerful force to recapture millions of youth adrift. (p. 8)*

This statement further underscores the importance of devoting adequate attention to resolve the *what* of the middle level school curriculum question. To do so will require our best use of curriculum approaches and procedures to plan and develop more responsively effective middle level school programs. The loss in further procrastination in moving that agenda could prove disastrous.

# References

Adelson, J. (1983). The growth of thought in adolescence. *Educational Horizons, 61*(4), 156–162.

Aiken, W. (1941). *The story of the eight year study.* New York: Harper & Row.

Alexander, W. M. (1973). An imperative for the curriculum worker: An historical perspective. *Impact on Instructional Improvement, 8*(20), 3–8.

Alexander, W. M., Williams, E. L., Compton, M., & Prescott, D. (1968). *The emergent middle school* (rev. ed.). New York: Holt, Rinehart and Winston.

Ames, L., Ilg, F., & Baker, S. (1988). *Your ten to fourteen year old.* New Haven, CT: Gesell Institute of Human Development.

Apple, M. (1986). *Teachers and texts.* New York and London: Routledge and Kegan Paul.

Arlin, P. (1984a). *Arlin test of formal reasoning.* East Aurora, NY: Slosson Educational Publishers.

Arlin, P. (1984b). Cognitive levels matching: An instructional model and a model of teacher change. In M. Frank (Ed.), *A child's brain* (pp. 99–109). New York: Haworth.

Baker, J. (Chairman). (1913). *Report of the committee on economy of time in education.* Washington, DC: National Council on Education, U.S. Bureau of Education Bulletin 1913 Number 38: 26–27.

Beane, J. (1990a). Rethinking the middle school curriculum. *Middle School Journal, 12*(5), 1–5.

Beane, J. (1990b). *A middle school curriculum: From rhetoric to reality.* Columbus, OH: National Middle School Association.

Beane, J., & Lipka, R. (1987). *When the kids come first: Enhancing self-esteem.* Columbus, OH: National Middle School Association.

Beane, J., Toepfer, C., Jr., & Alessi, S., Jr. (1986). *Curriculum planning and development.* Boston: Allyn and Bacon.

Becker, J. (1990). Curriculum and instruction in middle-grade schools. *The Kappan, 71*(7), 450–457.

Brooks, M. (1984). A constructivist approach to staff development, *Educational Leadership, 42*(3), 23–27.

Carnegie Council on Adolescent Development's Task Force on Education of Young Adolescents. (1989). *Turning points: Preparing American youth for the 21st century.* Washington, DC: Carnegie Council on Adolescent Development, a program of Carnegie Corporation of New York.

*Caught in the middle: Educational reform for young adolescents in California public schools: A report of the superintendent's task force.* (1987). Sacramento, CA: Bureau of Publications, California State Department of Education.

Eichhorn, D. (1966). *The middle school.* New York: The Central for Applied Research in Education.

Eliot, C. (1898). Shortening the elementary school and extending the high school. *Educational reform: Essays and addresses.* New York: Century Company.

Elkind, D. (1981). Adolescent thinking and the curriculum. *New York University Education Quarterly, 12*(2), 18–24.

Epstein, H. (1981). Learning to learn: Matching instructional to cognitive levels. *The Principal, 60*(5), 25–30.

Faunce, R., & Bossing, N. (1958). *Developing the core curriculum* (2nd ed.). Englewood Cliffs, NJ: Prentice-Hall.

Feldlaufer, H., Midgley, C., & Eccles, J. (1987). *Student, teacher, and observer perceptions of classroom environment before and after transition to junior high school*. Ann Arbor: The University of Michigan.

Florida Department of Education. (1990). *Coming of age: Impact of PRIME legislation on middle level schools in Florida*. Tallahassee, FL: Author.

Fusco, E. (1987). *Cognitive levels matching*. Columbus, OH: National Middle School Association.

Gardner, D. (Chairman). (1983). *A Nation at risk: The imperative for educational reform*. Washington, DC: U.S. Office of Education.

George, P., Spreul, M., & Moorefield, J. (1987). *Long-term relationships: A middle school case study*. Columbus, OH: National Middle School Association.

Gesell, A., Ilg, F., & Ames, L. (1956). *Youth: The years from ten to sixteen*. New York: Harper & Row.

Glass, J. (1923). The reorganization of the seventh, eighth, and ninth grades—Program of studies. *School Review, 30*(10), 519–520.

Glass, J. (1924). *Curriculum practices in the junior high school and grade 5 and 6*. Supplementary Education Monographs, No. 25. Chicago: University of Chicago Press.

Gruhn, W., & Douglas, H. (1947). *The modern junior high school*. New York: Ronald Press.

Hall, G. S. (1904). *Adolescence: It's psychology and its relations to physiology, anthropology, sociology, sex, crime, and education* (Volume 1). New York: Appleton & Company.

Hartwell, C. (1905). Economy of time in education. *Educational Review, 30*(3), 163–169.

Hass, G. (1980). *Curriculum planning: A new approach*. (3rd ed.). Boston: Allyn and Bacon.

James, W. (1890). *The principles of psychology*. New York: Henry Holt & Company.

Kliebard, H. (1986). *The struggle for the American curriculum: 1896–1958*. Boston and London: Routledge and Kegan Paul.

Koerner, T. (1989). Reform plans, implications for principals discussed by the chairman of the Carnegie Task Force on education of young adolescents. *Bulletin of the National Association of Secondary School Principals, 46*(518), 64–75.

Kramer, R. (1985). Adolescence: Is it necessary? *Transescence: The Journal on Emerging Adolescent Education, 13*(2), 44–50.

Lounsbury, J., & Vars, G. (1978). *A curriculum for the middle school*. New York: Harper & Row.

Moss, T. (1969). *The middle school*. Boston: Houghton-Mifflin.

NASSP Council on Middle Level Education. (1984). *An agenda for excellence at the middle level*. Reston, VA: National Association of Secondary School Principals.

National Education Association. (1894). *Committee of ten on secondary education*. New York: American Book Company.

National Education Association. (1907). Report of the committee on the equal division of the twelve years in the public schools between the district and the high school. *Journal of Proceedings and Addresses of the Forty-Sixth Annual Meeting* (pp. 705–706). Chicago: University of Chicago Press.

National Education Association. (1909). Report of progress by the committee on the culture element and economy of time in education. *Journal of Proceedings and Addresses of the Forty-Eighth Annual Meeting*. Chicago: University of Chicago Press.

*New York State board of regents policy on middle-level education and schools with middle-level grades*. (1989). Albany, NY: New York State Education Department.

Piaget, J. (1967). *The child's conception of the world.* Towota, NJ: Littlefield, Adams & Co.

Piaget, J., & Inhelder, B. (1958). *The growth of logical thinking from childhood to adolescence.* New York: Basic Books.

Popkewitz, T. (1987). *The formation of school subjects: The struggle for creating an american institution.* New York: Falmer.

Prevost, F. (1988a). Algebra isn't the answer: Alternatives to enrich eighth grade mathematics. *Schools in the middle.* Reston, VA: National Association of Secondary School Principals.

Prevost, F. (1988b). Are we accelerting able students out of math? *Middle School Journal, 15*(2), 8–10.

Slavin, R. (1989). In grouping for instruction. *ASCD Curriculum Update* (Available from the Association for Supervision and Curriculum Development, Alexandria, VA 22314-2798).

Stratemeyer, F., Forkner, H., McKim, M., & Passow, A. H. (1947). *Developing a curriculum for modern living.* New York: Bureau of Publications, Teachers college, Columbia University.

Toepfer, C., Jr. (1962a). *Evolving curricular patterns in junior high schools: An historical study.* Unpublished doctoral dissertation, Buffalo, NY: University of Buffalo.

Toepfer, C., Jr. (1962b). Historical development of junior high school organization in America. *National Association of Secondary School Principals Bulletin, 46*(271), 74–76.

Toepfer, C., Jr. (1982a). Junior high and middle school education. In H. Mitzel (Ed.), *Encyclopedia of educational research* (Vol. 3) (pp. 989–1000). New York: Free Press.

Toepfer, C., Jr. (1982b). Organizational strategies for two-grade middle schools. *Dissemination Services on the Middle Grades, 15*(9), 1–4.

Toepfer, C., Jr. (1986). Middle level transition and articulation issues. *Middle School Journal, 18*(10), 9–11.

Toepfer, C., Jr. (1988). Recognizing the capacities of teaming in middle level schools. *Dissemination Services on the Middle Grades, 19*(2), 1–4.

Toepfer, C., Jr. (1990). Revisioning middle level education: A prelude to restructuring schools. *Educational Horizons, 68*(2), 95–99.

Toepfer, C., Jr., Arth, A., Bergman, S., Johnston, J. H., & Lounsbury, J. (1989). *Middle level education's responsibility for intellectual development.* Reston, VA: National Association of Secondary School Principals.

Tompkins, E., & Gaumlitz, W. (1954). *The carnegie unit: Its origin, status, and trends.* Washington, DC: Department of Health, Education and Welfare Bulletin 1954, Number 7.

Vars, G. (1987). *Interdisciplinary teaching in the middle school.* Columbus, OH: National Middle School Association.

Vars, G. (Ed.) (1969). *Common learnings: Core and interdisciplinary approaches.* Scranton, PA: International Textbook Company.

Wright, G. (1952). *Core curriculum development: Problems and practices.* Department of Education Bulletin 1952, Number 6. Washington, DC: Government Printing Office.

# CHAPTER FOURTEEN

# Appropriate Grouping Practices for Middle Level Students

ROBERT C. SPEAR
*Southwick/Tolland Regional School District*
*Southwick, Massachusetts*

### Mike's Experience

*My name is Mike and I am 43 years old. I am a seventh-grade math teacher and I've lived in [Massachusetts] all of my life. When I first started [teaching], there was low, middle, and high [groups]. About five or six years [ago], we were homogeneously grouped. I was a staunch believer then, and now I am a reformed grouper. I noticed at the time that the low people began working with the middle people and it would tend to bring them up a little bit. They had higher expectations. I expected more of them and they did produce more. About five years ago we went entirely to heterogeneous grouping, which I kind of didn't like. I like to have a good top group and I believed at the time that was the way to go. We got away from that, and got into heterogeneous grouping. It was very difficult when we went to heterogeneous grouping. How to present the material to the students?*

*I could deal with moving the low group into the middle but when they had a big meeting and we had to get rid of the high group, we were just going to go completely heterogeneous, and oh my God, this is going to be really tough. This was the problem. How do I hit the top kids and hit the bottom kids all at the same time in the same classroom? How do I keep the top kids really interested, not to give them simple repetitive material like worksheets, something to tie it all together. It was very difficult for me, at least that first year.*

*The change in grouping really came down from administration. We wanted to get rid of the low stigma and a lot of kids thought "we're dumb guys," so we said let's get rid of that and put them in the middle. In the classroom everybody knew who the slow learners were, the ones that had difficulty, but you really didn't have the large stigma of everybody in the same class, and you didn't have somebody always cutting up as you did in the low, low class. The other kids just didn't pay attention to them, they didn't listen. They also help you keep classroom order; you had the peer pressure working for you.*

*In one of my bottom groups, a student came up with a fantastic way of solving a problem; it really amazed me. I really praised him, "That is fantastic." It was like the kids went "ha, ha, ha" and just because of the other kids laughing at him, it made him feel like, "I better not do this again." It made him feel bad for thinking of this great idea, showing that he was smart. They tried to put him down.*

*I had the same thing hapen in our heterogeneous groups. One of the low ones came up with a great idea of how to do a problem and he was talking within the group. One of top kids in the group said, "Hey, he's not dumb." It made him feel really good. It was a fantastic feeling not only for him but for me and the other kids in the group. You know everybody has something to contribute in the class, and that is why I wish way back then, we did have the heterogeneous groups.*

*After that first year we got into learning style material and that showed us different ideas of how to approach those kids who had difficulty. One thing we found [was] the low learners had an entirely different learning style. They were the kinesthetic people. They were the more global people. They always had trouble because I would say, "These are the rules to do division," and some kids just can't do that. You gotta picture the final answer, go through it going backwards. They were good with the word-type problems, and could come up with their own way of doing it.*

*I [also] had an in-service instructor showing us different ways to use manipulatives in mathematics. That is where I got all my games and things. [He] asked me, "What do you do with those kids who are done with the assignment for the day? Do you give them another worksheet?" I didn't have an answer. In this class I [got] an answer: "Games." There are a lot of mathematical, strategy, tactical, manipulative-type activities where the kids learn spatial relationships [and] that kids love. That is the extra stuff.*

*It was tough. It was very difficult, you know, to try to teach to everybody. I presented [to] an upper-middle class. That is what I taught. [Now] I see myself teaching with all the other things that we are doing, at a top level. I am teaching way up here and I see kids working cooperatively bringing the others up. There's a lot to say about students helping [one] another to understand. I had real trouble communicating with them, but now I know exactly how to explain [material] to them.*

*It was like beginning teaching. There were so many new things that you have to learn and it was very hard trying to meet everybody's needs in the classroom. After that first year, there were some good things and there were some bad things. I threw out the bad things and used the things that worked. The second year was easier, and after that second year I think it was when we got into the cooperative learning and that opened up our eyes a lot.*

*Peers helping peers — it has happened a lot where a bright student, a higher achiever would work out a problem [with] the lower achiever who knows very concrete stuff will have the answer. The other [student] says, "How did you do it so fast?" That person may just not be that dumb! They are really smart. We just have a respect for one another.*

Ability grouping is a common practice in schools across this nation, but it is a practice that has come under close scrutiny in the last decade. Grouping will most likely continue to be an important issue in the decades to come; both researchers and practitioners need to understand the perceived benefits and realities of ability grouping.

The issue is not *whether* we group students, but rather *how* we group students. In all schools that have more than 30 students, students will be grouped in some manner. Grouping is necessary for organizational reasons. The question of how we group, then, becomes pertinent. Should we group by ability? Should we group by age? Should we group at random? Should we group for specific reasons? Should we group for a specific duration of time? Should we group for interest? These questions are all pertinent to the central question: What is most appropriate method for grouping students to enhance the eduction of students?

In this chapter, I will (1) explore the knowledge base and history of grouping practices, (2) raise the question of its relevance to the present and speculate as to its potential relevance in the future, (3) explore the possible influence of ability grouping on the development of young adolescents, (4) consider the transition from inappropriate grouping practices to appropriate grouping practices and make suggestions for staff development, and (5) discuss appropriate grouping practices, looking at different ways of addressing individual needs, differentiating assignments, and learning strategies. This discussion of grouping practices may cause middle level educators to rethink the educational structures and organizations they provide for students "in the middle."

# Definitions

Terms commonly associated with ability grouping are often used synonymously. It may be helpful to fine-tune these definitions for educators who are attempting to understand appropriate grouping practices for middle level students.

### Tracking

"Tracking on the surface is an organizational arrangement by means of which students observed to be making varied progress in school are grouped so as to reduce the apparent range of achievement and performance in any one group" (Goodlad, 1984, p. 150). *Tracking* is one term that is frequently used relative to ability grouping. Paul George's (1988) definition of tracking is "dividing students into class sized groups based on a measure of a student's ability or prior achievement, and then attempting to design and deliver differentiated learning experiences to each group" (p. 1). Tracking, then, "is in essence sorting" (Oakes, 1985, p. 3).

### Ability Grouping

Bryson and Bentley (1980) stated that "ability grouping is the practice of prejudging students' ability based on some type of intelligence test and past educational performance and then assigning two or more students to a particular instructional setting for a sustained period of time" (p. 8).

*Homogeneous grouping* and *ability grouping* are terms that frequently are used interchangeably; however, they are not the same. Informally grouping students within the regular classroom for a short period of time for specialized instruction generally is not considered to be homogeneous grouping. Ability grouping simply refers to a clustering of students that have some relationship or common characteristic.

*Heterogeneous grouping* is a mix of abilities or other traits within the same grouping pattern. Low, high, and average ability students may be in the same heterogeneous class.

The differences between ability grouping and tracking should be noted. *Tracking* is more permanent; it is a method whereby students are grouped together and stay together for an extended time (a semester, a year, a school career). *Ability grouping* is a system whereby students remain together for a much shorter period of time: part of the school day, a few days, or a week. For example, during the school day, students might be ability grouped for reading instruction. In this scenario, when it is time for reading, students will go to their appropriate reading groups. The key words in this discussion, then, are *tracking, ability grouping, homogeneous,* and *heterogeneous grouping.*

## Assumptions about Ability Grouping

Educational practices are often difficult to investigate. "Ability grouping and tracking are more amenable to scientific study than are many things about schools. The research findings raise some serious questions about the benefits claimed for tracking and suggest some negative side effects" (Goodlad, 1984, p. 151). Those who endorse ability grouping defend its practice by citing the following assumptions: (1) students learn more or better in homogeneous groups, (2) students, especially the slower ones, feel more positively about themselves and school when they are in homogeneous groups, (3) student track placements are appropriate, accurate, and fair, and involve some fundamental considerations; and (4) teaching is easier (with respect to meeting both individual needs and managing classroom instruction in general) when students are in homogeneous groups (Oakes, 1985, pp. 7–13).

Educators have "deep seated beliefs and long held assumptions about the appropriateness of what happens in schools. These beliefs are so ingrained in our thinking and behavior, so much a part of our school culture, that we rarely submit them to careful scrutiny" (Oakes, 1985, p. 5). Oakes responds to the four assumptions regarding tracking and ability grouping.

The first assumption, that students learn more, is "simply not true, or at least we have virtually mountains of research evidence indicating that homogeneous grouping does not consistently help anyone learn better" (p. 7). The second assumption is that slower students feel more positively about themselves and is refuted by research that indicates that "students placed in average and slow tracks, do not develop positive attitudes. . . . The tracking process seems to foster lowered self-esteem among teenagers. . . . Students in upper tracks, on the other hand, sometimes develop inflated self concepts as a result of their track placements" (p. 8).

Regarding the assumption that placements are appropriate, the use of standardized tests are often coupled with guidance-counselor recommendations, grades, and parent input into the selection process for grouping. However, all of these methods of selection are suspect. Standardized tests are designed to separate students at a very specific, concrete level and to find the differences between students. They do not test what students know, but rather what they don't know; obscure questions are sometimes developed to identify these differences. Test makers do not use questions that everyone will get right.

Teacher and counselor recommendations are suspect in that they are often influenced not by a student's ability but by a student's appearance, manner, responsibility, or level of maturity. As human beings, we make judgments, and these judgments are subject to interpretation.

Parental choice raises other questions. Few parents would admit that their children are appropriately placed in classrooms of lower ability. All parents want the best for their children and see the uniqueness and special qualities of their children. They do not often see their children in relation to other children; therefore, their "objective" assessment of the student's achievement and capabilities are suspect at best.

The fourth assumption, that teaching is easier, may be harder to address. There are ways of organizing classrooms and ways of teaching students that are both effective and functional. Instructional strategies exist that make heterogeneity in a classroom a positive instructional resource. Further, "even if tracking students so teachers can work with homogeneous groups is easier, it is not worth the educational and social price we pay for it" (Oakes, 1985, p. 14). A brief historical perspective of grouping may be helpful to gain understanding of how this instructional practice came about and to help clarify thinking about appropriateness of grouping practices as it is practiced today and in the future.

## History of Ability Grouping

The history of tracking and ability grouping started with U.S. public schools in Massachusetts, in common schools, designed "to provide universal education that would increase opportunity, teach morality and citizenship, encourage leadership, maintain social mobility, and promote responsiveness to social progress. In short, to develop an intelligent mass citizenry" (Oakes, 1985, p. 16).

Toward the end of the 1800s, compulsory attendance became law in many states. While these laws were not strictly enforced until around 1900, even fewer students attended secondary school. For the most part, schools were for the white, Protestant, middle-class and upper-middle-class populations. Students continued to be of similar background and to attend secondary school in few numbers until the immigration period.

*With increased population of secondary school graduates came the first push for schools to sort and select students for higher education, as well as to prepare them for it. . . . In 1892 Charles Elliott chaired the Committee of Ten on secondary studies. It was Elliott's conviction that individual differences in intellect were not of such importance to require the design of special programs to accommodate them. . . . Under Elliott's influence the Committee of Ten recommended restructuring the secondary school curriculum based neither on the notion of curriculum differentiation to suit individual differences, nor the concept of a set of particular subjects best suited for college preparation. To the contrary, the Committee's report suggested four courses of study to be offered at the secondary level, each one to be acceptable for college admission. (Oakes, 1985, p. 18)*

Many immigrants in the early part of the 1900s came to America; by mid-1920 they numbered over 50 million. Enrollments in schools increased dramatically during this time. Particularly in urban schools, white, Anglo-Saxon, middle-class youngsters appeared to have lost their dominance. Schools during this time were under pressure to provide a greater variety of instruction. Diverse cultural groups had needs to be met. The immigrants, themselves, saw education as the key to improving their condition and blending into their new country. On the other hand, colleges were demanding new standards and core curricula to standardize admissions. This phenomenon gave birth to the comprehensive high school (a new secondary school that promised an education for everyone) but, of course, it did not promise the *same* thing for everyone.

Another factor that played an important role in school tracking and ability grouping was the Industrial Revolution. At the turn of the century, Americans had become enamored with industrial efficiency. With business leaders being part of school decision making on school boards, and the Industrial Revolution being the answer to many people's problems, it was only natural that this model be applied in the school setting: "It was seductive, as schools became large to think of them as factories that could use efficient and scientific methods to turn the raw material, children, into finished products, educated adults" (Oakes, 1985, p. 29).

Another influential factor at this time was the development of the Intelligence Quotient (IQ) test, which seemed to give a feeling of objectivity to the placement procedures used in separating children for instruction. One of the test pioneers, Louis Terman, commented that "this information would be of great value in planning the education of a particular child, and also in planning the differentiated curriculum recommended" (Terman, 1923, p. 27). These practices, then, in the first quarter of the century, paved the way and set precedents for U.S. schooling. The junior high school, created in the 1920s, was inspired partly by the desire to determine and to institute appropriate curriculum placements (vocational or academic) for students by the time children were 12 years old. The remnants of this 1920 philosophy remain with us today, which, of course, seems inadequate for today's society and intolerable for society in the future.

World War II contributed to the continuation of tracking. The military needed soldiers and capable officers. Aptitude and intelligence testing offered a quick and seemingly foolproof way to separate people efficiently.

These testing practices were adopted by the schools, and gave educators what seemed to be an accurate measure of a student's intelligence and other capabilities enabling the continued separation of students, only with more "accurate" data.

As the "Baby Boomer" generation came of school age, the great influx of students allowed for the expansion of schools and school programs and the necessity to manage large numbers. Generally, large high schools had four tracks: general, college preparation, business, and vocational. Junior high schools were to prepare students for what was perceived to be that student's expected course of study. Different level courses were developed at the junior high school, then, to accommodate this change.

The Vietnam War and increased media coverage of the events around the world made an impact on the grouping issue. Exposure to other world cultures and to other areas of the country broadened citizens' perspectives and enabled individuals to expand their thinking and their view of the world. This new perspective often challenged conventional thought and values, among them the issue of racial integration and methods of improving instruction.

Recently, the influence of technology and the corresponding reduction in industrial jobs have led educators and others to a renewed interest in education. This interest has also contributed to the separation of students. After years of plentiful, unskilled, industrial jobs, the current era is characterized by rapid displacement of such jobs and a strong demand for workers having high academic skills) Drucker, 1981; Etzioni, 1983; Leontief, 1982). The dropout rate, and unsuccessful students in the world of work, have placed new emphasis on the need for effective education for all.

Now more families of cultural backgrounds have access to the U.S. education system; therefore, the issue of accommodating the diversity of students within the educational setting becomes a greater challenge. The fallacy, of course, is that differences in learners, be they cultural, intellectual, or learning modality preferences, could be identified by any single sorting mechanism.

In June of 1989, the Carnegie Council on Adolescent Development released a report, *Turning Points: Preparing American Youth for the 21st Century,* that addressed ensuring success for all students. The goal of the task force was that "all young adolescents should have the opportunity to succeed in every aspect of the middle school program, regardless of previous achievement or the pace at which they learn" (p. 49). The authors of this report stated:

> *Grouping students by classes according to achievement level is almost universal in middle grade schools. In theory this between class tracking reduces the heterogeneity of the classes and enables teachers to*

*adjust instruction to students' knowledge and skills. Greater achievement is then possible for both low and high ability students. In practice this kind of tracking is proven to be one of the most divisive and damaging school practices in existence. Time and again, young people placed in lower academic tracks and classes, often during the middle grades, are locked into dull, repetitive instructional programs leading at best to minimum competencies. The psychic numbing these youth experience from a "dumbed-down" curriculum contrasts sharply with the exciting opportunities for learning and critical thinking that students in higher tracks or classes may experience. (p. 49–50)*

Often when students are placed in a lower track they do not move from this track. Minority youth, with their disproportionate numbers placed in lower academic groups, were a concern for the Task Force on Adolescent Development; likewise, those of higher socioeconomic levels more often than not appear in the upper-ability tracks. Today, *Turning Points* offers us a challenge: "to focus once again on the goal that tracking sought to achieve in the first place: Effectively teaching students of diverse ability and differing rates of learning" (p. 50).

## What Research Says: Directions from Educational Study

The underlying assumption of ability grouping is that teachers can create groups of children that are alike and that instruction with this homogeneous group will be more efficient and effective. This assumption has been challenged. Researchers have focused their attention on inequities that result from tracking: Minority and low-income children are overrepresented in low-achievement groups; students in low tracks often face low expectations and lack adequate peer models; and sometimes low tracks offer watered-down instruction. "An economic stratification develops within classes, the wealthier students dominated the gifted and talented classes, while the poorer ones often occupied the remedial classes, that reinforced a class difference the kids already felt" (Merina, 1989, p. 10).

Similar results are reported from many diverse sources. A number of reviews of research regarding tracking and practical application point to a factor that practitioner and researcher agree upon: there is no pervasive evidence that students benefit from tracking.

Slavin (1986) concluded that the average effect of grouping on achievement was zero. If forming classes on basis of student ability actually helped students to learn, we would by now have evidence supporting the practice.

Slavin's comment is further suported by a review conducted by the Harvard Education Letter (Organizing classes by ability, 1987) and concluded that "all this research taken together makes a reasonably strong case for reducing tracking and for supporting teachers who want to work with mixed groups" (p. 2).

In a study conducted by Trimble and Sinclair (1987), they stated,

> *In this study . . . little evidence emerged to suggest that the average and low ability students benefited from this organization. . . . Striking similarities in content and instruction across ability grouping seriously challenged the rationale for sorting students instead of widely varied educational practices, offered to help each student learn in the most appropriate way. We found a number of similarities of practices of content both within and across classes. . . . There is little evidence to suggest any group of students consistently benefits from ability grouping. . . . The findings in this study add to the mounting evidence that calls for a change in the present grouping practices in American schools. Only when schools stop sorting youth for learning by placing them into ability groups will it be possible to provide more equitable access to quality education for all students. (p. 20)*

In a research study on the effects of ability grouping, Noland and Taylor (1986) concluded that "the empirical evidence indicates that ability grouping does not improve overall student achievement and does damage overall student self concept" (p. 30). They further concluded that "we ought to be seeking policies and programs which enhance educational outcomes and which promote fairness in educational processes. Ability grouping does neither" (p. 30). Comments by Good and Marshall (1983) concluded that even allowing for some less than ideal studies, the research in this area in general indicated that

> *Tracking and ability grouping have few desirable consequences for low ability students. Research indicates that in many classrooms teachers err by holding expectations that are too low, by pacing instruction too slowly and by ignoring or underemphasizing the substantive expectation of task when instructing low groups. (p. 2)*

**Student Selection**

Low (1988) stated,

> *Practitioners revealed differences in their beliefs about the goals of ability grouping formation. Respondents employed sharply different place-*

*ment strategies. . . . Practitioners held different views of the selected student characteristics resulting in . . . students with the same characteristics were recommended for different classes. (p. 23)*

Low's study indicated that the reliability of teacher perceptions on students' abilities is not a constant variable upon which one can rely. Wilson and Schmits (1987) found that teachers generally believe that grouping students by ability is done fairly, is instructionally effective, makes teaching students at all ability levels easier, results in few discipline problems, and generates a better spirit of cooperation among students.

"Certainly students bring differences with them to school but by tracking schools [it] helps to widen, rather than narrow, these differences. . . . Everywhere we turn we find that the differentiated structure of schools throws up barriers to achievement for poor and minority students" (Oakes, 1986, p. 17).

One remarkable finding of research is that there is "relatively little change in the assigned ability group after the third grade" (Johnston & Markle, 1986, p. 56). In *What Research Says to the Middle Level Practitioner,* Johnston and Markel stated:

> *The practice of grouping students by ability for instructional purposes is not supported by research, even though a majority of teachers believe that ability grouping improves the effectiveness of schooling, the studies reviewed suggest the practice has deleterious effects on teacher expectations and instructional practices (especially for lower ability group students), student perceptions of self and others, and academic performance of lower ability students. It interferes with opportunities for students to learn from—and learn to accept—peers of different socioeconomic backgrounds, and may perpetuate notions of superior and inferior classes of citizens. The practice is especially antithetical to the goals and practices of the middle school. (p. 59)*

Although teachers generally believe that ability grouping helps students learn, assigning students to groups is problematic. Furthermore, it appears that once students are placed in lower tracks, it is difficult for them to escape.

### Student Ability

Gardner (1987) addresses the issue of ability. He proposes that seven intelligences exist in students:

1. Linguistic intelligence—a kind of ability exhibited in its fullest form, perhaps by poets
2. Logical-mathematical intelligence—logical and mathematical ability as well as scientific ability
3. Spatial intelligence—the ability to form a mental model of the spatial world and be able to maneuver and operate using that model
4. Musical intelligence
5. Bodily-kinesthetic intelligence—the ability to solve problems or fashion products using one's whole body or parts of the body
6. Interpersonal intelligence—the ability to understand other people, what motivates them, how they work, and how to work cooperatively with them
7. Intrapersonal intelligence—a correlative ability turned inward—is a capacity to form an accurate vertical model of one's self and to be able to use that model to operate effectively in life.

About these intelligences, Gardner stated,

> *I think all seven of the intelligences have equal claim to priority. In our society however we have put linguistic and logical mathematical intelligence, figuratively speaking, on a pedestal, . . . if you do well in language and logic you will do well in IQ tests and Scholastic Aptitude Tests, but whether you do well once you leave school, is probably going to depend as much on the extent to which you possess and use the other intelligences. . . . The purpose of school should be to develop intelligences and to help people achieve vocational and avocational goals that are appropriate to their particular spectrum of intelligences. People who are helped to do so, I believe, feel more engaged and competent and therefore more inclined to serve the society in a constructive way. . . . The design of my ideal school of the future is based upon two assumptions, the first is that not all people have the same interests and abilities, not all of us learn in the same way. . . . The second assumption is one that hurts, is the assumption that nowadays no one person can learn everything there is to learn . . . choice is therefore inevitable. . . . It is of utmost importance that we recognize and nurture all of the varied human intelligences, and all of the combinations of intelligences. We are all so different largely because we are different combinations of intelligences. (pp. 5–7)*

Ability, then, is varied and should not be limited to the commonly held definition. If Gardner's notion of intelligence is applied to the practice of ability grouping, it would bring an increasingly complex set of variables, which would render ability grouping of students virtually impossible. It also points to the limitations of present grouping practices that frequently use only one criteria for grouping. Intelligence can take many forms; all of which are legitimate and important in our society and in our schools.

## Impact of Ability Grouping on the Development of Young Adolescents

Grouping practices can have a profound influence on the social, emotional, and intellectual development of young adolescents. How schools organize for instruction defines the nature of interaction.

I will explore issues of a social development: peer influence, opposite sex interactions, achievement, independent learning, and sophistication. Issues surrounding the young adolescents' emotional development include: identity, change within students, self-concept development, and student self-centeredness. I will comment on issues of competence and excellence, and intellectual development of students, including abstract reasoning, uneven development, and imagination. It is my intent to investigate the influences of ability grouping on young adolescents utilizing these developmental characteristics. In this way, more direct links can be seen and appropriate decisions made regarding grouping practices in middle level schools.

### Social Development

Young adolecents are influenced by peers, boy-girl relationships, dependence-independence issues, and their search for sophistication: "The web of social contracts and interactions experienced by middle level students is intricate, involves an extensive amount of time to sustain, and has a potent impact on the way young people think, feel and act" (Van Hoose & Strahan, 1988, p. 27). Certainly peer influence and peer direction are universally accepted social development issues for young adolescents. Peer interaction is the bridge that moves individuals from parental control to self control: "Acceptance by friends and others who are the same age is a central concern in the lives of young adolescents. In the extreme, a young person may be willing to commit acts of violence, take drugs, become sexually precocious, or become dependent on alcohol to be accepted by peers" (Van Hoose & Strahan, 1988, p. 29).

If peer influence and peer associations are such powerful influences on the life of young adolescents, the implications for ability grouping become even more important. If peer role models are negative, then there is a greater likelihood that negative peer influence will cycle in negative ways and become problematic. Students in low groups tend to have behavioral problems and low self-esteem. If high groups are tracked, elitism often occurs. If both of these situations have negative consequences, the challenge then is to develop grouping practices with positive consequences.

It seems appropriate that flexible, changing, grouping practices should take place so that as young adolescents change, grouping practices change. If a student is having difficulty with a friend, a team of teachers operating within an interdisciplinary team organization can change that student's schedule until the issue is resolved. Grouping practices that allow for varied, broad peer interactions allow students to socialize with, model, and adjust to a variety of peer influences.

### Opposite Sex Interactions

Young adolescents are often concerned about boy-girl relationships. Much has been written about the impact of media, institutions, and parents on young adolescents. One recurring theme is the powerful pressure from these sources that encourage young people to grow up to be more like adults and, therefore, to do all that adults do at a younger and younger age. The tragedy in this scene is that childhood tends to slip away. Frequently, boys dominate lower-ability group classrooms, and higher-ability group classrooms tend to have more girls. If grouping practices are rigid, there are reduced opportunities for boys and girls to interact with each other in a learning environment. The implication of this situation is that gender interaction is reduced primarily to social settings, depriving both genders of intellectual interaction and appreciation.

The impact of a few girls in the low-ability track, and the influence of a few boys in the high-ability track, can also cause pressure on those particular students. The stereotype comes to mind of the extremely popular boy who has social pressures exerted on him by the girls in the upper-level groups and the other stereotype image of the "tough girl" who is in the lower-ability groups.

Ideally, mixed groups and flexibility can more effectively facilitate a natural relationship between boys and girls and help reduce the negative impact of gender bias and sex stereotyping. Although there are clear differences between boys and girls, flexible, appropriate grouping practices can reinforce characteristics and behaviors appropriately modeled for both sexes and can address issues of inequity.

### Achievement

Students often feel the pressure to grow up. The pressure on students in the top groups to achieve, to move ahead at a faster pace, and to learn more can be overwhelming for some students. Covering the curriculum is often the reason that certain concepts are pushed, chapters covered, terms learned, and ideas shared. The pressure mounts to take more advanced courses to get ready for high school, to gain an edge, and to move on in a competitive world.

Although some of these goals are worthwhile and appropriate, frequently they become negative for young adolescents. I believe we should allow students to explore the curriculum individually, allowing those with interest and skill to pursue specific learning, while avoiding in-depth or accelerated curriculum for groups of students. For the many students who are not ready, the curriculum becomes an application of skills to enrich curriculum and content. For middle level education, curriculum is not to be *covered,* but rather *uncovered,* enabling students to discover the meaning of learning.

### Independent Learning

"Because young adolescents are in a transitional stage, between childhood and late adolescence they vacillate in their behaviors from being childlike to being more like adults. . . . They shift in a heart beat from independence to dependence" (Van Hoose & Strahan, 1988, p. 30). Low-ability classrooms are often dominated by organizational issues and rote learning. High-ability classrooms generally offer greater opportunities for creative thought and independent learning. This, then, results in restrictive classrooms for both low- and high-ability groups — classrooms that may not be flexible enough to meet the changing characteristics of young adolescents.

Students of all ability levels need an opportunity for both kinds of learning. High-ability students may still benefit from organized, structured learning environments. Likewise, low-ability students need an opportunity for independent, self-directed, creative learning. Again, the issue of ability grouping seems in conflict with what we know about how young adolescents learn best.

### Sophistication

The last characteristic of social development to be considered is the search for sophistication. Young adolescents seem to strive to demonstrate that they are mature. Two areas in the search for sophistication illustrate this notion: the attempts by middle level students to demonstrate modern language usage, and the capacity for students to be very righteous and to defend a position (Van Hoose & Strahan, 1988, p. 31). Students will use their new-found abilities to experiment and use words to appear more sophisticated; frequently, they will misuse these words. If learning environments are not caring and sensitive to this experimentation, students will not venture out, experience, and try new vocabulary words or word meanings.

If learning in low-ability groups is structured and there is little opportunity for interaction and experimentation with language and learning, and if in high-ability groups the mood is competitive when sophisticated idea development occurs, then students of low and high groups will be hesitant to share their thought processes with the group. It is critical at all ability levels that students have an opportunity to discuss and search for ideas and shaping experiences in a supportive atmosphere. Tyler (1989) stated, "Learning does not come from the experience of an activity, it comes from the reflection upon that experience." We must provide classroom environments that will enable students to reflect on their experiences without the threat of punishment, ridicule, or sarcasm.

## Emotional Development

Early adolescence is characterized by emotional ups and downs. This roller coaster of emotions is partly due to increased hormone levels. But, as young adolescents pass from childhood to adulthood, they must answer the questions of Who am I? How much control do I have? and How competent am I and at what? These struggles naturally cause uncertainty at this age and many of the answers to these important questions are learned in school.

### Identity

The search for identity, so obvious during early adolescence, dominates much of what educators attempt to provide during this turbulent time of life. Middle level students need to achieve in order to develop a positive self-concept. Indeed, self-image often develops from successes and failures in the academic as well as social arena. If it is true that success breeds success, then this concept has implications for ability grouping. It seems that students who are in a low-ability group know that they are in a low-ability group, develop a poor self-image, and acquire a feeling that they cannot succeed. High-group students, on the other hand, develop the notion of inflated self-image. Middle level students may perceive themselves as average, never being "good" at anything. What may be more appropriate is to create climates in instructional settings that encourage experimentation, wherein failures are viewed as a necessary part of learning and are therefore treated as another basis upon which future success is built.

During this period of adjustment, young adolescents also try out different identities; they change their physical appearance and try new social roles. At times they may assume this new identity in total. The implication for grouping practices is that if students do not see diversity, they may be limited in their exposure, resulting in a warped sense of personal identity. Again, the notion of the greater variety and diversity within students can be celebrated as an enhancement of the learning environment and personal growth.

Certainly, early adolescence is a time of change and fluctuation; there is often an imbalance between needs that are satisfied and those that are unsatisfied: "Self concept first emerges as a global construct, that is students see themselves as able or unable, responsible or irresponsible, valuable or worthless" (Van Hoose & Strahan, 1988, p. 20). If self-concept first begins as a global construct, then the effects of ability grouping are extremely important. The implication for those young adolescents involved in low-ability groups or high-ability groups will bring about an unrealistic sense of who they are.

Low-ability groups will more than likely see themselves as unable, irresponsible, and worthless. We might expect higher-ability students to view themselves as able, responsible, and valuable. Students in both high- and low-ability groups may have their perceptions skewed by competition within those groups. This is especially apparent in the high groups, where young adolescents with admirable traits may view themselves in the mid to low range within their group and begin to see themselves as less than adequate, even though they may be capable, able, and very worthwhile.

The Poker Chip Theory, an analogy originated by Canfield and Wells (1976), suggests that students come to situations with their self-concepts conceptualized as a stack of poker chips. If their self-concept is well developed, they have many poker chips; if it is not, they have fewer poker chips. When it comes to gambling on a new experience, those who have many chips have more to gamble with, but those with fewer chips are less likely to gamble. Therefore, students with high self-concepts are more willing to risk in a learning situation. Implications for ability grouping seem obvious: If students are not willing to gamble/risk, they will not have the opportunity to win more chips. This situation sets up a spiral effect on students, with the direction going lower and lower or higher and higher.

In my opinion, tracking and ability grouping contribute to the spiraling effect. In a more heterogeneous arrangement this effect is not structured into the school organization: "As early adolescents come to believe they are inadequate, they develop patterns of behavior to attend to the perceived inadequacy" (Van Hoose & Strahan, 1988, p. 21). Students will take on roles and behaviors that are not theirs to compensate for what they perceive to be inadequacy. This is extremely important in a student's development. Many students let go of this experimentation during adolescence, and embrace a view of themselves as a competent person. Unfortunately, some students do not work through this sense of inadequacy and carry it with them for the rest of their lives.

### Self-Control
Middle level students attempt to move from parental control, through peer domination, to self-control. As students are making the transition to self-control from parental control, diversity and peer groups influence this process. If self-control is to be learned by trial and error, and peer influence

is highly important, it seems logical to conclude that diversity can be a positive aspect of student experiences.

If students in low groups exhibit less self-control and students in high groups exhibit more self control (Dentzer & Wheelock, 1990), high- and average-ability groups will have greater opportunities to model appropriate behavior. Students benefit from understanding how others process information and about how others view themselves.

### Competence

If there is always a group that is perceived as being more competent, then even when low- and average-level ability groups are trying to achieve and to be "the best of the best," they are never quite good enough. Educators want students to become competent learners and competent citizens, regardless of their ability grouping.

Willie (1987) contends that *excellence* is a personal choice. If one individual chooses to work hard, chooses to excel, then that is his or her choice. *Competence,* then, is the ability to perform a job adequately. All students can become competent in their learning; many may choose to be excellent. Most people feel less than adequate in some ways, but have resolved this and see their value as a person. They come to realize that they are indeed different, and they can be satisfied with those differences. But until that point is reached, most people will try to compensate for or deny perceived inadequacies and remain unsatisfied. Middle level educators must create environments where all students can succeed, where all students perceive themselves as worthwhile, and where differences, even in the attainment of excellence, are accepted.

## Intellectual Development

It is during early adolescence that students begin to develop the ability to reason abstractly. They begin to think of the world around them and themselves in new ways. For the first time, young adolescents can "think about thinking." Understanding the development of abstract reasoning and reflective thinking is especially important for successful teaching at the middle level. Students moving from concrete to formal stages in their development are often confused about their thought processes. This is further complicated by changes occurring at different times; all students do not move together in a magic moment that correlates with other aspects of adolescent development.

Intellectual development is also uneven across subject matter areas, which is to say that ability to think on a formal level may take place in one particular subject area but not in another (Smart & Smart, 1973). Abstract thinking development is uneven within students, day to day, and certainly is different between students. Piaget (1977) reports experimental studies showing as much as four years of "lag time" in students changing from concrete to formal operations (p. 36). Implications for grouping require that strategies for movement from concrete to formal operations be a concern for all teachers, and that perhaps frequent changing of grouping patterns and being flexible is appropriate and may facilitate intellectual growth.

Rigid tracking hinders the intellectual development of students. If one group stays together for the entire day, or in the entire academic subject core curricula, instruction is designed for only one level of cognitive development. It makes sense, then, that a variety of approaches to accommodate differing intellectual developments should be used in a variety of ways with all students. "Middle grade teachers need to be aware of the wide range of individual differences in reasoning development that are likely to occur in a given class. . . . Planning instruction is like shooting at a moving target, due to the rapid individual changes" (Van Hoose & Strahan, 1988, p. 16). Because of the vastness of individual differences, it would be nearly impossible to group according to each individual student's stage of development.

As young adolescents move from concrete to formal reasoning, they begin to think about how they are thinking. When presented with mental tasks that are difficult, they often dwell on their inability to perform them. This is especially the case when they know other students can solve them. One way that this awareness of not knowing is often demonstrated is in the "I could do it if I wanted to" defense mechanism. As a result, some students rarely attempt to think through challenging problems and miss opportunities to extend their reasoning potential. The only way to break this cycle is to create a climate in which students are willing to take chances and think about their own thinking in more productive ways. Appropriate grouping practices would be diverse within a class group and would enable students to observe and perhaps to model each other's thought processes.

As students think about how they are thinking, they develop what is called an "intensive introspection." Young adolescents seem to dwell on their lack of understanding and personalize feelings of inadequacy. Facilitating diversity in groups helps students reflect on a greater reality and a more diverse population so that they can determine where they fit in the larger picture that includes their peers.

The imagination of young adolescents reappears at this time. If the imagination becomes more vivid, students will be able to be more creative in how they solve problems, look at issues in different ways, and develop their own answers to issues of process. The notion of intelligence (amount of information and speed of processing) is different from that of creativity and imagination. If, as research indicates, creative learning environments are not developed in low-ability grouped classes, and are more prevalent in upper-ability classes, then students in the middle- and low-ability classes are frequently not exposed to creative problem solving.

It is important that all students receive this kind of instruction. Middle grades students enter a period in which they experience heightened intellectual capacities. Concepts and generalizations previously accepted at face value no longer stand unchallenged. Reason and logic begin to dominate the mind if these qualities of intellect are valued and nurtured. We must ensure that reason, logic, and the ability to generalize are developed in all students, and not limited to only a few students because of a selection process: "It can be a fragile time. it can also be an exciting time for adults who work with young adolescents. Because when human beings say for the first time, I have a future, I have a destiny, I am part of a generation, he or she is also ready to make a commitment to that future" (Lipsitz, 1979, p. 5).

## Moving to More Appropriate Grouping Practices

The discussion thus far has centered on ability grouping, an historical perspective, and its effects on young adolescents. As Dorman, Lipsitz, and Verner (1985) state, "There is a considerable lack of fit between what we know about early adolescents and what we do with them five days a week in schools" (p. 46). If one accepts the premise that ability grouping hinders the growth and development of young adolescents, then the question becomes how to move to more appropriate grouping practices.

Toepfer (1989) stated that nothing is more unequal than the equal treatment of unequals, which is what tracking perpetuates. We must find ways to treat all students with equality and to enhance their learning. There is no one "right" way to group, but flexible ways of grouping can be identified: "As strategies are developed in local settings, grouping can become a professional, decision making variable which teachers use to establish better learning and personal development environments in school" (Toepfer, 1989, p. 5). Again, the principle that may guide grouping practices in the middle school is not *whether* we group students for instruction, but rather *how* we group for instruction, that will make a difference.

Common sense dictates that effective grouping practice should be centered around the notion of flexibility. The reassessment of students and subsequent reassignment of students is an appropriate grouping strategy. Grouping students by specific, discrete skills to be learned as opposed to general overall achievement is appropriate. In addition to skill placement, it is important that the length of time in that placement be considered. Also, when students are placed by skill level, care must be taken to ensure that the level and pace of instruction matches the student's readiness level. Slavin,

Braddock, Hall, and Petza (1989) found that tracking plans have beneficial effects on student achievement when they incorporate the following features:

1. Students remain in heterogeneous groups most of the day and are grouped by performance level only in such subjects as reading and mathematics in which reducing heterogeneity is particularly important.
2. The grouping plan reduces heterogeneity in the specific skill being taught.
3. Group assignments are both flexible and frequently reassessed.
4. Teachers adapt their level and pace of instruction in regrouped classes to accommodate students' levels of readiness and learning rates.

A preponderance of evidence suggests that tracking is not effective in increasing achievement and it does not positively affect the student's development. Why does this practice continue to exist? Some educators believe that teachers do not know appropriate instructional strategies for a diverse group of students. Merina (1989) maintained that "the key to dismantling tracking is to explore alternative, appropriate ways of teaching the new groups. Switching the classes to heterogeneous groups and expecting the teacher to use teaching methods meant for homogeneous classes makes the teacher's job virtually impossible" (p. 11). Techniques and skills of instruction in homogeneous classrooms are not conducive to the heterogeneous classroom.

Additionally, if schools can create a culture that supports effort as much as achievement, less tracking would be needed.

> *Providing all children access to knowledge will require drastic alterations in instructional practice. . . . Students need to be clustered in small groups, exchanging ideas, sometimes working on separate but interrelated tasks and generally helping each other learn. . . . Teachers must function more like orchestra conductors than like lecturers, getting things started and moving them along, providing information and pointing to resources, coordinating a diverse, but harmonious, buzz of activity. (Goodlad & Oakes, 1988, p. 19)*

### Preparing for the Change

A study of the problems and issues surrounding ability grouping must occur as a preparation for change. Teachers are the ones who must change their behavior and it is teachers who must be the major players in this decision-making process. Moving to a more heterogeneous grouping of students requires tremendous individual reevaluation and change. Perhaps, however, many teachers are in the same boat. Although in-service can be provided for a group or school, for this specific issue it is the individual that must change to adjust to the appropriate teaching styles. Once the need for change is identified, the options for change must be explored.

When given time and support, teachers can solve problems. Leaders must find and create time to allow dialogue among teachers so that they may explore important concerns with each other. Teachers together can find answers to their difficult problems. Study of the current research helps lead to answers to this complex issue. Strategies and methodologies have been classroom tested with heterogeneous grouped students. The research is available and the answers are available; we must help teachers move to change their behavior in classrooms.

The change effort must move slowly; complete and abrupt abandonment of current grouping practices have not proven successful. A smooth and gentle transition toward a full incorporation of appropriate grouping practices is recommended. Teachers will need support as they implement the change effort. Reflecting on experience, there will be a time when the new practice will want to be abandoned or modified by those struggling with innovation, but with perseverance and support, new instructional methodologies can be adopted and implemented effectively so that they will be sustained.

Many schools across the country have successfully changed their grouping practices. In a study funded by the National Education Association, Slavin and colleagues (1989) found:

> *Teachers and administrators with whom we spoke were almost uniformly positive about their move to reduce ability grouping, but they also note that in making the change there were many obstacles they had to be overcome. . . . "It's the fear of failure in doing something different that upsets the experienced teacher,". . . "To me, commented a teacher, "it's just something to try," while another teacher said, "Once I got into it, it was the best thing that ever happened to my classes!"* (p. 15)

## Appropriate Grouping Practices

What, then, are appropriate grouping practices? Research and experience indicate that there are appropriate instructional methodologies to meet the needs of young adolescents. Slavin and colleagues (1989) reported, "When working with heterogenous groups in the same classroom, teachers from elementary to high school offered these suggestions: cooperative learning, peer teaching, whole class teaching, individualization of instruction, team teaching, and theme approach or integrated day" (p. 14).

### Instructional Issues

Commonly used instructional strategies including learning strategies, cooperative teams of learners, and individual tutorials as well as large and small group instruction. "Teachers are encouraged to match these strategies to their own teaching styles, to the learning styles of their students, and to the kinds of objectives for students" (Strother, 1985, pp. 309–310). These features form the basic characteristics of a renewed instructional approach in a more appropriate grouping arrangement.

Change to these kinds of instructional methodologies requires that teachers modify their activities within the classroom. Research indicates that teachers improve at their craft in part by examining whether or not they reach individual students:

> *Teachers can change the grouping within the class, choose and develop materials and assignments, vary the instruction in the classroom, and interact with students in variety of ways. In short, they can adjust instructional process to an individual student's responses, but also to their growing perception of student cognition and motivation with respect to the learning task at hand." (Corno & Snow, 1989, p. 613)*

The notion of individualization, or adopting learning to individual students, asks teachers to adjust their techniques and methodologies to find ways that match their own individual styles.

### Peer Tutoring

Peer tutoring is an effective way to meet student needs in a heterogenous classroom. In a report by the Massachusetts Advocacy Center titled *Locked In/Locked Out,* Dentzer and Wheelock (1990) suggested that, given limited opportunities for teachers to provide assistance, a promising alternative is a peer-tutoring model in which students tutor one another. They also suggested that possibilities for cross-age tutoring be explored, as it is less likely to have the potential stigmatizing effects of peer tutoring.

### Cooperative Learning

One of the most powerful methods of addressing diverse needs of students within a classroom is the use of cooperative learning. Cooperative learning has been suggested by numerous researchers and practitioners as an instructional method that has great promise as a viable solution to the issue of appropriate grouping practices. Coopertive learning, discussed fully in Chapter Seventeen, usually includes instrutional methods in which students learn in small, heterogeneous learning groups toward a group goal.

## Individualization

Techniques for individualization within regular classroom activities can help students. Allowing an oral presentation to be given in front of a teacher, counselor, and/or friend instead of the entire class can be an appropriate modification. When teachers utilize a lecture-direct instruction format, some techniques for individualization are allowing students to diagram rather than write or outline ideas and information; shortening the time requirement of a lesson into smaller segments or allowing some segments to be presented by tape; allowing for note cards; and providing an outline of points to be covered or learned.

Techniques to individualize reading assignments would include (1) providing lower-level texts for some students, (2) allowing students to highlight the regular textbook, (3) preparing taped presentations of text material, (4) assigning reading of specific points and providing vocabulary assistance, and (5) using visual clues to assist in comprehension.

Other approaches could include (1) permitting substitution of written assignments with projects, oral reports, and computer assignments; (2) allowing extra time; (3) emphasizing quality, not quantity; and (4) permitting students to tape lengthy assignments rather than write them. Listening can also be individualized by allowing students to tape oral presentations, to verify understandings by asking students to repeat or paraphrase directions, and by providing brief outlines of complex instructions. Countless methods of adapting instruction for individualized needs exist and can be effective in accommodating diverse abilities within a classroom.

Doda (1991) suggested approaches that can be used with students: (1) the interdisciplinary team unit of instruction that interrelates and correlates with curriculum objectives (these often involve hands-on activities and allow students to demonstrate different kinds of knowledge); (2) learning centers, stations, or areas within a classroom where students can go to investigate on their own specific topics related to classroom lessons or independent projects; (3) mastery learning, where students progress at their own rate to achieve specific mastery objectives; (4) small and large group experiences, ranging from pairs to groups of 4 or 5, or 25; and (5) the use of independent study, where students work independently to develop a project or product of interest.

Doda (1991) also suggested that individual learning contracts (where students and teachers together collaborate and identify exactly what will be done, when it will be done, and how success will be gauged) are particularly appropriate for young adolescents. Exploratory and mini-courses where grades are not given, but where students select courses of interest to them, are usually of short duration and are another example of appropriate options for students.

**Multiability Classroom**

Cohen (1986) stated,

*The multi-ability classroom means permanent changes in the organization of student work and evaluation practices. These changes are designed to increase active engaged learning behavior on the part of low status students, and to provide enriched detailed feedback to all students on how they are doing on different specific skills. (p. 145)*

Designing the multiability classroom requires a change in organization and planning strategies.

*In examining the kinds of tasks a teacher selects for instruction, one should ask the following questions:*

> *What opportunities do low achievers have for success in the classroom?*
>
> *Do classroom tasks and objectives provide multiple dimensions of competence?*
>
> *Is reading a prerequisite for successful participation in all important tasks?*
>
> *How often are multi-media tasks and small groups used?*
>
> *What are some ways that you can provide for students to evaluate their own competence and the competence of others?*
>
> *Is ability grouping used with more or less stable membership? Are competitive marks and grades the only basis that the children have for knowing how well they are succeeding? Are low achieving students successful? Do their classmates have a chance to see and evaluate their success?*
>
> *Do low achieving students know clearly what they have done and what is successful and what needs to be improved? (Cohen, 1986, p. 154)*

## Case Study: Powder Mill Middle School

Teachers and administrators at Powder Mill Middle School wanted to move toward a more flexible grouping pattern. Teachers decided that whatever the appropriate grouping practice was to be, it must be of short duration and for a speific purpose. Grouping options were explored in the preparation for change. Learning styles, modality preference, interest-based learning, talent areas, and skill development groups were all considered appropriate grouping options for young adolescents. Given the differences in people, and in young adolescents in particular, educators asked the question, How can Powder Mill Middle School work with this diverse population of students?

A guiding principle for this effort was stated as "schools don't need more bureaucracy, they need more creativity." Bureaucracy, which is what tracking can become, is a response to a problem. What we needed were more creative solutions to address this matter. Building and team schedules were analyzed and changed to eliminate inappropriate grouping practices. Teachers accepted responsibility for the educational program of the students they served, and, as such, had the ability and power to change student schedules as needed.

In this four-year process, one of the first changes was to "de-track" the unified arts subject areas. Students had been going to physical education, industrial arts, music, and art with the same students as their previous subject-tracked grouping system. In grades 7 and 8, there was a high and low group, and three groups in the middle (average, above average, and below average). Each of these groups went to "special subjects" together, meaning that those students saw only each other all day long. In the first year, the special area subjects were de-tracked. They then went to the unified arts classes in heterogenous homeroom groups.

The second major change was that five levels of tracking for the core subject classes were changed to three levels of tracking: high, medium, and low. The issue of grouping was tied to other significant change efforts in the school. In this case, curriculum revision was also addressed and studied. As curriculum was reviewed in mathematics and language arts, movement from teacher-centered classrooms to student-centered classrooms became a theme.

In language arts, a "whole language program," involving the writing and reading process, was implemented. Moving to literature-based instruction, individual goals and small work groups were the norm, and peer tutoring became accepted practice. This transition allowed the instructional focus to move from the group to the individual. As these techniques of instruction and other learning strategies became accepted and used, teachers with developing skills and new abilities to manage classrooms became resources for other teachers.

The unified arts teachers provided a model for other teachers. What principles of instruction could be learned from the art classroom as the teacher works with students with different art abilities? How did the art teacher handle those situations and allow for individual skill differences? How does the physical education teacher handle differing skills within the classroom and still allow for participation by all without ridicule? With these curricular changes taking place, other grouping practices changed as well.

Another guiding principle was "those teachers closest to the learners should make appropriate educational decisions for those students." New team schedules were developed, allowing for flexible grouping practices in each team. Ways were found to group students for ability in one or two subjects, and yet have mixed groups for other classes. This scheduling innovation, although somewhat complex, can be achieved and can be viewed as a transitional technique.

To clarify this team schedule, a group of 125 seventh-graders is thought of as one large class. Classrooms can be pictured with small groups and individuals in various parts of the classroom, working on different but related projects, readings, or activities. "Within-class ability grouping, which allows students in homogeneous subgroups to receive instruction at their own level and to progress at their own rate, is very common in elementary reading and mathematics, but is rarely seen in secondary schools (Barr & Dreeben, 1983; Hallihan & Sorensen, 1983). These plans generally conform to the four requirements for "effective ability grouping since students are grouped by specific rather than general skills and within-class groupings are easy to change, at least in principle" (Schneider, 1989, p. 8).

This concept of "one class" was transferred to the team organization. The team was then subdivided into five smaller groups based on appropriate educational activities and grouping practices. Individual student schedules were developed, with the end result being five different classes with five different student populations. With this team/class schedule, students would move with only three or four peers in each class, and all classes had mixed groupings. The focus for students was not the homeroom or the classroom, but the team.

Other scheduling changes took place to maintain a direction of reducing ability grouping and tracking. The eighth grade developed a schedule enabling a small group to take algebra and another group to take pre-algebra. No other subjects are grouped by ability within the eighth-grade team. Throughout the school, rigid structured reading groups are not scheduled by the office. This scheduling is done within the team, made possible by a renewed curriculum and changed instructional methods. Math groups can be developed by the team so that their only grouping practice is to accommodate a high level math ability group of students.

The process in this staff development effort was to find ways to support teachers as they changed their practices. Study teams, peer coaching, and time for the discussion of new methods were important to this process. New instructional methodologies and strategies, such as cooperative learning, were studied, assimilated, practiced, and adopted. Clearly, the experience of Powder Mill Middle School indicates that it is more than deciding not to group by ability; it is teachers deciding to risk a change as to how they want to work with students in the classroom. This change is motivated by what is known about young adolescents and the negative effects of rigid ability grouping: "Change is possible. Each school and district has to work out for itself whether, to what degree, and how it will dismantle its ability grouping arrangements" (Slavin et al., 1989, p. 18).

## Conclusion

Clearly, rigid homogeneous grouping patterns based on ability are not appropriate in schools. They are most inappropriate in a middle level school, where characteristics of student learners are in direct conflict with the negative aspects of ability grouping. Moving toward a more heterogeneous environment, and adopting appropriate instructional strategies and methodologies where heterogeneous methods can be successful, can facilitate higher achievement and enhance learning.

Middle school organization enhances the change of instructional strategies. Teaming itself allows for decisions in grouping practices to be decided at the closest level to the learner. Teaming provides appropriate collegial support for these change efforts. Teachers with common planning time can discuss their successes and concerns regarding new instructional strategies and approaches. The philosophy and foundations of the middle school organization enhance changes in grouping practices for students.

What, then, of the future, particularly the future of middle level education and this issue of ability grouping? As reported by Cawelti (1988), "The middle school form of organization is far more likely to provide those program characteristics needed by early adolescents" (p. 1). The author concluded that

> *Much remains to be done to ensure that schools serving students in the middle grades are responsive to their unique needs. But this study reveals that the efforts of middle school leaders have produced tangible results in shaping schools that serve their students effectively and help them prepare for many futures. (p. 12)*

To modify current practice and be instructionally effective, teachers must change their teaching strategies. Mike clearly substantiated the notion that teaching is difficult and that a teacher must be willing to implement new ideas. He allowed himself to investigate new techniques. He did this in a professional manner.

Appropriate grouping practice is a major issue facing middle schools of the future. As our society becomes more complex, with rapidly changing student conditions related to family structures, ethnic background, and cultural diversity, powerful strategies such as cooperative learning become absolutely necessary. It is vitally important that we do not continue to separate, but that we bring together—into one community—individual strengths to ensure that our schools function at their highest level.

### Mike's Thoughts on Changing Classroom Practice

*I see myself as changed, changed a lot since I first started teaching and getting more in tune with the kids and their feelings, feelings toward life and their feelings towards math and toward one another, and (long pause) I have learned more about myself. I have also been taking courses about how I tick and once you learn how you tick you can learn about how other people perceive themselves and also other people and their relationships with one another.*

*I think when we went from the homogeneous grouping to the heterogeneous grouping, I had a problem. At that point, I believed that we should have homogeneous groups and after we got into it [for] two years, that is the way to go. Support from the administration, . . . was more articles, educational articles on heterogeneous grouping and how that was really the way to be going. So that is where they were coming from, and explaining to the parents and [they] tried to explain to me too. (Laugh)*

*One of the difficult things is that there was a lot of theory connected with this but I need the practical applications. Show me how to do something, show me how to do it and let me try it and then tell me did I do it the right way. I can then feel confident and then I can go on. Myself—[pause] if somebody has a way to do something that looks good, I can take it and I can adjust it to what or how I want to present it in my classroom. Take his good ideas and combine it with what I want to do. I need that type of thing. The theory, I just couldn't deal with some of the material. Okay, great, now tell me what to do. Just give me an idea, which way to go, and then I can go with that and blossom out from that.*

*Kids learn that each one of them has something to offer to solve the problem and not just the math-type problems but working together they can help one another. Prior to cooperative learning, everything was done on your own, and it was you against the kids. To succeed, you always have to work with other people.*

*I love the job. (Laugh) The kids make it, kids really make it. Hopefully somewhere down the line, someone will say to you, "Thanks a lot" or see you on the street and say, "Yes, I remember you and I remember this is what happened. . . ." It makes you feel all choked up when you have a student come back and see you from high school.*

*That is the best part! I would work here for nothing, just volunteer work. (Laugh) It is great! It is a great occupation!*

## References

Barr, R., & Dreeben, R. (1983). *How schools work.* Chicago: University of Chicago Press.

Bernagozzi, T. (1988). One teacher's approval. *Learning, 17*(7), 39–43.

Bryson, J. E., & Bentley, C. P. (1980). *Ability grouping of public school students: Legal aspects of classification and tracking methods.* Charlottesville, VA: The Michie Co.

Canfield, J., & Wells, H. C. (1976). *One hundred ways to enhance self-concept in the classroom.* Englewood Cliffs, NJ: Prentice-Hall.

Carnegie Council on Adolescent Development's Task Force on Eduction of Young Adolescents. (1989). *Turning points: Preparing American youth for the 21st century.* Washington, DC: Carnegie Council on Adolescent Development, a program of Carnegie Corporation of New York.

Cawelti, G. (1988, November). Middle schools a better match with early adolescent needs, ASCD survey finds. *ASCD Curriculum Update.* (Available from the Association of Supervision and Curriculum Development, Alexandria, VA 22314-2798).

Cohen, E. G. (1986). *Designing group work: Strategies for the heterogeneous classroom.* New York: Teachers College Press.

Corno, L., & Snow, R. E (1989). Adapting teaching to individual differences among learners. *The Encyclopedia of Education: Research and Studies (Supplementary Vol. 1)* (p. 613). New York: Pergamon Press.

Dentzer, E., & Wheelock, A. (1990). *Locked in/locked out: tracking and placement practices in Boston public shools.* Boston: Massachusetts Advocacy Center.

Doda, N. (1991, January). *Middle school magic.* Presentation at Hampshire Educational Collaborative, West Springfield, MA.

Dorman, G., Lipsitz, J., & Verner, P. (1985). Improving schools for young adolescents. *Educational Leadership, 43*(6), 44–48.

Drucker, P. F. (1981). The next American work force: Demographics and U.S. economic policy. *Commentary, 77*(4), 3–10.

Etzioni, A. (1983). *An immodest agenda: Rebuilding America before the twenty-first century.* New York: McGraw-Hill.

Gardner, H. (1987). Beyond the IQ: Eduction and human development. *Harvard Educational Rerview, 57*(2), 187–193.

George, P. S. (1988). Tracking and ability grouping. *Middle School Journal, 20*(1), 21–28.

Good, T., & Marshall, S. (1983). Do students learn more in heterogeneous or homogeneous groups? In P. Peterson, L. Wilkenson, & M. Hillinan (Eds.), *The social context of instruction: Group organization and group process* (pp. 15–38). Orlando, FL: Academic Press.

Goodlad, J. I. (1984). *A place called school: Prospects for the future.* New York: McGraw-Hill.

Goodlad, J. I., & Oakes, J. (1988). We must offer equal access to knowledge. *Educational Leadership, 45*(5), 16–22.

Hallihan, M., & Sorensen, A. (1983). The formation and stability of instructional groups. *American Sociological Review, 48*(6), 839–851.

Johnston, J. H., & Markle, G. C. (1986). *What research says to the middle level practitioner.* Columbus, OH: National Middle School Association.

Leontief, W. W. (1982). The distribution of work and income. *Scientific American, 247*(3), 188–204.

Lipsitz, J. S. (1979). Adolescent development: Myths and realities. *Children Today, 8*(5), 1–9.

Low, D. (1988, April). *Ability grouping: Decision making at the secondary level.* Paper presented at Meeting of the American Educational Research Association, New Orleans.

Merina, A. (1989). Are we on the right track? *NEA Today, 8*(3), 10–11.

Noland, T. K., & Taylor, B. L. (1986, April). *The effects of ability grouping: A meta-analysis of research findings.* Paper presented at Meeting of the American Educational Research Association, San Francisco.

Oakes, J. (1985). *Keeping track: How schools structure inequality.* New Haven, CT: Yale University Press.

Oakes, J. (1986). Keeping track, part 1: The policy and practice of curriculum inequity. *Phi Delta Kappan, 68*(1), 12–17.

Organizing classes by ability. (1987). *The Harvard Education Letter, 3*(4), 1–4.

Piaget, J. (1977). *The science of education and psychology of the child.* New York: Penguin Books.

Schneider, J. M. (1989). Tracking: A current national perspective. Presentation at a Critical Issues Session on Academic Tracking in Schools to the National Education Association Board of Directors, *The NEA/Johns Hopkins Study of Academic Tracking: An Interim Report.*

Slavin, R. (1986). *Ability grouping and student achievement in elementary schools: A best evidence synthesis.* Baltimore, MD: The Center for Research on Elementary and Middle Schools, Johns Hopkins University.

Slavin, R. E. (1988). Ability grouping and its alternatives: Must we track. *Middle Grades Network, 3*(5), 1–7.

Slavin, R. E., Braddock II, J. H., Hall, C., & Petza, R. J. (1989). *Alternatives to ability grouping.* Baltimore, MD: The Center for Research on Elementary and Middle Schools, The Johns Hopkins University.

Smart, M. S., & Smart, R. C. (1973). *Adolescence.* New York: Macmillan.

Strother, D. B. (1985). Adapting instruction to individual needs: An eclectic approach. *Phi Delta Kappan, 67*(4), 308–311.

Terman, L. (1923). *Intelligence tests and school reorganization.* New York: World Book.

Toepfer, C. F. (1989). Differentiating middle level school programs. *Dissemination Service, 20*(6), 1–6.

Trimble, K., & Sinclair, R. L. (1987). On the wrong track: Ability grouping and the threat to equity. *Equity and Excellence, 23*(1–2), 12–21.

Tyler, R. H. (1989). Personal conversation. Amhearst, MA.

Van Hoose, J., & Strahan, D. (1988). *Young adolescent development and school practices: Promoting harmony.* Columbus, OH: National Middle School Association.

Willie, C. V. (1987). When excellence and equity complement each other. *Harvard Educational Review, 57*(2), 205–207.

Wilson, B. J., & Schmits, D. W. (1987). What's new in ability grouping. *Phi Delta Kappan, 59*(8), 535–536.

# CHAPTER FIFTEEN

# Motivation: Moving, Learning, Mastering, and Sharing

JULIA THOMASON
*Appalachian State University*

MAX THOMPSON
*Appalachian State University*

Throughout the history of education, much has been written on the subject of motivation. "Motivation—Getting students to move: move toward instructional goals, move into academic learning, move forward in the acquisition of skills and values" (McDaniel, 1985, p. 19). The critical nature of increased student motivation has become even more important in the last two decades. This is due in part, perhaps, because of the vast array of motivational needs displayed by our ever-changing clientele in U.S. public schools. Add to this the somewhat recent emphasis on young adolescents in middle level schools as a unique and legitimate third tier of education, and there is a need to study motivation even further, particularly for these students.

Lipsitz (1977) initiated the call to study early adolescent schooling in the benchmark publication, *Growing Up Forgotten*. She called to our attention the fact that there is a considerable lack of fit between what we know about young adolescents and what we do to and for them five days a week in school. She also pointed out that the change from elementary to middle school is perhaps the most abrupt and traumatic move in a student's educational experience. Her premise seemed to be that this lack of fit and the ramifications of the shift in educational setting cause students to become less involved in schooling, less motivated, and, thus, less likely to continue to perform as well academically as they once had in elementary school.

This illustration by Lipsitz was duplicated many times over in the middle school literature, but still there were initially only a few studies focusing on the differences in the classroom or school environment across grades or levels (Eccles & Midgley, 1989). However, looking at the relatively few studies that were conducted, four basic patterns emerged. First, many middle grades classrooms often evidenced a greater emphasis on teacher control and discipline, with fewer opportunities for teacher-student relationships than had been the case in the elementary school. Also, there seemed to be fewer opportunities for student decision making and personal independence. The transition was also associated with an increase in "practices such as whole class task organization, between classroom ability grouping, and public evaluation of the correctness of work; each of which may encourage the use of social comparison and ability self-assessment" (Eccles & Midgely, 1989, p. 164). Some observations suggested that many teachers began to use a different, and somewhat inappropriate, set of standards, to judge students' competence and in assigning grades.

In contrast, the more productive classroom settings at the middle level used what Brophy called "motivation to learn" (Marshall, 1987). "Within the classroom, motivation to learn refers to emphasizing to students the meaningfulness, value, and benefits of learning concepts and skills in order to engage students in academic tasks. This motivation to learn involves having the students engage in the task for endogenous rather than exogenous reasons" (p. 136). Endogenous reasons indicate that students perceive tasks as an ends to themselves, as contrasted to exogenous reasons wherein students see tasks as a means to some other end, such as a reward. Thus, motivation to learn has many similarities to intrinsic motivation.

The skills necessary to motivate students to learn become essential for teacher and school effectiveness. "Experience and research indicate that the performance of a student at school is influenced by the student's prior performance, by attitudes toward specific aspects of school learning, and by motivation to learn" (Keeves, 1986, p. 117). The challenge for middle level teachers is to capitalize on those prior performances when they have been successful and to counter when they have been less so. Plus, effective teachers become dedicated to enhancing students' attitudes about school and motivating them to learn the essential curriculum content in the most effective and efficient way possible for personal rather than mandated reasons. When these actions result in positive outcomes, only then has the student demonstrated the motivation to learn.

## Theoretical Principles for Motivation

Today, more than ever, teachers and administrators are challenged to analyze, translate, and apply findings from educational research to situations in the school and classroom, and to close the gap between research and practice.

The questions of why people elect to behave certain ways or pursue certain goals has been the subject of scholarly inquiry since the writings of Socrates, Plato, and Aristotle. However, it has only been in the last 25 to 30 years that the systematic study of motivational processes has yielded significant, sustained, and useful information for psychologists and educators. This section provides an short overview of the contributions of the study of motivation to education.

### Social Structures

Through sociological analyses, researchers and teachers have been able to identify social factors in the classroom. These social factors (group behavior, social roles, and teacher-student interrelationships) have a strong influence on the learning and motivation of students.

Johnson and Johnson (1985) described student motivation in three contrasting classroom social situations: (1) *individualistic:* individual achievement of goals has no influence on other persons achieving their goals; one individual's rewards are not dependent on another's; (2) *competitive:* the goals of each student depend on direct and indirect competition among students; one's goals are attained at the expense and subsequent negative feelings of others; (3) *cooperative:* the goals of students are so interrelated that a student can achieve his or her goals only with mutual cooperation and assistance from all members of the group to which the student belongs. Ames (1984) delineated the different meanings of success and effort within these structures and showed that motivation is qualitatively rather than quantitatively different within each structure.

Self-perceptions of positive and negative achievement orientation are reinforced in competitive and individualistic structures. That is, students who believe that they have the ability to achieve and succeed tend to reinforce that belief in those frameworks. Likewise, students who think that they do not have the ability to succeed and achieve in school will find that perception strengthened in individualistic and competitive settings. Not only do competitive structures accentuate the salience of ability but students' levels of satisfaction seem to be related to self-perceptions of ability (Ames, 1978; Covington & Omelich, 1979).

Other researchers (Covington, 1984; Nicholls, 1984; Stipek, 1984) noted that a self-concept of ability can be protected by exerting effort and succeeding (leading to an inference of high ability) or by withholding effort (procrastination) and failing (but nevertheless avoiding an inference of low ability because no effort to succeed was made). While attributions to ability may inhibit or enhance motivation, depending on the situational context, effort is seen as the cognitive element leading to proactive, intentional action.

The attribution theories of performance were developed by Weiner (1984) and Weiner and Sierad (1975), and, like motivation to learn, are closely related to concepts of intrinsic motivation. According to attribution theory, performance on various tasks is influenced by the extent to which persons attribute their success or failure to causal elements (e.g., their own ability or effort versus the difficulty of the tasks or chance/luck). Within this context, intrinsically motivated students may believe that performance is due to their own efforts, whereas extrinsically motivated students may believe that external factors that are outside their control (such as luck) determine success or failure. And, as Hunter and Barker (1987) pointed out, research has shown that students are better learners if they believe success depends on effort more than luck or ability.

Covington and Beery (1976) characterized competition as a situation where the most able are motivated and the less able students' sense of self-worth is threatened. Common to most competitive classroom situations is the emphasis on ability. The motivational disposition toward academic success held by an individual student does not exist in isolation from a wide range of experiences that the student has previously encountered.

Attitudes of academic motivation have their origins in previous learning experiences. Determining that one is able or not able to succeed has value if future situations are anticipated. Since ability is a stable trait, students tend to alleviate anxiety by attributing success and failure more to luck (Hunter & Barker, 1987). Particularly in the case of failure, a self-perception of low ability allows one to defend against future failure, for example, by not trying or by dropping out. In summary, in contrast to the popular notion held by many that competition leads to enhanced motivation, the research uniformly indicates that competition leads to a number of debilitating motivational impacts.

Individualistic structures have a strong task focus and the self-awareness that is endogenous to competitive structures is minimized (Nicholls, 1979). Several researchers (Ames & Felker, 1979; Garibaldi, 1979; Johnson, Johnson, Johnson, & Anderson, 1976; Nicholls, 1975) who have studied individualistic frameworks have found patterns of behavior similar to interpersonal competition and more extrinsically based motivation than cooperative structures. Taken together, these studies suggest that motivational consequences of individualistic and competitive structures are potentially rather negative (Ames, 1984).

There is some evidence that students are more process oriented in individualistic settings and tend to use more self-instructional statements (Ames, 1981). Part of the problem with competition in the classroom is simply the fact that there can be too few winners on too few types of outcomes (Berliner, 1989). White (1977) analyzed several research papers on competition and concluded that competitiveness is better suited in a society (classroom/school) where an educated elite is desired. It is not well suited to an environment or society that wishes to educate the vast majority of its members.

Cooperative situations tend to be achievement settings; and although performance outcome is important, unlike competitive situations, an individual's performance must be interpreted within the context of the group performance (Johnson & Johnson, 1985). Sanctions are directed to fulfill an obligation to the group by putting forth effort to assure group success (Slavin, 1983). The effects of cooperative frameworks on learning are influenced by motivational factors that involve the concept of "ought"—that one ought to put forth effort, to contribute, and to satisfy peer norms and sanctions. Inherent in cooperative structures, then, is a concept of shared effort, the positive interdependence among students implies shared goals and shared rewards.

Another concept that causes students to be more motivated for achievement in cooperative settings is the idea of safety (Keeves & Larkin, 1986). Low-achieving, academically at-risk students are usually less motivated to try academic tasks because of previous failure, and the differential treatment of low-achieving students and successful students has a detrimental effect on self-esteem, motivation, and learning (Good & Brophy, 1984). These students tend to be more willing to attempt and to complete academic tasks in a cooperative group rather than individually (Slavin, 1990).

Teacher-student relationships and interactions make up another social structure in the classroom. Advances in research methodology concerning teacher effectiveness have shown that specific teacher behaviors are related to students' academic achievement (Ashton, 1985). Teachers typically interact and communicate in different ways with different students. These interactions, both verbal and nonverbal, have been analyzed within classrooms and across grades and usually indicate the impact of the teacher as a leader and power figure.

Power is a prerequisite of classroom control and, therefore, motivation. As a teacher makes decisions on balancing the various types of power, the overall classroom climate is greatly affected. Teachers have distinct types of power available to them. They may choose to be the expert, to reward or punish, to serve as models, to coerce students in an autocratic atmosphere, or to share power in a democratic environment (White, 1977). Each of these patterns affects students' perceptions of the environment and, therefore, their responses. Balancing these powers and roles to best motivate individual students depends on each teacher's personality, pupils' expectations, and the subject matter. However, no matter how complicated it might be, it cannot be neglected since the instructor's role definition is one of the most fundamental variables in effective instruction (Brophy & Evertson, 1976).

## Academic Structures

The case is convincingly made by Eccles and Midgely (1989) that there is a developmental mismatch, with unfortunate consequences on motivation and achievement, between young adolescents and the school environments that they experience. This is true both in social interactions and in academic actions and environments. Research (Eccles, Midgely, & Adler, 1984) has demonstrated that declining opportunities for autonomy and choice, in combination with increased levels of teacher control, could undermine students' academic interest and motivation. Researchers have found that middle, junior, and senior level classrooms are characterized by higher levels of teacher control, more emphasis on discipline, and less trust of students than elementary classrooms (Brophy & Evertson, 1978; Highberger, 1976; Moore, 1983; Willower & Lawrence, 1979). The teacher-student relationship changes as students make the transition to middle and junior high schools. Students have perceived this change by characterizing the teachers as less friendly, less supportive, and more teacher-controlled (Midgely, Feldlaufer, & Eccles, 1988).

Student choice and self-management has been found to decrease in the transition from elementary settings to middle and junior high settings (Ward, Mergendoller, Tikunoff, Rounds, Dadey, & Mitman, 1982). They found that older elementary students were given more opportunities to take responsibility for various aspects of their schoolwork and were given more choices than were seventh-graders. Changes in task organization also occur when moving from the elementary setting. Teachers and observers have reported increases in whole class task organization in middle level schools, leading to almost all students working on the same homework and seat assignments at the same time and using the same textbooks (Midgely, Feldlaufer, & Eccles, 1988). These factors are likely to increase competitiveness, normative grading criteria, a greater emphasis on public evaluation, and homogeneous grouping, all of which may negatively impact some students' self-perceptions and motivation.

Viewing these studies across their findings leads us to conclude that many young adolescents encounter an increase in teacher control and a decrease in the affective relationships with their teachers as they move into middle level schools. They also experience an academic environment much more likely to stress conformity and only value rote achievement. Interestingly, some research has suggested that actual cognitive demands and the undertaking of higher order thinking and learning actually decrease in the transition (Mitman, Mergendoller, Packer, & Marchman, 1984; Rounds & Osaki, 1982; Sanford, 1985; Walberg, House, & Steele, 1973) More recitation, memorization, recall, recognition, and teacher-assigned seatwork is the norm for middle level classes versus elementary classes. All of these hasten a decline in student motivation and interest.

## Summary of the Literature

With the advances in research and the development of the related fields of psychology and pedagogy, we now have options related to motivation that were unknown just a short time ago. The motivational research reported here is just a small fragment of the literature available. However, it suggests that some commonly used educational practices may have debilitating effects on motivation. We also know now that we can increase mastery orientation and the achievement motivation of students.

# Motivational Issues Affecting Young Adolescents

As students move through early adolescence, they become more knowledgeable and skillful, develop cognitively, are able to use critical thinking to explore choices and dilemmas, become increasingly self-conscious about themselves in comparison to others, and place increased importance on their relationships with friends and adults. It does not make sense to set social conditions and educational expectations that are less demanding cognitively, that decrease opportunities for self-management and choice, and are more impersonal and formal. These are just a few of the many issues that particularly affect the motivation in school of young adolescents. This section describes these issues in more detail.

### Transition and Size

There are a number of motivational issues that the transition from elementary school to middle school can affect. For example, the size of the new school and the number of students in the middle school as compared with the elementary can be a motivationally stunning experience. Coming from relatively small elementary schools where student centeredness is much easier to cultivate and maintain does little to prepare the young adolescent for the large school experience. Being one of perhaps 300 elementary students is a much more personalized experience than being one of, say, 750 to 1,000 middle graders. The effect on motivation can be to demoralize and depersonalize the experience to the point where the student perceives that no one cares, so why try.

In its landmark publication, *Turning Points,* the Carnegie Council on Adolescent Development (1989) called for schools to respond to this depersonalization by creating smaller communities of learners under the charge of one or two teachers working as a team. A preferred approach is to create small communities for learning. The goal would be to "create responsive environments that provide students with care and support as well as challenging programs that will increase their learning" (Epstein, 1990, p. 439).

### Departmentalization and Ability Grouping

One major factor that can affect motivation to learn is the extent to which departmentalization and ability grouping come to be the norm at the middle level. In a major study conducted by The Johns Hopkins University Center for Research on Elementary and Middle Schools, the research team found that:

> *The use of between class-ability grouping in the middle grades is widespread: roughly two-thirds of middle-grade principals surveyed reported that their schools use the practice in at least some academic subjects, while more than one fifth said that their schools do so in all subjects. (Braddock, 1990, p. 449)*

Elementary schools, on the other hand, are more likely to use cross-ability arrangements, with one teacher responsible for teaching most or all of the basic subjects. These two strategies result in a more integrated approach to the subject matter and a greater consistency of effort on the part of students who have not been selected out of the group that is expected to perform. At the middle school level, if careful attention is not paid to these two factors, students find themselves in a loosely aggregated group of ability-alike learners, somewhat stigmatized with expectations of what they will or will not be able to do. Add to this the relative disconnectedness of subject matter taught by several different teachers who have no common thread to their disciplines, and it is reasonable to assume that confusion can prevail and the motivation to learn can be diminished. Again referring to the research of the CREMS team:

> *These are disquieting findings. They mean that learning opportunities in the middle grades remain highly stratified despite a middle school philosophy that encourages heterogeneous classes, despite various calls for school reform and restructuring to develop critical thinking skills among the nation's youth, and despite exhortations to insure that all children are provided equal access to learning opportunities. If schools serving early adolescents are ever to achieve their goals, they must find effective alternatives to tracking. (Braddock, 1990, p. 449)*

## Normative Rather Than Criterion-Referenced Standards

At the time of transition, there can be a dramatic shift to normative standards for evaluation. Rather than a teacher or school using criterion-referenced data to diagnose and prescribe for a particular student, at this point one's score in relation to scores of others of the same age, class, and grade becomes the standard. One is competing with others just as surely as if the room were filled with ability-alike students in the basic struggle to get the best score or finish first.

Additionally, a vast majority of middle grades schools give students letter or number grades for academic performance in each subject. Again, according to the research of the CREMS team (1990):

*Performance grades provide a means for schools to monitor and evaluate the attainment of their foremost goal—basic skills. While performance grades are standard, grades for progress and effort are rare. Only about one fourth (26%) of the schools that contain grade 7 give separate grades for effort in each subject. Still fewer schools (18%) recognize student improvement with grades for progress in each subject (p. 441).*

## Whole Class Instruction

Yet another motivational factor affected by the structure of the classroom and the expectation of the teacher involves whole class instruction. One might contend that the literature on effective schools, popularized during the last decade, was used by teachers and instructional supervisors to overgeneralize from the research. By using data collected on students determined to be academically disadvantaged and who typically study only the basic skills subjects of math and reading, schools may have overgeneralized to all students, all subjects, all grades. Unfortunately in many cases it has become the vogue to use whole group, teacher-directed instruction to teach all subjects to all students at all grades. This can cause problems, not only with motivation but in other areas as well. Becker (1990), writing for the CREMS team, pointed out that:

*Opportunities for students at any level of schooling to become competent and knowledgeable are largely determined by two things: the content and skills they are taught and the way their instruction is provided. . . . It is particularly important that schools serving the middle grades pay careful attention to the what and the how of instructional practice, because early adolescents are developing long-term attitudes toward the role of education in their lives. The effects of a narrow curriculum and of teaching approaches that emphasize memorization are likely to be especially harmful to those students. (p. 450)*

### Evaluation Procedures

A further motivational issue that can be affected by the move to the middle school is a different approach to evaluation in particular and the reward structure of the school in general. Simply stated, once a child gets to the middle school, the game of grades can change dramatically from counting the questions answered correctly to marking those that are wrong. Although this sounds simplistic, the results can be quite complex. Just when the curriculum becomes more difficult, subjects take on more sophistication, and teachers have greater expectations for mastery of complex problems, students find themselves graded by a different set of rules. They may no longer be rewarded for effort or partial correctness but instead be penalized for not getting all of the information at the required level of understanding. At the same time, opportunities for higher-level, cognitive problem solving may decrease because of an emphasis on limited content mastery. Grades often go down; and grades, like it or not, are often motivating factors for young adolescents.

These issues and factors are illustrations of things that can *increase* when a child moves to the middle school—increased size, increased departmentalization, increased rigor in grading. What, then, are similar factors that can *decrease* with the same move?

### Personal Contact

First, and perhaps foremost, there can be a significant decrease in the continuous, close, personal contact between student and teacher. With an increase in size there may be a decrease in personalization. There may be far too little emphasis put on the philosophy that students need to have prolonged, meaningful, personal relations with an adult on a nonacademic as well as a graded class basis.

Writing for the Association for Supervision and Curriculum Development and its recent middle schools survey research, Cawelti (1988) suggested a strategy for accomplishing increased personal contact. According to his findings:

*A "home base" plan gives teachers the opportunity to know their advisees better and to provide more continuity during their years in the middle school-especially when teachers retain responsibility for the same students during all three or four years. The plan does much to reduce the sense of anonymity and isolation many students feel, particularly in larger schools. (p. 6)*

### Relationships

The lack of emphasis on relationships and personal contact mentioned in the literature can result in considerable anonymity on the part of the student. When one perceives that "no one knows who I am so who is there to care?", the motivation to learn is quite likely to decline. Although no one would suggest that students at the middle level learn only for external reasons or for teacher-generated gratification, that is certainly the case to some extent and in some cases. Students need to perceive that they are known by their teachers and that those same teachers have a vested interest in their success. Delaney (1986) observed that most people who work with young adolescents believe that a strong attempt must be made to guide and help students through these difficult years.

### Student Autonomy

Another factor that can decrease following the transition to the middle school has to do with opportunities for student autonomy and teacher trust. In contrast to increasing age and maturity, middle level schools and teachers can adopt rules and regulations that put the student out of control of even the simplest actions and decisions. For example, elementary classrooms may have in-room toilet facilities that students may use without the embarrassment of having to get permission; middle schools most often do not. Therefore, students are reduced to having to ask for and actually announce a personal hygiene need. They are not allowed to control this act of leaving the classroom because of a perceived lack of trustworthiness.

The same situation may occur in relation to the media center. In many elementary schools, library access is quite open and based on a perceived need on the part of the student. In the middle grades, however, library hours may be by appointment only. Thus, students are in control of neither access nor time. How can we doubt that motivation can decrease when students view themselves as reflected by a system that tells them they are mere children who cannot be trusted or left in control of their own basic needs?

This, however, need not be the case. According to George and Oldaker (1985), writing about a national survey of middle school effectiveness:

> *Certainly one of the long-espoused goals of the middle school has been to focus on the unique nature and needs of young adolescents. Our results indicate that exemplary middle schools have been very successful in promoting student personal development. Ovr 80% of the respondents testified that student emotional health, creativity, and confidence in self-directed learning were positively affected by reorganization. Over 90% believed that student self-concept and social development also benefitted. (pp. 80–81)*

These changes, along with the normal developmental characteristics of young adolescents, can interact adversely to affect student motivation. In terms of developing from concrete to abstract reasoners, students may be hindered by the school's concentrated effort on the mastery of limited content. As the students move from an egocentric to a sociocentric perspective, their development may well be delayed when they are not allowed experiences that enable them to view the world with a greater sense of community. In light of their increasing abilities to understand human motivation, students who are kept in ability-alike groups have only that perception of what is normal. It is only when schools provide opportunities for broadening horizons in dealing with others that students begin to be able to see issues with a deeper sense of understanding based on motive or intent.

So we find ourselves in a "so what?" situation. If the data on motivation suggest certain implications for students, and if the developmental and transitional nature of young adolescents is accepted, so what? What can teachers do to increase the probability of enhancing motivation, especially motivation to learn, given the constraints of an organizational system historically too often out of touch with student needs and capabilities?

## Desired Practices for Increasing Student Motivation

### What Teachers Can Do: Preinstructional Decisions

Theorists, researchers, and practitioners agree that conditions in the environment must be established that the student perceives as healthy and motivating. The following are a few of the types of decisions needed that have been found to have a motivational effect.

1. *Create an inviting environment:* Most educators recognize that students need a positive learning environment that capitalizes on encouragement. This environment is determined to some degree in terms of being visually pleasant, creative, stimulating, and inviting. For many years Purkey (1978) has been an advocate of and proponent for invitational learning

based on teaching and learning as an invitation rather than as an expectation or chore. He uses the concepts of warmth, cooperative spirit, and positive expectations to illustrate his point. Within these classrooms, teachers are dedicated to setting an optimistic tone where there is ample evidence of fairness and relevance. Students are helped to foster their own sense of personal competence through activities that call, for example, for diverse and changing leadership roles.

2. *Allow for a participatory democracy:* In motivationally sound classrooms, teachers allow for a democratic exchange of ideas and for participatory activities that use student input in decision making. Decisions about the order of activities and experiences can be left, in some cases, to student judgment. Alternative methods for completing assignments present still other opportunities for student decision making. Formulating classroom rules, expectations, rewards, and sanctions present further experiences for students to participate and have practice in making choices and decisions. At this particular developmental stage, young adolescents are in need of these opportunities to broaden their capacities to reason at higher levels and to begin to see issues from other points of view.

3. *Implement heterogeneous grouping:* Teachers have often been the first to recognize that ability grouping is detrimental to almost every child at every level. The labeling factor not withstanding, there are pressures to perform for some students and permissions not to perform for others. All of these factors get in the way of motivation to learn. Basing their actions on the research of Slavin (1987) and Johnson and Johnson (1985), more and more teachers realize that developing activities and learning environments that use heterogeneous grouping are more effective for more students. They also realize that grouping with positive expectations for success for everyone has a much greater likelihood of fostering personal motivation for each student.

### What Teachers Can Do: Expect Success

The literature places a great deal of emphasis on the motivational effect of teacher *and* student expectations for success. Many of the behaviors of nonmotivated students are caused by either the students' previous lack of success and the resulting avoidance behaviors, or the teachers' lack of understanding of what an important role their expectations play on the students' performance. Teachers can change the success expectations of themselves and students.

1. *Connect success to effort:* Many students have an external locus of control that causes them to believe that success and failure are not dependent

on effort but instead on pure and simple luck. They can speak with great conviction about their beliefs that it does not matter how hard they try, they just are not lucky enough to get a passing mark or a higher grade. Much of their sense of personal control is based on whether or not they think the teacher likes them rather than on how hard they have worked on a task. Thus, teachers who are trying to capitalize on motivation to learn set up conditions where students recognize that there will be a reward for effort-effect rather than ability-effect. In this way, students are encouraged to see for themselves that trying really does pay off and that effort is more significant to success than simple luck.

2. *Help students redefine success:* For the most part, success in school is like a tennis metaphor. To be successful, one has to beat an opponent. But now change the metaphor from tennis to golf. To be successful in golf, one must beat the course and outperform one's own personal best score. When students can begin to redefine their personal success in light of exceeding their own goals rather than in being in competition with others, motivation to learn can be increased dramatically.

### What Teachers Can Do: Use Extrinsic Incentives Appropriately

Although extrinsic incentives have been found to have a detrimental effect on students' intrinsic motivation, there are several ways to use extrinsic incentives for motivation.

1. *Provide equal opportunity to win:* For some students, the idea that success is only a matter of luck is coupled with the idea that the competition will always be too strong. When competition is the motivator, and few can argue that for some children in some situations this can be a powerful tool, teachers will want to structure the activity so that everyone perceives there is an equal opportunity to win. This may involve a series of possible activities, completing any three of which can be considered as criteria for winning. It may mean a team or group competition as well as individual games where students have a responsibility to the group or themselves for winning. Selected pairings may also be effective. Whatever the mechanism, the intent is for all children to perceive that they can have at least a fair and possible chance to win. In this sense, whereas the original middle school literature called for decreasing the star system, perhaps this effort could result in an expansion of the same system whereby all students could begin to perceive themselves as stars.

2. *Provide a variety of rewards:* Just as young adolescents are different from each other developmentally, they also differ in their opinions about what constitutes success and what is viewed as a "good" reward. For some students, quiet time in the library may be a top priority; for others, getting to play their favorite music in the cafeteria would rate near the top. From experience with middle school students, we know that one reward selected quite frequently is free time. Because of the pressures both within and external to the school to be involved and busy much of the time, students often select this "down time" reward just to be able to have time with friends and to unwind a bit.

The point here is that teachers who are using extrinsic motivators will want to be aware that the rewards offered should be based to some extent on student choice and should represent different perspectives of what is a "good" reward. Additionally, there should be opportunities to receive a reward for improved performance. For some students, having to make a certain percentage appropriate to the entire class or reach a certain level measured by the expectation of what the academically able students will be able to do will always produce a sense of failure. However, being judged in light of individual improvement is more likely to produce success.

3. *Reward effort:* In some cases, teachers may well recognize that it initially may be only the students' effort that is the desired result rather than more depth or thoroughness. When teachers are trying to get students to attempt something, to take a risk, or simply to start a task, extrinsic rewards would be most effective. One caveat, however: The effort must be viewed by students as feasible, and the teacher must remain trustworthy by not rearranging the standards of what constitutes a good effort once the students have begun. This is not the place for a dangling carrot to be held just out of a student's reach in the hope that it will make him or her work a little bit more and more and more.

4. *Clearly define the task:* Students who are having difficulty with their motivation to learn may have a subconscious sense of mistrust of teachers in particular and schooling in general. Over their years in school, they may have developed the conviction that no matter what teachers say, the rules can change at a moment's notice. Even when the students think they know exactly what is expected, many of them tell us that the teachers change the task, and their efforts do not receive appropriate reward. This happens most frequently when students fail to understand clearly what teachers have in mind as a successful way to complete the assignment. Teachers who are working on the trust factor as well as the motivation to learn issue devote an extraordinary amount of time clarifying expectations for the assignment in advance, so that the students can perceive that they will get it right and thus have a chance to earn the expected reward.

## What Teachers Can Do:
## Capitalize on Intrinsic Incentives

Teachers need to select or design activities that students will perceive as enjoyable or rewarding to do. This is usually more difficult than it seems, which explains why many teachers completely neglect intrinsic incentives. There are, however, strategies for capitalizing on intrinsic incentives as much as possible.

1. *Have a balance between too hard and too easy:* When all the assignments are perceived by the student to be too hard and therefore not feasible, there is little incentive to do the work. When the tasks are determined by the student to be too easy and therefore not worth the effort, there is, again, little incentive. It is when the balance between too hard and too easy is achieved that students decide that the work is likely to get done and it is worth the effort to begin. This balance creates the perception of creative tension, where students have a chance to succeed without thinking that the task or assignment is beneath their status or expectations for themselves. When one is tested a bit and still succeeds, there is a feeling of developing and increasing competence. Motivation to continue the effort is thus nurtured.

2. *Use novelty:* Educators seem to dislike our perceived competition with the media and technological extravaganzas. However, reality is that we are educating a media generation who is used to high-tech, rapid change and stimulating experiences. In terms of motivation to learn the expected content within the school curriculum, this predisposition may cause teachers to capitalize on novelty, interest, curiosity, and surprise as enhancements in the learning process. Anyone who has seen the 1980s movie, *Teachers,* remembers the substitute teacher who dressed up as characters from history and portrayed their exploits through roleplay and dramatization. The effect on the students was mesmerizing. Their motivation to learn about historic figures and events was greatly enhanced by the novelty of the presentation and the surprise of seeing what had been so dull for so long presented in a new and exciting manner.

3. *Provide for peer interaction:* Active learning and active involvement are of paramount interest to most young adolescents. What we used to term *hands-on learning* has been broadened in concept to include relevant experiences, completed in heterogeneous groups, utilizing cooperative learning strategies. The middle school literature is becoming replete with examples of projects and activities done through both the core classes and within the exploratory block that capitalize on this desire for active learning with peer interaction. Descriptions of the outcomes of these activities serve as graphic accolades for the success of all students in terms of motivation to learn.

4. *Promote autonomy and personal control:* Young adolescents have

as a primary developmental task to establish a sense of personal independence from parental and other adult control. During this time, students need practice, under supervised conditions, to make choices, select from alternatives, and assert their own personalities. When school fails to provide opportunities for this to happen constructively, the imperative is so strong that it sometimes manifests itself destructively. How can we expect students to be able to make effective choices in light of such situations as drug and alcohol abuse or potential suicide if they have little or no practice on less life-threatening matters?

Teachers who are dedicated to enhancing motivation to learn will seize every opportunity to allow students to control, to some extent, the how, when, and why of tasks and assignments, as opposed to relying on autocratic decision making. They will create activities that foster student choice, alternatives, and autonomy.

5. *Foster higher-order thinking skills:* One all-encompassing aspect of the motivation to learn issue concerns the middle grade students' increasing ability to process information and data at ever-higher functioning levels. Students need constant practice in evaluating information and evaluating themselves in relation to that information. Students will begin to respond well, after practice, to opportunities that require synthesis, analysis, and application. For the first time in their developmental history, young adolescents will be ready to begin to think at more abstract levels and to process more sophisticated information. Motivating them to learn these processes, as well as the content resulting from being able to use higher level thinking strategies, will provide substantial evidence of cognitive growth and affective maturity.

## Conclusion

Successful, effective teachers understand the importance of motivation, although they cannot "teach" motivation as they do concepts or skills. We believe that motivation should have a central role in the decision-making activities of teachers, especially when considering academically at-risk students and students of different cultural, racial, and ethnic backgrounds. Making research-based choices will greatly enhance the learning and performance outcomes of students.

## References

Ames, C. (1978). Children's achievement attributions and self-reinforcement: Effects of self-concept and competitive reward structure. *Journal of Educational Psychology, 70*(3), 345–355.

Ames, C. (1981). Competitive vs. cooperative reward structures: The influence of individual and group performance factors on achievement attributions affect. *American Educational Research Journal, 18*(3), 273–287.

Ames, C. (1984). Competitive, cooperative, and individualistic goal structures: A cognitive-motivational analysis. In C. Ames & R. Ames (Eds.), *Research on motivation in education: Vol. 1. Student motivation* (pp. 177–207). San Diego: Academic Press.

Ames, C., & Felker, D. (1979). Effects of self-concept on children's causal attributions and self-reinforcement. *Journal of Educational Psychology, 71*(5), 613–614.

Ashton, P. (1985). Motivation and the teacher's sense of efficacy. In C. Ames & R. Ames (Eds.), *Research on motivation in education: Vol. 2. The classroom milieu* (pp. 141–171). San Diego: Academic Press.

Becker, H. J. (1990). Curriculum and instruction in middle-grade schools. *Phi Delta Kappan, 71*(6), 450–457.

Berliner, D. (1989). Furthering our understanding of motivation and environments. In C. Ames & R. Ames (Eds.), *Research on motivation in education: Vol. 3. Goals and cognitions.* (pp. 317–342). San Diego: Academic Press.

Braddock, J. H., II. (1990). Tracking the middle grades: National patterns of grouping for instruction. *Phi Delta Kappan, 71*(6), 445–449.

Brophy, J. E., & Evertson, C. M. (1976). *Learning from teaching: A developmental perspective.* Boston, MA: Allyn and Bacon.

Brophy, J. E., & Evertson, C. M. (1978). Context variables in teaching. *Educational Psychologist, 12*(3), 310–316.

Carnegie Council on Adolescent Development's Task Force on Education of Young Adolescents. (1989). *Turning points: Preparing American youth for the 21st century.* Washington, DC: Carnegie Council on Adolescent Development, a program of Carnegie Corporation of New York.

Cawelti, G. (1988, November). Middle schools a better match with early adolescent needs, ASCD survey finds. *ASCD Curriculum Update.* (Available from the Association of Supervision and Curriculum Development, Alexandria, VA 22314-2798).

Covington, M. (1984). The motive for self-worth. In C. Ames & R. Ames (Eds.), *Research on motivation in education: Vol. 1. Student motivation* (pp. 78–113). San Diego: Academic Press.

Covington, M., & Beery, R. (1976). *Self-worth and school learning.* New York: Holt, Rinehart and Winston.

Covington, M., & Omelich, C. (1979). Effort: The double-edged sword in school achievement. *Journal of Educational Psychology, 71*(2), 169–182.

Delaney, J. D. (1986). Developing a middle school homeroom guidance program. *NASSP Bulletin, 70*(11), 96–98.

Eccles, J., & Midgely, C. (1989). Stage environment fit: Developmentally appropriate classrooms for young adolescents. In C. Ames & R. Ames (Eds.), *Research on motivation in education: Vol. 3. Goals and cognitions* (pp. 139–186). San Diego: Academic Press.

Eccles (Parsons), J., Midgley, C., & Adler, T. F. (1984). Grade-related changes in the school environment: Effects on achievement motivation. In J. G. Nicholls (Ed.), *Advances in motivation and achievement* (pp. 283–331). Greenwich, CT: JAI Press.

Epstein, J. L. (1990). What matters in the middle grades—Grade span or practice? *Phi Delta Kappan, 71*(6), 438–444.

Epstein, J. L., & Mac Iver, D. (1990). *Education in the middle grades: An overview of national practices and trends.* Columbus, OH: National Middle School Association.

Garibaldi, A. (1979). Affective contributions of cooperative and group goal structures. *Journal of Educational Psychology, 71*(6), 613–614.

George, P. S., & Oldaker, L. L. (1985). *A national survey of middle school effectiveness.* Alexandria, VA: Association of Supervision and Curriculum Development.

Good, T. L., & Brophy, J. E. (1984). *Looking in classrooms* (3rd ed.). New York: Harper & Row.

Highberger, J. H. (1976). Attitude toward student control and school climate in middle schools and junior high schools. *Dissertation Abstract International, 37,* 2537A–2538A.

Hunter, M., & Barker, G. (1987). If at first: Attribution theory in the classroom. *Educational Leadership, 45*(2), 50–53.

Johnson, D., Johnson, R., Johnson, J., & Anderson, D. (1976). The effects of cooperative vs. individualized instruction on student prosocial behavior, attitudes toward learning and achievement. *Journal of Educational Psychology, 68*(4), 446–452.

Johnson, D. W., & Johnson, R. T. (1985). Motivational processes in cooperative, competitive, and individualistic learning situations. In C. Ames & R. Ames (Eds.), *Research on motivation in education: Vol. 2. The classroom milieu* (pp. 249–286). San Diego: Academic Press.

Keeves, J. (1986). Motivation and school learning: Different methods of analysis and different results. *International Journal of Educational Research, 10*(2), 117–126.

Keeves, J., & Larkin, A. (1986). The context of academic motivation. *International Journal of Educational Research, 10*(2), 205–214.

Lipsitz, J. (1977). *Growing up forgotten: A review of research and program concerning early adolescence.* Lexington, MA: Heath.

Marshall, H. H. (1987). Motivational strategies of three fifth-grade teachers. *The Elementary School Journal, 88*(2), 135–149.

McDaniel, T. R. (1985). The ten commandments of motivation. *Clearinghouse, 59*(1), 19–23.

Midgely, C., Feldlaufer, H., & Eccles, J. (1988). The transition to junior high school: Beliefs of pre- and post-transition teachers. *Journal of Youth and Adolescence, 17*(6), 543–562.

Mitman, A. L., Mergendoller, J. R., Packer, M. J., & Marchman, V. A. (1984). *Scientific literacy in seventh-grade life science: A study of instructional process, task completion, student perceptions and learning outcomes: Final Report.* San Francisco, CA: Far West Laboratory.

Moore, D. W. (1983, April). *Impact of school grade-organization patterns on seventh and eighth grade students in K-8 and junior high school.* Paper presented at the Annual Meeting of the New England Research Association, Rockport, ME.

Nicholls, J. (1975). Causal attributions and other achievement related cognitions: Effects of task-outcomes attainment value and sex. *Journal of Personality and Social Psychology, 31*(3), 379–389.

Nicholls, J. (1979). Quality and equality in intellectual development: The role of motivation in education. *American Psychologist, 34*(11), 1071–1084.

Nicholls, J. (1984). Conceptions of ability and achievement motivation. In C. Ames & R. Ames (Eds.), *Research on motivation in education: Vol. 1. Student motivation* (pp. 39–73). San Diego: Academic Press.

Purkey, W. W. (1978). *Inviting school success: A self-concept approach to teaching and learning*. Belmont, CA: Wadsworth.

Rounds, T. S., & Osaki, S. Y. (1982). *The social organization of classrooms: An analysis of sixth- and seventh-grade activity structures* (Report EPSSP-82-5). San Francisco: Far West Laboratory.

Sanford, J. P. (1985). *Comprehensive-level tasks in secondary classrooms* (R&D Rep. No. 6199). Austin, TX: Research and Development Center for Teacher Education, University of Texas at Austin.

Slavin, R. (1983). *Cooperative learning*. New York: Longman.

Slavin, R. (1987). Mastery learning reconsidered. *Review of Educational Research, 57*(2), 175–213.

Slavin, R. (1990). *Cooperative learning: Theory, research, and practice*. Englewood Cliffs, NJ: Prentice Hall.

Stipek, D. (1984). The development of achievement motivation. In C. Ames & R. Ames (Eds.), *Research on motivation in education: Vol. 1. Student motivation* (pp. 145–174). San Diego: Academic Press.

Walberg, H. J., House, E. R., & Steele, J. M. (1973). Grade level, cognition, and affect: A cross-section of classroom perceptions. *Journal of Educational Psychology, 64*(2), 142–146.

Ward, B. A., Mergendoller, J. R., Tikunoff, W. J., Rounds, T. S., Dadey, G. J., & Mitman, A. L. (1982). *Junior high school transition study: Executive summary*. San Francisco, CA: Far West Laboratory.

Weiner, B. (1984). Principles for a theory of student motivation and their application within an attributional framework. In C. Ames & R. Ames (Eds.), *Research on motivation in education: Vol. 1. Student motivation* (pp. 15–38). San Diego: Academic Press.

Weiner, B., & Sierad, J. (1975). Misattribution for failure and the enhancement of achievement strivings. *Journal of Personality and Social Psychology, 31*(3), 415–421.

White, M. (1977). Social motivation in the classroom. In S. Ball (Ed.), *Motivation in education* (pp. 147–172). New York: Academic Press.

Willower, D. J., & Lawrence, J. D. (1979). Teachers' perception of student threat to teacher status and teacher pupil control ideology. *Psychology in the Schools, 16*(4), 586–590.

# CHAPTER SIXTEEN

# Developmentally Appropriate Instruction: The Heart of the Middle School

JUDITH L. IRVIN
*Florida State University*

Restructuring has occurred in middle level schools of our nation (Alexander & McEwin, 1989; Epstein & Mac Iver, 1990); little has changed, however, in the heart of the middle school—the classroom. Although more schools are organized in interdisciplinary teams, have active teacher advisory programs, and have a commitment to exploration, many middle level schools have stopped short of implementing change in curriculum and instruction for middle level students. Beane (1990) maintained that "the movement has succeeded partly because it has not taken on substantive change would touch deep subject matter loyalties" (p. 6). Part of those subject matter loyalties lie in the instructional methods of teachers.

During the last two decades, learning theorists have produced research to help educators understand the processes of learning. *Schema theory* (everything we know and everything we have experienced) helps middle level educators understand how to connect with the world of the young adolescent and how connecting new knowledge with prior knowledge is essential for meaningful learning. *Metacognitive theory* (thinking about your own thinking) helps middle level educators understand that students can learn about how to learn and become more independent. The concept of *strategic learning* (acquiring a repertoire of strategies to aid in learning) helps middle level educators understand that the process of learning endures and can be applied to new learning situations.

As a result of the research on learning in the past two decades, educational movements have swept the country, many of which have had a significant impact on middle level schools. Whole language, process reading and writing, literature-based language arts, integrated instruction, and authentic testing, to name just a few, have implications for middle schools.

In this chapter, I will (1) discuss implications for instruction drawn from what we know about the characteristics of young adolescents; (2) discuss the problems with learning that most students encounter when entering a middle level school; (3) describe some of the research on learning of the last two decades and the implications for instruction at the middle level; (4) explain some research-based, classroom-tested strategies that are particularly successful with middle level students; and (5) present components necessary for a successful middle level instructional program.

## Developmentally Appropriate Instructional Methods for Middle Level Students

The experiences of early adolescence have lasting effects in terms of the young adolescents' emerging personality characteristics and self-concept (Drash, 1980). To educate this unique group of children effectively, teachers must use learning strategies that accommodate their special and varied needs. That is, it is imperative that teachers use instructional methods that are *developmentally appropriate.* Instruction should be designed based on what we know about young adolescents and based on what we know about effective learning strategies.

A veteran middle school teacher once told me that you might as well assign students to groups, plan for movement, and plan the changing of activities, because "they will talk and walk anyway." Apparently, she felt it was better to control the interaction and channel students' desire for social interaction and activity into productive academic pursuits. Small group work, cooperative study groups, and paired readings are all instructional techniques that accommodate students' needs at this age. Every middle school teacher intuitively knows that, *physically,* middle grades students need to move and change activities and, *socially,* they need to interact with each other.

A positive learning environment, one of acceptance on the part of the teacher and other students, is essential. *Emotionally,* students need to feel competent and they need to achieve. They need to participate in school and classroom decisions, but they also require structure and clear limits.

I am occasionally struck by the double standard with which adults, whether they are educators or not, treat young people. Adults frequently make mistakes. What adult has never forgotten the laundry in the washing machine until it soured, or never gotten a speeding ticket, or run out of gas, or bought a piece of clothing one size too small in anticipation of the time when 10 pounds would be shed? Adults somehow seem to grant themselves some latitude, forgive themselves, learn from their mistakes, and move on. In the same way, students should be given the opportunity to make mistakes in an environment where they can reflect on those mistakes and learn from them.

Classrooms should be emotionally safe places where taking risks is not only acceptable but encouraged. Without risk, a first draft of a story or report will never be improved, the metric system never learned, or a book that looks a little more difficult with a little bit smaller print may never be read. Teachers hold the key to students taking academic risks and creating a learning environment that is emotionally safe.

*Intellectually,* we know that most middle level students function primarily at the concrete level of thinking. Given some time and some prompting, however, many more students can perform such operations as problem solving, synthesis, analysis, and evaluation. I am reminded of Thomas, a sixth-grade student, who accompanied my family on a water skiing trip. The boat arrived at the dock where Thomas was standing and he was told to hold the rope (connected to the bow of the boat). So, Thomas jumped in the boat holding the rope. He was then reminded by every adult nearby that holding the boat *with the rope* was really more effective if he stood on the dock. Every middle level educator has a similar story.

Young adolescents think concretely, even literally, most of the time; however, the middle grades is the appropriate time for students to experiment with and become more comfortable with abstract thinking. This introduction should be nonthreatening and success oriented. That is, abstract thinking for middle level students should be encouraged but not expected. Consideration of the intellectual capabilities of young adolescents should be made for another important reason—helping students move beyond their egocentrism.

Elkind (1978) believed that young adolescents need to consider the viewpoints of others to move beyond the egocentrism, or focusing on one's self, that characterizes early adolescence. Students must understand that others may think differently or hold differing points of view. Through discussion with teachers and peers, students eventually begin to evaluate their own thinking in light of the points of view of others.

Instruction for middle level students must be different from that of the elementary and high schools because young adolescents have unique needs. Students should be provided with:

1. The opportunity to work cooperatively in groups (social needs)
2. A vehicle for connecting new information to what is already known, thus helping students to feel more confident about learning new material and recognizing and validating their own experience (intellectual and emotional needs)

3. Success-oriented experiences in abstract thinking that may help students move gradually from the concrete to the abstract levels of reasoning (intellectual needs)
4. An opportunity to move and change activities (physical needs)
5. Successful experiences that help students feel better about themselves as learners (emotional needs)
6. Motivation to learn through the use of strategies that heighten students' curiosity about learning (emotional and intellectual needs)

## The Problem of Adjustment

When students move from an elementary to a middle level school, they must adjust to a myriad of new situations. The nature of the school structure, the mode of instruction, the number of independent activities, and the nature of reading materials all change as students move into this new environment.

### Changes in School Structure

Middle level schools are departmentalized to some degree and always more departmentalized than elementary schools. Gone is the security of one or two teachers looking out for students. Students often have difficulty seeing the relationship between the content taught in science and the content taught in social studies.

### Changes in Instruction

Very few teachers at the middle level were trained to teach in a middle school. Most were certified in secondary education with an emphasis in a content area or certified in elementary education with an emphasis on child-centered curriculum. The majority of secondary trained teachers simply do not feel comfortable teaching the strategies students need to read and write successfully, even when these abilities are necessary to learn the content they teach.

### Changes in Expectations of Independent Learning

The leap between elementary and middle school in terms of teachers' expectations of student independence is too wide for some students. Thus, students who appear to be unmotivated or disinterested may simply lack the ability or confidence to approach a task independently. Keeping track of a number of books, making it to class with a pencil *and* notebook, organizing homework, managing time, and adjusting to the teaching style of at least six different teachers is sometimes overwhelming for students entering a middle level school; the expectations are too great for some students.

### Changes in Reading Material

Textbooks are more difficult in the middle grades; there are also more of them and students are expected to understand them with less assistance from the teacher. Studies by Armbruster and Anderson (1984) have shown that many of the texts students are given to read are poorly written and "inconsiderate." That is, they are written in such a way that the text is not easily understood or remembered, even by a proficient reader.

In contrast, elementary students most often read from basal readers, which are generally written in narrative style. Expository text, which is most often found in content area texts, is more factual and usually contains a hierarchical pattern of main ideas and details. Teachers, however, do not spend much time teaching students to read from this kind of a book.

In fact, after almost 300 hours of classroom observation in grades 4 through 6, Durkin (1978–79) found that *no* time was spent in social studies lessons teaching students to comprehend expository text. Teachers taught only content and facts. With the exception of literature class, middle grade students are expected to read almost exclusively expository text as found in their science and social studies textbooks. But who takes the responsibility to teach students to acquire the reading abilities necessary to facilitate the comprehension of these texts?

Most often, the responsibility for teaching reading in the middle grades falls on the language arts teacher who is often secondary trained in English education. After a review of practices and perceptions among content area teachers, Witte and Otto (1981) concluded that few English educators "express any concern for . . . [having students read] the expository materials of social studies, sciences, and other content areas" (p. 154).

The pictures of story scenes typically found in narrative text are replaced by tables, graphs, diagrams, and flowcharts. Therefore, while middle level students are expected to read more expository text, no one, it seems, teaches them how to understand this type of text. Herber and Nelson-Herber (1987) stated that "attaining independence in reading the basal in elementary grades does not prepare students to read the expository material in their science or social studies or arithmetic texts independently" (p. 586).

Students need to learn to adapt their reading ability to a variety of material. Ideally, students should receive a gradual introduction to reading expository text beginning in the elementary grades. At each grade level, in each subject area, teachers must help students learn "to read to learn" with increasing sophistication. Becoming an independent learner is a lifelong process. For this reason, continued and systematic reading instruction at the middle level and maximizing the potential of middle school organization is imperative.

## Two Decades of Research on Learning

During the last two decades, educators have witnessed unprecedented advances in knowledge of the basic processes of learning. The more teachers understand the learning process, the better they will be able to evaluate and improve the learning environments they create. Three concepts—schema theory, metacognition, and strategic learning—may help shape meaningful middle level instruction in the future.

### Schema Theory

Meaningful learning occurs when a student relates new information to prior knowledge. That is, it is nearly impossible to learn new information that has no connection to what is already known. *Schemata* comprise all of the information and all of the experience that the reader has stored in memory. A particular schema, then, represents all of the associations that come to mind when a person reads about a certain subject.

For example, you probably have a schema for the object we label *computers.* You have a mental picture of what does or does not characterize a computer. You also bring to that basic picture many other associations. If you are a "user," your schema of computers may be merged with positive feelings of limitless possibilities. If the computer revolution has left you behind with your yellow legal pads and typewriter, you may have feelings of anxiety or frustration as you approach a computer. Our schema determines the sum total of all our thoughts about and reactions toward a certain subject. A reader cannot separate his or her schema from what is learned; thus, schema influences the interpretation of what is learned.

Thelen (1986) likened schema to a filing cabinet. Everyone has a unique and personal way of organizing cognitive structures (the cabinet). The schemata are the ideas contained within the file folders. Learners must be shown where and how new material fits into the existing structures. Because each student has his or her own organization, it is important that teachers help students engage their schema to connect new information to what is already known. For this process to occur, students must be able to determine what is known and what is *not* known. The process of metacognition helps learners assess their own knowledge.

### Metacognition

Much of the content that middle grade students learn in school today will be out of date by the time they are adults. It seems only logical, then, to focus our attention and instruction on teaching them how to learn rather than focus on content only. Learning is often referred to as a "cognitive" event. It is that, but it is also a "metacognitive" event. *Cognition* refers to using the knowledge possessed; *metacognition* refers to a person's awareness and understanding of that knowledge. "Cognition refers to having the skills; metacognition refers to awareness of and conscious control over those skills" (Stewart & Tei, 1983, p. 36).

For example, when a student enters class and sees that the topic for study is volcanoes, metacognition is involved when she assesses what she knows and does not know about the topic. While watching a movie about volcanoes, she makes a mental note of the new information she has learned and makes it "fit" with the prior knowledge or schema for volcanoes. When the teacher explains the terms *molten ash* and *lava,* she notices that she does not completely understand these terms and may be somewhat disturbed because the new information "doesn't fit."

Younger and less proficient learners do not have developed metacognitive abilities. They continue to read, listen, or watch with no knowledge that they do not understand the content being presented. They plow merrily (or not so merrily) along without stopping to assess, question, or correct the condition.

Metacognitive skills usually do not fully develop in students until late adolescence, but much can be done to enhance this ability during the middle level years. Before students can use metacognitive skills, they must become aware of the learning context (text or lecture), their own ability, how to interpret the demands of a learning task, and the best ways to react in order to maximize learning. Metacognitive skills include (1) clarifying the purposes of learning, understanding both the explicit and implicit task demands; (2) identifying the important aspects of a message; (3) focusing attention on major content rather than trivia; (4) monitoring ongoing activities to determine whether comprehension is occurring; (5) engaging in self-questioning to determine whether goals are being achieved; and (6) taking corrective action when failures in comprehension are detected (Brown, 1982).

At the middle level, metacognitive skills can be facilitated but not expected. A math teacher asked students to write a short journal entry assessing their daily understanding to help them become more aware of their own learning. Periodically, students were asked to write journal summaries in order to facilitate drawing conclusions about their learning. One student wrote about getting stuck "at about problem 12" in every assignment. Upon further examination, the teacher noticed that problem 12 is about where the problems begin to vary significantly from the example given in the book and more application is needed from students. This particular student could perform the task as long as the problem looked like the example, but was having difficulty applying the same process to a slightly new situation.

Metacognition, then, is knowing how and when to use one's skills to solve problems in understanding. "Thinking about one's thinking is at the core of strategic behavior" (Paris, Lipson, & Wixson, 1983, p. 295).

Metacognition develops as a student matures, usually during adolescence, but it can be taught and strengthened by explicit instruction and practice (Palincsar & Brown, 1983). Young adolescents are just beginning to be able to consider their own thinking in relation to the thoughts of others. The middle level years are an ideal time to develop metacognitive abilities in students and to teach them a repertoire of learning strategies to become more independent learners.

### Strategic Learning

Suppose that during a racquetball game you hit a straight shot down the right side of the court and your opponent misses the ball. The point is yours. This well-placed shot may have been a lucky one, or it may have been the result of a strategy. Before you hit the ball, you noted that your opponent was standing in the middle of the court and you remembered that she is left-handed with a weak backhand. You hit the ball deliberately and strategically.

This analogy can be applied to learning. Strategic learning involves analyzing the task, establishing a purpose for learning, and then selecting strategies for this purpose (Paris, Lipson, & Wixson, 1983). A strategy is a conscious effort on the part of the learner to attend to comprehension. Srategic learners know whether or not they are understanding and are willing to use any of a number of available strategies to help them understand better.

For example, while watching a videotape of proper diet, one student did not understand the function of vitamins. She wrote "vitamins??" on her paper and later asked a member of her group for clarification. This is a simple act, but necessary to understand the content. Another student stopped his reading of a chapter on igneous rocks because he became confused. He went back to the beginning of the chapter, flipped through the pages of the chapter to provide an overview, read the chapter summary, and studied the pictures. This activity helped him to reorient his learning and he proceeded in his reading. Over a period of years (and, it is hoped,beginning with early learning experiences), efficient learners develop a "repertoire of cognitive and metacognitive strategies" (Jones, Tinzmann, Friedman, & Walker, 1987, p. 38). These strategies, then, are the ones that will be applied to new learning situations in the future.

# Enhanced Instruction with Middle School Organization

Interdisciplinary team organization, advisory programs, and full and rich exploratory experiences were implemented in middle level schools as a response to the developmental needs of young adolescents. These middle school elements, however, also lend themselves to enhanced instruction because they provide the vehicle for a more relevant and a more integrated curriculum. Personal experience convinced me of their power to deliver more responsive instruction to students.

Before our middle school was organized in teams where I taught social studies for a number of years, I was teaching a unit on environment to seventh-graders. After about two weeks, one of my students asked me if the "environment" we were studying in social studies was the same "environment" they were studying in science. Sure enough, the science teacher, one period earlier and two doors down the hall, was teaching a unit on environment. It was sobering to realize that only one of the brightest students figured that out. It probably would have been helpful to our students if their two teachers had planned that unit together.

I participated in a Shadow Study last March. Hundreds of educators across the country participated and each followed an eighth-grader for one day. The reports were compiled and published by the National Association of Secondary School Principals in *Inside Grade Eight: From Apathy to Excitement* (Lounsbury & Clark, 1990). I followed a nice, quiet boy. He did his work, he answered questions, he turned in assignments; and he learned about dangling participles, Jack London, fission, the Antebellum south, and how to head his paper — all before lunch. He was expected to remember that in language arts the papers are turned in to the teacher, in science they are placed in a basket (blue for 3rd period), in social studies they are turned in only when requested. Papers are folded in science, headed in the upper-right corner in math, and kept in a notebook in social studies. He had to remember his book number for home economics, his locker number and combination in physical education (which incidentally is different from his locker number and combination in the hallway). High school students, even adults, sometimes have trouble seeing the connection between concepts. Many young adolescents are still concrete in their thinking. I wondered, as we zoomed through participles and on to the Antebellum south, how he was ever supposed to make sense of all of these isolated bits of information.

### Interdisciplinary Team Organization

Middle school organization lends itself to integrated instruction. For example, a team of five sixth-grade teachers in one school handles the science fair project in the following manner. The *science teacher* helps students identify a topic. The *reading teacher* teaches the students Cornell Notetaking System and helps them use the library to take notes from text. Then students take their notes to the *language arts teacher,* who works with them on writing a report. They go through the draft, editing, groups of students responding to each others reports, and end up with a completed report. The *math teacher* requires at least one chart or graph. When their report is finished, the *science teacher* uses them to discuss the content and they get four grades on the project. The focus of instruction is on the process — notetaking, writing, learning about graphs and charts — but the vehicle is the content (the science report).

With interdisciplinary team organization, there are limitless opportunities to teach thematic units — science and social studies, science and math, social studies and literature. For example, while teaching about Australia in social studies, one language arts teacher read aloud *A Fire in the Stone,* a tradebook about a mining town in central Australia, and she and her students wrote response journals. Through the use of literature, the characters, issues, and geography came alive while they were studying the actual events and facts in social studies class.

### Advisor/Advisee

The time that students spend exploring value issues during advisor/advisee time can enhance learning. One teacher I know used her Advisor/Advisee time to introduce a unit on comparative governments. She began by asking students to agree or disagree to statements like "I think that it is fair for some people to have more money than other people." After discussing different points of view, students then had more of a vested interest when they read about the political structure of different governments. The initial value discussion set up a dissonance of sorts as a background for reading. Some researchers (Irvin, 1980; Lunstrum & Irvin, 1979) concluded that discussion of value issues prior to new material presented improves comprehension of that material.

Problem solving helps develop thinking ability that is helpful in science and math, and analyzing value conflicts helps students understand literature and events in history. Students learn empathy for others, which can be used to improve the quality of writing. Teachers can use the topics discussed during advisor/advisee time throughout the day to reinforce academic pursuits.

### Exploration

A commitment to exploration, usually seen in a middle school, can also be used to enhance instruction. Unified arts courses, such as industrial arts or home economics, are one way to facilitate exploration. Another way is through mini-courses, scheduled periodically, such as photography, oceanography, or journalism. However, the entire curriculum in a middle school should embrace the spirit of exploration so that courses can go beyond the typical topics covered in the textbook. When one moves beyond the Table of Contents in textbooks, students can then study themes such as relationships, institutions, or exploration. These themes cut across disciplines and embrace the true spirit of exploration.

Exploratory experiences help to reinforce concepts and to develop vocabulary. Concrete or hands-on experiences are best for helping young adolescents learn. The more experiences students have, the better they can relate those experiences to academic subjects. Students do not readily see the application of one concept to a different content. These learning experiences can help students link learning experiences.

To be responsive to the needs of young adolescents and to help prepare students for the demands of a new century, curriculum and instruction at the middle level need to be (1) more process oriented, (2) more integrated, and (3) more relevant to the lives of students. When students study themes and solve problems that relate to their lives, they are more likely to remember, relate, and apply this learning to a new learning context.

### Suggested Practice

In the last three decades, it has become increasingly clear that organizing a school in interdisciplinary teams and providing for the affective and exploration needs of young adolescents is the best way to educate middle level students. Developmentally appropriate instructional methods are less defined, however. Many research-based and classroom-tested learning strategies are available that facilitate movement and interaction among students, provide for successful experiences in an emotionally safe environment, and provide a challenging introduction to abstract thinking: The time has come to orchestrate change in the classroom.

Developmentally appropriate instruction includes learning how to learn, learning how to think, and learning how to cooperate. Learning how to learn includes reading, writing, speaking, listening, and problem solving. Many books provide full descriptions of learning strategies that help students become more independent learners and more independent thinkers (Irvin, 1990; Readance, Bean, & Baldwin, 1985; Vaughn & Estes, 1986). Cooperative learning has proven successful in middle level classrooms. For more information, turn to Chapter Seventeen of this book for a rationale and practical suggestions on how to implement cooperative learning in middle level classrooms.

Although cooperative learning is very effective for student learning, many cooperative strategies that work on the same principle of cooperation in the classroom, but may not involve a group goal or group processing, can be used in a simple and just as effective way.

In the remainder of this section, I will briefly explain two strategies that are developmentally appropriate for middle level students: Think-Pair-Share and Mapping.

### Think-Pair-Share

Developed by McTighe and Lyman (1988), Think-Pair-Share is a simple, yet elegant, strategy to help all students become involved in the subject at hand. The strategy has a few simple steps:

1. Students *listen* while the teacher poses a question.
2. Students are given time in which to *think* of a response.
3. Students are then cued to *pair* with a neighbor and discuss their responses.
4. Finally, students are invited to *share* their responses with the whole group.

Students have time to think through their own answers to questions before the questions are answered and the discussion moves on. They rehearse responses mentally and verbally with another student before being asked to share with the entire class. All students have an opportunity to share their thinking with at least one other student, thereby increasing their sense of involvement.

Think-Pair-Share can be used in a number of interesting ways. After explaining a math procedure, the teacher may ask students to *think* about a problem (solve an application of the concept by themselves), then *pair* with a neighbor to compare answers, and, finally, *share* the answer with the whole group. A science teacher may ask students to Think-Pair-Pair-Share what they know about the surface of the moon prior to reading about the topic in the textbook. Basically, students spend two minutes writing what they know about the surface of the moon, then they pair with a neighbor to expand the list, then each pair joins another pair to form a foursome. Each foursome can then share with the total class through the use of a map, or a summary, or a simple listing of facts. The teacher would, of course, use these rich sharings of knowledge to stimulate a discussion of what the class knows about the surface of the moon. Questions, or what the students want to know (or think they know but are not sure of), can be listed separately for further reference.

Prereading (or prelistening) strategies operate on the same principle. It is important to activate what the learner knows about a topic and build background information before the new learning experience begins. Think-Pair-Share is particularly effective used in this way because all students have a role and a stake in the discussion. The activity provides students with an opportunity to interact and contribute in a nonthreatening environment.

Students are learning metacognitive abilities by assessing what they know and what they think they know or want to learn, and are thus motivated to learn more about the topic.

### Mapping

Maps are merely diagrams that help students see how words or ideas are related to one another. Circles and lines are used to show relationships between concepts. Hanf (1971) suggested mapping as a way to help students learn how to think critically, because in order to create a map, students must receive, organize, and evaluate information so that it makes sense to them. The map becomes a graphic display of main points, subcategories, and supporting details. *Semantic Mapping: Classroom Applications* (Heimlich & Pittleman, 1986) is an excellent publication that explains the many classroom applications of mapping. This strategy can be used as a prereading or prewriting activity, a vocabulary-building activity, or as a study skill. That is, it can be used before reading (or listening) to active prior knowledge and build background information, during reading (or listening) to take notes, and/or after reading (or listening) to synthesize information for later recall.

*Chapter mapping* is a powerful tool to help students comprehend and remember the important ideas in a text or lecture (Armbruster & Anderson, 1980). Mapping helps students to understand the important relationships in the text by providing them with a visual outline of the logical connections between key ideas. This strategy helps students be more active readers or listeners, thus facilitating the all important "deep processing." Mapping can also help students organize texts that are difficult to understand or poorly written. Sample maps created by Brandon, an eighth-grader, show how maps can be used before and after reading a few pages in his science book on the surface of the moon (see Figure 16–1).

Mapping is just as flexible as Think-Pair-Share. Mapping can be used as a first step to outlining, summarizing, or other writing assignments. Maps can be generated individually or in small or large groups. They can be shared, revised, and used as a study guide. But, most importantly, mapping is a developmentally appropriate learning strategy for young adolescents.

## Components of a Successful Middle Level Instructional Program

Those who agree with the tenet that learning is a lifelong process and that it is impossible for a student to attain all of the skills to learn new material in the first six or seven years of school must endorse systematic attention to instructional methodology at the middle level. Students at the middle

**FIGURE 16–1  •  *Brandon's Map Before Reading***

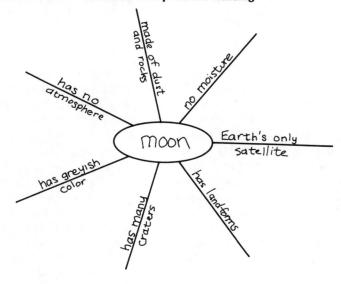

Brandon's Map After Reading

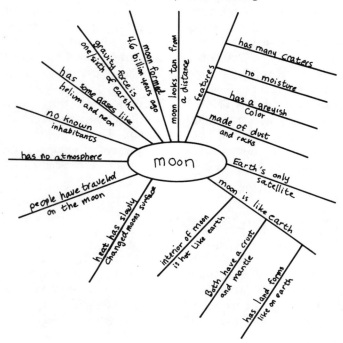

level are expected to read increasingly difficult material and increasingly more expository (versus narrative) material. Textbooks at the middle level often require students to understand abstract concepts for which they may not be cognitively and developmentally ready.

Middle level students are also expected to do more with what they learn. Students are expected to read increasingly longer assignments, take notes, and do homework assignments based on what they read. It is difficult for most middle level students to accomplish all of these feats on their own; they need guidance.

What, then, are the components of a successful instructional program at the middle level? The following recommendations are based on (1) the testimony of educators who have implemented successful middle level programs, (2) the knowledge of experts, (3) an understanding of the characteristics of middle grade students, and (4) my own experience as a teacher and consultant in middle level schools.

1. *Total school/district and building level leadership commitment:* A commitment to improved instruction at the middle level means providing leadership and support for new instructional methods at both school and district levels. Leadership and support at the district level means that programs will be provided with an overall organization, with funding, and with careful consideration. Leadership at the building level includes supporting staff development activities, creating an environment where it is safe for teachers to experiment, and clearing roadblocks for improved instruction.

2. *Content area teachers who are committed to teaching students and not just content:* In order to facilitate learning, teachers are expected to understand (1) their students, (2) their content, (3) the learning process, (4) learning strategies (when and how to use them), and (5) the materials they are using and how to adapt the text to their students. Effective teachers keep all of these things in mind as they plan for instruction.

3. *An instructional program guided by learning strategies rather than by a set of materials:* In many middle level classrooms, the organization of the textbook determines the organization of the program. Such programs do little to meet the needs of individual students and of specific content requirements. Instruction at the middle level should help students match learning strategies with the demands of content area instruction. Learning strategies should be taught directly through the content text in coordination with a developmental reading class or by content area teachers.

4. *Instruction that integrates all of the content areas and learning objectives that are taught through integrated content:* Interdisciplinary teams naturally lend themselves to integrated instruction if teachers will avail themselves of this opportunity. Teachers can design themes to study that are of interest of young adolescents. Content can be taught and the processes

of reading, writing, speaking, listening, computing, and problem solving can be learned through this integrated instruction. Through integrated instruction, content begins to make sense to students because it is connected to other content and to their own store of prior knowledge.

5. *One or more resource teachers or curriculum facilitators in the school:* A learning specialist or curriculum facilitator who does not have a student assignment can provide guidance to content area teachers by modeling learning strategies, by assessing text material that may be too difficult for students, or by providing diagnostic information about students.

These support teachers must have special qualities. They must have (1) knowledge of latest research and its classroom application, (2) excellent human relations skills and leadership qualities, (3) the ability to function as a catalyst for change, and (4) the ability to provide support at the school and district level.

6. *Evaluation that is consistent with the instruction:* Content area teachers who have incorporated the teaching of learning strategies into their curriculum sometimes continue to evaluate student outcomes in a way that is not consistent with their teaching. That is, their teaching is for process and main idea; their testing is still objective and detail oriented. Therefore, the students fail, but for good reasons; the evaluation was not consistent with their instruction. Evaluation and instruction should be tailored to the needs of the students and be consistent with each other.

7. *A strong staff development program:* Once it has been determined by a school, a district, or a classroom teacher that change is desirable, staff development generally begins. Ideally, teachers should identify the needs for staff development. Sometimes, however, the decision to change is made before teachers are consulted. One key element in the implementation of successful change is ownership or a feeling that the teacher is a part of the change process. "Ownership must be established for any change to survive" (Gallagher, Goudvis, & Pearson, 1988, p. 36). Ownership can be facilitated by teachers setting goals, teachers having input into the process, and mutual respect for all of the people involved in the process.

It is important in this stage, as with all stages of staff development, that those who are involved in the process consider *teacher growth* and not *teacher deficit.* All of us in our personal and professional lives cherish growth experiences. Professional growth happens in a supportive, positive environment. After ownership and a sense of respect and mutual integrity is established, growth and understanding can occur.

The second key element of change is knowledge. New knowledge can be gained through workshops, reading, discussion, observation, modeling, coaching, or attending conferences. The format is not as important as the support network that is established that will help the new ideas grow into eventual application in the classroom. The most successful staff development efforts seem to be guided by teachers, school based, and supported by the school district. However, changes toward improved instruction can happen team by team, as they adopt particular learning strategies and support one another in the implementation of those strategies.

8. *Classroom action research:* Although "teachers work hard and are constantly searching for methods and strategies that will help students achieve better, seldom do they receive proof that a different method worked effectively enough to keep at it" (Monahan, 1987, p. 678). One type of classroom action research consists of keeping track of how a particular method (such as graphic organizers) works with one class while continuing to teach other classes in the "old way." Pre- and posttesting is used to determine which group of students performed the best. Charts can be constructed to dramatize the results. Teachers take ownership of a strategy when they see that its use brings results in improved achievement. Classroom action research is a vehicle for facilitating ownership of new strategies and methods and professional growth.

9. *Peer coaching:* An interdisciplinary team is an excellent vehicle for offering support to teachers trying new instructional methods. When hearing about a new instructional method at a workshop, the likelihood of actually implementing that strategy is about 10 percent. When peer coaching is involved, the likelihood of implementing the innovation rises to 90 percent (Joyce & Showers, 1988). It seems logical that teachers will take ownership in a strategy if supported and reinforced by teammates. in fact, teams can decide which strategies to emphasize and reinforce during a school year and arrange their schedule to accommodate two teachers working together for a day to coach each other in the use of that strategy.

## Conclusion

As middle level schools implement organizational structures that are more conducive to meeting the needs of young adolescents, it is time that the curriculum and instruction are transformed to be more meaningful to students. Interdisciplinary team organization as well as advisory and exploratory programs naturally lend themselves to enhanced instruction for middle grades students. Good middle schools are not those that are organized in teams, provide for student exploration, and have remarkable advisory programs; exemplary programs do all of these things *and* strive to provide curriculum and instruction that is process oriented, integrated, and relevant to students. These schools deliver this curriculum in a developmentally appropriate manner to accommodate young adolescents' need to move, to explore, to debate, to interact, and to relate new learning to what they know and what they will need to know to be productive citizens in the twenty-first century.

## References

Alexander, W. M., & McEwin, C. K. (1989). *Schools in the middle: Status and Progress.* Columbus, OH: National Middle School Association.

Anderson, R. C., Hiebert, E. H., Scott, J. A., & Wilkinson, I. A. G. (1985). *Becoming a nation of readers.* Urbana, IL: Center for the Study of Reading.

Armbruster, B. B., & Anderson, T. H. (1980). *The effect of mapping on the free recall of expository text.* Urbana, IL: Center for the Study of Reading. (ERIC Document Reproduction Service ED 182 735).

Armbruster, B., & Anderson, T. (1984). *Producing "considerate" expository text: Or easy reading is damned hard writing.* (Reading Education Report No. 46). Champaign, IL: Center for the Study of Reading.

Beane, J. A. (1990). *A middle school curriculum: From rhetoric to reality.* Columbus, OH: National Middle School Association.

Brown, A. L. (1982). Learning how to learn from reading. In J. H. Langer and M. T. Smith-Burke (Eds.), *Reader meets author, bridging the gap: A psycholonguistic and sociolinguistic perspective* (pp. 26–54). Newark, DE: International Reading Association.

Drash, A. (1980). Variations in pubertal development and the school system: A problem and a challenge. In D. Steer (Ed.), *The emerging adolescent characteristics and educational implications* (pp. 15–26). Columbus, OH: National Middle School Association.

Durkin, D. (1978–79). What classroom observations reveal about comprehension instruction. *Reading Research Quarterly, 14*(6), 481–533.

Elkind, D. (1978). *A sympathetic understanding of the child: Birth to sixteen.* Boston: Allyn and Bacon.

Epstein, J. L., & Mac Iver, D. J. (1990). *Education in the middle grades: Overview of national practices and trends.* Columbus, OH: National Middle School Association.

Gallagher, M. C., Goudvis, A., & Pearson, P. D. (1988). Principles of organizational change. In J. Samuels & P. D. Pearson (Eds.), *Changing school reading programs: Principles and case studies* (pp. 11–39). Newark, DE: International Reading Association.

Hanf, M. B. (1971). Mapping: A technique for translating reading into thinking. *Journal of Reading, 14*(4), 225–230, 270.

Heimlich, E., & Pittleman, S. D. (1986). *Semantic mapping: Classroom applications.* Newark, DE: International Reading Association.

Herber, H. L., & Nelson-Herber, J. (1987). Developing independent learners. *Journal of Reading, 30*(7), 584–589.

Irvin, J. L. (1980). *The effects of value analysis procedures upon students' achievement in reading comprehension.* Unpublished doctoral dissertation, Florida State University, Tallahassee, FL.

Irvin, J. L. (1990). *Reading and the middle school student: Strategies to enhance literacy.* Boston: Allyn and Bacon.

Jones, B. F., Tinzmann, M. B., Friedman, L. B., & Walker, B. B. (1987). *Teaching thinking skills: English/Language arts.* Washington, DC: National Education Association.

Joyce, B., & Showers, B. (1988). *Student achievement through staff development.* New York: Longman.

Lounsbury, J., & Clark, D. (1990). *Inside grade eight: From apathy to excitement.* Reston, VA: National Association of Secondary School Principals.

Lunstrum, J. P., & Irvin, J. L. (1979). Improving reading comprehension through value analysis. *Selected Articles on the Teaching of Reading, 30.* New York: Barnell-Loft.

McTighe, J., & Lyman, F. T., Jr. (1988). Cueing thinking in the classroom: The promise of theory-embedded tools. *Educational Leadership, 45*(7), 18–24.

Monahan, J. N. (1987). Secondary teachers do care . . . ! *Journal of Reading, 30*(8), 676–678.

Palincsar, A. S., & Brown, A. L. (1983). *Reciprocal teaching of comprehension monitoring activities.* (Technical Report No. 269). Champaign, IL: Center for the Study of Reading.

Paris, S., Lipson, M. Y., & Wixson, K. K. (1983). Becoming a strategic reader. *Contemporary Educational Psychology, 8*(3), 293–316.

Readance, J. E., Bean, T. W., and Baldwin, R. S. (1985). *Content area reading: An integrated approach.* Dubuque, IA: Kendall/Hunt.

Stewart, O., & Tei, O. (1983). Some implications of metacognition for reading instruction. *Journal of Reading, 26*(1), 36–43.

Thelen, J. N. (1986). Vocabulary instruction and meaningful learning. *Journal of Reading, 29*(7), 603–609.

Vaughn, J. L., & Estes, T. H. (1986). *Reading and reasoning beyond the primary grades.* Boston: Allyn and Bacon.

Witte, P. L., & Otto, W. (1981). Reading instruction at the postelementary level: Review and comments. *Journal of Educational Research, 74*(3), 148–158.

# CHAPTER SEVENTEEN

# Meeting the Needs of Young Adolescents Through Cooperative Learning

KAREN D. WOOD
*University of North Carolina at Charlotte*

For decades, finding the best approaches for meeting the needs of individual students has been a major concern of educators. One highly touted attempt to meet student needs is programmed learning, which emerged in the 1960s under the influence of behaviorism. In programmed learning each student is given an assignment in a commercially prepared workbook or "machine" and allowed to work through the material at his or her own pace. Immediate knowledge of results is usually provided so students can determine if their chosen answers are correct or incorrect.

Highly prevalent in the 70s and in existence today is the mastery learning concept, with its diagnostic-prescriptive approach and classroom management systems. This and similar approaches took over many subject area classrooms, especially in math, reading, and language arts. The diagnostic-prescriptive approach shares some similarities with programmed learning in that students proceed through material at their own pace. First, however, a student is given a diagnostic pretest on a specific skill. If the criterion level is not met, the student is assigned additional work in that area. A posttest is then administered, and if mastery is achieved, the student exits from that task and proceeds to the next hierarchically arranged skill.

Although some of the elements of these approaches for individualizing

This chapter is a compilation and expansion of the "Out of Research — Into Practice" Column written by the author for the *Middle School Journal* during the 1988–1989 volume year.

instruction have merit, many infractions of good teaching practices have resulted from their implementation. For example, in a typical classroom based on these notions of individualized instruction, students enter the room at the start of the period, pick up their assigned folder, and proceed to work through the skills exercises assigned. Students have no excuse to ask for assistance from a peer or share an idea since all are given different assignments. Consequently, no student-to-student interaction is observed and none is encouraged. Likewise, since the assignments for the class are varied, there is no room for teacher demonstrations, modeling, and guided practice—components that we have come to recognize as essential to good teaching.

With the emphasis in the 80s on effective teaching and "best practices," we must reconceptualize our thinking about previous concepts of individualized instruction. We now know that little can be learned in an atmosphere that is constricted with silence, and that the best approach to learning is to allow students to help other students. Indeed, in middle level schedules, where teachers may be responsible for over 150 students, it is empirically unsound and humanly impossible to give everyone a different assignment. What can be done is to employ a variety of grouping strategies so that students can be responsible for helping their peers. In this way, the teacher is using the best resource available for individualizing instruction: the students themselves.

Therefore, the purpose of this chapter is to show how cooperative learning can be used to meet individual student needs at the middle level. It begins with a section on the research-based benefits of cooperative learning, along with what research reveals about the social needs of adolescents. The remainder of the chapter is devoted to a discussion of how to integrate cooperative learning experiences with subject area instruction.

## What Research Reveals about the Benefits of Cooperative Learning

The earliest study on cooperative learning reported in the professional literature dates back to 1897. Since that time, hundreds of studies have been conducted attesting to the validity of employing grouping techniques in the classroom. Prominent educators such as John Dewey and Colonel Frances Parker long ago advocated classrooms in which learning is a cooperative enterprise. More recently, Pearson and Raphael (1990) have suggested that information can be conveyed via the notion of a *cognitive apprenticeship,* which is based on the model of "mentor helping novice" that has characterized entry into certain crafts and professions.

Interest in grouping has extended beyond the United States into an international effort, with countries such as Israel, West Germany, Canada, and Nigeria, to name a few, involved in research. According to Johnson and Johnson (Brandt, 1987), there is more evidence for cooperative learning than any other aspect of education.

Through an analysis of the voluminous research on grouping (Johnson, Maruyama, Johnson, Nelson, & Skon, 1981; Slavin, 1983), it has been consistently shown that students in cooperative learning situations score higher on achievement tests than students learning by other methods. Further, according to reviews by Lehr (1984) and Johnson and Johnson (1985), many other benefits of cooperative learning have emerged. Specifically, students consistently engaged in cooperative learning arrangements have

1. A higher motivation to learn
2. Greater intrinsic motivation
3. Shown improvement for both tutor and tutee
4. Demonstrated more positive perceptions about the intentions of others
5. Displayed a decrease in negative competition
6. Shown a greater acceptance of differences in their peers
7. More positive perceptions about the intentions of others
8. Shown improvement in their attitude to persons of different races
9. Displayed greater self-sufficiency and a decrease in dependence on the teacher

Despite the magnitude of these research findings, Johnson and Johnson (1985) have estimated that group learning strategies are used only 7 to 20 percent of classroom time. Some of the primary assumptions offered for these low figures are that (1) teachers often are afraid that chaos will result if the room is rearranged; (2) middle level teachers, in particular, were often trained on a secondary model of education, which promotes the lecture approach, with its straight rows and assigned seats; and (3) teachers lack a knowledge of the many grouping strategies from which to choose.

## What Research Reveals about the Social Needs of Young Adolescents

The professional literature abounds with calls for less individual learning and more cooperative learning arrangements (e.g., Doda, George, & McEwin, 1987; Lounsbury, 1985; Nickolai-Mays & Goetsch, 1986). Frequently, the rationale cited in these articles surrounds the social needs of adolescents.

In a report from a series of conferences on adolescent development funded by the Ford Foundation and other agencies (Lipsitz, 1979), participants recommended that institutions can best meet the needs of young adolescents by fostering peer interaction. Specifically the report stated, "Schools should provide an opportunity for peer and community interaction. Youth educating other youth should be encouraged. Ethnic and cultural identities should be emphasized" (p. 49)

Despite this theoretical emphasis, classroom observational research indicates that the lecture method, where the teacher is the primary purveyor of information and the students the passive recipients, continues to predominate in our schools today (Cuban, 1984; Goodlad, 1984; Lounsbury & Johnston, 1985; Ratekin, Simpson, Alvermann, & Dishner, 1985). When the lecture method is employed, the social and physical needs of adolescents are ignored. Instead, students sit in straight rows, often assigned seats, with little opportunity to share an idea with a friend or discuss a newly learned concept (Wood & Muth, in preparation).

Often accompanying the lecture method are directives such as, "Do your own work," "Stay in your seat," and "Be quiet." Lounsbury (1985) commented that these directives ought to be used more sparingly and only under testing situations. He further suggested that as social beings, adolescents will resort to whispering and even writing notes to meet their need to communicate with others.

The social needs of students are greatest between the ages of 11 and 15. During these years, a sense of acceptance and a need to belong to a group is at variance with the need to be recognized as a unique individual (George & Lawrence, 1982). Small group situations address these conflicting needs by providing an atmosphere for self-expression less threatening than the risk taking that occurs when an individual speaks to an entire class.

Unless teachers have a variety of grouping techniques from which to choose, the employment of any one technique can become as ineffective and unmotivating as sole reliance on the lecture method. Therefore, the remainder of this chapter will describe a variety of cooperative learning arrangements that are easily implemented and appropriate for all subject areas, in addition to an explanation of how cooperative learning can be incorporated within a daily and weekly schedule (adapted from Wood, 1987, 1988a, 1988b).

## Strategies for Implementing Cooperative Learning Experiences

### Group Retellings

One method for ensuring classwide participation is through the use of group retellings (Wood, 1987). In this approach, students work in pairs or groups of three or more, with each member reading a different type of topically related material. For example, a science or health teacher might select three varied selections on the topic of the cardiovascular system. One piece of material might be a brochure from the local health department on recognizing a heart attack, another could be an excerpt from an encyclopedia, and yet another might be an article from a magazine or newspaper. Each student in the group reads his or her piece and is responsible for retelling it in his or her own words to other group members, who may interject with related information from their own readings or past experiences. In addition, one way to individualize this group activity is to assign the shorter, easier material to the less able students.

### Buddy System

The buddy system approach (Fader, 1976), as the name implies, involves grouping students of varied abilities together and making them responsible for each other's learning. In this approach, before turning in any assignment, buddy system group members must read each other's work, edit, and offer assistance.

Fader suggested rearranging the class role from the "most prepared" for this class to the "least prepared." In a hypothetical class of 30 students, this list would be divided into thirds. Then, the top student from each of the three divisions would work together; next, the number 2 students from each division, the number 3 students, and so on, until the last group would be composed of the last member of each of the three divisions.

The results are 10 heterogeneous groups of three students in which the differences in ability levels are minimized to avoid both boredom and intimidation. Yet, the differences are still sufficient to ensure that they all can benefit from each other's experiences.

### Research Grouping

At any stage of the instructional lesson, before, during, or after the reading, students can work in groups to investigate an issue in more depth. Whether the choice is laboratory research involving actual scientific experiments, or library research for the purpose of solving unanswered questions, research grouping is an excellent method to employ. For example, a social studies class may be divided into groups to gather more information on Civil War battles, generals, or everyday life. Or groups in a health class may seek varied sources to find more information on poison control or childhood diseases.

When employing research grouping, it is helpful to give students a collaborative sequence to follow, with roles and tasks assigned to each group member. The sequence might begin with students in each group taking on the responsibility of searching varied sources, either encyclopedias, books, pamphlets, or magazines for information on a topic. One student serves as a recorder while the group decides how to synthesize the sources. A rough draft is then compiled, with group members editing where necessary. (Any subsequent drafts can be written by a different recorder). Finally, group members become editors, reading the paper for mechanical and content modifications. Figure 17-1 shows how this process can be depicted in abbreviated format to aid groups in understanding their roles and meeting their objectives. Ideally, this sequence (or one similar) should be written on the board and explained thoroughly prior to the lesson.

### Cybernetic Sessions

Maztal (1986) developed cybernetic sessions in which small groups of students respond to predetermined questions during a specified period of time. Cybernetic sessions can be used before a new lesson as a means of eliciting students' prior experiences with a topic. Or they can be used after a lesson as a form of review. The four phases of cybernetic sessions will be described next.

#### Preplanning Phase

Begin by writing one question on poster board and hanging the boards around the classroom. Some questions can be developed for science on the digestive system; in literature on the setting, problem resolution, or characters in a novel; or in mathematics on everyday uses of the decimal system.

**FIGURE 17-1  •  *Research Group Assignments***

| | |
|---|---|
| Each member: | Assign research roles: encyclopedia, magazines, card catalog |
| Entire group: | Combines notes |
| Individual: | Rough draft recorder |
| Each group: | Read and revise |
| Individual: | Second draft recorder |
| Each member: | Assign editorial roles: grammar, punctuation, content |
| Entire group: | Final copy reading and revision |

*Source:* K. D. Wood, "Meeting the Social Needs of Adolescents through Cooperative Learning: Part I," *Middle School Journal, 20*(1).

Regardless of the subject area, the questions should be thought provoking, eliciting much discussion, brainstorming, and interaction.

### Response Generating Phase

Students are assigned to groups of four to six and are then seated around each of the question stations. Then they are instructed to write down on a separate sheet of paper as many responses as possible to the given question. A different student can serve as a recorder for each question. At the end of the allotted time, the groups move to the next question and the process is repeated.

### Data Synthesis Phase

In this phase, students get the chance to hear the responses of all their classmates. The teacher or an appointed student writes the various answers under each posted question, thereby leading the way to a whole class discussion of new concepts and ideas.

### Final Presentation Phase

The completed posters can be placed on the bulletin board, reread later for review purposes, or typed as handouts.

Cybernetic sessions are useful for all subject areas. Because they require a certain degree of movement, they appeal to middle level students' inherent need to be active.

## Tutorial Grouping

When students are in need of assistance, tutorial grouping is the next best alternative to direct teacher-to-student interaction. In tutorial grouping, two students work together and are responsible for each other's learning. As such, the disparity between them should not be so great as to intimidate a partner. Likewise, pairs should not be so similar in terms of ability that they are unable to aid each other's progress. Learning or reading disabled, ESL, or educable mentally handicapped students are often unable to handle grade level material. Therefore, the teacher may choose to assign the majority of the class the textbook reading while tutorial groups work in topically related alternative materials written at an easier grade level.

I find the management device in the lesson plan form excerpted in Figure 17–2 very useful. This form is filled out initially by the teacher and then later taken over by the tutor and tutee as more responsibility is allotted to them. The figure shows how the form may be used in a science class.

Tutorial grouping is most effective when it is not used excessively. Otherwise, the chosen students may feel isolated from their classmates. When

**FIGURE 17–2** • *Excerpt from Lesson Plan Form*

Names: John/Doug
Subject: Science

| Date | What I Plan to Do Today | What I Did Today |
|------|------------------------|------------------|
| 9/4 | Read *Gateways to Science* pages 24–27 with partner. Write down 10 new ideas. | I finished reading and wrote down 5 ideas. Doug wrote 3 more. |
| 9/6 | Study display case on insects in room with partner. Choose 3 insects. Write 3 facts about each from *Gateways*, Chapter 2. | I chose spiders, roaches, and flies. I wrote my facts from the book. |

deemed necessary, the teacher may say something like, "For the first half of the period, form your tutorial groups and begin your next assignment. The remainder of the class will work in pairs on the textbook assignment. I will be around to assist all of you. Then we will all see a demonstration on insect life."

### Social Grouping

Allowing students to work with peers of their own choosing can be most beneficial behaviorally and academically. The reward of such a grouping arrangement may be all that is needed to quiet a restless class after lunch or prior to an assembly program. The teacher need only say, "You may choose a partner with whom to work if you do so quietly." Or an alternative is to ask the class to write down the names of three preferred partners, then, as Johnson, Johnson, Holubec, and Roy (1984) have suggested, those students not selected can be grouped with others who are known to be compassionate and supportive.

### Interest Grouping

Capitalizing on the specific interests of young adolescents is often a sure way to motivate them to undertake an assignment. After the introduction of a particular unit in any subject area, the teacher can provide a list of activity or content-based choices. Some content-based choices in social studies, for example, may include collecting more information and objects related to Greece, including food, climate, dress, or government. Some activity-based choices might involve presenting a skit, making a demonstration, engaging a speaker, developing a project, or writing a report.

### Dyadic Learning

Larson and Dansereau (1986) recommend having students work in dyads (pairs) to study their subject area assignments. Each must read a segment (from a paragraph up to two pages) of their textbook or assigned selection. The other partner assumes the role of "listener/facilitator" by correcting errors, adding information, or clarifying concepts. Together they can draw charts, maps, outlines, graphs, pictures, or anything that will assist in furthering their understanding and recall. After each segment of text is read and discussed, the partners switch roles. At any point in the lesson, the teacher may call for a classwide discussion of the textbook concepts.

### Group Communal Writing

The improvement of students' writing proficiency is gaining widespread emphasis throughout the country. Group communal writing is a means of incorporating writing practice throughout all subject areas with minimal preparation, instruction, and evaluation time. In this approach, each heterogeneous group of four students composes only one product between them. Students are able to contribute their individual strengths to the composition process, which may range from spelling to proofreading to topical knowledge. Consequently, the process of writing is modeled for those with less experience, and everyone, regardless of ability level, can make a contribution.

Group members can be assigned different roles, such as content editor, researcher, proofreader, or recorder, and these roles can be rotated periodically. After the assignment is completed, group members sign the paper to indicate their agreement. A grade is given to the group to further recognize the collaborative effort. Thus, a teacher of any subject area can offer one or more writing assignment choices and circulate around the groups to provide assistance.

### Associational Dialogue

The associational dialogue is a component of a strategy called *free associational assessment* (Wood, 1985), which uses students' free recalls as a means of evaluation. The dialogue portion can be used separately as an aid to the oral review process.

The teacher begins by preparing a list of the most significant concepts in the lesson to be taught. Students are to take notes on these concepts from class demonstrations and the textbook until they have "associational clusters" of relevant information. The teacher should encourage them to use information from their own experiences to further assist in retention. Figure 17–3 shows an abbreviated list for a social studies lesson. Although students A and B have responded to the stimulus *continental divide* differently, both have sufficiently captured the essence of the concept. Note how both students have included familiar information to extend their understanding.

Next, with the original list unmarked, the students can look at each concept and then mentally or subvocally recite as much of the associated content they can recall. This recitation continues until they feel they can comfortably associate the word with the related content. The process can be done at home, in class under teacher guidance, or both.

Class time should be provided for students to work in pairs, engaging

**FIGURE 17–3** • *Free Associational Assessment Using the Land and Climate of the Mountain West States*

### *"The Mountain West States: Land and Climate"*

*List of Concepts, Events, Places, People*

> timberline
> intermontane
> continental divide
> arroyo
> semidesert
> rain shadow

*Student Free Recalls or "Associational Clusters"*
> Continental Divide

*Student A:*  An imaginary line like the Prime Meridian, but it's located in the Rockies. It divides the flow of rivers. Rivers on the east side flow east. Rivers on the west side flow west. On our trip out west, people called it the Great Divide.

*Student B:*  The continental divide determines which way rivers will flow. The Snake River, on the west side, flows west. The Yellowstone River, on the east side, flows east. The Blue River, near us, most flow to the east because it is east of the continental divide.

in the associational dialogue by discussing each concept in their own words. With concept lists in hand, the students recall from memory their individual associations, elaborating on each other's contributions with their own anecdotes. The teacher can circulate among the pairs to clarify important terms and provide further content.

After the student dialogue review, the teacher may choose to discuss selected concepts with the class as a whole, eliciting their contributions and filling in gaps where needed.

### Generic Lesson Grouping

Nelson-Herber (1988) described a method for grouping that is appropriate for a variety of purposes. Although Nelson-Herber did not name this procedure, it can be called *generic lesson grouping* because of its versatility in making any reading assignment more comprehensible to all students and because it extends across the prereading, reading, and postreading phases of the instructional lesson. A distinguishing characteristic of this form of grouping is the nature of the roles assigned to each group member before the lesson proceeds. Roles such as *checker* and *encourager* ensure that compassion is shown for fellow students and that no one's needs are overlooked.

To implement generic lesson grouping, begin by asking students to move into groups of five and to write down as many words they can think of on the specified topic. In a social studies class, such a topic might be "Life in Japan." This brainstorming activity serves to activate students' prior knowledge of the topic before reading, thereby establishing a firm foundation on which to base the new learning. A *recorder* for each group writes down the contributed words or phrases. Next, the groups share their contributions and the class, as a whole, discusses how each word relates to the topic. From these words, the teacher and students construct a graphic organizer or web, a visual representation that uses connecting lines to show the relationships between key concepts.

A web in social studies, for example, may include categories such as climate, food, people, government, and the history of Japan. After the teacher asks the students to make predictions about the selection, they can begin the reading assignment. The teacher can develop a set of five or six questions to accompany the reading. The questions should be answered collectively by the group members. In each group a *leader* is designated to read the questions and start the reading and searching process. During the reading, the more proficient readers can assist the less able readers with difficult words and concepts. Group members then address each question, presenting evidence from the text for their responses.

A *recorder* writes down the answers as a *checker* ensures that everyone understands the answers offered and where they can be found. Then, an *encourager* is designated to make sure that all group members have a chance to participate and that they are praised for their contributions. During the grouping process, the teacher circulates, answering questions and providing assistance or supervision when needed.

Finally, all of the groups merge their answers by engaging in a discussion. Students are asked to explain variations in their responses by presenting evidence from the text or their prior experiences. What results is an activity in which all ability levels, even the less abled readers, can participate and benefit from the group interaction and multiple recitations of the content.

### Random Grouping

In some instances, it may be necessary to group students randomly. Merely directing the students to "pair up with someone seated near you" or "get into groups of four" can make the math word problems, the grammar exercises, or the science textbook questions more understandable to more students. Another way of randomizing students is to have them count off by 2s, 3s, or 10s, depending on the group size needed.

### Base Grouping

Johnson and Johnson (1985) have found what they call base groups or home groups very useful. Students within a class are assigned to a base or home group at the beginning of the year. Then, when deemed necessary, usually 5 to 10 minutes before the beginning of the lesson, the teacher calls the students into their base groups. Here, they have the opportunity to greet classmates, discuss the previous night's homework, confer on a project, or relate an anecdote relevant to an assignment. After trying it with graduate students, Johnson and Johnson maintain that this time begins the class on a positive note, since it allots students an opportunity to interact informally with their peers on academic matters.

### Needs Grouping

Sometimes it is necessary to group students according to their strengths and weaknesses in a particular area. Unless the teacher has a systematic plan for ongoing assessment, these needs can go unnoticed until the first test or even later. Two methods for determining students' needs are (1) pre- and posttesting and (2) arranging assessment tests topically.

Pretests can be developed before teaching a unit on grammar, for example, to determine students' knowledge of comma usage, end-of-sentence punctuation, or rules of capitalization. Similarly, they can be used to preassess students' understanding of math concepts and computations. In this way, the teacher can eliminate the teaching of unnecessary material and find out who has specific needs. Posttests can be used after the instructional lesson to ascertain who has or has not mastered particular skills or concepts.

By arranging chapter or unit tests topically, the teacher can evaluate what students have learned and what they still need to know. A grammar test arranged topically would have categorically grouped the items related to subjects, predicates, or verbs together. By using a grid such as the one shown in Figure 17–4, the teacher can judge if additional explanation of concepts is needed for the entire class or for specific students. The teacher can use a simple " + " if the majority of items on a particular topic were mastered or a " − " if they were not. As the grid in Figure 17–4 indicates, the students profiled could be grouped for more instruction in causes of and controlling pollution, which are their weakest areas. Another possibility is to have students who performed better on the test explain the concepts to those whose test performance suggests a lack of understanding. (See Wood, 1985, for a fuller discussion of the procedure.)

**FIGURE 17–4** • *Partial Class Profile: Science Unit*

Topics

| Student's Name | Air | Water | Soil | Noise | Solid Water | Causes | Controlling |
|---|---|---|---|---|---|---|---|
| 1.  Ryan | + | + | + | + | + | − | + |
| 2.  Eric | + | + | − | + | − | + | − |
| 3.  Shannon | + | − | − | + | − | − | − |
| 4.  Tara | + | + | − | + | − | − | − |
|  |  |  |  |  |  |  |  |
| 30. |  |  |  |  |  |  |  |

## The Interactive Reading Guide

The interactive reading guide is similar to a typical reading or study guide in that it uses questions as an accompaniment to reading text to reduce the amount of print students must deal with at a given time. It is unlike the typical guide in that students are not sent off to work individually or merely asked to turn in their assignment when finished. Instead, the teacher-directed guide is designed to lead students through the reading of textbook material in orchestral manner, sometimes requiring responses from them as individuals, small groups, pairs, or class. Also, students are asked to do much more than answer the literal level, multiple-choice or fill-in-the-blank questions that are typically found at the end of textbook chapters. At various points in their guided reading, students may be asked to predict what may occur next, develop associations, discuss a segment of information with their partner, read and retell the content in their own words, or contribute their free recalls of the material to the class.

Figure 17–5 is an illustration of an interactive reading guide developed for a middle school social studies chapter on "The Middle Atlantic States Today." Figure 17–6 shows how the guide can be adapted for a general science lesson on "Water: A Basic Resource."

As can be seen, the textual material is divided into manageable units. After each segment is completed by the pairs, groups, or individuals, the class as a whole may discuss the responses. Although designed for the class to proceed through the guide together, the teacher may want to make adjustments by permitting advanced students to proceed ahead or by setting a time limit on certain segments to expedite the guide's completion.

A most efficient way to develop several interactive reading guides, especially if a teacher is responsible for more than one subject area, is to use the stem of the questions, as shown in Figures 17–5 and 17–6, and then add the relevant content and page numbers. In science, for example, a question might read, "Before reading, write down everything you can think of on the topic of pollution." Similarly, a guide for a chapter in a health class might include questions such as, "With your partner, jot down five things you have learned after reading the section on 'Components of the Eye.'"

An interactive reading guide could be developed to assist students in understanding a literature selection. Such a guide could be used to point out figures of speech or stylistic conventions such as foreshadowing or flashbacks, or it could stimulate students' predictive abilities by asking them to guess what a character might do next or suggest some alternative endings.

Yet another way the elements of the interactive guide can be used is to assist students in following directions. Every teacher has experienced the frustration of explaining the directions of a lesson, only to have hands go up requesting that the same information be repeated, or to have groups of

**FIGURE 17–5** • *Interactive Reading Guide*

*"The Middle Atlantic States Today"*

*Interaction Codes:*

 Individual    Pairs    Group    Whole Class

1. In your group, write down everything you can think of on the following topics related to the Middle Atlantic States. Be prepared to share these associations with the class.

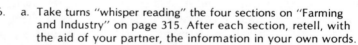

Middle Atlantic States

Land    Climate & Natural Resources    Farming & Industry    Cities

2. With your partner, discuss and record some things you have learned about the Middle Atlantic region after studying the map on page 311.

3. In your own words, define "bay" and "harbor." Locate the New York, Chesapeake, and Delaware Bay areas.

4. After reading each section on pages 311–312, jot down three things you have learned about the mountains, rivers, and lakes of this region. Share this information with your group.

5. Read to remember all you can on pages 313–314 about the climate and national resources of the Middle Atlantic region. The associations of the class will be written on the board.

6. a. Take turns "whisper reading" the four sections on "Farming and Industry" on page 315. After each section, retell, with the aid of your partner, the information in your own words.
   b. What have you learned about the following: poultry farms, truck farms, the manufacturing belt, petrochemical industries, and still manufacturing?

7. With your partner, use your prior knowledge to predict if the following statements are true or false before reading the section on "Cities." Return to these statements after reading to see if you have changed your view. In all cases, be sure to explain your answers. You do not have to agree with your partner.

   a. New Jersey is the most densely populated in the country.
   b. The majority of people in the Middle Atlantic region reside in the rural areas.
   c. Ports help commerce.
   d. The area from Boston to Washington is one big city.

8. Read the section on "Cities." Each group member is to choose a city, show its location on the map on page 32, and report some facts about it.

9. Return to the major topics introduced in the first activity. Skim over your chapter reading guide responses with these topics in mind. Next, be ready to contribute, along with the class, anything you have learned about these topics.

**FIGURE 17–6 • *Interactive Reading Guide***

### *"Water: A Basic Resource"*

Interaction Codes:

Individual        Pairs        Group        Whole Class

1.  In your groups, write down everything you can think of related to resources. (A resource is something in nature that is valuable to mankind.)

    Each group will offer at least one resource to be written on the board and the whole class will discuss the various resources.

2.  Read the topic "From Land to Sky" (p. 280). Close your books and answer the following questions:

    a. Where is most of the earth's water stored?
    b. How does water move from the earth to the sky?
    c. How does water move from the sky to the earth?
    d. What is this water movement called?

    In your groups, check and discuss your answers.

3.  In your pairs, "whisper read" the three paragraphs under the section "Evaporation" (pp. 280–281). With the aid of your partner, retell this information in your own words.

4.  Read to remember all you can about "Downhill to the Ocean" (pp. 281–282). The associations of the class will be written on the board and discussed.

5.  Read "The Underground Route" (pp. 282–283) and write three questions on the topic for your partner to answer.

6.  Read the section "Aquifers and the Water Table" (p. 283). Answer and discuss the following questions:

    a. Discuss the relationship between porous and impermeable rock in forming aquifers.
    b. What is occurring in an aquifer when the water table is dropping?
    c. What is occurring in an aquifer when the water table is up?
    d. How do aquifers affect your life?

*Source:* Contributed by David Lowe, Knox Middle School, Salisbury, NC.

students whispering amongst themselves because they did not hear the directions. To circumvent this problem in math class, for example, the teacher may list the day's directions on the board in the following manner:

- In your groups, try to recall everything you can remember about yesterday's lesson on fractions. Refer to the class notes and the introductory lessons on page 192 has needed.
- With your partner, read the directions on page 193. If you still have questions, ask your group members for assistance. Do the first five problems in pairs.
- Do the last five problems on page 193 individually.

During this time, the teacher is available for assistance by continually circulating among the groups or pairs as needed. Students have been taught from the beginning of the year to rely first on their peers for assistance and next on their teacher. With teacher-granted permission to request help from their peers, lesson pacing is maintained. Students who understand the assignment can proceed without being deterred by the questions of their classmates. In addition, since middle level students are often reluctant to admit in front of a class that they do not understand an assignment, they are less threatened in a pair or small group situation.

It is imperative that the small groups or pairing arrangements be predetermined before a lesson begins. These arrangements can and should be flexible, with changes made whenever the teacher feels it is warranted. In addition, guides should not be developed for every chapter in a textbook. When used judiciously, the interactive reading guide can be a welcome vehicle for fostering peer cooperation and for motivating students to want to read assigned material.

## Integrating Cooperative Learning Experiences with the Instructional Program

Table 17–1 shows how grouping techniques can be incorporated throughout the week in language arts, social studies, science, and math. Figure 17–7 shows a sample schedule for a middle level student and how grouping techniques may be engaged in throughout the day and across subject areas. Notice how a combination of whole class, small group, and individual work has been employed with each subject area. Notice, too, how various forms of grouping have been used throughout the day, emphasizing the importance of cooperation in all learning tasks.

## Suggestions for Successful Implementation

Without ample guidelines to follow, the implementation of cooperative learning in the classroom could be a negative experience for both teacher and

**TABLE 17–1 · A Sample Weekly Schedule for a Seventh-Grade Class**

| | Monday | Tuesday | Wednesday | Thursday | Friday |
|---|---|---|---|---|---|
| Language Arts | Introduce point-of-view paragraph. Model writing assignment for whole class. | Students work in buddy system groups to compose/edit. | Students are paired randomly to compose a single descriptive paragraph. | Students work individually and then share compositions with original buddy system group for editing. | Students' individual efforts with whole class work is displayed. |
| Social Studies | Teacher builds background on "India." Whole class. | Group retellings of varied, topically related material. | Students begin interactive reading guide on textbook chapter. | Students continue interactive reading guide. | Teacher poses topics for future interest groups. |
| Science | Demonstration on "Source of Pollution." Whole class. | Students read relevant textbook section. Dyadic learning. | Whole class discussion of textbook content. | Students choose related topics and form research groups. | Research groups continue. |
| Math | Teacher models percentages on overhead. Whole class. | Students practice in pairs. Tutorial grouping. | Students practice individually. | Progress test given. | Students grouped according to need. |

331

**FIGURE 17–7 • A Sample Daily Schedule for a Middle or Secondary Level Student**

| Period | Class | Grouping Strategy |
|--------|-------|-------------------|
| First | Math | Based on previous unit pretesting on equations, students work in small groups on their specific needs. |
| Second | Biology | After seeing a film and watching a demonstration on dissecting earthworms, students are assigned to buddy system groups to begin their own dissecting experiments. |
| Third | English | Group communal writing groups are employed to complete an assignment on persuasive writing. |
| Fourth | History | Students continue working through the interactive reading guide displayed in Figure 3. |
| Fifth | Health | An outside speaker, engaged to discuss stress, assigns students to random groups to work on various stress reduction techniques. |
| Sixth | Computer Science | Students select a programming assigment based on their interests and then are assigned to research groups to solve the problem posed. |

students. The following suggestions are designed to help teachers plan strategically for cooperative learning in advance of implementation to ensure successful classroom application.

1. Begin the year by establishing an atmosphere of responsible learning and caring in which negative comments are not tolerated. Explain to the students that, for the remainder of the year, they will be asked to help and receive help from their peers, share ideas, and encourage one another through projects and assignments.
2. It will be necessary to extend or reemphasize existing classroom rules such as "Stay in your groups," "Speak softly," "Respect others," or "Avoid criticism." Such rules can be posted in the classroom and reinforced when needed before the start of a group assignment.

3. To ensure success and avoid chaos, the teacher will want to make decisions about placement in groups before beginning the lesson. This preparedness communicates to students that the teacher is well organized and expects the same from them.

4. Specify in advance the academic objectives of the lesson; that is, explain, demonstrate, and model any skills to be learned or strategies to be employed. Lessons run smoothly when students have a thorough understanding of the tasks involved.

5. Specify in advance the collaborative objectives of the lesson; that is, tell students how to interact to complete a task and determine the individual roles and responsibilities to be undertaken. For example, a research group would assign roles related to researching the topic, recording the content, revising, proofreading, and editing.

6. While students are engaged in group learning, continually circulate and monitor to oversee the social interactions and provide academic assistance.

7. Be sure to use a variety of grouping strategies throughout the curriculum to avoid boredom and apathy and to allow students the opportunity to work with all class members.

8. In some instances, it may be beneficial to have students (a) summarize the academic content to determine if objectives have been met and (b) evaluate the collaborative objectives to assess the group's use of effective interpersonal skills. This process is a valuable way to make continuous improvement and ensure lasting success.

## Conclusion

As demonstrated in this chapter, the benefits of cooperative learning are varied and numerous. Of particular benefit to the middle level student is the extent to which cooperative learning experiences contribute to their need for social interaction. Inherent in every human being is the need to interact, communicate, and share ideas with our peers. As Glasser (1987) has said, "Working alone . . . is totally contrary to the basic human need to belong" (p. 656).

## References

Brandt, R. (1987). On cooperation in schools: A conversation with David and Roger Johnson. *Educational Leadership, 45*(3), 14–19.

Cuban, L. (1984). *How teachers taught: Constancy and change in American classroom 1890–1980.* New York: Longman.

Doda, N., George, P., & McEwin, K. (1987). Ten current truths about effective schools. *Middle School Journal, 18*(3), 3–5.

Fader, D. (1976). *The new hooked on books.* New York: Berkeley.

George, P., & Lawrence, G. (1982). *Handbook for middle school teaching.* Glenview, IL: Scott, Foresman.

Glasser, W. (1987). The key to improving schools: An interview with William Glasser. *Phi Delta Kappan, 68*(9), 56–62.

Goodlad, J. (1984). *A place called school: Prospects for the future.* New York: McGraw-Hill.

Johnson, D. W., Johnson, R. T., Holubec, E. J., & Roy, P. (1984). *Circles of learning: Cooperation in the classroom.* Alexandria, VA: Association for Supervision and Curriculum Development.

Johnson, D. W., Maruyama, G., Johnson, R. T., Nelson, D., & Skon, L. (1981). Effects of cooperative, competitive and individualistic goal structures on achievement: A meta-analysis. *Psychological Bulletin, 89*(1), 47–82.

Johnson, R. T., & Johnson, D. W. (1985). Student-student interaction: Ignored but powerful. *Journal of Teacher Education, 36*(4), 22–26.

Larson, C. O., & Dansereau, D. F. (1986). Cooperative learning in dyads. *Journal of Reading, 29*(6), 516–520.

Lehr, F. (1984). Cooperative learning. *Journal of Reading, 27*(5), 458–461.

Lipsitz, J. (Ed.). (1979). *Barriers: A new look at the needs of young adolescents.* New York: Ford Foundation.

Lounsbury, J. (1985). Do your own work? *Middle School Journal, 17*(1).

Lounsbury, J., & Johnston, J. H. (1985). *How fares the ninth grade?* Reston, VA: National Association of Secondary School Principals.

Maztal, N. B. (1986). Cybernetic sessions: A high involvement teaching technique. *Reading Research and Instruction, 25*(2), 131–138.

Nelson-Herber, J. (1988). Cooperative learning: Research into practice. *Reading Today, 5*(6), 16.

Nickolai-Mays, S., & Goetsch, K. (1986). Cooperative learning in the middle schools. *Middle School Journal, 18*(1).

Pearson, P. D., & Raphael, T. E. (1990). Reading comprehension as a dimension of thinking. In B. F. Jones & L. I. Idol (Eds.), *Dimensions of thinking and cognitive instruction: Vol. 1. Implication for reform.* Hillsdale, NJ: Erlbaum.

Ratekin, N., Simpson, M. L., Alvermann, D. E., & Dishner, E. K. (1985). Why teachers resist content reading instruction. *Journal of Reading, 28*(5), 432–437.

Slavin, R. E. (1983). *Cooperative learning.* New York: Longman.

Thomason, J. (1984). Nurturing the nature of early adolescents—Or a day at the zoo. *Middle School Journal, 15*(4), 3–6.

Wood, K. D. (1985). Free associational assessment: An alternative to traditional testing. *Journal of Reading, 19*(2), 106–111.

Wood, K. D. (1987). Fostering cooperative learning in middle and secondary level classrooms. *Journal of Reading, 31*(1), 10–18.

Wood, K. D. (1988a). Guiding students through information text. *The Reading Teacher, 41*(9), 912–920.

Wood, K. D. (1988b). Meeting the social needs of adolescents through cooperative learning: Part I. *Middle School Journal, 20*(1), 21–23.

Wood, K. D. (1988c). Meeting the social needs of adolescents through cooperative learning: Part II. *Middle School Journal, 20*(2), 32–34.

Wood, K. D. (1989a). Using cooperative learning strategies in middle school classrooms: Research and suggestions. *Middle School Journal, 20*(5), 24–25.

Wood, K. D. (1989b). Promoting cooperative learning through the interactive reading guide. *Middle School Journal, 20*(4), 38–39.

Wood, K. D., & Muth, D. (in preparation). The case for improved instruction at the middle level.

# CHAPTER EIGHTEEN

# Humanizing Student Evaluation and Reporting

GORDON F. VARS
*Kent State University*

"Does this count toward our grade?"
"How many points is this assignment worth?"
"How come you gave me a C on my report?
    I worked hours on it!"

Countless questions like these attest to the importance of marks or grades in the minds of middle level students.

Grades are no less important to parents. What middle level teacher has never been confronted by an irate parent, angry over the "poor grade" received by a son or daughter? And that "poor grade" might not have been a D or an F, but a B or a C, if the parent thought the child deserved an A.

Assigning marks to students is one of the most distasteful aspects of teaching. Conflicts over grades often pit students against teachers, and parents against schools. One eighth-grade science teacher was ordered by his principal to give no more than 25 percent of his students Ds or Fs, after a conflict that went all the way to the West Virginia state hearing examiner. On the other hand, many teachers "shade" some students' grades, knowing that a poor mark will result in either physical or psychological abuse of the child by one or both parents. It is no wonder that report cards have been compared to guided missiles, often creating explosions when they hit (Vars, 1983).

In an era when accountability and excellence are stressed at all levels of the education establishment, it is not surprising that students, parents, and teachers have their eyes on the "bottom line"—learning outcomes measured in standardized test scores and grade point averages. Student-centered middle level programs, such as teacher advisory groups, exploratory activities, integrated curriculum, and even interdisciplinary team organization, have little chance of success when student evaluation, marking, and reporting practices fail to reflect appropriate attention to the nature and needs of young adolescent learners.

## Conventional Marking and Reporting

Nearly all schools (99 percent) use some kind of letter or number grade to report middle level students' academic performance, according to Epstein (1990). About one-fourth (26 percent) of the schools in her large-scale study also gave separate grades for "effort," and 18 percent gave "progress grades." About half the schools graded student conduct or sent home written comments in each subject. Computer-generated comments were used in about 30 percent of the schools. Epstein concluded:

> *Virtually every middle grade school in the country uses report cards, but relatively few have designed the form and content of the cards to be responsive to the needs of early adolescents for strong support and for recognition of their effort and progress in learning. (pp. 441–442)*

Marking and reporting practices at the middle level have changed little over the years, despite the shift from junior high to middle school organization. In 1977, Kunder and Porwall found that ABC marks were used by 90.9 percent of the junior highs and middle schools in the 319 schools systems they studied. In an earlier large-scale study of educational practices in schools containing grades 7, 8, and 9, Wright and Greer (1963) found similarly high percentages of schools using letter or number symbols. Roelfs (1955) surveyed junior high school reporting practices in 1948 and 1953, comparing his results with other surveys conducted in 1925, 1935, and 1943. He concluded then that symbols or symbols expressed as percentages were the predominant method of reporting student progress through the years, and it is still true today.

Alexander and McEwin (1989) also found very little change in student progress reporting practices between their 1968 and 1988 surveys of middle schools (Table 18–1). The letter scale (A to E and so forth) was most prevalent, being used in more than 84 percent of the schools. Note that even in 1988, 29 percent of the schools used percentage marks, a practice widely criticized and presumably on its way out in the 1950s.

In addition to marks or symbols, middle schools in the Alexander and McEwin study used a variety of other reporting procedures, such as

**TABLE 18–1 • Percents of Middle Schools Using Various Types of Pupil Progress Reports**

| | Percent | |
|---|---|---|
| Types | 1968 | 1988 |
| Letter Scale | 86 | 84 |
| Word Scale (excellent, good, etc.) | 6 | 21 |
| Number Scale (1–5, etc.) | 13 | 14 |
| Satisfactory/Unsatisfactory Scale | 26 | 41 |
| Informal Written Notes | 46 | 62 |
| Percentage Marks | 36 | 29 |
| Dual System (progress compared with (1) class, (2) student's own potential) | 14 | 9 |
| Parent Conference | 42 | 68 |
| Self-Evaluation | — | 5 |

*Source:* From *Schools in the Middle: Status and Progress* (p. 38) by W. M. Alexander and C. K. McEwin, Columbus, OH: National Middle School Association. Copyright 1989 by National Middle School Association. Reprinted by permission.

informal written notes and parent conferences, often in combination with standard symbols. These person-centered procedures, more common in the lower grades, reflect the middle school's position between the typically child-centered elementary school and the subject-centered high school. Their increased use between 1968 and 1988 is encouraging. On the other hand, Alexander and McEwin report a decrease in the use of the dual marking system, which combines achievement marks with ratings of some other factor, such as effort or progress.

## Critiques of Conventional Marking and Reporting

It seems that the familiar comment about the weather applies equally well to marking and reporting: "Everybody complains but nobody does anything about it!"

Marks and marking systems have been heavily criticized for decades, dating back at least to the Starch and Elliott studies of 1912 and 1913. They demonstrated the wide variability in grades that different teachers assign to the same piece of student work. In 1925 Pressey pointed out the fallacy of grading on a curve, and in 1947 Wrinkle reported 10 years of a largely fruitless search for suitable alternatives to marks. Kirschenbaum, Simon, and Napier (1971) made a strong case against conventional marking and they presented a fictional scenario of how a high school might develop more suitable alternatives. The attack continued in 1976 (Simon & Bellanca) and 1977 (Bellanca).

In 1987, Natriello summarized the research up to that date, pointing out the limitations of all three approaches to evaluation employed by the schools: norm referenced, criterion referenced, and individualized. Criticism continues to this day. Canady and Hotchkiss (1989) set forth a 12-count indictment of conventional evaluation and reporting procedures, ranging from "varying grading scales" through "ambushing students" to "establishing inconsistent criteria."

Dyer (1989) eloquently described the anguish felt by both middle school teachers and their students at report card time. He suggested that the system continues because people embrace the following highly questionable principles: (1) grades adequately symbolize academic progress, (2) grades are objective (i.e., reliable and valid), and (3) grades are uniform and consistent. He identified three reasons why conventional marking systems continue: tradition, fear of change, and convenience.

The side effects of grade-dominated education also can be harmful. Marking and reporting consume teacher time that might otherwise be spent in planning and teaching. Student learning time is diminished by the need for testing or other assessment. Marking practices also may distort the curriculum. Both students and teachers may be reluctant to engage in valuable experiences like community service or cooperative learning because of difficulties in arriving at a grade. Indeed, it has been asserted that we have created a generation of "grade junkies," who will do nothing in school unless it is rewarded by a grade.

Unqualified defenses of conventional marking are rare, although a number of authors try to present the advantages and disadvantages of various approaches (Gronlund, 1974; National Education Association, 1970; Terwilliger, 1971). Ebel (1974) listed 22 common criticisms of grades, then argued that many of them are mutually inconsistent, others are not supported by research and experience, and still others are inaccurate or irrelevant. Where the criticisms are valid, he said, the remedy is not to get rid of grades but to do a better job of grading. To minimize the discouraging effects of low grades, he advocated an individualized approach such that "the basis for evaluating achievement is appropriate to the pupil in question." He further asserted that "any pupil who has done as well as can be reasonably expected should never be given a low or failing grade." He would handle the problem of inappropriate parent response to their children's grades by attempting to educate the parents or, if that fails, withholding grades from particular parents!

### Marks and the Middle Level Student

Another perspective on the limitations of conventional marking and reporting systems may be gained by considering the special characteristics and needs of middle level students (Vars, 1976b). A primary developmental task or need of this age group is to establish a healthy self-concept (Beane & Lipka, 1986, 1987). Yet for many students, report cards regularly confront them with failure or the threat of failure. Since hardly anyone is willing to be considered "average," Cs carry a stigma for most students, and even Bs are not satisfactory to many parents. Thus, as many as two-thirds of the students in a typical reporting period receive some kind of bad news. At the time when a young person's self-concept is in flux and very vulnerable to insult, this is an intolerable situation.

A second major need or developmental task during the middle school years is to achieve a satisfactory status with one's peers. Yet most conventional marking systems are based on class averages and hence are competitive. Many a capable student has deliberately "played dumb" to curry favor with his or her peers. Although the women's liberation movement has helped the situation somewhat, this "dumbing down" seems especially prevalent among girls. Marking systems based on class comparison run directly counter to the young person's striving for peer status.

A third prominent characteristic of middle level students is their wide range of individual differences. Diversity brought on by differing rates of maturation reaches its peak in the middle grades. It has been said that middle level classes are made up of men, women, and children. What greater argument is needed for an individualized marking and reporting system? Yet we find in most middle schools a uniform system, applying the same standards and procedures to all students.

Too often the only way a teacher can modify the grading system to meet the needs of an individual student is to "fudge" the grade. For example, of the hundreds of teachers I have asked over a period of 13 years, not one would give a failing mark to a student who gave evidence of trying his or her level best. Any system that has to be subverted to be fair to students leaves a great deal to be desired.

Thus, in terms of three major characteristics and needs of the middle level student, the conventional competitive marking system has very serious limitations. Conventional marking and reporting systems may not be good for elementary or high school students, but they may be especially devastating for students going through the highly impressionable middle school years.

### Research Findings

Research attempting to document the charges against conventional marking systems has been carried out sporadically since the early 1900s. Since few studies deal specifically with middle level students, we shall also consider research involving upper elementary and lower high school grades. Studies at all levels, elementary through college, have verified the variability and unreliability of teachers' marks (see, for example, Evans [1976], Hull [1980], Lewis, Dexter, & Smith [1978], Smith & Dobbin [1960], and Yauch [1961].) There seem to be many reasons for this variability. Many attribute it to the fact that different types of evaluation data, often based on widely varying standards of comparison, are all lumped together in one mark or symbol. (See Leese [1961] and Johnson [1962].) This issue is explored in greater detail later in this chapter.

Ability grouping further confounds the problem, with various schemes being used to assign higher weights to grades earned in honors classes when calculating a grade point average (Saville, 1983). The "halo effect" of ability grouping also affects grades, as Schwartzapfel (1981) discovered when he examined the grades awarded to 1,236 ninth-graders. He found that students in high-ability groups obtained significantly higher grade point averages than students who had equivalent standardized test scores in reading and mathematics but who were in average ability groups.

Personality factors also influence teachers' grades. For example, Matlin and Mendelsohn (1965) found that marks given to fifth-graders were more highly correlated with student scores on the California Test of Personality than with their scores on the Stanford Achievement Tests. Russell and Thalman (1955) likewise found that grades given by seventh- and eighth-grade teachers in six Illinois schools correlated positively with the teachers' personality ratings of the students. Hadley (1954) found that "most-liked" students in grades 4 through 6 were graded higher than their achievement appeared to justify.

Personality, in a very broad sense, probably lies behind differences in grades received by boys and girls. For example, Carter (1952) examined the marks given by both men and women teachers to students taking high school algebra for the first time. He found that girls received significantly higher marks than boys, even though their scores were equivalent on a standardized algebra test. Men tended to assign lower marks than women, also.

Students are aware that teachers give higher grades to students that they like, according to Hull (1980). He administered a 57-item opinionnaire to 345 junior high students in grades 7, 8, and 9. As might be expected, students who received higher grades were more likely to view teachers as fair than those who received lower grades.

Even physical appearance may affect a student's grade. Salvia (1977) submitted photographs of third-, fourth-, and fifth-graders to graduate students who were not acquainted with the children. Those rated "attractive" by this panel received significantly higher grades than those rated "unattractive," even though scores on the Iowa Tests of Basic Skills were not significantly different.

How grades affect student motivation depends a great deal on whether students believe they have any control over them; that is, whether they attribute their grades to their own effort and ability or to external factors such as luck or teacher bias. In a major study of these "attribution effects," Evans and Engelberg (1988) administered an 88-item questionnaire to 304 students in grades 4, 6, 8, 9, and 11 in four schools, two of which were middle schools. They found that older and higher-ability students attributed their school success to their own efforts, whereas students who were younger or who had lower ability blamed external factors. Moreover, they found that even the older students lacked understanding of the grading system being used.

In a later study, Engelberg (1989) administered a questionnaire to 42 students in grades 4 through 8 in two urban and two suburban schools. Here again, lower achievers were more likely to attribute their success, or lack of it, to external factors. On the other hand, most of the students in this sample indicated that they believed grades were more influenced by characteristics of the learner such as effort, ability, learning, and interest, than by classroom factors such as task characteristics, teacher favoritism, or luck.

In one of the few studies that examined directly the possible linkages between marking practices and student self-esteem and achievement, Hughes (1971) studied four groups of fourth-, fifth-, and sixth-graders. Each group received a different kind of report card, ranging from "very traditional" (based on set standards or class comparison) to "very progressive" (based on individual ability or progress). Student achievement was measured using the Iowa Tests of Basic Skills, and self-esteem was determined using the Piers-Harris Self-Concept Scale. Questionnaires also were administered to students, teachers, and parents.

The most traditional reporting system used the symbols A, B, C, D, and F to report individual achievement compared to class norms. This was supplemented by a checklist that could be marked to indicate that the student was working beneath his or her ability in a particular skill. The "modified traditional" report used no failing marks, only A, B, or C. "E" was used to indicate that the student was "experiencing difficulty." This report also carried a number indicating whether the student was exerting "strong, average, or little effort." The "somewhat progressive" report form used four ratings of how well the student was working with respect to his or her ability, ranging from O (outstanding) to U (unsatisfactory). The "very progressive" report form merely listed the subjects and rated the student as "successful" or "needs improvement."

Students receiving the "most traditional" (A–F) reports had the lowest achievement and lowest self-esteem of any group, although all comparisons were not statistically significant. These students also showed the most negative attitude toward the reporting process on the opinionnaire.

The highest self-esteem scores were registered by students receiving the "modified traditional" reports. This group also had higher achievement scores and more positive attitudes toward the reporting system than those receiving either "progressive" report. Parent attitudes favored the more traditional reports, whereas the teachers tended to favor more "progressive" procedures.

Hughes concluded that self-esteem is more closely related to achievement rather than to the way it is reported. She also attributed the success of the "modified traditional" reporting system to the fact that it rewarded success (A–B–C) but did not punish failure, and that it provided more feedback to students than either of the "progressive" systems. It should be pointed out that this system also gave students and parents a general effort rating in each subject, thus combining both competitive and individualized evaluation. It might better have been characterized as a "dual marking system" rather than merely "modified traditional." At any rate, this important study demonstrates that sorting out the effects of a marking system is no simple matter.

In a more recent study, Bachman and O'Malley (1986) examined social context as well as grades for their possible effects on self-esteem. They used data from the Youth in Transition study that followed 1,487 tenth-graders through high school and five years after high school. They concluded that the "school mean ability," the general level of academic performance in a school, was less important in determining self-concept of ability than the individual student's measured ability. They did say, however, that grades were "quite important" in shaping self-concepts of ability.

In summary, researchers as well as students recognize that many factors affect the grade a student receives, including how well that student gets along with the teacher. Moreover, those who get good grades consider them fair and believe that they have earned them. Those who receive lower grades are less likely to accept responsibility for them. In other words, grades as motivation work least well with students who most need encouragement.

As yet, it has not been conclusively demonstrated that conventional marking systems are harmful to student self-concepts, although the Hughes study in grades 4, 5, and 6 is suggestive. To date, there appear to have been no studies of grading effects on students' status with their peers. Efforts to individualize marking systems will be considered later in this chapter.

## Issues in Middle Level Marking and Reporting

What, then, are the major issues in marking and reporting at the middle level? Five appear to be most crucial.

- *Issue 1: What standards or bases of comparison should be used in determining student marks?*

Resolving this issue is complicated by the fact that marks are expected to serve several different functions, some of them mutually exclusive. The sorting function is best accomplished by some kind of competitive marking system, whereas encouragement of personal growth requires a more individualized approach. Years ago, Hiner (1973) pointed out that grading is a cultural function and that various approaches could be laid out on a continuum from those that stress achievement (sorting) to those that stress equality (personal growth) (see Figure 18–1).

In one of the few studies that compared practices from both ends of the continuum, Yarborough and Johnson (1980) located 51 seventh-graders who had gone through a nongraded elementary school where students received no marks of any kind and where there were no promotions or retentions at the end of the year. They compared these students with three carefully structured control groups of students who had experienced conventional marks in elementary school. There were no consistent significant differences between the nongraded group and any of the others with respect to 31 variables, including achievement, self-concept, and a number of attitude measures.

They did find, however, that "brighter" seventh-graders from the graded elementary schools had higher adjustment scores and more positive attitudes toward school than equally bright students who attended the nongraded elementary. On the other hand, the slower students from the nongraded elementary school had higher adjustment scores and more positive attitudes toward school than equivalent students who had received grades in elementary school. These differential effects on students of various abilities continue to plague efforts to assess the impact of various approaches to marking and reporting.

### Criterion-Referenced Marking

At the extreme "achievement end" of the Hiner continuum is criterion-referenced evaluation and grading. In this approach, a uniform performance standard or criterion is determined, and students are evaluated according to how close they come to meeting this absolute standard. This approach makes no allowance for individual differences, and hence, would seem least appropriate for students in the middle grades, where variability is at its peak. Gronlund (1974) succinctly stated other problems with this approach:

1. The problem of delimiting and defining the domain of learning tasks to be achieved by students
2. The problem of stating the instructional objectives in performance terms
3. The problem of setting appropriate standards of student performance
4. The problem of obtaining criterion-referenced measures of student performance

**FIGURE 18–1** · *Grading Systems as Cultural Phenomena*

| No<br>Grades | Blanket<br>Grades | According<br>to Effort | Norm-<br>Referenced | Criterion-<br>Referenced | |
|---|---|---|---|---|---|

Equality——————————————————————————————————————Achievement

*Source:* N. R. Riner, "An American Ritual: Grading as a Cultural Function," *Clearing House, 47*(6), p. 358, February 1973. Reprinted with permission of the Helen Dwight Reid Educational Foundation. Published by Heldref Publications, 4000 Albemarle St., N.W., Washington, DC 20016. Copyright © 1973.

Terwilliger (1971) pointed out that pass-fail marking is a special case of the application of an absolute standard, and that even teachers using A–B–C marks must decide what they will accept as minimum acceptable performance. This decision, in turn, is based on the teacher's conception of what, for example, a seventh-grader "ought" to be able to do, a highly idiosyncratic judgment that is heavily influenced by the teacher's prior experience.

Arbitrary standards also are likely to affect student motivation. If the student perceives that good marks are beyond reach, he or she may refuse to try. A student who achieves the criterion easily may cease working (Natriello, 1987).

So-called blanket grading is similar to pass-fail, in that everyone in class receives a certain mark provided that certain criteria are met (Curwin, 1978). Contract grading is an extension of this, with specific criteria set for attaining each mark. The same contract may be offered to all class members, or small groups within the class may each develop a contract, or each student may negotiate an individual contract with the teacher. The latter approach has some of the same advantages and disadvantages as the individual-referenced marking procedures described later. A problem with any of these approaches is that criteria usually are stated in terms of quantity rather than quality of work, thus short circuiting the important factor of teacher judgment.

Since 1969, Roosevelt Middle School in Eugene, Oregon, has used "credit," "no credit," and "incomplete" to report student progress. Teachers use a variety of evaluation forms to specify what the student has done during the term. Students who receive no credit have the option of retaking the course, and students who receive an incomplete usually have two weeks to complete the work and receive credit. Rubinstein (1989) reports that these and other ways of recognizing student accomplishments have created a school that is "remarkably congenial, cooperative, and informal, and there is an atmosphere of mutual trust and respect between students and staff members" (p. 329).

In some middle schools, A–B–C marks are used for so-called academic subjects and something like pass-fail for exploratory courses such as art, music, and physical education. Alexander and McEwin (1989) expressed disappointment that only 23 percent of their respondents made a distinction in the type of reporting used for academic and exploratory courses. Unfortunately, students, teachers, and parents may see this differentiation as clear evidence that exploratory subjects are less important than the others. Exploratory teachers obviously are not happy with that situation!

Despite these limitations, criterion-referenced evaluation may have a place for certain clearly specified learning objectives. In mastery learning (Bloom, 1976), the criteria are uniform for all students, but the amount of instruction is varied to enable each student to meet them. Students themselves may take part in setting the criteria, helping to ensure that they are within reach of all or nearly all the class. For example, a class may agree that each student should read five library books during a given grading period, but the length and difficulty of the books chosen would be worked out individually by the teacher and student.

Criterion-referenced evaluation is suggested in Glasser's *The Quality School* proposal (1990), in which the only grades listed would be As and Bs and there would be no record kept of how long it took the student to reach the B level. The mastery approach also appears to underlie some of the proposals to base evaluation on students' "portfolios" or "performances," an approach promoted by Sizer (1984) and the Coalition of Essential Schools. For example, Vermont's Commissioner of Education would have a statewide sample of students' writing portfolios evaluated by trained teacher assessors. These portfolios "would be calibrated against standards the profession shares and the public understands" (Mills, 1989). It will be interesting to see if either the profession or the public can even approach the consensus that Commissioner Mills seeks!

Of course, performance evaluation does not have to be based on arbitrary standards, but instead on individual students' ability or on their progress since a previous assessment. Portfolio or performance evaluation may be either criterion referenced, norm referenced, or individual referenced, depending on how standards are determined.

As an overall method of grading students at the middle level, most criterion-referenced approaches should be used with caution, because they typically make little allowance for the wide-ranging individual differences among students at this time of life.

### Norm-Referenced Marking

Although conventional marks usually represent a mix of various factors, by far the dominant factor is comparison of a student's performance with that of other students, usually those in the same class. Occasionally, teams or departments will base their grades on the performance of all the students in a team of perhaps 120 to 150 students, or even all the seventh-graders in a school. This practice increases the reliability of the grades, but requires time and a degree of staff coordination that are rare in most public schools. Hence, most teachers must determine their own grades based on the particular students they have at the time.

Experts in educational measurement have for years been recommending sound procedures for treating the data used to determine a grade (see, for example, Terwilliger [1971] and Gronlund [1974].) After 40 years of working with middle level teachers, I have concluded that few teachers use or are aware of these procedures. For example, since the 1960s, teachers have been admonished to convert test scores to stanines or standard scores before combining them, in order to minimize differences in the tests' variability. Moreover, different assignments should be weighted according to their importance before combining them at the end of a grading period (Glock & Millman, 1963).

Some teachers determine grades on the basis of total points earned during a grading period, with more important assignments or tests being allocated a larger number of points. Although this may handle the weighting problem, Madgic (1988) has pointed out that it may tempt the teacher to make distinctions with an unwarranted degree of precision. Just how different are point totals of 143 and 145 for six weeks of work, for example? Moreover, merely adding points makes no allowances for variability in student scores on a particular test, the problem that stanines or standard scores are designed to correct.

Even though percent grades are not widely used by themselves, many schools still set percent equivalents for A–B–C marks, usually based on some kind of normal curve. Since classroom groups are never large enough to warrant application of a normal curve, Terwilliger (1971) has stated flatly that "it is impossible to justify the practice of grading on the curve" (p. 78). Nottingham (1988) also criticized the use of percent equivalents for letter grades and recommended that teachers instead convert scores to grades based on how the scores cluster when arranged from high to low. Teacher judgment is the issue here, and arbitrary percent equivalents take away the teacher's authority to make those judgments.

In summary, despite the many years that norm-referenced grading has been the dominant pattern, mathematically sound ways of calculating grades are still not in widespread use. Moreover, there is danger that the advent of computer grading programs (Hively, 1984, 1986) will simply make it faster and easier for teachers to do what they should not be doing in the first place.

In other words, the main problem with norm-referenced grading is not the mathematical calculations but the fact that it is based on comparing one student with another. The Children's Defense Fund (1988) put it this way:

> The way students are evaluated in the middle grades can be particularly damaging for young adolescents, who have a keen need to establish their sense of identity. Students who received high marks in the middle-grades school, despite equal effort, because they are more likely to be graded on a curve rather than on their individual progress. (p. 7)

Consider also the evidence of teacher bias cited earlier and its potential for harming student self-concepts. The result is a strong case against the use of norm-referenced grading as the primary way of reporting student progress.

### Individual-Referenced Marking

Individual-referenced marking systems compare a student's achievement with some measure of his or her own ability or previous accomplishments, rather than with some arbitrary standard or group norm. How well a student is making use of potential is often referred to as an effort mark. It may be found on many report cards along with a conventional comparative mark. For example, Robinson and Craver (1989) found that effort was "not graded but noted separately" for grades 4 through 6 in 43.4 percent of the districts and 28.7 percent for grades 7 through 9. So-called dual marking systems, for example, may use ABCs to report norm-referenced achievement and numbers 1 to 3 to indicate effort. Thus, a grade of C/1 might mean average achievement as compared with the class but above-average effort, but an A/3 might mean top level achievement but a low level of effort. Epstein and Mac Iver (1990) cite the advantages of this approach:

> *Such a dual evaluation system may encourage a greater number of students to make the most of their opportunities to learn. Similarly, such a system may cut down on the number of students who lose confidence in their ability to master the subject matter and thus, over time, reduce the likelihood that students will drop out of school. (p. 8)*

Rupert Nock Middle School in Newburyport, Massachusetts, for years has used two different report forms in the four academic subjects. On the form labeled "Individual Achievement," the teacher checks the students' "progress in terms of his own ability" as excellent, good, fair, or unsatisfactory. The other form applies the same four descriptors to the student's "progress in comparison with his group" (Case, 1982).

Individual-referenced marking would appear to be tailor-made for the middle grades, where students vary so widely. It also would appear to have the greatest potential for motivating students. Yet few schools use this method exclusively, or even as the primary means of reporting student progress. In their 1988 survey, Robinson and Craver found that "progress toward learning objectives for individual students" was the standard applied in only 25.3 percent of the school districts in grades 4 through 6 and 18.6 percent in grades 7 through 9. Evaluating "relative to individual pupil ability" was even less common, being reported in only 7.6 percent of the districts in grades 4 through 6 and 6.0 percent in grades 7 through 9.

In large part, these small percentages are probably due to a widespread expectation that school marks will refelct class comparison, but there are other problems. How does one determine a student's potential? How much progress is it reasonable to expect of this student? Will not teacher bias confound both kinds of evaluation, even more than norm-referenced grading?

We have already seen evidence that a student's sex and attractiveness may influence a teacher's grade. Pringle (1980) verified that speech patterns also affect teachers' judgments of student potential. She asked teachers to estimate the academic potential of fifth-grade students on the basis of brief recorded samples of their speech. The student who spoke "Black English" was rated lowest, and the white male who spoke "Appalachian dialect" was rated lower than the white female who spoke standard English.

After carefully analyzing problems like these, Terwilliger (1971) rejected both individual growth and ability as a basis for evaluation. With respect to progress grading, he said, "Despite its intuitive appeal and apparent advantages, growth is a logically and technically unsound basis for assigning grades to students" (p. 51).

His case against grading on ability is based largely on the sorting function of grades:

*There is little logical support for the concept of achievement with respect to ability. The person who uses school grades as a basis for decisions is interested in what the student has achieved, not what he has achieved in relationship to the teacher's expectations for him. Once he is out of school, a student will be judged largely on his achievements, regardless of his reputed abilities. It is unfair to a student (and to those who must interpret his grades) when a teacher gives a high grade for over-achievement or a low grade for under-achievement. Separate teacher ratings of student work habits are much more desirable. (p. 71)*

Two classic studies by Baker and Doyle (1957, 1958) are often cited as evidence that a change from grading based on class comparison to one based on individual effort makes little difference in student achievement, either in grades 7 and 8 or later after they have gone on to high school. The authors report that, although the basis of determining grades was officially changed, there were few differences in teachers' evaluation and grading practices. Halliwell (1960) obtained similar results in a study of fourth- and sixth-graders.

On the other hand, Butterworth and Michael (1975) found significant differences between sixth-graders who received conventional marks and those who received individualized narrtive reports without symbols. Students receiving the individualized reports had higher reading scores, more positive attitudes toward school, and higher scores on a survey of Intellectual Achievement Responsibility. Moreover, low-ability children receiving the individualized reports indicated greater self-responsibility than their peers in the other group. Using two different kinds of marks also has its limitations. Halliwell and Robitaille (1963) examined marks received by sixth-graders under a system in which students received two marks, one based on achievement and the other on ability. The researchers reported that both marks were very similar, so that capable students were rewarded twice and the less capable were punished twice.

Beady and Slavin (1980) reported the results of three studies of the effects on middle grade students of a grading system based on individual progress. In one study, sixth-, seventh-, and eighth-graders in the experimental group gained significantly more in language arts achievement that control students who received percentage scores. In the second study involving seventh-grade mathematics classes, the students receiving recognition for individual progress did not score significantly better than those recognized for achievement compared with classmates. The third study of seventh- and eighth-grade mathematics classes also was inconclusive, but suggested the possibility of "race by treatment interaction effects." The authors suggest that this individualized approach to grading might have potential for increasing student motivation, especially for blacks in desegregated schools.

Vars (1976a) reported a nine-year experiment with a marking and reporting system based primarily on evaluation of achievement compared with estimated ability. Both teachers and students rated the student's achievement as: (1) working at or near capacity, (2) making moderate use of ability, or (3) working substantially below ability. Teachers also had the option of reporting class comparison (without the use of A–B–C marks) and also student performance compared with specified criteria. In addition, they held regular parent conferences and sent home frequent narrative reports. Parents, students, and teachers reported general satisfaction with the total system, and were even more satisfied when queried seven years after its initial installation.

In summary, individual-referenced marking systems, despite their potential for motivating students, have serious limitations when used as the sole means of reporting student progress. They are best used in conjunction with other systems. In any case, teachers will need help in distinguishing the different kinds of evaluation required in a multifaceted evaluation and reporting system. Symbols other than the conventional ABCs should be used for individual-referenced evaluation to avoid confusion with norm-referenced grades.

### Other Alternatives

Numerous other grading systems have been proposed from time to time. Powell (1981) has suggested an A–B–C Incomplete system for the middle grades, with promotion to high school contingent upon removal of all incompletes. Wiggins (1988) made several proposals, including a multilevel "sliding" grading system that incorporates in various proportions "mastery, effort, and progress." Another alternative, according to Wiggins, is to give all students the same assignments but set different expectation levels according to students' "need and ability levels."

Frierson (1975) proposed a variety of clever techniques to equalize a student's chances of earning a good grade, even in very heterogeneous classes. One proposal was for "handicap grading," using procedures adapted from bowling, golf, horseracing, and track and field competition. Other alternatives included "incentive grading," "inventory grading," "interactive grading," and "probability grading."

Saints Peter and Paul Middle School in St. Cloud, Minnesota, began using the following marking system in 1988:

C = Consistently performs at the level of expectation relative to ability
U = Usually performs at the level of expectation relative to ability
S = Seldom performs at the level of expectation relative to ability
N = Does not perform at the level of expectation relative to ability

In addition, teachers of classes that "include quantifiable information" record an "average raw percentage score" on the report card (M. A. Mullin, personal communication, October 12, 1988).

Even more unusual was the experiment conducted at Gulf Middle School in New Port Richey, Florida. At this school, students all started with As (100 points). Points were deducted for not completing assignments, not taking tests, being tardy, or being disruptive in class. There also were procedures for earning back lost points (Koop, 1988).

As innovative as these approaches may sound, they all must address the basic question proposed at the beginning of this section: What standards or bases of comparison should be used in determining student marks? This question, in turn, must be viewed within the context of a sound philosophy of middle level education.

### Summary

This review of research and informed opinion makes clear that no single standard is completely satisfactory in determining student marks. Instead, middle level schools should develop carefully orchestrated combinations of marking and reporting procedures, emphasizing individual progress but also indicating how a student's work compares with group norms and other appropriate criteria. Student self-evaluation, written comments, and parent-teacher conferences also have an important role to play, as we shall discuss later in this chapter.

- *Issue 2: What should be the role of the student in determining marks?*

Since one purpose of marks is to encourage student growth, it seems only reasonable that students have some input into the process. When they do this and then compare their evaluations with those of the teacher, students come to understand their strengths and weaknesses, an important part of developing an accurate self-concept. Teachers also benefit from knowing how students perceive their achievement, since self-concept of ability is an important component of student motivation that needs to be taken into account when planning instruction.

From the very beginning of the evaluation process, students should have input into the criteria used for determining marks. This ensures that the criteria are public and more apt to be understood by the students. They also are much more likely to work toward those goals if they have had some say in establishing them.

Students should be invited to evaluate their own progress from time to time, not just at report card time. Corrective feedback from the teacher can help students make mid-course corrections, and the student comments can help the teacher adjust the work of the class to make it more meaningful for the students.

Formal self-evaluation is especially desirable at the end of a grading period. Student self-evaluations should accompany the teacher's progress reports, and both should include explanatory comments. At the Kent State University Middle School (Vars, 1982), report forms had space for both teacher and student ratings of how well students were achieving with respect to their ability. Marked discrepancies between teacher and student ratings were discussed in individual conferences, which often turned out to be valuable for both teacher and student.

Research on student self-evaluation in the middle grades is sparse. Blade (1967) examined the relationships among achievement, expected grades, and actual grades with sixth-grade students. Pupils grade expectations were highly correlated with the grades actually received, especially for students in heterogeneous classes. This confirms observations of most teachers, who find that the grades students assign themselves usually match what the teacher has determined. Capable and highly conscientious students tend to underrate themselves, however, whereas students of lower ability and/or indifference to the process tend to overrate themselves. Accurate or not, the process of self-evaluation is a very important learning experience that should be available to all students.

- *Issue 3: How should nonacademic outcomes be reported?*

There is much more to education than academic achievement. From the earliest days, schools have reported students' deportment, citizenship, work habits, and the like. Report cards often have lists of these personal-social traits and behaviors, with a space for teachers to mark those that need improvement. For maximum benefit, students should also have the opportunity to evaluate themselves on these outcomes.

Instead of traits, a report card may carry standardized comments, such as "Completes work on time" or "Gets along well with others." Hevern and Geisinger (1983) identified 136 nonredundant comments on a sample of forms used in grades 4 through 6 in metropolitan New York City. Cluster analysis and ratings by psychololgists, teachers, and other educators were used to sort the comments into two categories: task orientation and interpersonal relationships. The researchers point out the "psychometric unreliability" inherent in such a large number of possible comments, plus the fact that few teachers have received any instruction in how to carry out this kind of assessment.

Even more unreliable and idosyncratic are the individual comments teachers may write on report cards. Rothe (1980) conducted a content analysis of 450 anecdotal comments written by elementary teachers in British Columbia. Categories ranged from "Praise," which a student might find it hard to live up to, all the way to "Challengers" (belittling comments), which would be likely to provoke an angry confrontation with parents. He also found "glosses," statements that sound positive but have little substantive content. On the other hand, teachers used four other types of comments that appeared to be "acceptable in social terms because they are substantive, yet allow parents to retain positive images of themselves and their children" (p. 21). He concluded by listing questions teachers should be aware of when writing individual comments, lest the substance of the comment be lost in the emotional reaction to the communication.

Although exceedingly time consuming and fraught with danger of misunderstanding, teacher comments help to personalize the report card, especially if all it carries otherwise is a single symbol or mark. Kingsley (1960) found that more than 75 percent of the parents of junior high students wanted comments on student effort and work habits. There seems little likelihood that parents today would want any less information.

With the advent of computer-generated progress reports, teachers can now choose from literally hundreds of standardized comments and save themselves the labor of writing them by hand. The list for one middle school in Ohio ranged from the highly positive, "Pleasure to have in class" to "Does not complete required work." How much more meaningful would be a note from the teacher indicating exactly what work was overdue. Fleming (1988) indicated that letters containing that kind of specific information are already within the capability of modern computers.

Schools also are linking computers with telephone answering machines to increase home-school communication (Bauch, 1989). When Carter Lawrence Middle School in Nashville, Tennessee, instituted such a system so that parents could call in and find out their child's homework assignments, the rate of student homework completion increased significantly (Bissell, 1989). Of the "frequent user" parents, 93 percent also noticed improvements in the attitudes and skills of their children.

Although Ebel (1974) asserted that conferences may provide less information for parents than a grade, most teachers and parents would disagree. Note that the proportion of middle schools using parent conferences rose from 42 percent in 1968 to 68 percent in 1988 in the study reported by Alexander and McEwin (1989). Robinson and Craver (1989) found similar high percentages in their 1988 survey: 79 percent in grades 4 through 6 and 58.7 percent in grades 7 through 9.

Georgiady and Romano (1982) call parent-teacher conferences "indispensable for the middle school" and offer valuable guidelines for carrying them out. They also say that students should be included in at least part of the conference. Over the years, numerous guides have been published to help teachers conduct effective conferences with parents (National School Public Relations Association, 1961; Stephens & Wolf, 1989). Although these typically are aimed at elementary school teachers, the general principles set forth apply at all levels.

Guidelines for parents also are available. For example, the National Committee for Citizens in Education (n.d.) distributes a folder that lists materials to review at home, questions to ask during the parent-teacher conference, conference followup, things to look for in an annual review of the child's confidential school records, and suggestions for further action and appeals. No longer can teachers expect parents merely to sit passively and accept without question anything the teacher says!

Scheduling parent conferences is complicated at the middle school level, where each student may have up to 8 or 10 different teachers. Interdisciplinary teams find that team conferences with parents and/or students are very effective but also time consuming. Such conferences seldom include the exploratory teachers, who also can benefit from and contribute to parent conferences. Some middle schools place major responsibility for parent conferencing in the hands of the homeroom teacher or student advisor. Before the conference, teachers communicate the student's progress to the advisor, who shares it with the parents. The other teachers also need to be on hand so that parents can follow up on specific problems identified in the overall conference.

Like the symbols placed on a report card, words used in checklists, comments, and conferences are subject to misinterpretation, but that does not eliminate the need for communication among all those concerned about the welfare of the student. Although those efforts may consume some of the teacher's precious time, the results in the long run justify the effort.

- *Issue 4: How frequently should student progress be reported?*

Whenever this issue comes up, debate often ensues between teachers and parents. Parents want their children's progress reported frequently, every week if possible. Teachers, on the other hand, do not want to spend all their time filling out progress reports, so they favor longer marking periods.

Another factor to consider is the school policy on interim reports, which are sent home during the middle of a marking period to alert parents about potential problems. Some schools send interim reports home for all students, in essence doubling the number of times a teacher must sum up a student's progress. Under a six-weeks' reporting cycle, this means calculating marks every three weeks. This is a real chore for teachers, especially specialists like physical education teachers, who may have as many as 200 different students. When formal reports are sent home every nine weeks, the burden is not quite so heavy.

Most schools send home full progress reports on either a six-week or a nine-week cycle. Robinson and Craver (1989) found that between 1977 and 1988 a number of districts changed their schedule from nine weeks to six weeks. For example, in grades 4 through 6, the percentage sending reports every six weeks rose from 18.3 to 26.7 percent, whereas those on a nine-week cycle dropped from 69.7 to 61.4 percent. In grades 7 through 9, the six-week cycle rose from 22.4 to 29.7 percent and the nine-week cycle dropped from 70.5 to 60.1 percent. No doubt the current stress on accountability has been a factor in this change.

One innovative middle school established the policy of sending home progress reports whenever the teacher considered it appropriate, as long as there was at least one report each nine weeks (Vars, 1982). The school was small and most parents kept in close touch with the school, so the irregular schedule did not create any noticeable inconvenience.

- *Issue 5: What format is best for student progress reports?*

Whenever schools undertake to change their reporting system, the results are most noticeable in the format. Here again, research is of little help, although Wrinkle (1947) and colleagues demonstrated long ago that all formats have their strengths and weaknesses.

Computer-printed report forms save much teacher time, but they inevitably appear cold and impersonal. Even if the teacher makes the same comment about 27 different students, it seems more personal to the parent if it is handwritten rather than machine-printed. Checklists of frequently used comments, such as "Needs to contribute more in class," are another way of saving time, but they too lack the personal touch.

Widespread availability of photocopy machines opens up a compromise. At Harmon Middle School in Aurora, Ohio, each department creates its own progress report form. At Shoreham-Wading River Middle School in New York state, each individual teacher has that freedom.

At the Kent State University Middle School (KSUMS) in Ohio, teachers were free to design their own progress reports as long as they incorporated the standard rating scale adopted by the entire faculty. Many included a brief description of what the class had accomplished since the last report. Two copies were made for each student, one to go home and the other for the office files. Teachers often left space for individual comments by both the teacher and the student, thus combining mass production of the forms with personal comments (Vars, 1982).

Student self-evaluation was an important part of this KSUMS system, both with respect to academic achievement and personal-social development. At report card time, students entered their names, the date, and the subject, topic, or skill being evaluated on both copies of the blank forms. They then checked the self-rating scales and wrote in any comments they wished to make. The teacher collected them, added his or her ratings and comments, filed on copy, and sent the other to the parents. Parents also were encouraged to write back their responses on a special form included with each envelope of student progress reports.

Whatever the format, a progress report should meet the following criteria, which are adapted from those set forth many years ago by Strang (1947):

1. Does the report emphasize the broad goals of education in a democratic society? In other words, does it go beyond academics, important as they are, to include citizenship skills, acceptance of responsibility, positive attitudes?
2. Does the report reflect an awareness of the unique characteristics and needs of the age group? For example, does it contribute to wholesome self-concept development and satisfactory peer relations?
3. Does the report make proper allowance for individual differences? For example, does it report how well the student is utilizing his or her ability, as well as how his or her achievement compares with others?
4. Is the report diagnostic? That is, does it indicate specifically what the student has done and what he or she can do to improve?
5. Does the report accentuate the positive? In other words, is the general tone positive and encouraging? Consider the tone of a checklist item or comment that says flatly: "Does not turn in homework." Much better would be this checklist item: "Turns in homework: ___ always ___ usually ___ seldom ___ never." Better yet would be a list of assignments with a checkmark indicating those completed and a comment on their quality.
6. Is there opportunity for personal comments, either on the form itself or through letters, checklists, or other communications included with the report? Are there regular provisions for parent-teacher and parent-teacher-student conferences?

7. Is the report easily understood by students and parents? Does it speak their language, or does it require a college degree to interpret?

8. Can the report be prepared without placing an undue burden on teachers? Although careful evaluation and reporting are important parts of the teacher's job, they should not take so much time as to detract substantially from other aspects of planning and teaching.

9. Do students have appropriate input into the evaluation and reporting process? Only in this way can students become genuine partners in the education enterprise.

10. Is the report designed to be used by students, teachers, and parents to promote student growth? All who have any relationship with the student need to downplay the traditional perception of reports as judgments and to emphasize their use as a means of guidance. The report should trigger a parent-child conference, not a beating or a cash payoff.

Developing a marking and reporting system tht meets these criteria is no easy task. We turn now to some suggestions for accomplishing this.

## Improving the Marking and Reporting System

Changing anything about an educational system is exceedingly difficult, and modifying the marking and reporting system is hardest of all, or so it seems. Students, teachers, parents, future employers, and general citizens usually view student marks as measures of success, not only of the individual student but of the entire school system. Moreover, there is tremendous ego involvement. Students and parents too often view school marks as evidence of personal worth. Teachers may be personally hurt when parents or students question their judgments of student progress, and administrators get upset when their school or school system is criticized because student grade point averages are too low. The "Lake Woebegon effect" applies here with a vengeance: All students are expected to be above average!

Over the years, numerous authors have suggested steps to take in improving a marking and reporting system (Association for Supervision and Curriculum Development, 1956; Bellanca, 1977; Kirschenbaum, Simon, & Napier, 1971; Miles, 1977; Kozuch, 1979; Simon & Bellanca, 1976; Strang, 1947, 1955; Vars, 1982). Kozuch (1979), in particular, emphasizes that marking and reporting are part of a complex social system, and therefore any change will necessarily affect nearly all other parts of the system.

In brief, here are five guidelines for improving a marking and reporting system to make it more appropriate for middle level students in a democratic society:

1. Involve all interested parties in the improvement project: teachers, administrators, parents, students, and representatives of the larger community. Involvement means having some appropriate and meaningful input, not just listening to what the professional staff plans to do or, the opposite extreme, exercising veto power over the outcome of a genuine cooperative effort.

2. Begin by making a thorough study of the characteristics and needs of middle level youngsters. The primary justification for a special kind of education at the middle level rests on the fact that young people between the ages of 10 and 15 are going through tremendous changes, physically, intellectually, socially, and emotionally. These, in turn, cause certain personal-social needs or developmental tasks to become especially acute during these years. The entire middle level education program, including the marking and reporting system, should help students to make this crucial transition with as little trauma as possible, while not neglecting the acquisition of the basic skills and knowledge deemed essential for their successful functioning in contemporary society.

3. Evaluate the current marking and reporting system to determine how appropriate it is for middle level students. In all likelihood, this analysis will identify at least some aspects of the system that need improvement. In many cases, a drastic overhaul will be warranted.

4. Develop a strategy for change, depending on the amount of change proposed and the readiness of the entire school and community to accept the change. Curriculum development experts disagree on whether it is best to introduce change gradually, in small increments, or to change everything at once. Too fast or drastic a change may provoke backlash and resentment that will take years to overcome—the so-called burnt-over-territory effect.

On the other hand, changes introduced too gradually may lose their momentum. School leaders move around a good bit, too, so key people may leave the school system before the new procedures are fully implemented. Any change must be fully implemented before any valid judgment can be made of its effects.

School systems making a transition from the junior high to the middle school organization, for example, might make a new marking and reporting system part of the package. Indeed, it may be that unless the marking and reporting system is changed, none of the other reforms can be fully effective. This requires a lot of change in a short period of time, but it usually is best to take advantage of the state of flux in a district reorganization to put into place the most ideal system the planning group can envision, even if they must back off a bit in future years.

On the other hand, where resistance to change is strong or there is no major upheaval that loosens up the system, some changes can be phased in gradually. Progress reports using conventional comparative marks can be supplemented with checklists, narrative reports, and conferences, all designed to communicate in a more individualized manner. As teachers, students, and parents get used to these approaches, the traditional marks can be deemphasized, perhaps by moving them to the bottom of the report form and placing individualized ratings or comments at the top. "Phase in the better and phase out the less appropriate" is the advice of those who favor the gradual approach.

5. Whatever strategy is chosen, be prepared for the long haul. Changes in something as important as marking and reporting take a long time to become established, so the planning group and administration must persist in the face of the inevitable questions and objections. Both Kozuck (1979) and Halliwell (1960) have documented the fact that just announcing a policy change does not necessarily change the way teachers actually operate. Continual staff development and input are essential to establish, maintain, and improve the new system.

Only after new policies and procedures have been in place for several years is it appropriate to conduct a full-scale evaluation to determine whether the new system is better for young people than the old. No doubt that evaluation will reveal additional ways that the system can be improved, so the entire self-renewal process starts all over again. Improving education is a never-ending task.

## Conclusion

This review of research and informed opinion on marking and reporting has culminated in 10 criteria for a developmentally appropriate marking and reporting system and 5 guidelines for revising and improving the system. It remains here only to reiterate the paucity of research on nearly all aspects of this important topic. Natriello (1987) has cited the need for research that focuses on group effects, not just the effects of marking systems on individual students. Also needed, he says, are studies of the multiple effects on students of all the teachers a student encounters during the day. In other words, research on marking and reporting procedures should look at the institutional context in which marking and reporting take place, as Kozuch (1979) has pointed out.

The broader social context of U.S. society also must be considered. The bibliography reveals a burst of writing and research on this topic in the late 1970s, but things have been relatively quiet ever since. One wonders why. On the other hand, the rationale behind the various approaches to marking have changed only slightly over the years, so that the 1982 article in the *Encyclopedia of Educational Research* (Geisinger, 1982) adds little to what Thorndike said in 1969 or Smith and Dobbin in 1960. The National Education Association's Research Summary entitled *Marking and Reporting Pupil*

*Progress* (1970) might even pass for a 1990s document with little chance of detection.

It is almost as if the "back to basics" and accountability movement of the 1980s wiped out all memory of the reform efforts of earlier years. When leaders of the Progressive Education Association designed the classic Eight Year Study of the 1930s and 40s, they wisely built in careful plans for evaluating the results (Smith & Tyler, 1942). Many efforts to reform and humanize student marking and reporting systems grew out of the child-centered emphasis of that era of progressive education. The renewed attack on conventional marking systems that took place in the 1960s and 70s apparently sprang from the ferment generated by those characterized as the "compassionate critics" by Van Til (1970). Their student-centered approach to marking and reporting is best exemplified by three works published in the late 1970s (Simon & Bellanca, 1976).

What will the 1990s bring? Where are the reformers who will once again seek to develop marking and reporting systems that are both compassionate and reasonably objective, that will motivate without leading to false illusions, that will communicate clearly yet not swamp teachers with an overwhelming amount of paperwork? Above all, where are the leaders who will engage teachers, students, parents, and others in the difficult task of implementing improved marking and reporting systems and keeping them in place long enough to prove their worth? The task is huge but the rewards for students are great. Let us hope that middle level educators will rise to the challenge.

## References

Alexander, W. M., & McEwin, C. K. (1989). *Schools in the middle: Status and progress.* Columbus, OH: National Middle School Association.

Association for Supervision and Curriculum Development. (1956). *Reporting is communicating: An approach to evaluation and marking.* Washington, DC: Author.

Bachman, J. G., & O'Malley, P. M. (1986). Self-concepts, self-esteem, and educational experiences. The frog pond revisited (again). *Journal of Personality and Social Psychology, 50*(1), 35–46.

Baker, R. L., & Doyle, R. (1957). A change in marking procedures and scholastic achievement. *Educational Administration and Supervision, 43*(4), 223–232.

Baker, R. L., & Doyle, R. (1958). Elementary school marking practices and subsequent high school achievement. *Educational Administration and Supervision, 44*(3), 158–166.

Bauch, J. P. (1989). The Trans*Parent* school model: New technology for parent involvement. *Educational Leadership, 47*(2), 32–54.

Beady, C., & Slavin, R. (1980). Making success available to all students in desegregated schools. *Integrated Education, 18*(5–6), 28–31.

Beane, J. A., & Lipka, R. P. (1986). *Self-concept, self-esteem, and the curriculum.* New York: Teachers College Press.

Beane, J. A., & Lipka, R. P. (1987). *When kids come first: Enhancing self-esteem.* Columbus, OH: National Middle School Association.

Bellanca, J. A. (1977). *Grading.* Washington, DC: National Education Association.

Bissell, P. (1989). A study of the effects of a home/school communication model on improving parent involvement. (Doctoral dissertation, George Peabody College for Teachers, Vanderbilt University.) *Dissertation Abstracts International, 50,* 2869A.

Blade, G. A. (1967, Summer). An exploration of the relationships between grading practices of teachers, grades received by pupils, and pupils' levels of expectancy. In *Report of the Northern Illinois University Junior High School Workshop.* DeKalb: Northern Illinois University.

Bloom, B. S. (1976). *Human characteristics and school learning.* New York: McGraw-Hill.

Butterworth, T. W., & Michael, W. B. (1975). The relationship of reading achievement, school attitude, and self-responsibility behaviors of sixth-grade pupils to comparative and individualized reporting systems: Implications for improvement of validity of the evaluation of pupil progress. *Educational and Psychological Measurement, 35*(4), 987–991.

Canady, R. L., & Hotchkiss, P. R. (1989). It's a good score! Just a bad grade. *Phi Delta Kappan, 71*(1), 68–71.

Carter, R. S. (1952). How invalid are marks assigned by teachers? *Journal of Educational Psychology, 43*(4), 218–228.

Case, E. (1982). Reporting pupil progress. *New England League of Middle Schools Journal,* 113–120.

Children's Defense Fund. (1988). *Making the middle grades work.* Washington, DC: Author.

Curwin, R. (1978). The grades of wrath: Some alternatives. *Learning, 6*(6), 60–64.

Dyer, D. (1989). The report card system is a menace. *The Cleveland Plain Dealer.*

Ebel, R. L. (1974). Shall we get rid of grades? *Measurement in Education, 5*(4), 1–5.

Engelberg, R. A. (1989). The student perspective on grades (Doctoral dissertation, University of Washington, 1988). *Dissertation Abstracts International, 50:* 63A.

Epstein, J. L. (1990). What matters in the middle grdes—Grade span, or practices? *Phi Delta Kappan, 71*(6), 438–444.

Epstein, J. L., & Mac Iver, D. J. (1990). *Responsive education in the middle grades: Teacher teams, advisory groups, remedial instruction, school transition programs, and report card entities.* Report No. 46. Baltimore, MD: Center for Research on Elementary and Middle Schools, Johns Hopkins University.

Evans, E. D., & Engelberg, R. A. (1988). Student perceptions of school grading. *Journal of Reading and Development in Education, 21*(2), 45–54.

Evans, F. B. (1976). What research says about grading. In S. B. Simon & J. S. Bellanca (Eds.), *Degrading the grading myths: A primer of alternatives to grades and marks* (pp. 30–50). Washington, DC: Association for Supervision and Curriculum Development.

Fleming, D. J. (1988). Report card follow-up: Going beyond the facts. *NASSP Bulletin, 72*(507), 50–52.

Frierson, E. C. (1975). *Grading without judgment: A classroom guide to grades and individual evaluation.* Nashville, TN: EDCOA Publications.

Geisinger, K. F. (1982). Marking systems. In H. E. Mitzel (Ed.), *Encyclopedia of educational research* (5th ed.) (pp. 1139–1149). New York: Macmillan.

Georgiady, N. P., & Romano, L. G. (1982). Parent teacher conferences: Indispensable for the middle school. *Middle School Journal, 14*(1), 7, 30–31.

Glasser, W. (1990). *The quality school: Managing students without coercion.* New York: Harper and Row.

Glock, M. D., & Millman, J. (1963). *The assignment of school marks.* Cornell Miscellaneous Publication No. 44. Ithaca, NY: New York State College of Agriculture, Cornell University.

Gronlund, N. E. (1974). *Improving marking and reporting in classroom instruction.* New York: Macmillan.

Hadley, S. T. (1954). School mark—fact or fancy. *Educational Administration and Supervision, 40*(5), 305–312.

Halliwell, J. W. (1960). The relationship of certain factors to marking practices in individualized reporting programs. *Journal of Educational Research, 54*(2), 76–78.

Halliwell, J. W., & Robitaille, J. P. (1963). The relationship between theory and practice in a dual reporting program. *Journal of Educational Research, 57*(3), 137–141.

Hevern, V. W., & Geisinger, K. F. (1983). *An initial classification of non-cognitive student behavior grading items.* Paper presented at the 91st Annual Convention of the American Psychological Association at Anaheim, CA, August, 1985. (ERIC Document Reproduction Service No. ED 241 166).

Hiner, N. R. (1973). An American ritual: Grading as a function. *Clearing House, 47*(6), 356–361.

Hively, W. (1984). Putting the computer to work. *Electronic Education, 3*(7), 42, 54.

Hively, W. (1986). Grade book programs pass the test. *Electronic Education, 5*(8), 18–19.

Hughes, C. S. (1971). Self-esteem and achievement as related to elementary school reporting instruments. (Doctoral dissertation, Kent State University, 1971). *Dissertation Abstracts International, 32:* 5106A.

Hull, R. (1980). Fairness in grading: Perceptions of junior high school students. *Clearing House, 53*(7), 340–343.

Johnson, M., Jr. (1961). Solving the mess in marks. *New York State Education, 49*(2), 12–13, 30.

Johnson, M., Jr. (1962). Solving the mess in marks. *Education Digest, 27*(6), 12–14.

Kingsley, H. H. (1960). Communication between the school and home: A study of teacher-pupil-parent reaction to a variety of reporting procedures and technique. (Doctoral dissertation, Boston University.) *Dissertation Abstracts International, 20:* 3152–3153.

Kirschenbaum, H., Simon, S. B., & Napier, R. W. (1971). *Wad-ja-get? The grading game in American education.* New York: Hart.

Koop, R. E. (1988). *Unearning grades: An affective approach to grading.* Paper presented at the meeting of the National Middle School Association, Denver, CO.

Kozuch, J. A. (1979). Implementing an educational innovation: The constraints of the school setting. *High School Journal, 62*(5), 223–231.

Kunder, L. H., & Porwall, P. J. (1977). *Reporting pupil progress: Policies, procedures, and systems.* Arlington, VA: Educational Research Service.

Leese, J. (1961). The mess in marks. *New York State Education, 48*(8), 9–11.

Lewis, W. A., Dexter, H. G., & Smith, W. C. (1978). Grading procedures and test validation: A proposed new approach. *Journal of Educational Measurement, 15*(3), 219–227.

Madgic, R. F. (1988). The point system of grading: A critical appraisal. *NASSP Bulletin, 72*(507), 29–30, 32–34.

Matlin, A. H., & Mendelsohn, F. A. (1965). The relationship of personality and achievement variables in the elementary school. *Journal of Educational Research, 58*(10), 457–459.

Miles, W. R. (1977). *Simformation 5: Reporting student progress.* Madison, WI: Reearch and Development Center for Cognitive Learning, University of Wisconsin.

Mills, R. P. (1989). Portfolios capture rich array of student performance. *The School Administrator, 46*(11), 8–11.

National Committee for Citizens in Education. (n.d.). *Annual education check-up.* (Available from The Committee, 410 Wilde Lake Village Green, Columbia, MD 21044.)

National Education Association. (1970). *Marking and reporting pupil progress.* Research Summary 1970-S 1. Washington, DC: Author.

National School Public Relations Association. (1961). *Conference time for teachers and parents: A teacher's guide to successful conference reporting.* Washington, DC: National Education Association.

Natriello, G. (1987). The impact of evaluation processes on students. *Educational Psychologist, 22*(2), 155–175.

Nottingham, M. (1988). Grading practices—Watching out for land mines. *NASSP Bulletin, 72*(507), 24–28.

Powell, W. (1981). Middle schools without failure. *Clearing House, 55*(1), 5–8.

Pressey, S. L. (1925). Fundamental misconceptions involved in curent marking systems. *School and Society, 21*(547), 736–738.

Pringle, C. A. (1980). The effects of teachers' attitudes toward dialects on their expectations for students' academic competence. (Doctoral dissertation, Kent State University, 1980.) *Dissertation Abstracts International, 41,* 3927A.

Robinson, G. E., & Craver, J. M. (1989). *Assessing and grading student achievement.* Arlington, VA: Educational Research Service.

Roelfs, R. M. (1955). Trends in junior high school progress reporting. *Journal of Educational Research, 49*(4), 241–249.

Rothe, J. P. (1980). *Teacher evaluation comments within program evaluation: An analysis of negotiation structures.* Paper presented at the Annual Meeting of the Evaluation Network, Memphis, TN. (ERIC Document Reproduction Service No. ED 194 586).

Rubinstein, R. E. (1989). Building an atmosphere for success in a middle school. *Phi Delta Kappan, 71*(4), 328–329.

Russell, I. L., & Thalman, W. A. (1955). Personality: Does it influence teachers' marks? *Journal of Educational Research, 48*(8), 561–564.

Salvia, J. (1977). Attractiveness and school achievement. *Journal of School Psychology, 15*(1), 60–67.

Saville, A. (1983). Ability grouping and grading systems—What are the alternatives? *NASSP Bulletin, 67*(467), 80–82.

Schwartzapfel, H. B. (1981). Adaptation level as an explanation for differentiated standards in junior high school grading (Doctoral dissertation, St. John's University). *Dissertation Abstracts International, 42:* 948–949A.

Simon, S. B., & Bellanca, J. A. (Eds.) (1976). *Degrading the grading myths: A primer of alternatives to grades and marks.* Washington, DC: Association for Supervision and Curriculum Development.

Sizer, T. R. (1984). *Horace's compromise: The dilemma of the American high school.* Boston: Houghton Mifflin.

Smith, A. Z., & Dobbin, J. E. (1960). Marks and marking systems. In C. W Harris (Ed.), *Encyclopedia of educational research* (32rd ed.) New York: Macmillan.

Smith, E. R., & Tyler, R. W. (1942). *Appraising and recording student progress.* New York: Harper.

Starch, D., & Elliott, E. C. (1912). Reliability of the grading of high school work in English. *School Review, 20*(7), 442–457.

Starch, D., & Elliott, E. C. (1913a). Reliability of grading work in mathematics. *School Review, 21*(4), 254–295.

Starch, D., & Elliott, E. C. (1913b). Reliability of grading work in history. *School Review, 21*(10), 676–681.

Stephens, T. M., & Wolf, J. S. (1989). *Effective skills in parent/teacher conferencing* (2nd ed.). Columbus, OH: School Study Council of Ohio, College of Education, Ohio State University.

Strang, R. (1947). *Reporting to parents.* Practical Suggestions for Teaching No. 10. New York: Bureau of Publications, Teachers College, Columbia University.

Strang, R. (1955). *How to report pupil progress.* Chicago, IL: Science Research Associates.

Terwilliger, J. S. (1971). *Assigning grades to students.* Glenview, IL: Scott, Foresman.

Thorndike, R. L. (1969). Marks and marking system,. In R. L. Ebel (Ed.), *Encyclopedia of Educational Research* (4th ed.). New York: Macmillan.

Van Till, W. (1970). The compassionate critics. *Contemporary Education, 42*(2), 94–96.

Vars, G. F. (1976a). Student evaluation in the middle school: A second report, *Clearing House, 49*(6), 244–245.

Vars, G. F. (1976b). Evaluating and reporting pupil progress in the middle school. *Transescence, 4,* 9–13.

Vars, G. F. (1982). *Evaluating and reporting student progress in the middle school: A case study and teachers' manual.* Kent, OH: Cricket Press.

Vars, G. F. (1983). Missiles, marks, and the middle level student. *NASSP Bulletin, 67*(463), 72–77.

Wiggins, G. (1988). Rational numbers: Toward grading and scoring that help rather than harm learning. *American Educator, 12*(4), 20–25, 45–47.

Wright, G. S., & Greer, E. S. (1963). *The junior high school: A survey of grades 7-8-9 in junior and junior-senior high schools, 1959-60.* (U.S. Office of Education Bulletin 1963, No. 32.) Washington, DC: U.S. Government Printing Office.

Wrinkle, W. L. (1947). *Improving marking and reporting practices in elementary and secondary schools.* New York: Holt, Rinehart and Winston.

Yarborough, B. H., & Johnson, R. A. (1980). Research that questions the traditional elementary school marking system. *Phi Delta Kappan, 61*(8), 527–528.

Yauch, W. A. (1961, May). What research says about school marks and their reporting. *N.E.A. Journal, 50*(5), 50, 58.

# PART FOUR

# Developing a Support System for Continued Improvement

A Delphi Study conducted by the National Middle School Association (Jenkins & Jenkins, 1991) revealed that achieving legitimacy for the middle school was the leading issue among its members. These educators considered it imperative for the middle level to be recognized as a level distinct from elementary and high school. As a distinct level, unique staff preparation and a solid research base are required.

For many years, C. Kenneth McEwin, author of Chapter Nineteen, has studied middle level teacher education and certification. He reports that although only a small minority of middle school teachers have had specific preparation for teaching at this level, great strides have been made over the last decade to further a separate certification for the middle level. Most middle level educators believe that if the school specifically designed for young adolescents is to endure, then teachers and administrators must be specially prepared to work in it. Part of the preparation of middle level educators is understanding why certain practices are best for young adolescents.

Cross (1990) emphasized the importance of research in supporting quality middle schools. He stated that "research must lead to results—significant gains in learning . . . [and] the education research community must lead the charge on restructuring" (p. 21). Clearly, the nature of schooling in our nation must change if it is to meet the needs of youth and society. Research may be the key to providing an adequate direction for change. Middle level education, over the years, has suffered from a paucity of quality research. Now is the time to conduct, facilitate, and disseminate research on topics vital to the education of young adolescents.

367

David Strahan, former Chair of the Research Committee of the National Middle School Association, traces the history of middle level research in Chapter Twenty. He relates middle level research to the rest of the field of education, describes the current status of research at the middle level, and sets forth guidelines on how investigators can improve research efforts at the middle level. Without a substantial research base, claims for the legitimacy of middle level education are bound to fall on deaf ears.

Middle level educators have accomplished much in the move to provide schools that are more responsive to the needs of young adolescents. Much work remains, however, in two areas that will support continued improvement for middle level schools: providing a separation preparation and certification for educators at the middle level and pursuing a research agenda that lays the foundation for practice in middle level schools. The issue of legitimacy lies at the heart of both preparation and research. Until the education community accepts the middle level as a distinct level of education, providing adequate preparation of educators and a credible research base will be difficult.

## References

Cross, C. (1990). National goals: Four priorities for educational researchers. Educational Researcher, 19(8), 21–24.

Jenkins, D., & Jenkins, K. (1991). The NMSA Delphi report. Middle School Journal, 22(4), 23–36.

# CHAPTER NINETEEN

# Middle Level Teacher Preparation and Certification

## C. KENNETH McEWIN
*Appalachian State University*

A perennial roadblock to excellence in middle level education is the practice of staffing middle level schools with teachers and other professional personnel who have no special preparation for teaching or working in other ways with young adolescents. Teacher preparation institutions, state departments of education, and the profession itself have largely failed to recognize the importance of designing specific preparation programs for middle level teachers and other professionals who are responsible for the education and welfare of these youth. As a result, many of today's middle level teachers are simply unprepared for the challenging task of understanding, coping with, and effectively educating young adolescents.

The realization of the importance of specially designed middle level teacher education programs is not a recent phenomenon. Calls for the establishment of these programs have been found in the literature for over 50 years (Carnegie, 1989; Floyd, 1932; George & McEwin, 1978). Yet, teacher preparation institutions have been reluctant to establish these programs and certification agencies have permitted teachers with a great variety of preparations to teach at the middle level. This long-standing practice has created, or at least perpetuated, one of the most serious problems in middle level education—that of making middle level schools miniature versions of senior high schools or glorified extensions of elementary schools. This situation persists today, despite overwhelming evidence that neither model fits (McEwin, 1990a).

One unfortunate result of this situation is that many middle level teachers do not put forth serious efforts to become master middle level teachers. Although there are many dedicated middle level teachers, some are waiting to be "promoted" to the senior high school or assigned to elementary classrooms to teach younger children. The often prevailing attitude of "no specialized preparation needed" causes many middle level teachers largely to ignore opportunities to improve their skills and acquire knowledge focused directly on the middle level. Furthermore, those who seek specialized middle level preparation often find it unavailable at institutions of higher education. This dilemma will remain a major one until specialized teacher preparation programs are widely available and required for those teaching young adolescents. This chapter provides an exploration of the major trends and issues surrounding middle level teacher preparation and certification.

## An Historical Perspective of Middle Level Teacher Preparation

Calls for specialized middle level teacher preparation programs remained largely unheeded during the junior high school movement. Koos stated in 1927,

> Professional colleges are sympathetic with the junior high school movement, but are more disposed to emphasize the training of administrators and other leaders in the field than the training of junior high school teachers. They also stress the training of secondary-school teachers, but the tradition is for these trainees to look forward to work in senior and four-year high schools rather than in junior high schools. (p. 454)

This statement, although over 50 years old, remains valid and descriptive of the situation as it currently exists in many states.

Pedagogical considerations were a part of the rationale for the establishment of junior high schools at the turn of the century (See Chapter One.) However, these schools were primarily established as administrative reorganizations of the secondary school. It is generally accepted that the true educational and curricular rationale for the establishment of separate junior high schools did not develop until the 1920s (Gruhn & Douglas, 1947; Toepfer, 1982; Van Til, Vars, & Lounsbury, 1967). This legacy is one that is difficult to overcome and continues to contribute to the popular practice of employing large numbers of secondary prepared teachers in middle level schools. It has also caused, at least to some extent, the relegation of the middle level of schooling to a secondhand status and the view of it simply as a place to "get students ready" for the senior high school. Preparation for being successful at the senior high school is one function of middle level education, but it should not override other important purposes and functions (McEwin, 1984).

Another problem that was apparent in the early days of the junior high school movement was the low prestige given to teaching at the "junior" school. Junior high school teachers were allowed to teach with lower levels of preparation than were those at the "senior" high school and were paid lower salaries than their senior high school colleagues. Although salary parity has been accomplished in more recent years, a lack of prestige continues to be associated with middle grades teaching.

Additional factors have contributed to the lack of widespread development of specialized middle level preparation programs, past and present. They include: (1) the popular tradition regarding the appeal of teaching young children; (2) an interest among many in teaching a single subject area "in-depth"; (3) a general lack of understanding concerning the goals and functions of middle level schooling; (4) ignorance about the nature and needs of young adolescents, which at times borders on fear and dislike; (5) a low confidence level in the ability to teach this age group effectively; and (6) the absence of middle level teacher certification to encourage and require the development of specialized teacher preparation programs (Eccles & Midgley, 1990; Howard & Stoumbis, 1970).

In summary, employment and assignment practices in junior high schools and the dearth of specialized middle level teacher preparation programs and teacher certification practices indicate that a widespread commitment to excellence at the middle level did not exist during the junior high school movement. The residue of many of the actions and "in-actions" that occurred during the first decades of junior high school movement remain with us in contemporary times. Barriers established by tradition are extremely difficult to overcome in education. Those associated with teacher preparation are certainly no exception.

## Contemporary Middle Level Teacher Preparation

Renewed interest in the special preparation of middle level teachers has once again surfaced, with significant progress being made in some states. A major reason for this new interest is a dramatic growth in the number of middle schools and a corresponding decline in the number of junior high schools. For example, in the 1989–1990 school year there were 6,451 grades 5 or 6 through 8 middle schools and only 1,680 grades 7 through 9 junior high schools. By comparison, there were 6,606 junior high schools in 1964 (Van

Til, Vars, & Lounsbury, 1967) and only a few hundred 5 or 6 through 8 middle schools.

This encouraging growth in the number of middle level schools, especially grades 6 through 8 middle schools, has not been paralleled by a corresponding increase in middle level teacher preparation programs. A national study of 670 middle level schools found that 61 percent of all responding schools reported that less than 25 percent of teachers at those schools had special preparation for teaching at the middle level (Alexander & McEwin, 1989). An earlier survey of over 1,400 middle level principals revealed that 41 percent of respondents reported having *no* teachers with special preparation in their schools (Valentine, Clark, Nickerson, & Keefe, 1981).

It seems logical that this clear lack of teachers specifically prepared to teach young adolescents would result in such programs being widely available at teacher preparation institutions. However, this is not the case. A study of programs of 504 teacher preparation institutions found that only 168, or 33 percent, had any type of special preparation program for middle level teachers (Alexander & McEwin, 1988). The results of these surveys provide little encouragement when compared with those conducted earlier. For example, Krinsky and Pumerantz (1972) conducted a survey in 1970 and found 23 percent of accredited teacher preparation institutions responding had specialized middle level preparation programs. Clearly, middle level teacher preparation programs have not kept pace with the demand for specially prepared middle level teachers.

## Middle Level Teacher Certification

A major reason for this lack of specially prepared middle level teachers is directly related to the absence of mandatory middle level teacher certification/licensing in the majority of states. As long as distinctive certification does not exist, middle level classrooms will continue to be staffed primarily with teachers who have no special preparation for their task and, in many cases, do not even prefer to be teaching at the middle level. The practice of allowing almost anyone with any kind of professional certification to teach at the middle level has perpetuated the mediocrity evident in all too many middle level classrooms.

Representatives from teacher preparation institutions without specialized middle level teacher preparation programs quite often state that their institution does not plan to institute specialized middle level teacher preparation programs until special middle level teacher certification exists. Conversely, representatives from many state departments of education state that no specialized teacher certification/license plan will be adopted until specialized middle level teacher programs are established. This dilemma must be overcome through the combined efforts of teacher preparation institutions, state certification agencies, and the teaching profession itself. Otherwise, there may be several more decades of inaction and avoidance behavior regarding this matter. *Certification does have a direct effect on the establishment of middle level teacher preparation programs.* For example, in 1987, 83 percent of all specialized middle level teacher preparation programs were located in states with specific middle level teacher certification or endorsement plans.

State certification agencies that fail to initiate special certification for middle level teachers are neglecting their obligation to protect the public welfare when they allow teachers who have completed no specialized preparation to teach young adolesents. A key function of certification in education is the protection of the public from incompetence. Secondary certified and prepared teachers are not allowed to teach elementary children in the vast majority of states, and elementary prepared teachers are seldom, if ever, allowed to teach senior high school students. In the majority of states, however, young adolescents have been offered no such assurance that the teachers who teach them are specially prepared to do so.

There is some room for encouragement when certification patterns are considered. A 1990 survey conducted by McEwin (1990b) reported that 28 states had established some form of middle level teacher license/certification or endorsement. This compares with 2 states having special certification plans in 1968, 15 in 1978, and 25 in 1982 (Gillan, 1978; McEwin & Allen, 1983; Pumerantz, 1969). When results from middle level teacher certification studies conducted in 1987 and 1990 are compared, an identical number of states reported having a special certification/license for middle level teachers. In the intervening three years, however, five states discontinued middle level certification programs and five states established them (Alexander & McEwin, 1988). These data reflect the relative instability surrounding the middle level certification issue.

The most popular grade spans for states having special middle level teacher certification in 1990 are shown in Table 19-1. The 5 through 8 grade span is the most popular, representing 32 percent of all plans, with grades 5 through 9 being second most popular with 29 percent. The majority of states with specialized middle level teacher certification (51 percent) include grades 5 through 8 or 9. This grade span is likely the most popular because it includes the grades most frequently found in the vast majority of the nation's separately organized middle level schools.

A common problem among states that have discontinued middle level teacher certification plans is that of overlapping certification patterns. When the certification levels in a state are grades K through 8, 5 through 9, 7 through 12, for example, there is little chance that sufficient numbers of prospective teachers will select programs leading to grades 5 through 9 certification. By selecting the K-8 plan, they can be licensed to teach in the elementary *and*

**TABLE 19–1 • *Patterns of Middle Level Teacher Certification***

| Patterns | Frequency of Use | Percent |
|---|---|---|
| 4–8 | 5 | 18 |
| 4–9 | 2 | 7 |
| 5–8 | 9 | 32 |
| 5–9 | 8 | 29 |
| 6–9 | 1 | 3 |
| 7–8 | 2 | 8 |
| Other* | 1 | 3 |

*Depends on individual school organization

middle grades, including those middle grades most often found in middle schools. The problem with this decision is that programs that lead to K–8 certification are ones that traditionally focus almost exclusively on teaching young children. The grades 7 through 12 secondary certification is perhaps the greatest roadblock to the universal adoption of the specialized certification and preparation of middle level teachers. As long as teachers prepared to teach at the senior high school are permitted to teach at the middle level, many middle schools will continue to operate as pale reflections of senior high schools.

Overlapping certification plans, which include a specialized middle level certification or endorsement, open the door of opportunity for the establishment of specialized middle level teacher preparation programs. They stop short, however, of requiring these sorely needed programs. Perhaps only when the school districts that employ teachers demand that teacher preparation institutions establish middle level teacher preparation programs will they become a reality. The middle level teacher preparation programs that have been established in states with mandatory middle level teacher certification are popular with prospective teachers and their employers. Middle level administrators who no longer have to employ teachers who are prepared to teach different developmental age groups at levels other than the middle are very supportive of such programs.

The only apparent way to assure that quality middle level preparation programs are established is adoption of mandatory middle level teacher certification plans that have little or no overlap with those of the elementary and/or secondary grades. For example, North Carolina's plan is K–6, 6–9 subject specific, 9–12 subject specific. (Areas such as music, physical education, and home economics are K–12.) This certification plan has led to the almost universal establishment of middle level teacher preparation programs at both private and public institutions. Prospective teachers in the state must decide which of the three levels of education they prefer as a career goal and prepare themselves specifically for that level. This, along with other important occurrences, has led to middle level education being recognized as a respected third level of education in North Carolina.

In summary, middle level teacher certification and teacher preparation programs are very closely related. Prospective and in-service teachers are unlikely to prepare for careers for which there is no license to practice. Altruism alone will not bring the majority of middle level teachers back to teacher preparation institutions, or to other sources, to refine their skills and increase their knowledge about teaching more effectively at the middle level. Sound certification requirements should reflect strong middle level teacher preparation programs.

## Essential Components of Middle Level Preparation Programs

A clear consensus exists regarding the essential components of middle level teacher education programs, and current programs largely reflect this consensus (Alexander & McEwin, 1988; George & McEwin, 1978). Middle level principals (Valentine et al., 1981) middle level teachers (Boyer, 1983; DeMedio & Kish, 1983) and middle level professors (DeMedio & Helms, 1984) agree that these components are desirable and essential. The problem with middle level teacher preparation programs lies not in their poor design but rather in their scarcity and low enrollments. Elements considered essential for middle level teacher preparation programs include: (1) a thorough knowledge of the nature and needs of early adolescents; (2) a study of middle level curriculum and instruction; (3) a broad academic background, including concentrations in at least two academic areas at the undergraduate level; (4) specialized methods and reading courses; and (5) early and continuing field experiences in good middle level schools (Alexander & McEwin, 1988, p. 48).

### Graduate Programs

The primary focus of this chapter is on undergraduate teacher preparation. It should be noted, however, that specialized middle level graduate programs are also essential to the success of middle level education. Middle level graduate programs are not widely available. A national survey of teacher preparation institutions conducted by Alexander and McEwin (1988) found that only 13 percent of responding institutions reported having master's level programs and only 2 percent having doctoral level ones. Therefore, middle level teachers returning to institutions to pursue graduate work frequently find few opportunities to focus their graduate study on courses and programs that address the unique knowledge, skills, and teaching strategies appropriate for teaching young adolescents. Graduate middle level courses and programs must become more widely available if middle level education is to reach its full potential.

## National Middle Level Teacher Preparation Guidelines

Undergraduate and graduate middle level teacher education guidelines are having a significant impact on the provision of specialized middle level preparation. These guidelines, developed by the National Middle School Association and approved by the National Council for Accreditation of Teacher Education, provide needed guidance for institutions establishing new middle level teacher preparation programs or evaluating and updating existing ones.

Institutions of higher education that have middle level teacher preparation programs, and are participating in the National Council for Accreditation of Teacher Education folio program review process, submit their programs to the National Middle School Association for possible approval. This process provides the National Middle School Association with the opportunity to have a significant impact on the nature of middle level teacher preparation at all levels. Guidelines for the master's level are provided in the next section of this chapter. The undergraduate ones are more extensive and not included here because of space considerations. They, as well as the educational specialist and doctoral level ones, closely parallel the essential elements of middle level preparation programs as presented in this chapter.

## NMSA/NCATE Master's Level Guidelines

The master's degree program should enhance the general expertise of middle level educators by ensuring a deeper, more comprehensive understanding of young adolescent learners and schooling that is responsive to students' developmental nature and needs. The program should provide further expertise in teaching field content and pedagogy.

1. The curriculum for the master's degree shows depth and breadth in the study of the theoretical base and exemplary practice of middle level education. The plan of study for each student builds upon prior professional preparation and experience.

2. Programs leading to the master's degree in middle level education include the following components:

    2.1. Major theories and research findings concerning early adolescent development: physical, social, emotional, intellectual and moral.

    2.2 The history, philosophy, and future development of middle level education.

    2.3 Curriculum theories and research focusing on the middle level.

    2.4 Pedagogy appropriate for early adolescent learners.

    2.5 Advanced study in one or more broad teaching fields.

    2.6 A culminating examination, project or thesis that links theory and practice.

The National Middle School Association/National Council for Accreditation of Teacher Education middle level teacher preparation guidelines represent an important and historical step in the effort to establish quality middle level teacher preparation programs. They provide a framework for planning and include the essential components that have so long been absent from the professional preparation of the nation's middle level teachers.

## The Professional Preparation of Other Middle Level Personnel

Middle level principals, counselors, and other professional personnel seldom have specialized preparation for working at the middle level. Problems associated with this lack of preparation are compounded by the fact that many principals and other educators assigned to work at middle level schools have had little or no previous middle level administrative or teaching experience.

This unfortunate situation is reflected in professional preparation programs. In a national study of these programs, only 13 percent of responding institutions reported specialized classes or programs for middle level administrators. Even fewer reported specialized middle level preparation courses or programs for middle level counselors (Alexander & McEwin, 1988). The practice of ignoring the unique nature of working with middle level youth must be altered. It is unfair to both the professionals involved and the young adolescents with which they work to proceed as if no specialized knowledge or skills are needed.

## Looking to the Future

What does the future hold for middle level teacher preparation? Will those who teach young adolescents in the next century be specially prepared to do so? Will all states institute middle level teacher certification/licensing requirements, or will some continue to allow almost anyone with any teaching certification to teach at the middle level? Definitive answers for these questions are not known. However, some encouraging trends have emerged.

Growing concerns about U.S. public education have focused attention on the performance and preparation of teachers. This, in turn, has helped draw attention to the lack of specialized licensing requirements and professional preparation programs for middle level teachers. This new awareness, coupled with an increasing recognition of the uniqueness of the stage of early adolescence, has resulted in middle level education receiving unprecedented attention in recent years. For example, the Carnegie Council on Adolescent Development in their landmark publication, *Turning Points: Preparing American Youth for the 21st Century* (1989), strongly recommended that middle grades classrooms be staffed "with teachers who are expert at teaching young adolescents and who have been specially prepared for assignment to the middle grades" (p. 9).

An additional significant factor lies in the actions of the National Board for Professional Teaching Standards. The establishment of separate voluntary national certification standards for middle level teachers is a significant step in establishing the importance and uniqueness of teaching young adolescents. The NBPTS Board also recognized the importance of middle level teaching by beginning the development of these new standards with the middle level certification areas. These actions, along with others discussed in this chapter, give hope to the possibility that despite over 70 years of uncertainty, procrastination, and frustration, middle level teacher preparation programs will in the future become the rule rather than the exception.

In summary, significant progress has been made, but much remains to be accomplished. The practice of employing teachers whose career goals and professional preparation lie in areas other than the middle level is still widespread and readily accepted as "effective practice" by many. The full success of middle level education awaits middle level classrooms that are staffed by specially prepared teachers who choose the middle level and are willing to extend the effort necessary to provide excellent, developmentally appropriate instruction for these youth. This will likely occur only when mandatory licensing plans for middle level teachers are established in all states.

As noted earlier, the large majority of middle level teachers and other professional personnel have no special preparation for teaching or working in other ways with young adolescents. To compound the problem, the majority of those preparing to enter the profession do not have the option of preparing specifically for the middle level. This dilemma will not be resolved until dynamic middle level teacher preparation programs are more universally established. There are many excellent middle level teachers who have spent years seeking role definition and attempting to compensate for their lack of appropriate preparation. However, middle level education cannot afford to depend solely on the possibility that large numbers of teachers will be successful in this struggle. Poorly prepared and uncommitted school personnel cannot do the job required.

Exemplary middle level teacher preparation programs are likely to be established only if a coalition of representatives from teacher preparation institutions, policy-making bodies, the profession, state department of education representatives, and others work together cooperatively and intensely. The cost of avoidance behavior regarding this issue is high with the educational opportunities and welfare of young adolescents at stake.

Will significant progress in the establishment of quality middle level teacher preparation programs and the specialized middle level licensing requirements that sustain them be made in the near future? I remain cautiously optimistic.

## References

Alexander, W. M., & McEwin, C. K. (1988). *Preparing to teach at the middle level.* Columbus, OH: National Middle School Association.

Alexander, W. M., & McEwin, C. K. (1989). *Schools in the middle: Status and progress.* Columbus, OH: National Middle School Association.

Boyer, J. A. (1983). *A study of middle level teacher education components.* Unpublished doctoral dissertation, State University of New York, Buffalo, NY.

Carnegie Council on Adolescent Development's Task Force on Education of Young Adolescents. (1989). *Turning points: Preparing American youth for the 21st century.* Washington, DC: Carnegie Council on Adolescent Development, a program of Carnegie Corporation of New York.

DeMedio, D., & Helms, B. (1984). What North Carolina professors say about middle grades teacher education. *Journal of the North Carolina League of Middle/ Junior High Schools, 5*(1), 28–29.

De Medio, D., & Kish, J. (1983). What North Carolina teachers say about teacher preparation for the middle grades. *Journal of the North Carolina League of Middle/Junior High School, 4*(1), 23–24.

Eccles, J. S., & Midgley, C. (1990). Stage/environment fit: Developmentally appropriate classrooms for early adolescents. In C. Ames & R. Ames (Eds.), *Research on motivation in education: Vol. 3. Goals and cognitions.* San Diego: Academic Press.

Floyd, O. R. (1932). *The preparation of junior high school teachers* (U.S. Office of Education Bulletin No. 20). Washington, DC: U.S. Government Printing Office.

George, P. S., & McEwin, C. K. (1978). Middle school teacher education: A status report. *Journal of Teacher Education, 29*(5), 13–16.

Gillan, R. E. (1978). *Teacher preparation and certification for the middle school grades.* Unpublished doctoral dissertation, Northwestern University. (ERIC Document Reproduction No. 178463).

Gruhn, W. T., & Douglas, H. R. (1947). *The modern junior high school.* New York: Ronald Press.

Howard, A. W., & Strombis, G. C. (1970). *The junior high school and middle school: Issues and practices.* Scranton, IL: Intext Educational Publishers.

Koos, L. V. (1927). *The junior high school.* Boston: Ginn.

Krinsky, J. L., & Pumerantz, P. (1972). Middle school teacher preparation programs. *The Journal of Teacher Education, 23*(4), 468–470.

McEwin, C. K. (1984). Preparing teachers for the middle school. In J. H. Lounsbury (Ed.), *Perspectives: Middle school education, 1964–1984* (pp. 109–120). Columbus, OH: National Middle School Association.

McEwin, C. K. (1990a). How fares middle level education? A research-based status report. *Educational Horizons, 68*(2), 100–104.

McEwin, C. K. (1990b). *Middle level certification practices: Report of a national study.* Boone, NC: Appalachian State University.

McEwin, C. K., & Allen, M. G. (1983). *Middle level teacher certification: A national survey.* Boone, NC: Appalachian State University.

Pumerantz, P. (1969). Few states certify teachers for growing middle schools. *Phi Delta Kappan, 5*(2), 102.

Toepfer, C. F. (1982). Junior high and middle school education. In H. E. Mitzel (Ed.), *Encyclopedia of educational research* (pp. 989–1000). New York: The Free Press.

Valentine, J., Clark, D. C., Nickerson, N. C., & Keefe, J. (1981). *The middle level principalship: A survey of middle level principals and programs (Vol. 1).* Reston, VA: National Association of Secondary School Principals.

Van Til, C. F., Vars, G. F., & Lounsbury, J. H. (1967). *Modern education for the junior high school years.* New York: Bobbs-Merrill.

# CHAPTER TWENTY

# Turning Points and Beyond: Coming of Age in Middle Level Research

DAVID B. STRAHAN
*The University of North Carolina*

*A major reason why research methodology in education is such an exciting area is that education is not itself a discipline. Indeed, education is a field of study, a locus containing phenomena, events, institutions, problems, persons, and processes, which themselves constitute the raw material for inquiries of many kinds. (Shulman, 1988, p. 5)*

Life in middle level classrooms certainly provides raw material for inquiries of many kinds. The chapters in this text have explored many of the phenomena, events, institutions, problems, persons, and processes that constitute life at the middle level. In so doing, this text provides a status report on many of the most pressing issues in middle level education, issues that have characterized the middle school era to date and that are likely to continue to do so. This chapter focuses on the nature of our research as we project the possibilities into the future.

Each of the chapters have chronicled a growing body of research related to middle level education. As studies have proliferated, patterns of results have emerged to such a degree that we are nearing a consensus about what middle level schools should be and about what needs to be done to improve middle level schools. I see the publication of *Turning Points: Preparing American Youth for the 21st Century* (Carnegie, 1989) as a milestone in focusing this emerging consensus. In this chapter, I will explain why I believe a consensus has emerged and suggest ways to focus our research efforts based on that consensus. In doing so, I find it helpful to reflect on our context in the educational research community—a context that, like so many other characteristics of middle level education, makes us unique.


## How Does Middle Level Research Relate to the Rest of Education?

Shulman (1988) reminds us that education is a field of study rather than a discipline. He noted,

> *Disciplined inquiry not only refers to the ordered, regular, or principled nature of investigation, it also refers to the disciplines themselves which serve as the sources for the principles of regularity or canons of evidence employed by the investigator.*
>
> *What distinguishes disciplines from one another is the manner in which they formulate their questions, how they define the content of their domains and organize that content conceptually, and the principles of discovery and verification that constitute the ground rules for creating and testing knowledge in their fields. (p. 5)*

Shulman's description of education as a field of study on which the "perspectives and procedures of many disciplines can be brought to bear" (p. 5) is helpful in thinking about the relationship of middle level reserch to the rest of educational research. If we think of education as a field of study, we can begin to think of the various formal disciplines and other areas of inquiry as strands that pass through the field. We can begin to think of the middle level as a major "zone" of the field that encompasses these areas of inquiry. Figure 20–1 represents an attempt to diagram this notion of the "middle level zone" in the field of education.

In Figure 20–1, I have represented the K–12 continuum of public education as lines that extend up and down the "field" of education. Major portions of the field extend beyond the K–12 continuum to include preschool and postsecondary education. I have presented a sampling of the areas of inquiry that pass through the middle level zone. Recognized disciplines, such as psychology and anthropology, investigate events that occur in the middle level zone of inquiry. Less formalized areas of inquiry, such as curriculum and instruction, teacher education, and leadership, explore topics and issues related to the middle level in the developmental fashion. I included literacy development and numeracy development as areas of inquiry to suggest that although the development of the 3 Rs may be the focus of many of our

**FIGURE 20–1 • A Sampling of Areas of Inquiry in the Middle Level Field**

| | K | 1 | 2 | 3 | 4 | 5 | 6 | 7 | 8 | 9 | 10 | 11 | 12 | |
|---|---|---|---|---|---|---|---|---|---|---|---|---|---|---|
| Psychology | | | | | | ░ | ░ | ░ | ░ | ░ | | | | |
| Anthropology | | | | | | ░ | ░ | ░ | ░ | ░ | | | | |
| Curriculum and Instruction | | | | | | ░ | ░ | ░ | ░ | ░ | | | | |
| Teacher Education | | | | | | ░ | ░ | ░ | ░ | ░ | | | | |
| Leadership | | | | | | ░ | ░ | ░ | ░ | ░ | | | | |
| Literacy Development | | | | | | ░ | ░ | ░ | ░ | ░ | | | | |
| Numeracy Development | | | | | | ░ | ░ | ░ | ░ | ░ | | | | |

efforts, all of the traditional academic disciplines pass through the middle level zone to some degree. These are but a few of the many disciplines and areas of inquiry encompassed by the middle level zone.

Representing the middle level as a zone in the field of education can help clarify several essential features of middle level research. One feature is the emphasis on *transition* in much of the research at the middle level. In developmental psychology, for example, we have made great progress in recognizing early adolescence as a distinct stage of the lifespan. The more we learn about early adolescence, the more information we have to guide our efforts in curriculum and instruction, leadership, and other areas of research and development. At the same time, the more we learn about early adolescence, the better we understand lifespan development.

By studying developmental issues that first emerge during puberty, psychologists have extended our understanding of how these issues occur in early and later adulthood. Similar interactions occur in literacy development. Everything we learn about emerging literacy during childhood and extended literacy during adulthood helps us understand more about how young adolescents think, read, and write. Again, everything we learn about the unique ways that young adolescents interpret and employ language helps us better understand the processes of literacy development.

Another feature emphasized by the conceptualization of education as a field is the need for middle level *identity*. The various areas of inquiry that explore the field of education need to acknowledge and to investigate the middle level as a recognized zone of inquiry. Although such recognition is beginning in psychology and literacy, it is not as evident in other areas. One area of inquiry that has not fully acknowledged the middle level is curriculum.

As Beane (1990) has suggested, "The middle school curriculum is not really 'a curriculum' in the sense of having some clearly identifying purpose or theme" (p. 2). One reason for this is that curriculum studies are often organized into elementary and secondary. Other areas of inquiry, such as leadership and teacher education, need to recognize the middle level as a unique zone in the field of educational research.

A third feature is the opportunity to draw from many different *research traditions.* While the various academic disciplines have developed recognized modes of inquiry with shared standards for conducting and evaluating research, a field of study has no one single way of knowing. Within the disciplines of psychology and anthropology, for example, recurring modes of inquiry have developed over time and, with them, expectations regarding information gathering and analysis. Other areas of study have developed different research strategies, such as historical analysis and philosophical inquiry.

In describing education as a field of study, Shulman (1988) reminded us that all of the areas of research encompassed by the field of education, whether formal disciplines or less formal areas of study, share a common grounding in "disciplined inquiry" and a common commitment to rigorous scholarship in pursuing such inquiry. After reviewing several definitions of *disciplined inquiry,* Shulman (1988) concluded that "what is important about disciplined inquiry is that its data, arguments, and reasoning be capable of withstanding careful scrutiny by another member of the scientific community" (p. 5). Research that focuses specifically on the middle level zone may draw from many different modes of inquiry, and from the many different ways of knowing that accompany those modes.

When we think about the studies that have been most influential to the middle level, such has clearly been the case. In their commitment to improve the quality of life in classrooms, middle level practitioners have drawn freely from almost every type of research. Correlational studies in development have helped us define the needs of our students. Examples include Tanner's (1962) studies of growth patterns, Purkey's (1970) analysis of self-concept and school achievement, Toepfer's (1978) longitudinal analysis of the "turn off syndrome," and Arlin's (1984) analysis of patterns of concrete and formal reasoning.

A series of survey studies have shaped our definitions of successful practices. Examples include Alexander's 1968 review of organizational patterns and Alexander and McEwin's (1988) update, George and Oldaker's (1985) survey of effective schools, and Strahan and Van Hoose's (1988) assessment of inviting teaching. Meta-analyses of experimental studies have helped guide our conclucions regarding practices such as ability grouping (Kulik & Kulik, 1982; Marsh, 1984) and cooperative team learning (Johnson, Johnson, & Stanne, 1986).

Although we have drawn conclusions from these scientific studies, interpretive studies have shaped our agenda for action in very powerful ways by providing descriptive studies of successful schools. Lipsitz's (1984) *Successful Schools for Young Adolescents* and Johnston and Ramos de Perez's (1985) "Four Climates of Effective Middle Level Schools" have been especially influential in describing the underlying dynamics of successful programs in varied settings. A series of shadow studies (*How Fares the Ninth Grade?* [Lounsbury & Johnston, 1985], *Inside Grade Eight: From Apathy to Excitement* [Lounsbury & Clark, 1990], *Life in the Three Sixth Grades* [Lounsbury & Johnston, 1988], and *The Middle School in Profile: A Day in the Seventh Grade* [Lounsbury, Marani, & Compton, 1980]) have provided a rich portrayal of the ways students have experienced life in middle level schools over the past 30 years. As we continue to draw from many different types of research at the middle level, it becomes increasingly important to define research standards, a topic I will address later in this chapter.

## What Is the Current Status of Research in the Middle Level Zone?

In his chapter in *Perspectives: Middle School Education 1964–1984,* Johnston (1984) observed that "research on and about the middle level school has begun to proliferate" and emphasized the importance of looking outside "middle school research *per se*" to identify "information that is useful in making professional decisions that enhance the educational program for young adolescents" (p. 135). Noting that increasing attention to middle level education made it impossible to synthesize related research in a single chapter, Johnston provided a synopsis of research in nine clusters of studies that has helped guide "research into practice" connections since its publication.

In the years that have passed since that chapter, research relating to the middle level has proliferated at an even faster rate, making it impossible for any chapter, book, or series of books to claim to provide a complete synthesis of research. This book, *Transforming Middle Level Education,* represents an attempt to synthesize a portion of this growing body of research as it relates to the most pressing concerns of middle level educators.

Several indicators suggest that we are coming of age in middle level research. Among these are the growing emphasis on research in our professional organizations, the increasing frequency of research reports on middle level issues, the quality of research reports, and an emerging consensus regarding an agenda for action and inquiry.

Research has certainly become an important emphasis within the National Middle School Association. NMSA may be unique in its establishment and support of a research committee. I was privileged to attend the very first of the research symposia of the National Middle School Association at the Denver conference in 1977. J. Howard Johnston, Sherrel Bergman, and others had perceived the need to establish a research committee and had issued a call for papers related to middle level issues. Six of us presented papers to an audience of 50 or so, a turnout we considered rather large given the "first time" nature of this event. Our papers were published in *The Middle School Research Annual,* a mimeographed and stapled publication, a few copies of which have managed to survive. Looking back, our topics seem rather timely: organizational structures of middle schools and junior highs and the attitude of teachers and students; a comparison of the attitudes of elementary, middle, and high-school teachers; students' perceptions of science; cognitive style and classroom climate in algebra; writing apprehension and attitudes toward literature among eighth-graders; and trait anxiety, peer presence, and skill acquisition of sixth-grade boys.

In the years that followed, the *Middle School Research Annual* became a tradition. Fifteen volumes have been published, including over 100 research reports on middle level topics and issues. As editor from 1984 to 1989, I noted that the number of submissions continued to grow and the quality of the studies of themselves continued to improve. Interest in research presentations at the annual conference has also continued to grow. At each national conference since 1977, at least three symposia sessions have been featured. Since 1986, each conference has highlighted an "invited presentation" of research synthesis. During this same time period, reports of research at the middle level have appeared with increasing frequency in other professional publications and at other national conferences.

During the past decade, funding agencies have focused more of their attention on middle level issues. As a result, several large-scale, longitudinal studies of middle schooling are underway at research centers across the country. Involving hundreds of schools and thousands of students, these are the types of studies we dreamed about back in the early years of the research committee.

Drawing on many of the efforts of middle level researchers, members of the Carnegie Council Task Force on Education of Young Adolescents conducted a very thorough review of research on middle level education and commissioned a series of special reports that addressed concerns generated in their review. The result of these efforts, published in *Turning Points: Preparing American Youth for the 21st Century* (Carnegie, 1989), provides an "agenda for action" at the middle level, an agenda that is based on research and that provides a foundation for new research initiatives.

Reactions to these recommendations have indicated a strong consensus among middle level educators. Participants at various professional conferences highlighting the report have responded enthusiastically. Articles in professional journals, newspapers, and periodicals have embraced the recommendations. Few objections have been raised and the general response has been to call for rapid implementation of the recommendations. A number of states have formed their own "turning points task forces" to begin formulating agendas for action based on the report.

To me, this consensus is another unique feature of middle level education. We seem to agree on our goals for middle level schooling. Paraphrasing the recommendations of the *Turning Points* report, we want to encourage our students to become more intellectually reflective, healthy, caring people on their way toward lifetimes of meaningful work and active citizenship (p. 415). We want our schools to create smaller communities for learning, teach a meaningful academic core, ensure success for all students, empower all professionals to make decisions, employ middle level experts, foster health and fitness, and connect families and communities with the day-to-day processes of education (p. 9). These goals reflect those articulated earlier in *This We Believe* (NMSA, 1982) by the National Middle School Association and *An Agenda for Excellence at the Middle Level* (NASSP, 1986) by the National Association of Secondary School Principals.

A recent report by Epstein and Mac Iver (1990) gave us some estimate of the degree to which many of the practices advocated in *Turning Points* have been implemented. Conducted by the Center for Research on Elementary and Middle Schools at the Johns Hopkins University and published by the Research Committee of the National Middle School Association, this report provided a detailed analysis of survey responses from 1,753 public schools in the United States with seventh-grade students. Data reported are weighted to provide an equal probability (representative) sample of schools in the country. Results summarized responses from principals regarding 16 different aspects of middle grade education. Results related to the recommendations from *Turning Points* are summarized in Table 20–1.

A review of these recommendations in comparison with data regarding levels of implementation underscores the urgency of *Turning Points'* call for action. For each of the eight recommendations, data indicate a discrepancy between what is advocated and the experience of the majority of seventh-graders in the country. Very few students attend schools within formally designated "houses" or "schools within schools." More than half of the seventh-graders in the sample have no experience with interdisciplinary teams of teachers. More than one-third have no advisor/advisee program. Very few are "adept" readers or score well in mathematics. Very few have classes that are grouped for instruction in predominantly heterogeneous fashion. Few teachers have common planning time with teammates or special certification at the middle level. Almost half of the teachers receive no staff development specially designed for the middle level. Fewer than half of the schools have intensive parental involvement programs or work consistently with youth agency programs.

**TABLE 20–1 • Frequency of Implementation of Practices Recommended in Turning Points, as Reported by Epstein and Mac Iver (E&M) and by the Carnegie Council on Adolescent Development (CCAD)**

| Recommendations (paraphrased) | Implementation |
|---|---|
| 1. Create small communities for learning. | The average size of schools with seventh-graders is 452 (E&M, p. 9). |
| | 6 percent of seventh-graders attend schools with "schools within schools" (E&M, p. 59). |
| | 42 percent of middle schoolers have some experience with interdisciplinary teams of teachers; only 36 percent of these teams have common planning time (E&M, pp. 27, 30). |
| | 66 percent of middle schoolers have some "advisory" time (E&M, p. 21). |
| 2. Teach a core academic program. | 11 percent of 13-year-olds are "adept" readers, able to understand complex passages; fewer than 20 percent write adequate or better essays; average mathematical proficiency is at the level of basic operations, lowest of nine industrialized countries assessed by NAEP (CCAD, p. 31). |
| 3. Ensure success for all students. | 7 to 15 percent of students have *no* classes grouped homogeneously; 25 to 30 percent have *all*; 57 to 64 percent have *some* (E&M, p. 12). |
| | 98 percent of schools have some remedial program; 50 to 60 percent have pullout programs in reading and math (E&M, p. 49). |
| | 20 percent of the schools offer cooperative team learning on a regular basis (E&M, p. 59). |
| 4. Empower teachers and administrators. | Middle level teachers and students perceive fewer opportunities to make decisions than at elementary level (CCAD, P. 34). |
| | 10 percent of schools have interdisciplinary teams with common planning time *and* use that time to integrate academic activities (E&M, p. 31). |
| | 19 percent of the schools have flexible schedules (E&M, p. 59). |
| 5. Staff middle schools with experts in working with young adolescents. | 22 states have middle-level certification (E&M, p. 54). |
| | 51 percent of schools offer staff development specific to the middle level (E&M, p. 58). |

*Continued*

**TABLE 20–1** • *Continued*

| Recommendations (paraphrased) | Implementation |
| --- | --- |
| 6. Foster health and fitness. | As many as one-fourth of the nation's adolescents may be extremely vulnerable to high-risk behaviors, such as school failure, substance abuse, and unprotected intercourse (CCAD, p. 27). |
| 7. Reengage families. | 35 to 50 percent of schools offer workshops for parents and recruit and train parents as volunteers (E&M, p. 59). |
| 8. Connect schools with communities. | The extent to which youth-agency programs are closely integrated with school programs is unclear (CCAD, p. 70). |

Although we must remember that the Epstein and Mac Iver's data are limited to responses from administrators, results from their survey raise compelling questions for research. In fact, inherent in each of the recommendations from *Turning Points* is a series of urgent questions for research. Among the many questions we might ask are the following.

- What are the long-range effects of practices like interdisciplinary team organization and advisor/advisee programs for students? For teachers? For school improvement?
- What are the barriers to interdisciplinary teaming and advisor/advisee programs?
- Why do we seem to be making little progress in improving literacy and numeracy?
- Given the evidence against tracking, why are so many students grouped for instruction according to ability?
- How do teachers and administrators perceive efforts toward empowerment?
- What types of decision-making processes accompany efforts to enhance team-based management?
- What are the barriers to team-based management at the middle level?
- What types of staff development experiences are most meaningful to teachers?
- How can schools encourage health and fitness in more meaningful ways?
- How can schools encourage more meaningful participation by parents?
- How can the school and community work together more successfully?

While many of these questions are being investigated, the urgency of our agenda for action and the need for information regarding that agenda is such that we need to find better ways to share information and organize our research.

## How Can We Improve Middle Level Research?

As we consider the current status of middle level research and how we might proceed to improve it, it is once again helpful to think about the middle level as a zone of the education field in which many types of research occur. Given the apparent consensus regarding the agenda for action, we should be able to initiate a wide-ranging dialogue regarding an agenda for related research — research that should draw from each of the areas of inquiry that our field encompasses. As one more step toward such dialogue, I propose the following general suggestions for improving our level of research productivity and practice:

1. *We need to accelerate our efforts to develop an agenda for research to guide our agenda for action:* As I have indicated, the discrepancies between practices most advocated for middle schools and the apparent degree of implementation of the practices are dramatic and troubling. The questions I have raised regarding those discrepancies are only a few of the many we might raise. Perhaps the most basic of these questions necessitate two essential types of research.

One type of research is the search for *patterns*. Many of our most urgent questions address the efficacy and implementation of recommended middle level practices: (a) the long-range effects of interdisciplinary team organization and of advisor/advisee programs, (b) the barriers to implementation of interdisciplinary teaming and advisor/advisee programs, (c) the effects of student-centered curriculum reform, (d) the success of efforts to differentiate instruction and implement alternatives to ability grouping, (e) perceptions of efforts toward empowerment, (f) the effects of staff development experiences that focus on the middle level, (g) the effects of efforts to encourage health and fitness, and (h) the success of strategies for promoting participation by parents and community involvement. More sophisticated investigations of patterns among these practices will not only help us know more about what works but also will help us understand more about what works best in various types of settings under varied conditions. Such studies will help us communicate more effectively with each other, our colleagues in education, and scholars in the academic disciplines.

At the same time that we search for patterns that cross school boundaries, we also need to explore the uniqueness of individual school *settings*.

Knowing more about patterns among practices may help us develop better policies and make better curricular decisions, but it may not tell us much about how practices will work in a particular school or how to improve the day-to-day life of that school. While the topics of interest may remain similar, the questions have a contextual focus.

- How do interdisciplinary teams function in this school?
- How does this particular team function?
- How do they conduct their advisor/advisee program and develop activities?
- How do students in this class approach literacy and numeracy tasks?
- How can we group these students differently and what happens when we try a particular alternative?
- How do teachers and administrators in this building perceive efforts toward empowerment?
- What types of decision-making processes accompany their efforts to enhance team-based management?
- What types of staff development experiences are most meaningful to teachers on this team? In this building?
- How can this school encourage health and fitness in more meaningful ways?
- How can this school encourage more meaningful participation by parents?
- How can this school and the surrounding community work together more successfully?

More sophisticated investigations of questions like these will help us learn more about context, contextual interactions, and action research. Such studies can help us make local decisions and communicate more effectively with our internal audiences of fellow teachers, parents, and schoolboard members.

2. *We need to be more innovative in investigating the "intangibles" of middle schooling:* Many of the questions raised regarding patterns among practices and the uniqueness of individual middle schools have been explored and many others are currently being investigated. Many have been addressed in preceding chapters in this text. Underlying each of these questions is a mystery much more difficult to investigate: Why is it that the practices we advocate have not been implemented more frequently and more successfully? This basic question addresses some of the "intangibles" of schooling:

- Why do students, teachers, and administrators make the decisions they make?
- How can ineffective teachers become more effective?
- How can successful teachers become more successful?
- How do good schools get better?

A growing number of analyses of these "intangibles" have begun to explore *school culture* as a way of examing how schools function and how they change — or do not seem to change — over time. Deal (1990) offers one of the most insightful of these analyses. In "Reframing Reform," he describes the failure of many of our attempts to reform education and makes a compelling case for transformation. Reform, which focuses on correcting weaknesses in existing practices, is often reduced to tinkering with structural features of schools. Transformation, in contrast, addresses alterations in fundamental character. "For the most part, efforts to improve public schools have concentrated on correcting visible flaws. However, deep structures and practices cannot be reformed, they have to be transformed" (p. 9).

In this respect, the basic problems of schools are "more spiritual than technical" (Deal, 1990, p. 12). If we are to transform schools, we must acknowledge that schools are "complex social organizations held together by a symbolic webbing" rather than "formal systems driven by goals, official roles, commands, and rules" (p. 7). Deal suggests that real transformation must begin by addressing the unique symbolic webbing of a particular school. Such symbolic webbings have much to do with the "zeitgeist" of the school, the prevailing intellectual, moral, and cultural climate. The symbolic webbing that Deal describes encompasses the trappings, folklore, and emblems of the school culture, the school spirit that transcends pep rallies, physical climate, and the intuitive "feel" of a school. The symbolic webbing that must be addressed is the way the members of the school culture represent themselves, who they are collectively, how the underlying zeitgeist of the school is defined and transmitted.

Deal (1990) suggested that we can begin to address this symbolic webbing by sharing the stories that have shaped the culture of that school. Only when participants have clarified core values and have a shared sense of identity will they be able to embrace new views. Deal described transformation as the "trapeze-like process of letting go and grabbing on" (p. 9). Essential to this effort are our collective rituals. In some cases, we need to grieve for the past, articulate our historical connections, and invent celebrations of our new identity.

> *The first is to reach back, in research rather than nostalgic quest, to our historical roots. There we must refind and rekindle basic values, stories, rituals, or other symbols that may have been lost, forgotten, or allowed to atrophy. . . . The second is to refocus and renegotiate the myths and values about schooling. (p. 12)*

Deal's analysis may provide us a working hypothesis for addressing the question of why the practices we advaocate have not been implemented more frequently and more successfully. It may well be that we have focused so intently on *restructuring* and *reorganizing* middle level schools that we have not fully considered the processes of *transformation*. Many of the middle level schools that have been most successful have been newly formed, some beginning in new buildings with faculty recruited from an entire district. These schools have had an opportunity to develop a fresh "zeitgeist" and to develop their own stories, rituals, and semantic webbing. Other successful schools have probably been transformed in the manner Deal describes. Schools struggling to become successful may be hampered in their efforts by a fixation on reorganization or restructuring. Other schools may have developed cultures that discourage change.

Certainly, all of our studies of highly successful middle level schools have emphasized the importance of *vision*. In her analysis of the essential characteristics of the four schools profiled in *Successful Schools for Young Adolescents,* Lipsitz (1984) concluded that "becoming a good middle-grade school requires a change in vision about the possibilities of educating young adolescents" (p. 200). Vision is certainly one of the "intangibles" that form the "zeitgeist" of a school. Deal's analysis suggests that, if powerful visions are to emerge in a particular setting, they must somehow emanate from the prevailing zeitgeist and then begin to transform it.

Given the essential nature of vision and other intangibles in schooling, it would seem that we must begin to try to study the dynamics of cultural change. How such change occurs remains unclear. Even so, a growing body of cultural studies in education may provide us with guidance in our efforts to learn more about cultural change, and we may draw clues to the nature of such change from some of the stories of transformation in the literature on schooling.

One of the most revealing of these stories is Goldberg's (1990) "Portrait of Dennis Littky." Littky is well known to middle level educators as the founding principal of Shoreham-Wading River Middle School, one of the most acclaimed schools in the country. As Goldberg described the early years at Shoreham-Wading River, Littky and a select group of teachers literally "invented" a school. In Littky's words, "I gathered together 23 teachers that first year who were all pretty much superstars in their own schools" (p. 29). According to Goldberg,

> *Dennis worked 80 hours a week, and many of his young teachers worked with him. He generated excitement in the new school by introducing book talks, a working farm, frequent field trips, a community service program, sustained silent reading, a student advisory program, integrated learning, and team teaching. (p. 29)*

After six years, Littky left Shoreham-Wading River and "retired" to Winchester, New Hampshire. There, he "fell in love with the town" and "grew to understand the nuances of rural poverty and to admire the dignity of the town's residents" (p. 29). He gradually reentered schooling, organizing a community newspaper, joining the PTA, and serving on the school board. In 1981, he became principal of Thayer Junior-Senior High (grades 7 through 12) in Winchester, a school of 310 students with a dismal physical setting, poor attendance, and many discipline problems. The dropout rate was 20 percent; only 11 percent of the students went on to college. After eight years, the dropout rate is 6 percent, attendance rose sharply, and half of the students went to college. In the meantime, Littky once again became a national figure, drawing intensive attention from the national media and inspiring local controversy. The subject of heated debate, he was fired by the school board, became the focus of the next school board election, and was subsequently rehired.

Perhaps the most meaningful portions of Littky's story are the illustrations of his attempts to improve Thayer School. Although he may not have used the language of transformation, he seemed to address very clearly the dynamics of cultural change. His first phase of action was to try to understand the culture of the community. He spent a great deal of time in Winchester before becoming principal, talking with residents, listening, and learning about the community through his work on the newspaper. When hired, he met with students and recruited many of them to clean and repair the school over the summer. He worked on each student's schedule individually; held conferences with each teacher; and talked with them about their wishes, dreams, and problems. He led the development of a student advisory program, and spent most of his time as principal "talking with kids" and meeting with parents in informal "coffees" held in homes and diners. He brought in a varied group of educational leaders to conduct community workshops. These efforts would seem to be driven by a desire to tap, articulate, and extend the "semantic webbing" of the community and rechannel the culture of the school.

Littky's story provides a number of clues regarding the dynamics of transformation, but, in its presented format, may not be fully "research." As Shulman (1988) has insisted, research is "disciplined inquiry" in which data, arguments, and reasoning must be able to withstand the rigorous scrutiny of other members of the research community. If we are to understand transformation, we need both stories and studies. Stories provide us with insights and inspiration. We need to learn all we can about individual people and innovative activities. At the same time, we need scholarly inquiry that can be examined, debated, tested, and refined.

As difficult as it may be to conduct this type of inquiry, two different types of research may be especially helpful in learning more about the "intangibles" of middle schooling. One type is *historical* analysis of schools and their communities; not necessarily the typical who, what, and when of chronology but rather the thematic analysis of the meanings of schooling to the members of school communities over time, the recurring stories, struggles, and successes that have shaped the culture of the school as a living entity. Deal was careful to note the need to "research" the past rather to rely on "nostalgia" (p. 412).

Another type of research is description of school *culture*. Culture, in its broadest sense, includes "almost everything that has been learned or produced by a group" (Spradley & McCurdey, 1972, p. 7) or, as Johnston suggested in an earlier chapter, "the way we do things around here." As a working construct, *culture* may be defined as "the knowledge members of a given group are thought to more or less share; knowledge of the sort that is said to inform, embed, shape, and account for the routine and not-so-routine activities of the members of a culture" (Van Maanen, 1988, p. 3). As Van Maanen suggested, describing culture is often difficult.

> *The ends of fieldwork involve the catchall idea of culture; a concept as stimulating, productive, yet fuzzy to fieldworkers and their readers as the notion of life is for biologists and their readers. Culture is akin to a black hole that allows no light to escape. The observer knows of culture's presence not by looking, but only by conjecture, inference, and a great deal of faith. (p. 3)*

Whereas culture is thus an "intangible," expressed only by what members of a culture do and say, cultural description may provide very helpful representations of shared constructs. "To portray culture requires the fieldworker to hear, to see, and most important to our purposes, to write of what was presumably witnessed and understood. . . . Culture is not itself visible, but is made visible only through its representation" (p. 3).

Cultural studies of schools and schooling, when drawn from the rich research traditions of anthropological investigation, can help us better understand how teachers and students represent shared ways of knowing—how they construct and interpret the symbolic webbing of their school, create stories, attach meaning to their emblems—how the underlying "zeitgeist" of the school is defined and transmitted. We can learn more about rituals and celebrations, and, through them, refind and rekindle basic values, refocus and renegotiate the myths and values about schooling (Deal, 1990, p. 12).

3. *We need to continue to articulate more explicit standards for conducting and reporting research:* As our research agenda grows more sophisticated, we find ourselves increasingly involved in efforts to improve the quality of research in education. During the past decade, the entire community of educational research has been embroiled in a series of discussions, debates, and disagreements regarding modes of inquiry and expectations for conducting research. Gage (1989) and others have referred to these discussions and disagreements among "positivists," "antinaturalists," "interpretivists," and "critical theorists" as the "paradigm wars." At issue are basic questions regarding how we conduct, report, and interpret investigations.

Although advocates of differing perspectives may disagree on many of the particulars, consensus is growing regarding common expectations. Many of these stem from the types of shared commitments to disciplined inquiry and rigorous scholarship that were discussed earlier in the chapter, the essential feature of which may be that any study be capable of withstanding careful scrutiny by another member of the scientific community (Shulman, 1988, p. 5).

As the paradigm wars have raged in the literature and the varying "camps" have debated at professional meetings, a growing number of researchers have begun to advocate "paradigmatic rapproachment," a meeting of the minds, so to speak, in which scholars begin to realize that "paradigm differences do not require paradigm conflict" (Gage, 1989, p. 7). Whether or not the "wars" subside, disagreements about assumptions and expressions of research have encouraged dialogue about expectations.

One of the most helpful analyses of the issues at stake in this debate is the "prolegomenon" (preliminary observations) offered by Howe and Eisenhart (1990). They contend that while "a variety of specific standards are legitimate" for conducting and interpreting research, given differences in disciplines, interests and purposes, it may be possible to identify general standards that apply to the design and an analysis of qualitative and quantitative research in education (p. 3). They propose five standards as the basis for a common ground in educational research, acknowledging that such standards must be abstract to cut across disciplines and focus on educational issues.

Because education is a field of study, which cuts across different logics in use, it presents special problems regarding standards for research. Standards applicable to any research that can be called "educational" will have to be relatively abstract and will have to turn certain questions of standards over to individuals possessing various kinds of expertise. Their standards (with general explanations) are as follows:

- *The fit between research questions and data collection and analysis techniques:* The data collection and techniques employed in a study should be determined by the nature of the research questions themselves (p. 6).
- *The effective application of specific data collection and analysis techniques:* Data collection and analysis techniques should be applied in a competent fashion that follows principles of practice and fits the particular characteristics of the research situation (p. 7).
- *Alertness to and coherence of background assumptions:* Studies should be judged against a background of existing knowledge with assumptions clarified and the researchers' role defined (p. 7).
- *Overall warrant:* To be "warranted," conclusions should be drawn after

"robust and respected theoretical explanations have been tentatively applied to the data" ("triangulated by theory") (p. 7).

- *Value constraints:* Reports of studies should address both internal and external value constraints, describing how research ethics have been addressed and how contributions to educational practice considered (p. 7).

Standards like these seem especially important in conducting research in the "middle level zone." Many of our questions are so pressing that it is sometimes tempting to conduct studies quickly or to seek affirming results. Teachers, administrators, and school board members often want to know what works, especially when considering new programs or initiating new policies. Confronted with such expectations, we need to be sure that our studies are grounded in theory, designed to explore the complexities at hand, conducted with techniques sophisticated enough to address the questions raised, and written with conclusions that are triangulated by theory and that express ethical and practical values.

## Conclusion

I believe we are coming of age in middle level research. We are identifying an agenda for research that can inform and extend our agenda for action. We are raising common questions and beginning to identify the types of studies we need to address those questions. We are searching for patterns of effects and interactions among common practices and, at the same time, exploring and describing the unique features of individual schools. We are more aware of the ways that our most urgent questions address the "intangibles" of schooling and are beginning to develop more sophisticated approaches to studying those intangibles. We are articulating clearer expectations for conducting and reporting our studies and sharing them in more visible and productive ways.

As we do so, we are reminding ourselves of the importance of our work. Although education is a field of study, it is certainly not a "playing" field. Our work is energizing, compelling, and urgent. One of the most eloquent expressions of this urgency was offered by N. L. Gage in his address as the recipient of the 1988 AERA Award for Distinguished Contributions to Educational Research. Gage (1989) concluded that our ultimate concern must be the betterment of schooling for students and teachers, the "moral obligation" of educational research.

*I find myself better motivated to succeed at this difficult task whenever I remind myself of what we are all about. Educational research is no mere spectator sport, no mere intellectual game, no mere path to academic tenure and higher pay, not jut a way to make a good living and even to become a big shot. It has moral obligations. The society that supports us cries out for better education for its children and youth—especially the poor ones, those at risk, those whose potential for a happy and productive life is all too often going desperately unrealized. (p. 10)*

The moral obligations that Gage has described have been the basis for most of our research at the middle level. The middle school movement and the original junior high movement were predicated on the effort to develop school practices that meet the needs of young adolescent students. Given that foundation, we are in a position to design, conduct, and report studies that enrich the well-being of students in the middle grades and beyond.

## References

Alexander, W. M. (1968). *A survey of organizational patterns of reorganized middle schools.* Final report, USDOE project 7-D-026. Gainesville, FL: University of Florida.

Alexander, W. M., & McEwin, K. (1988). *Schools in the middle: Status and progress.* Columbus, OH: National Middle School Association.

Arlin, P. K. (1984). *Arlin test of formal reasoning.* East Aurora, NY: Slosson Educational Publications.

Beane, J. (1990). Rethinking the middle school curriculum. *Middle School Journal, 21*(5), 1-6.

Carnegie Council on Adolescent Development's Task Force on Education of Young Adolescents. (1989). *Turning points: Preparing American youth for the 21st century.* New York: Carnegie Council on Adolescent Development, a program of Carnegie Corporation of New York.

Deal, T. E. (1990). Reframing reform. *Educational Leadership, 47*(8), 6-12.

Epstein, J., & Mac Iver, D. (1990). *Education in the middle grades: An overview of national practices and trends.* Columbus, OH: National Middle School Association.

Gage, N. L. (1989). The paradigm wars and their aftermath: A "historical" sketch of research on teaching since 1989. *Educational Researcher, 18*(7), 4-11.

George, P., & Oldaker, L. (1985). A national survey of middle school effectiveness. *Educational Leadership, 43*(4), 79-85.

Goldberg, M. F. (1990). Portrait of Dennis Littky. *Educational Leadership, 47*(8), 28-31.

Howe, K., & Eisenhart, M. (1990). Standards for qualitative (and quantitative) research: A prolegomenon. *Educational Researcher, 19*(4), 2-9.

Johnson, R., Johnson, D., & Stanne, M. (1986). Comparison of computer-assisted, cooperative, competitive, and individualistic learning. *American Educational Research Journal, 23*(3), 382-393.

Johnston, J. H. (1984). A synthesis of research findings on middle level education. In J. Lounsbury (Ed.), *Perspectives: Middle school education 1964-1984.* Columbus, OH: National Middle School Association.

Johnston, J. H., & Ramos de Perez, M. (1985, January). Four climates of effective middle level schools. *Schools in the middle.* Reston, VA: National Association of Secondary School Principals.

Kulik, C., & Kulik, J. (1982). Effects of ability grouping on secondary school students: A meta-analysis of findings. *American Educational Research Journal, 19*(3), 415–428.

Lipsitz, L. (1984). *Successful schools for young adolescents.* New Brunswick: Transaction Books.

Lounsbury, J. H., & Clark, D. C. (1990). *Inside grade eight: From apathy to excitement.* Reston, VA: National Association of Secondary School Principals.

Lounsbury, J. H., & Johnston, J. H. (1985). *How fares the ninth grade?* Reston, VA: National Association of Secondary School Principals.

Lounsbury, J. H., & Johnston, J. H. (1988). *Life in the three sixth grades.* Reston, VA: National Association of Secondary School Principals.

Lounsbury, J. H., Marani, J., & Compton, M. (1980). *The middle school in profile: A day in the seventh grade.* Columbus, OH: National Middle School Association.

Marsh, H. (1984). Self-concept, social comparison and ability grouping: A reply to Kulik and Kulik. *American Educational Research Journal, 21*(4), 799–806.

National Association of Secondary Principals. (1986). *An agenda for excellence at the middle level.* Reston, VA: Author.

National Middle School Association. (1982). *This we believe.* Columbus, OH: Author.

Purkey, W. (1970). *Self-concept and school achievement.* Englewood Cliffs, NJ: Prentice Hall.

Shulman, L. (1988). Disciplines of inquiry in education: An overview. In R. Jaeger (Ed.), *Complementary methods for research in education* (pp. 3–18). Washington, DC: American Educational Research Association.

Spradley, J. P., & McCurdey, D. W. (1972). *The cultural experience: Ethnography in complex society.* Chicago: Science Research Associates.

Strahan, D., & Van Hoose, J. (1988). Inviting student and teacher renewal. *Middle School Journal, 19*(3), 3–7.

Tanner, J. M. (1962). *Growth at adolescence.* Oxford: Blackwell Scientific Publications.

Toepfer, C. F. (1978). Brain growth periodization — A new dogma for education. *Middle School Journal, 10*(3), 18–21.

Van Maanen, J. (1988). *Tales of the field: On writing ethnography.* Chicago: University of Chicago Press.

# Epilogue

Howard Johnston was sharing the results of the 1987 sixth-grade shadow study with a class of middle level students in Cincinnati. After listening to the findings, one boy asked, "If you know all those things, how come it doesn't change?" (Lounsbury & Clark, 1990). That's a good question. *Transforming Middle Level Education: Perspectives and Possibilities* ranged from historical reviews, to reports of the status quo, to peeks of and bold assertions about the future. This book is an attempt to provide a foundation for the serious thinking that will be needed if middle level educators are to move beyond organizational reform to real programmatic transformation.

In the now limited waking hours before the new century arrives, we have the opportunity to create environments that respond to the needs of young adolescents and engage them actively in learning. We have the option of grouping students in a ways that are fair to all. We have the understanding needed to develop a curriculum that is fully integrated and relevant to students. We have adequate reasons for seeking legitimacy for the middle level of education so that the proper education and certification of teachers for middle schools is ensured. We have the skills needed to establish a solid research base for this distinct level of education.

Middle level schools should be about the business of developing a true identity, a sense of responsiveness, a curriculum of relevance, and the support systems needed for continued improvement. Many already have, to a marked extent, but the movement has a long way to travel. In a recent meeting of the Research Committee of the National Middle School Association, the members were hammering out goals for the committee and struggling to set a research agenda that made sense for the twenty-first century. At one point, Doug Mac Iver, a member of the committee, said, "You know, I don't want to be sitting in a hotel room like this one 10 years from now not having answered the questions we are raising today." We accepted the implied challenge, for none of the rest of the committee wanted to assemble in another decade and raise the same research needs.

The restructuring of schools is now widely advocated in educational literature. Middle level schools are well into this process. This book is offered in the hopes that it will stimulate thorough discussion and informed action as the needed transformation in education's most critical level takes place.

## Reference

Lounsbury, J. H., & Clark, D. C. (1990). *Inside grade eight: From apathy to excitement.* Reston, VA: National Association of Secondary School Principals.

# Name Index

# Subject Index